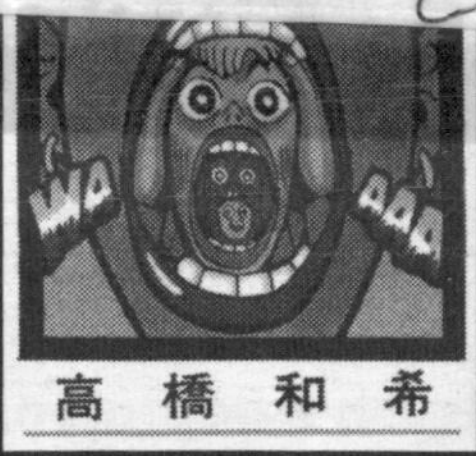
WA
AAA
高橋和希

MAN, IT REALLY IS HARD WORKING ON A WEEKLY DEADLINE! I'M SO BUSY, I CAN'T PLAY THE GAMES I LIKE. I WANNA SIT BACK AND GET SOME GAMING TIME IN, AND THE GAME I WANT TO PLAY MOST RIGHT NOW IS... *TABLETOP ROLEPLAYING GAMES* (RPGS)! IN THE PAST, ME AND MY FRIENDS WOULD GET TOGETHER AND HAVE A GOOD OL' TIME DOING THIS. WE'D STAY UP ALL NIGHT AND HAVE TONS OF FUN. I DEFINITELY RECOMMEND TABLETOP RPGS TO ANYONE. RECENTLY, I HAVEN'T BEEN ABLE TO HOOK UP WITH MY FRIENDS, BUT SOON WE GOTTA GET TOGETHER AND FIRE IT UP AGAIN!

—KAZUKI TAKAHASHI, 1997

Artist/author K[...] break into th[...] success eluded h[...] in the Japanese **Weekly Shonen Jump** magazine in 1996. **Yu-Gi-Oh!**'s themes of friendship and fighting, together with Takahashi's weird and wonderful art, soon became enormously successful, spawning a real-world card game, video games, and two anime series. A lifelong gamer, Takahashi enjoys Shogi (Japanese chess), Mahjong, card games, and table-top RPGs, among other games.

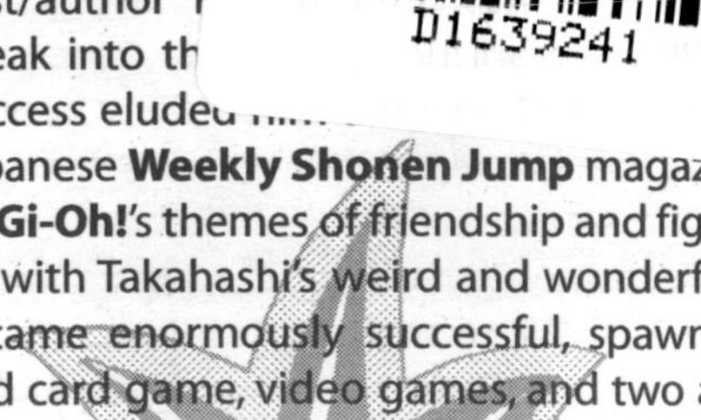

13

THE STORY SO FAR...

When an Egyptian museum exhibit came to Tokyo, an unwelcome visitor came along with it: Shadi, the keeper of the Millennium Items, who sought to kill the archaeologist and museum owner who had desecrated the tomb. But Shadi was startled to discover that the Millennium Puzzle had been solved for the first time in 3,000 years—by Yugi Mutou! Using the Millennium Key to go inside Yugi's soul, Shadi fought the "other" Yugi—and was defeated. Determined to have a rematch, Shadi turned the archaeologist into a mindless zombie, to terrorize Yugi's "other self" into coming out!

DARK YUGI

武藤遊戯

YUGI MUTOU

The main character. When he solved the ancient Egyptian Millennium Puzzle, he developed an alter ego, "Dark Yugi," which emerges in times of stress. Afterwards, the regular Yugi doesn't remember what happened.

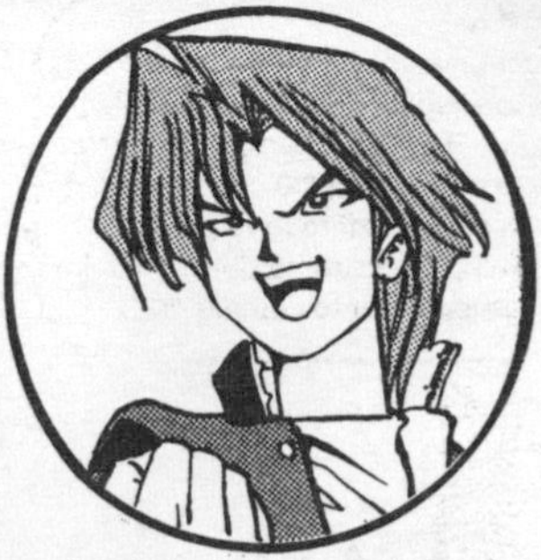

城之内克也

KATSUYA JONOUCHI

Yugi's classmate, a tough guy who gets in lots of fights. He used to think Yugi was a wimp, but now they are good friends. In the English anime he's known as "Joey Wheeler."

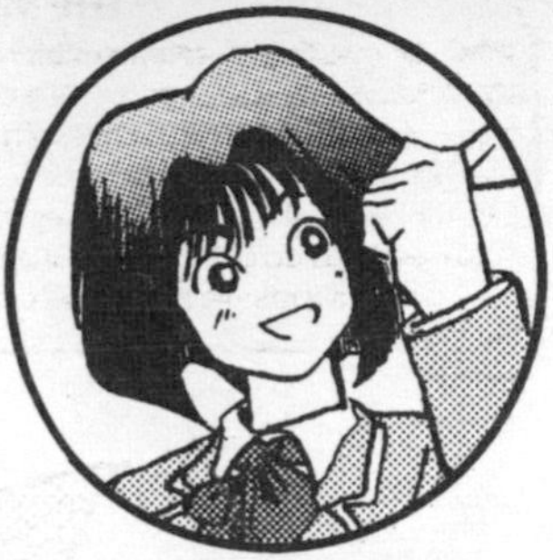

真崎杏子

ANZU MAZAKI

Yugi's classmate and childhood friend. She fell in love with the charismatic voice of Yugi's alter ego, but doesn't know that they're the same person. Her first name means "Apricot." In the English anime she's known as "Téa Gardner."

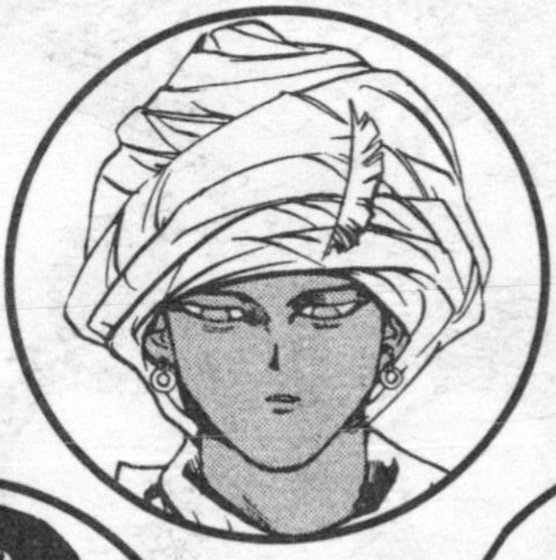

SHADI

A mysterious mystic whose bloodline has guarded the tombs of Egypt for 3000 years. He owns the Millennium Scales, which can weigh a person's sins, and the Millennium Key, which he can use to look inside people's souls and control them.

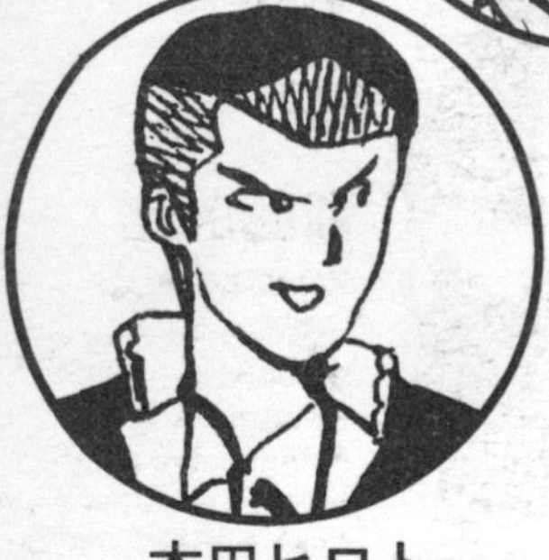

本田ヒロト

HIROTO HONDA

Yugi's classmate, a friend of Jonouchi. In the English anime he's known as "Tristan Taylor."

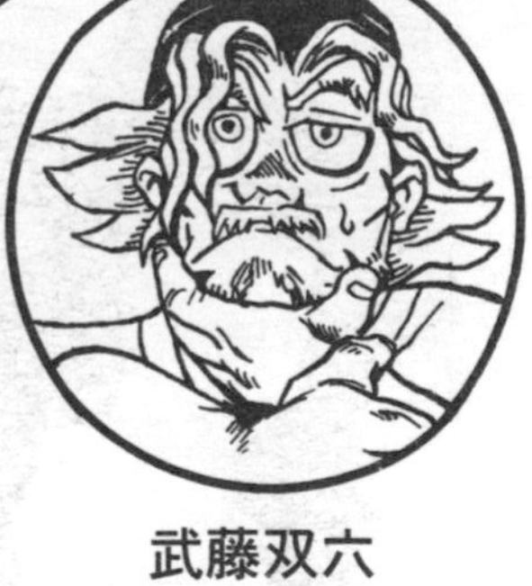

武藤双六

SUGOROKU MUTOU

Yugi's grandfather, the owner of the Kame ("Turtle") game store, and a friend of the archaeologist Professor Yoshimori.

Vol. 3

CONTENTS

Duel 16 Shadi's Challenge 7

Duel 17 Game Start! 33

Duel 18 Second Stage 57

Duel 19 Final Stage 79

Duel 20 Game Over 99

Duel 21 Digital Pet Duel 121

Duel 22 American Hero (Part 1) 141

Duel 23 American Hero (Part 2) 161

Duel 24 Capsule Monster Chess 182

Duel 16: Shadi's Challenge

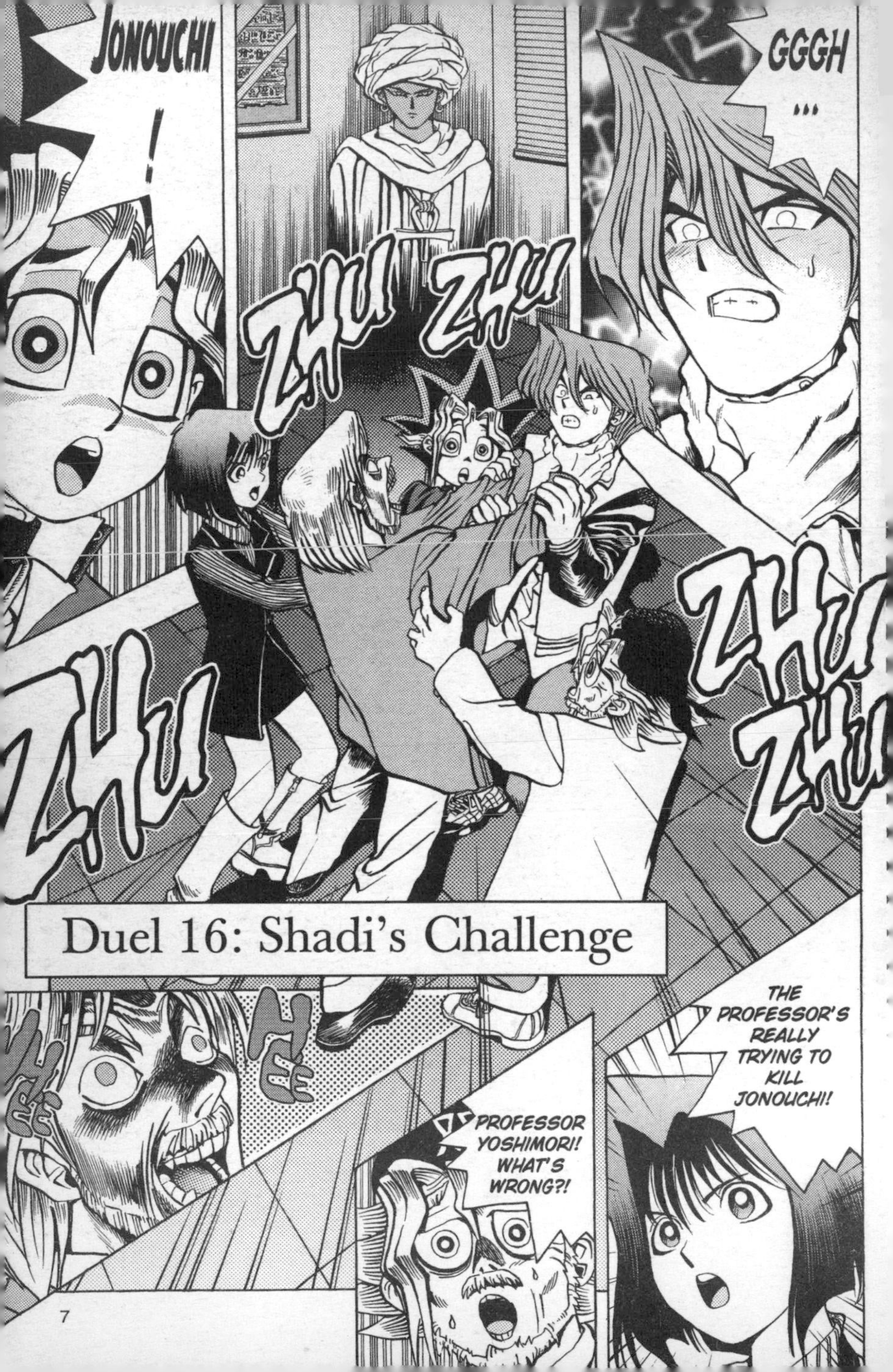
GGGH ...
JONOUCHI !
ZHU ZHU
ZHU ZHU
ZHU
THE PROFESSOR'S REALLY TRYING TO KILL JONOUCHI!
PROFESSOR YOSHIMORI! WHAT'S WRONG?!

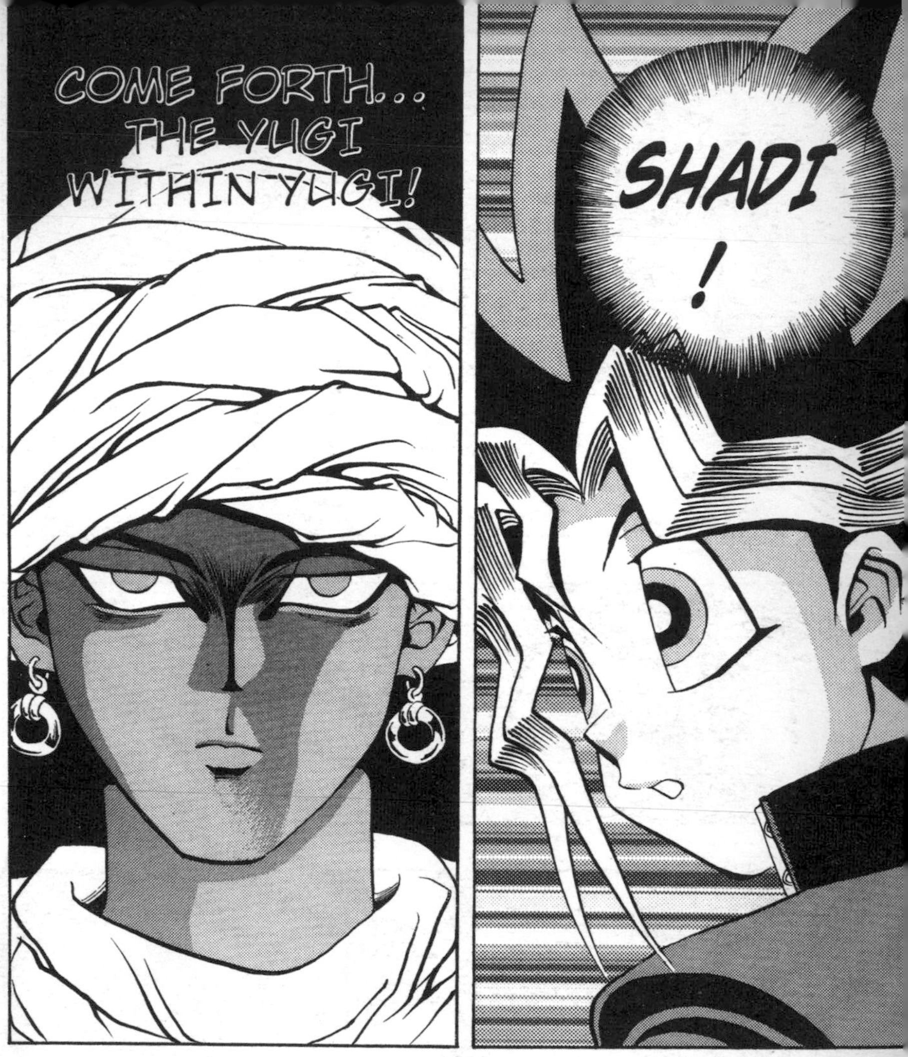
SHADI!
COME FORTH... THE YUGI WITHIN YUGI!

Duel 16: Shadi's Challenge

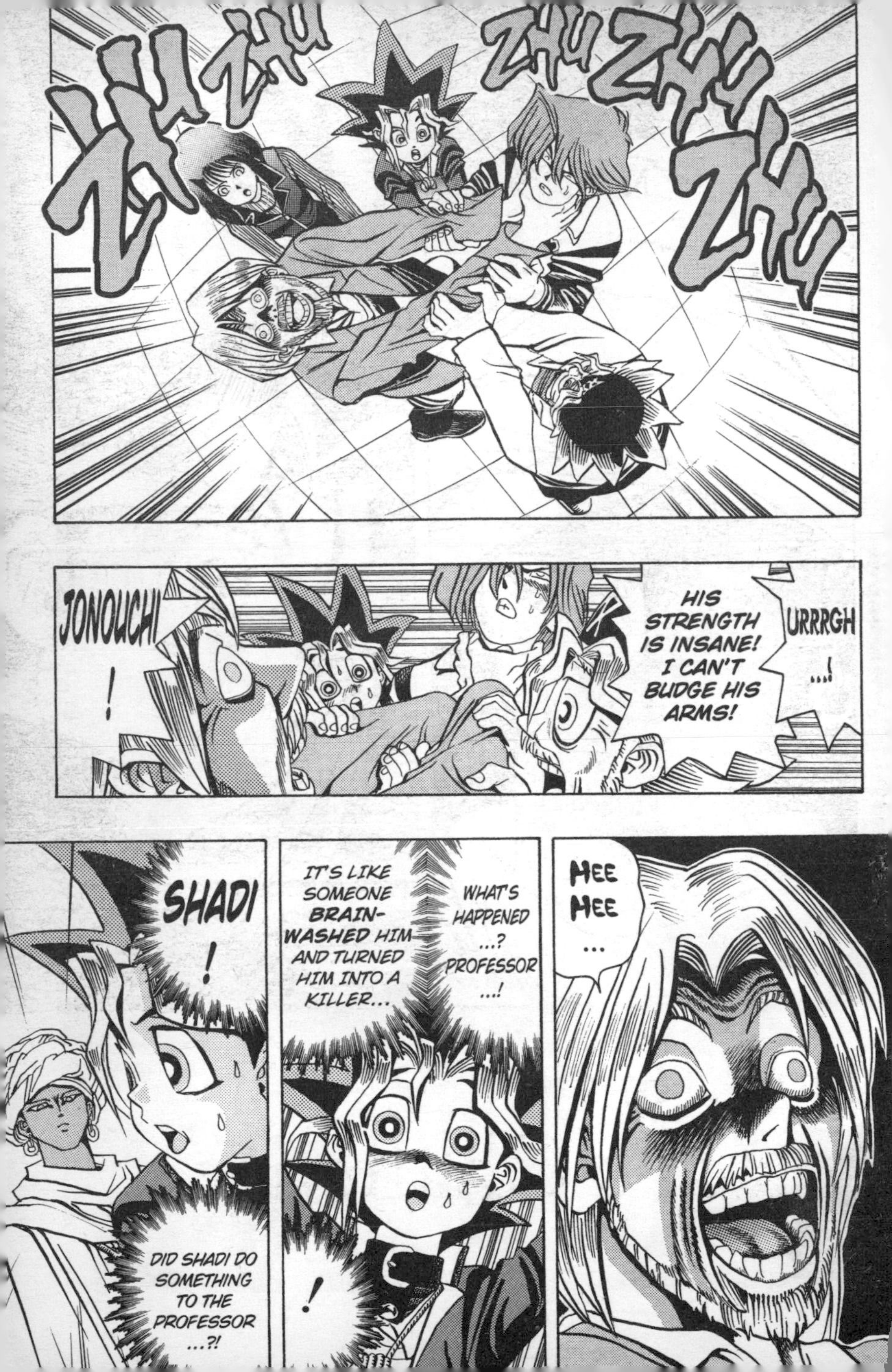
ZHU ZHU ZHU ZHU
ZHU ZHU
URRRGH ...!
HIS STRENGTH IS INSANE! I CAN'T BUDGE HIS ARMS!
JONOUCHI !
HEE HEE ...
WHAT'S HAPPENED ...? PROFESSOR ...!
IT'S LIKE SOMEONE BRAIN-WASHED HIM AND TURNED HIM INTO A KILLER...
!
SHADI !
DID SHADI DO SOMETHING TO THE PROFESSOR ...?!

READ THIS WAY

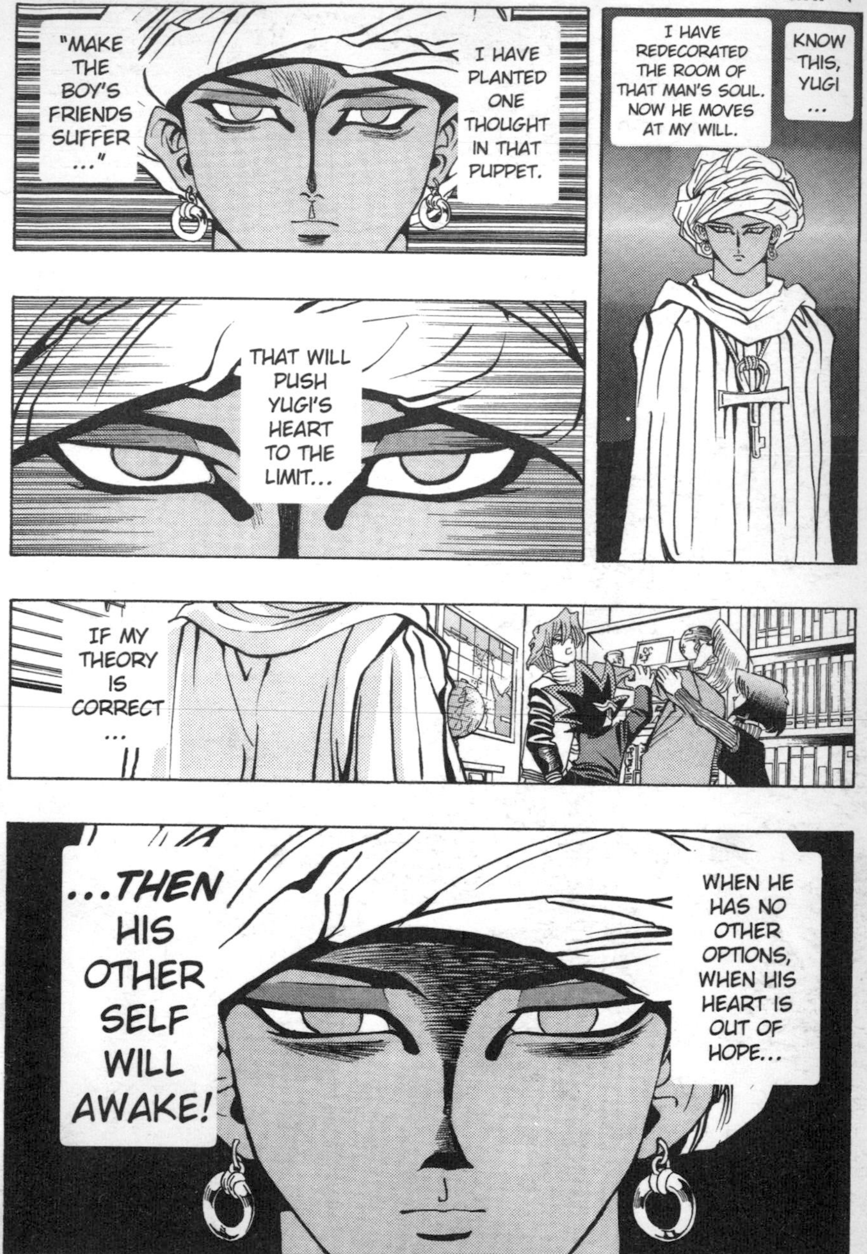
KNOW THIS, YUGI ...
I HAVE REDECORATED THE ROOM OF THAT MAN'S SOUL. NOW HE MOVES AT MY WILL.
I HAVE PLANTED ONE THOUGHT IN THAT PUPPET.
"MAKE THE BOY'S FRIENDS SUFFER ..."
THAT WILL PUSH YUGI'S HEART TO THE LIMIT...
IF MY THEORY IS CORRECT ...
WHEN HE HAS NO OTHER OPTIONS, WHEN HIS HEART IS OUT OF HOPE...
...THEN HIS OTHER SELF WILL AWAKE!

READ THIS WAY

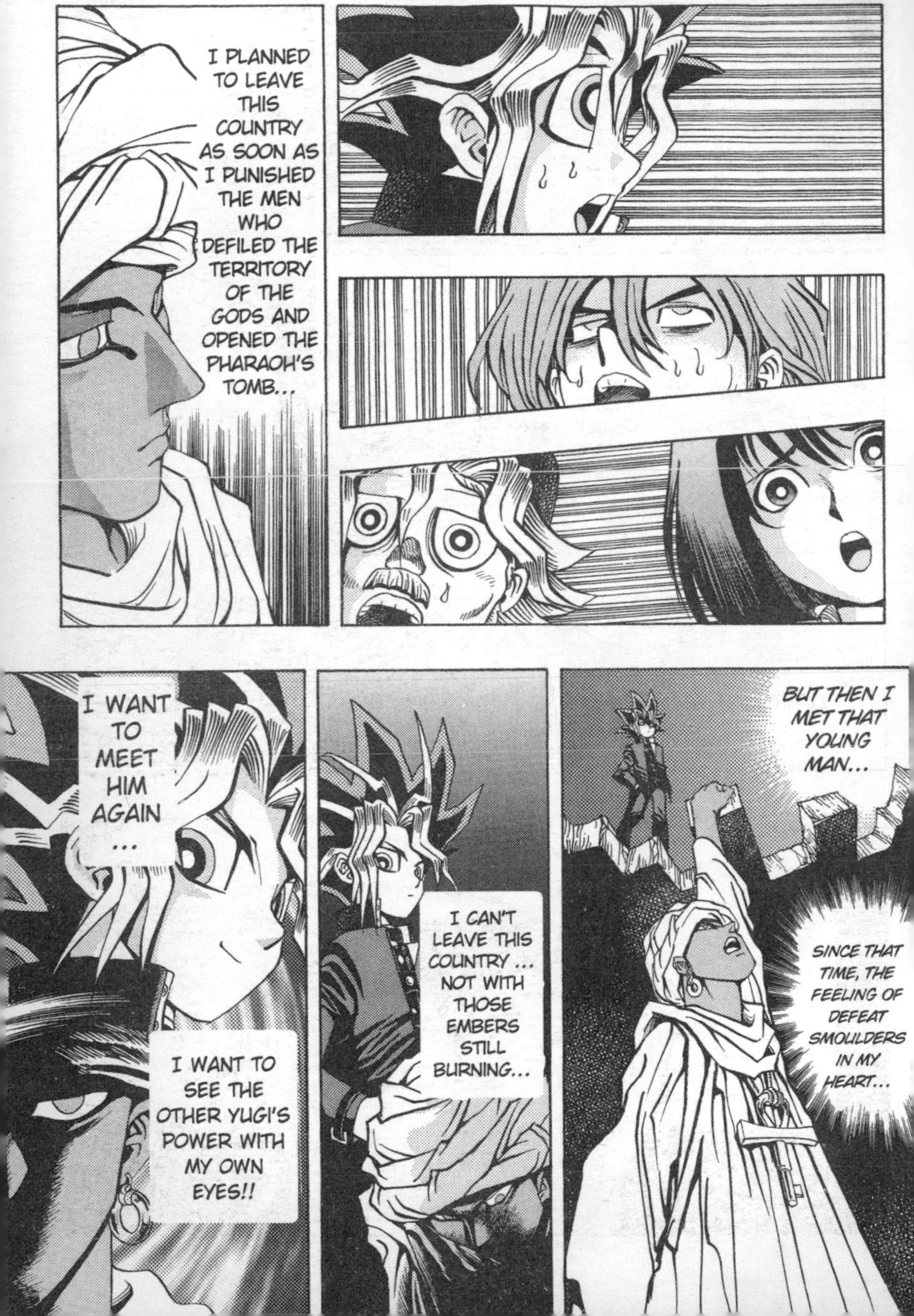
I PLANNED TO LEAVE THIS COUNTRY AS SOON AS I PUNISHED THE MEN WHO DEFILED THE TERRITORY OF THE GODS AND OPENED THE PHARAOH'S TOMB...
BUT THEN I MET THAT YOUNG MAN...
SINCE THAT TIME, THE FEELING OF DEFEAT SMOULDERS IN MY HEART...
I CAN'T LEAVE THIS COUNTRY ... NOT WITH THOSE EMBERS STILL BURNING...
I WANT TO MEET HIM AGAIN ...
I WANT TO SEE THE OTHER YUGI'S POWER WITH MY OWN EYES!!

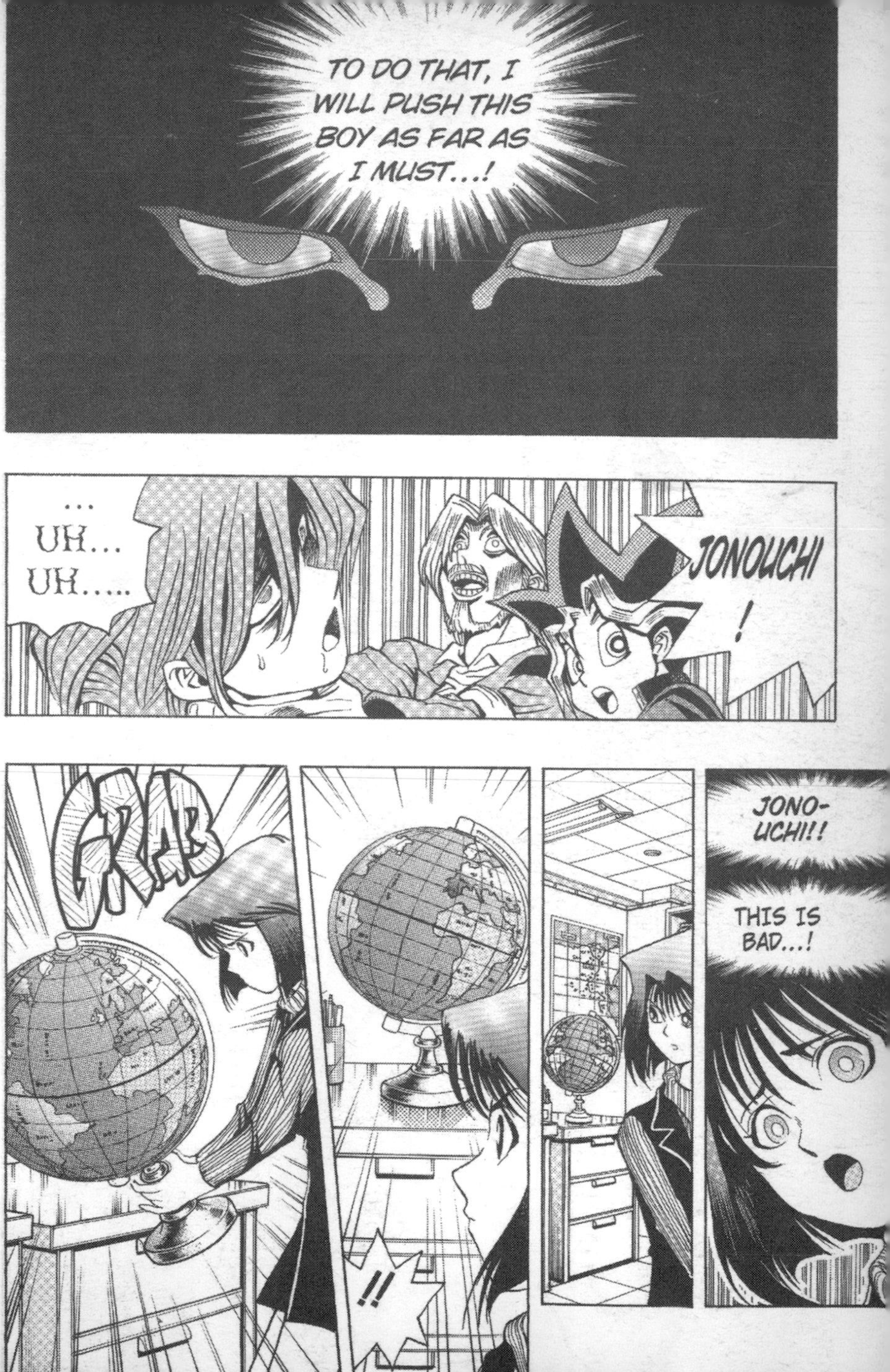
TO DO THAT, I WILL PUSH THIS BOY AS FAR AS I MUST...!
JONOUCHI !
... UH... UH.....
JONO-UCHI!!
THIS IS BAD...!
!!
GRAB

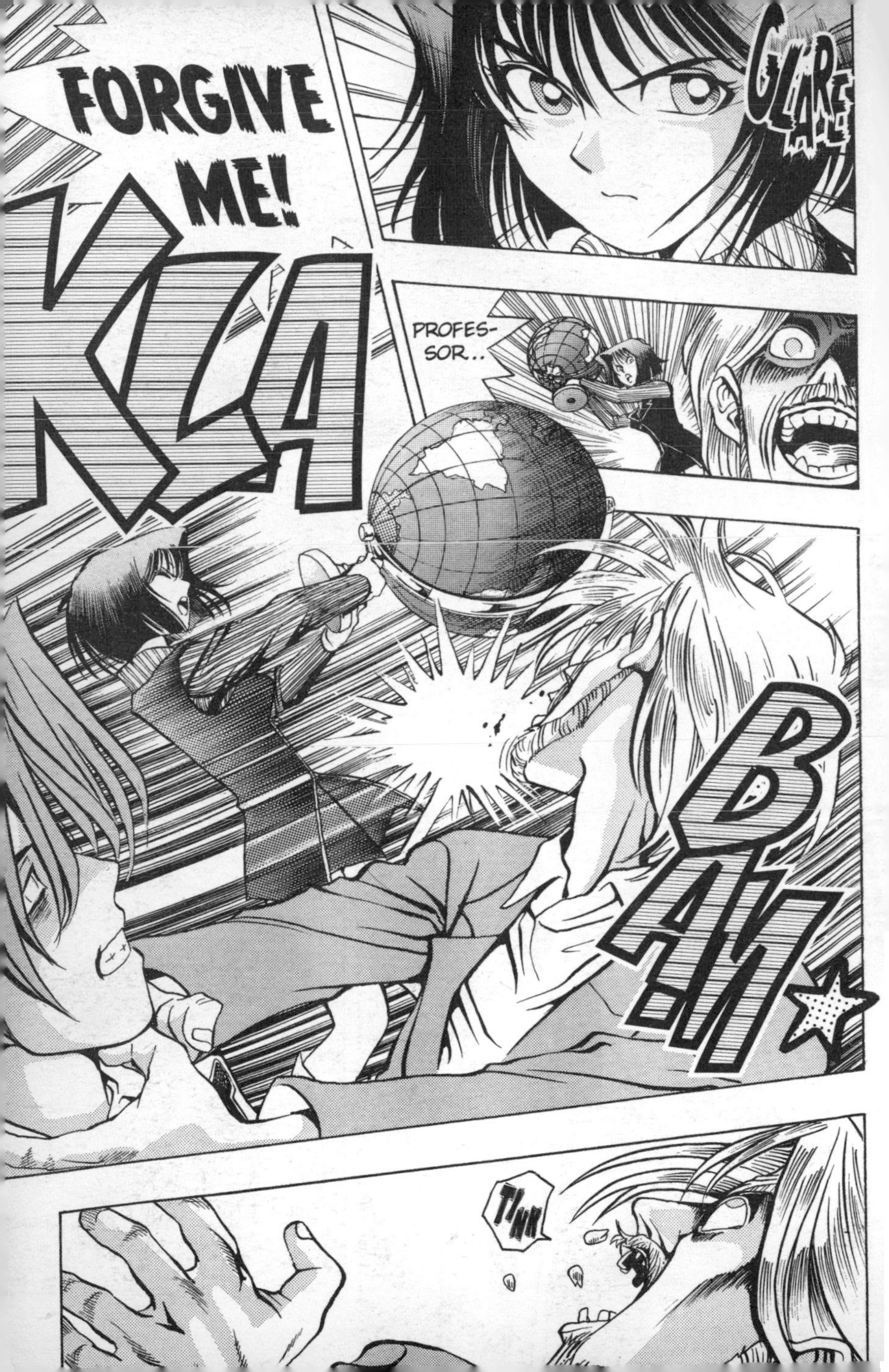
GLARE
FORGIVE ME!
PROFES-
SOR...
BAM
TINK

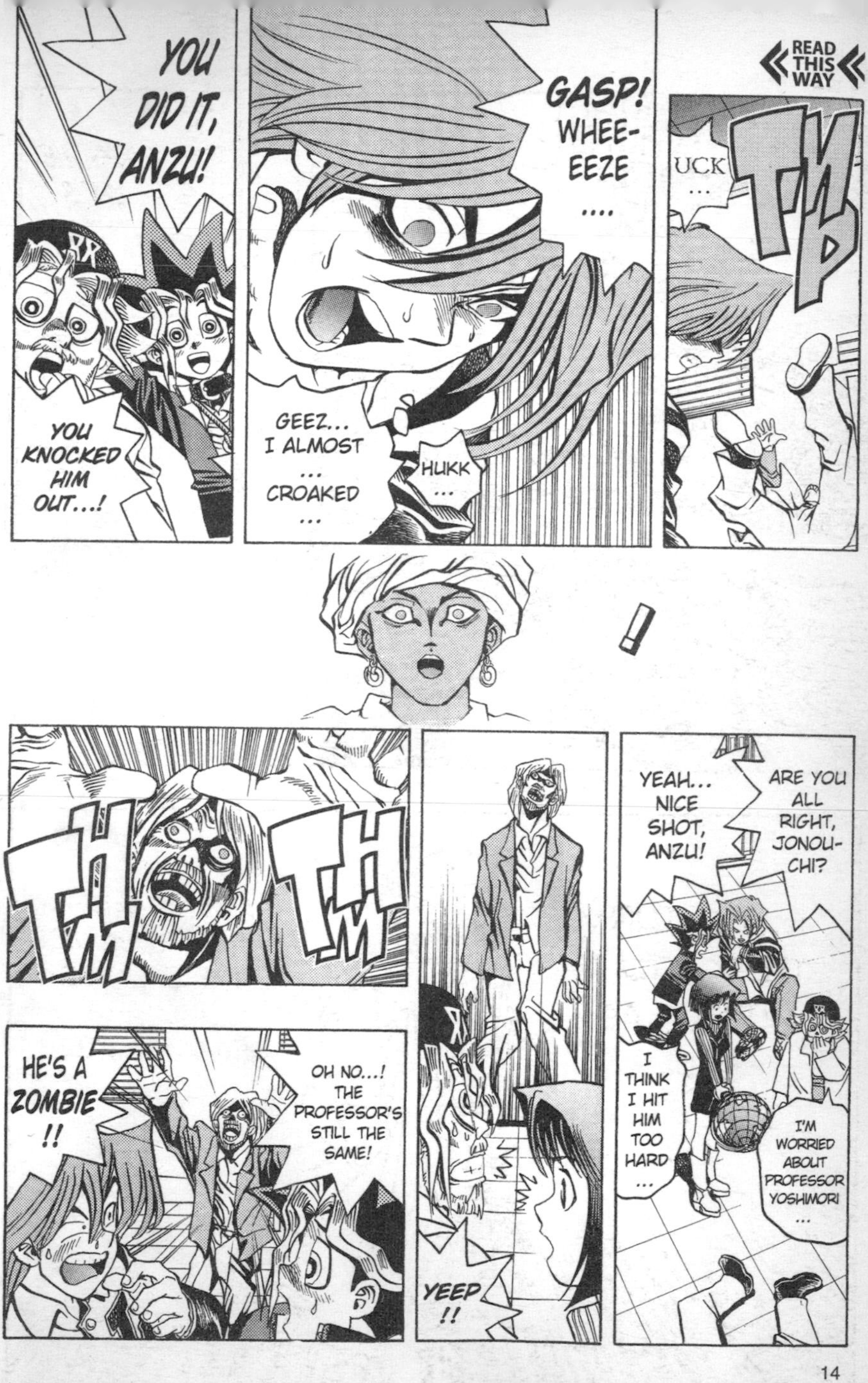
READ THIS WAY
UCK ...
GASP! WHEEE-EEZE ....
GEEZ... I ALMOST ... CROAKED ...
HUKK ...
YOU DID IT, ANZU!
YOU KNOCKED HIM OUT...!
!
ARE YOU ALL RIGHT, JONOUCHI?
YEAH... NICE SHOT, ANZU!
I'M WORRIED ABOUT PROFESSOR YOSHIMORI ...
I THINK I HIT HIM TOO HARD ...
YEEP !!
OH NO...! THE PROFESSOR'S STILL THE SAME!
HE'S A ZOMBIE !!

READ THIS WAY

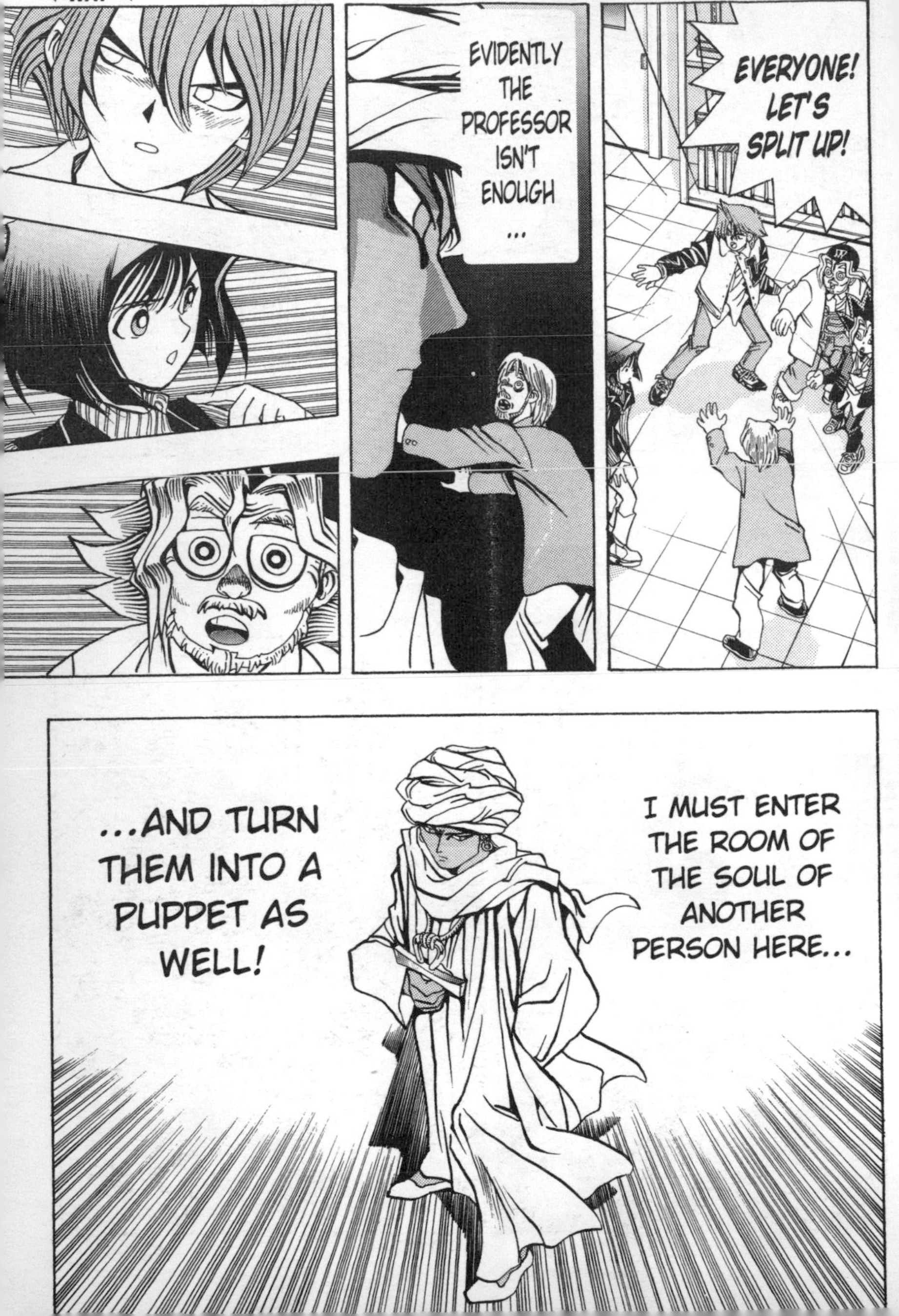
EVERYONE! LET'S SPLIT UP!
EVIDENTLY THE PROFESSOR ISN'T ENOUGH ...
I MUST ENTER THE ROOM OF THE SOUL OF ANOTHER PERSON HERE...
...AND TURN THEM INTO A PUPPET AS WELL!

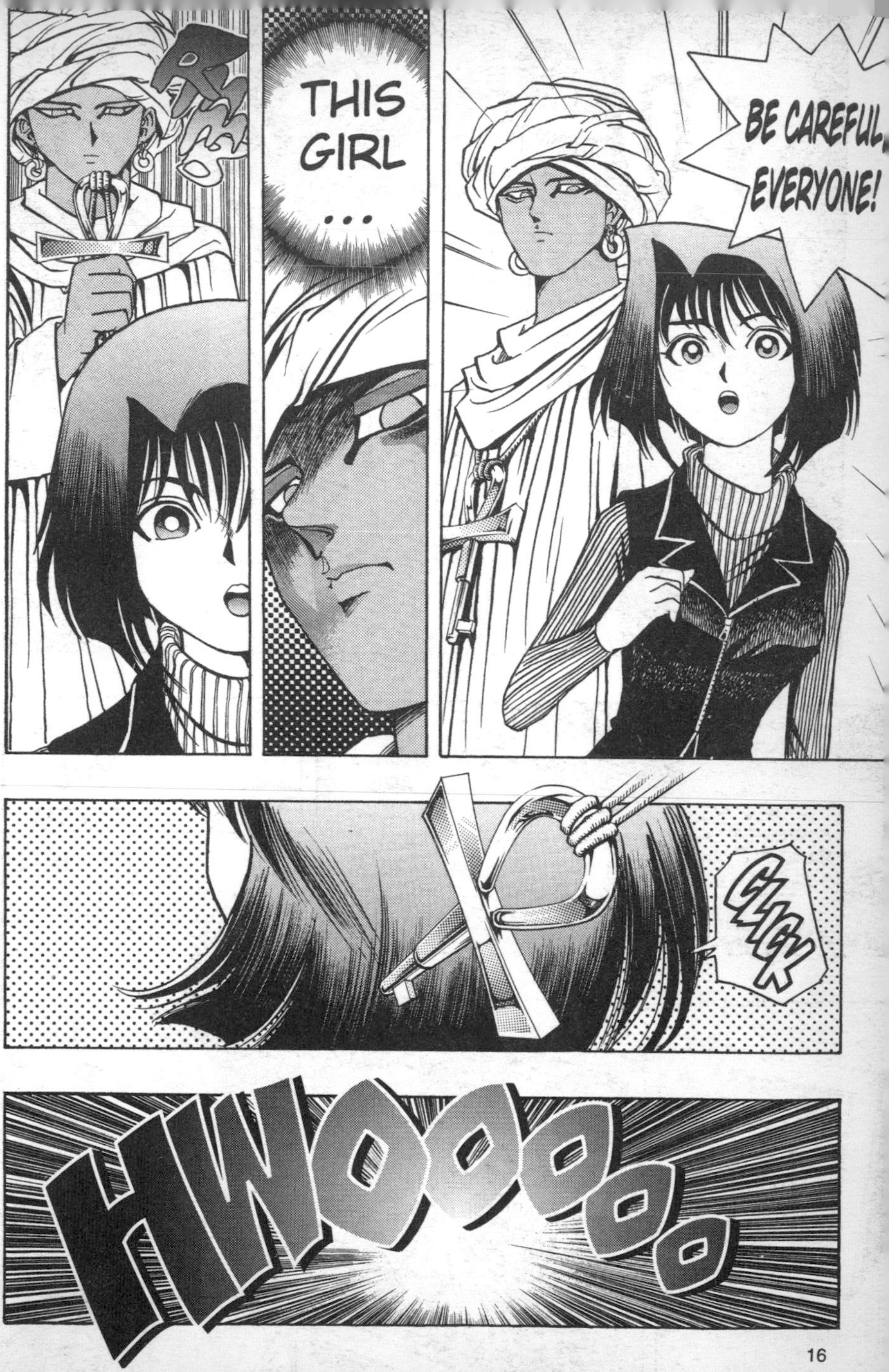
BE CAREFUL, EVERYONE!
THIS GIRL ...
CLICK
HWOOOOOO

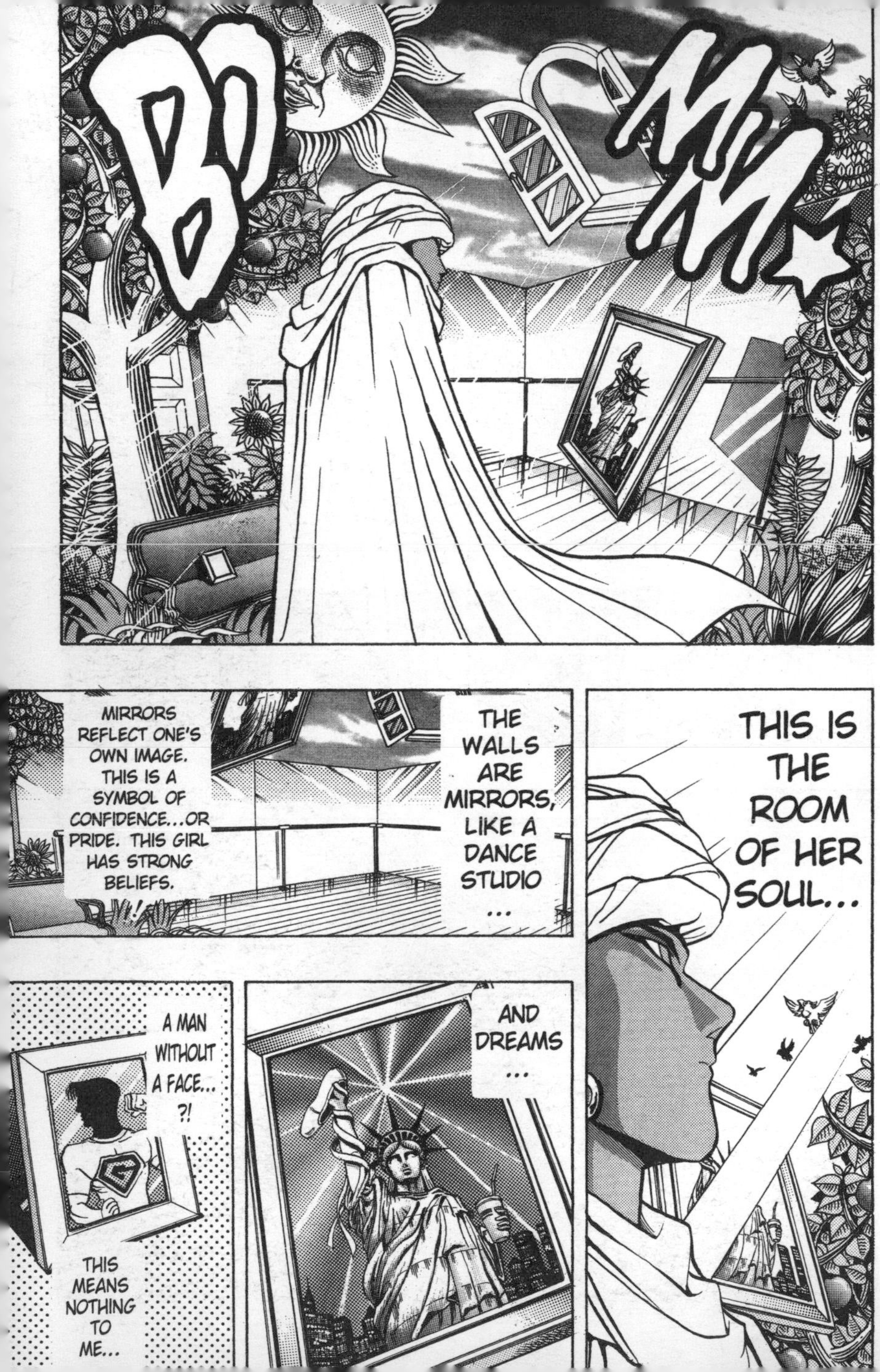
B
MM
THIS IS THE ROOM OF HER SOUL...
THE WALLS ARE MIRRORS, LIKE A DANCE STUDIO...
MIRRORS REFLECT ONE'S OWN IMAGE. THIS IS A SYMBOL OF CONFIDENCE...OR PRIDE. THIS GIRL HAS STRONG BELIEFS.
AND DREAMS...
A MAN WITHOUT A FACE...?!
THIS MEANS NOTHING TO ME...

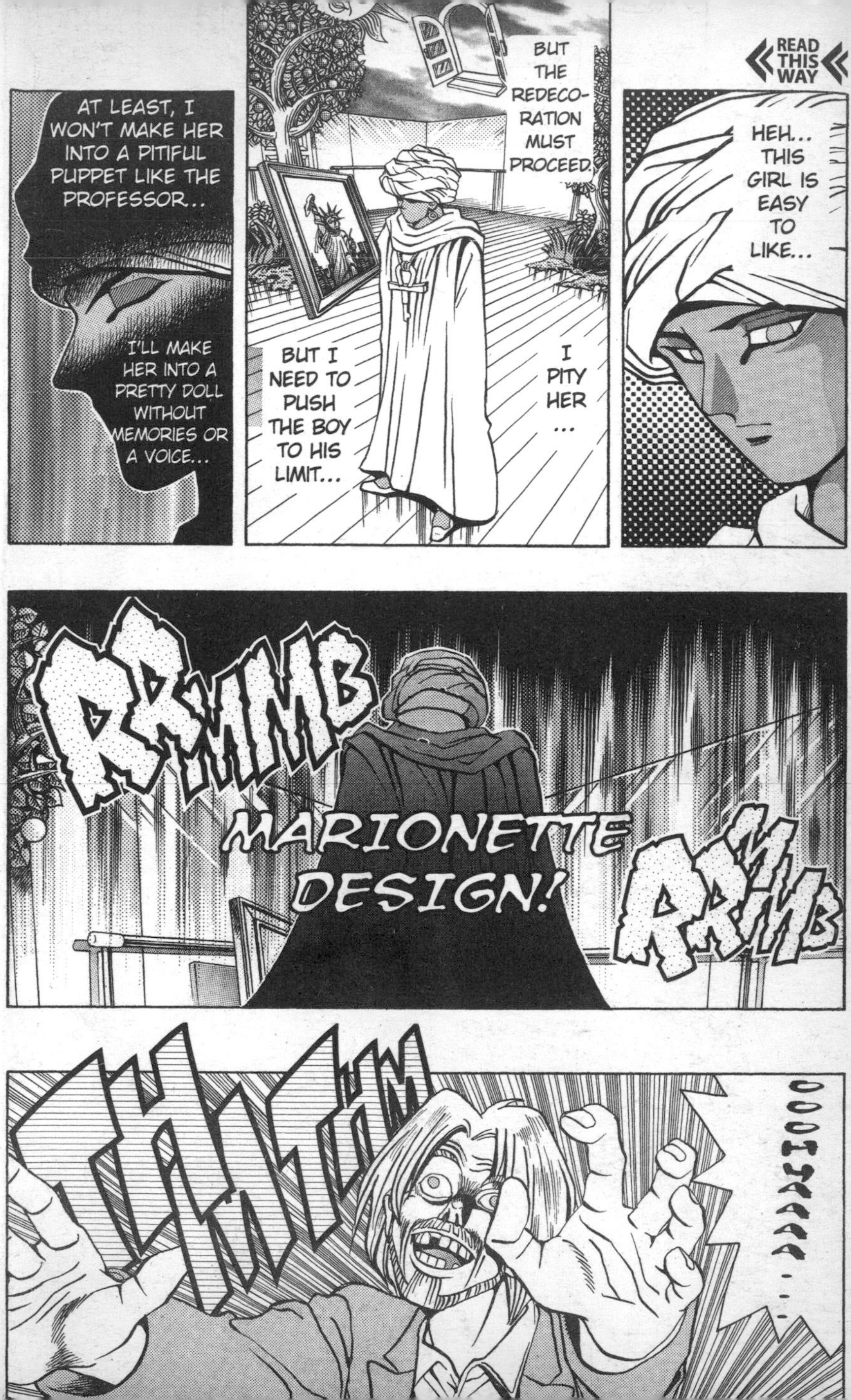
READ THIS WAY
HEH... THIS GIRL IS EASY TO LIKE...
BUT THE REDECORATION MUST PROCEED.
I PITY HER...
BUT I NEED TO PUSH THE BOY TO HIS LIMIT...
AT LEAST, I WON'T MAKE HER INTO A PITIFUL PUPPET LIKE THE PROFESSOR...
I'LL MAKE HER INTO A PRETTY DOLL WITHOUT MEMORIES OR A VOICE...
RRMMB
MARIONETTE DESIGN!
RRMB
OOOHWAAAAA...
THMTHM

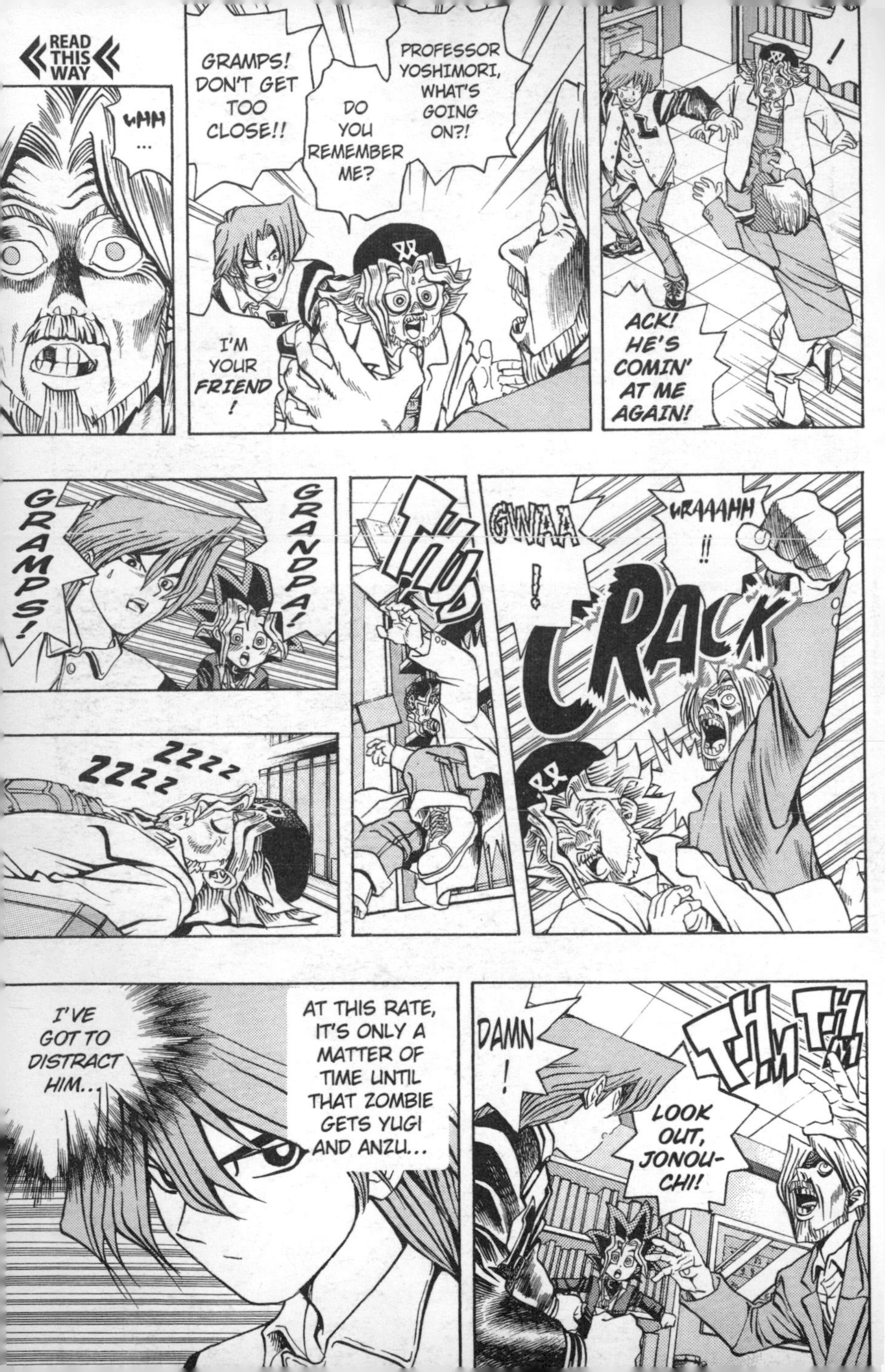
READ THIS WAY
!
ACK! HE'S COMIN' AT ME AGAIN!
PROFESSOR YOSHIMORI, WHAT'S GOING ON?!
DO YOU REMEMBER ME?
GRAMPS! DON'T GET TOO CLOSE!!
I'M YOUR FRIEND!
UHH ...
URAAAHH!!
GWAA!!
CRACK
THUD
GRANDPA!
GRAMPS!
ZZZZ ZZZZ
LOOK OUT, JONOUCHI!
DAMN!
AT THIS RATE, IT'S ONLY A MATTER OF TIME UNTIL THAT ZOMBIE GETS YUGI AND ANZU...
I'VE GOT TO DISTRACT HIM...

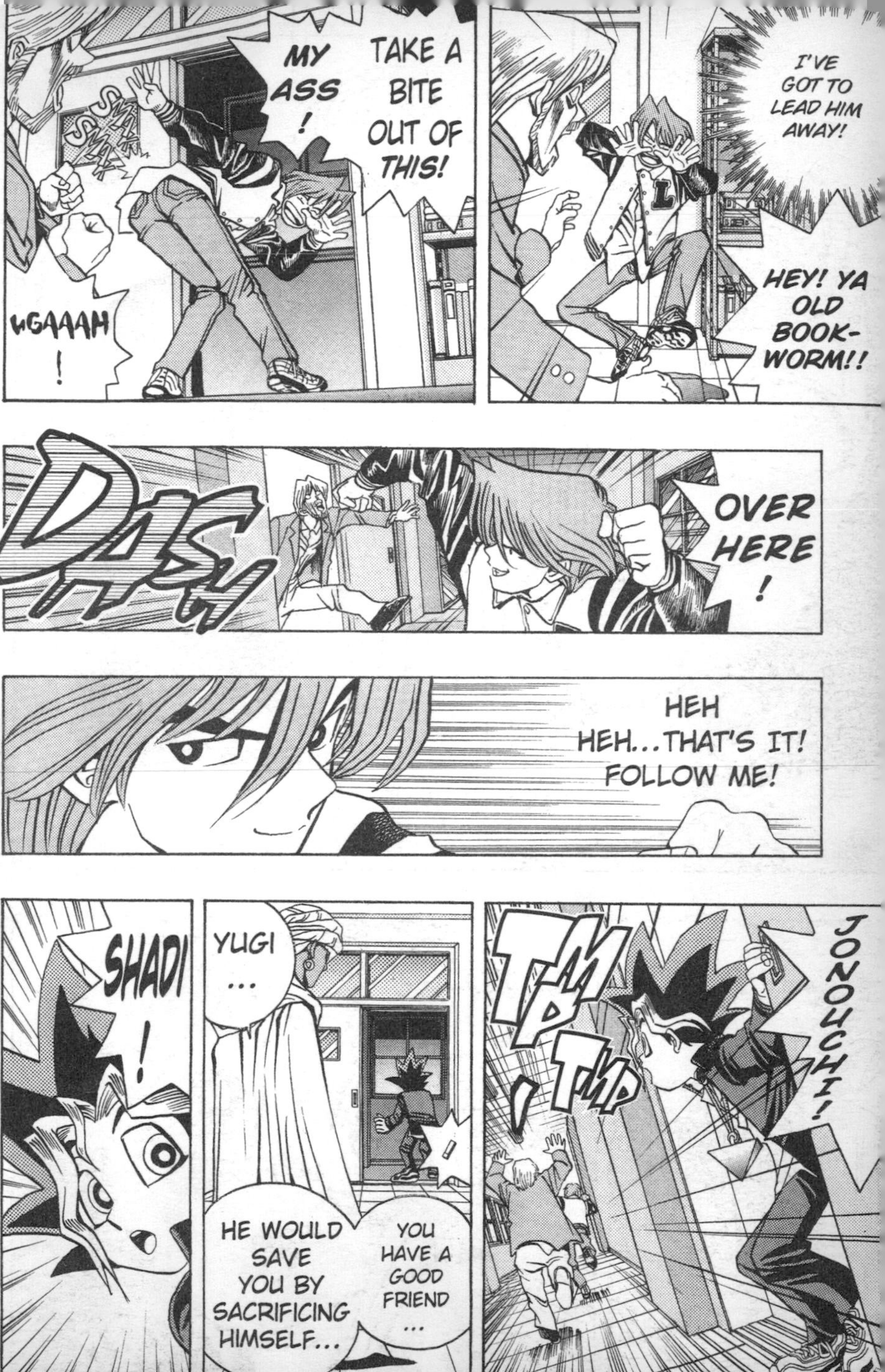
I'VE GOT TO LEAD HIM AWAY!
HEY! YA OLD BOOK-WORM!!
TAKE A BITE OUT OF THIS!
MY ASS!
UGAAAH!
OVER HERE!
DASH
HEH HEH...THAT'S IT! FOLLOW ME!
JONOUCHI!
YUGI ...
YOU HAVE A GOOD FRIEND ...
HE WOULD SAVE YOU BY SACRIFICING HIMSELF...
SHADI!

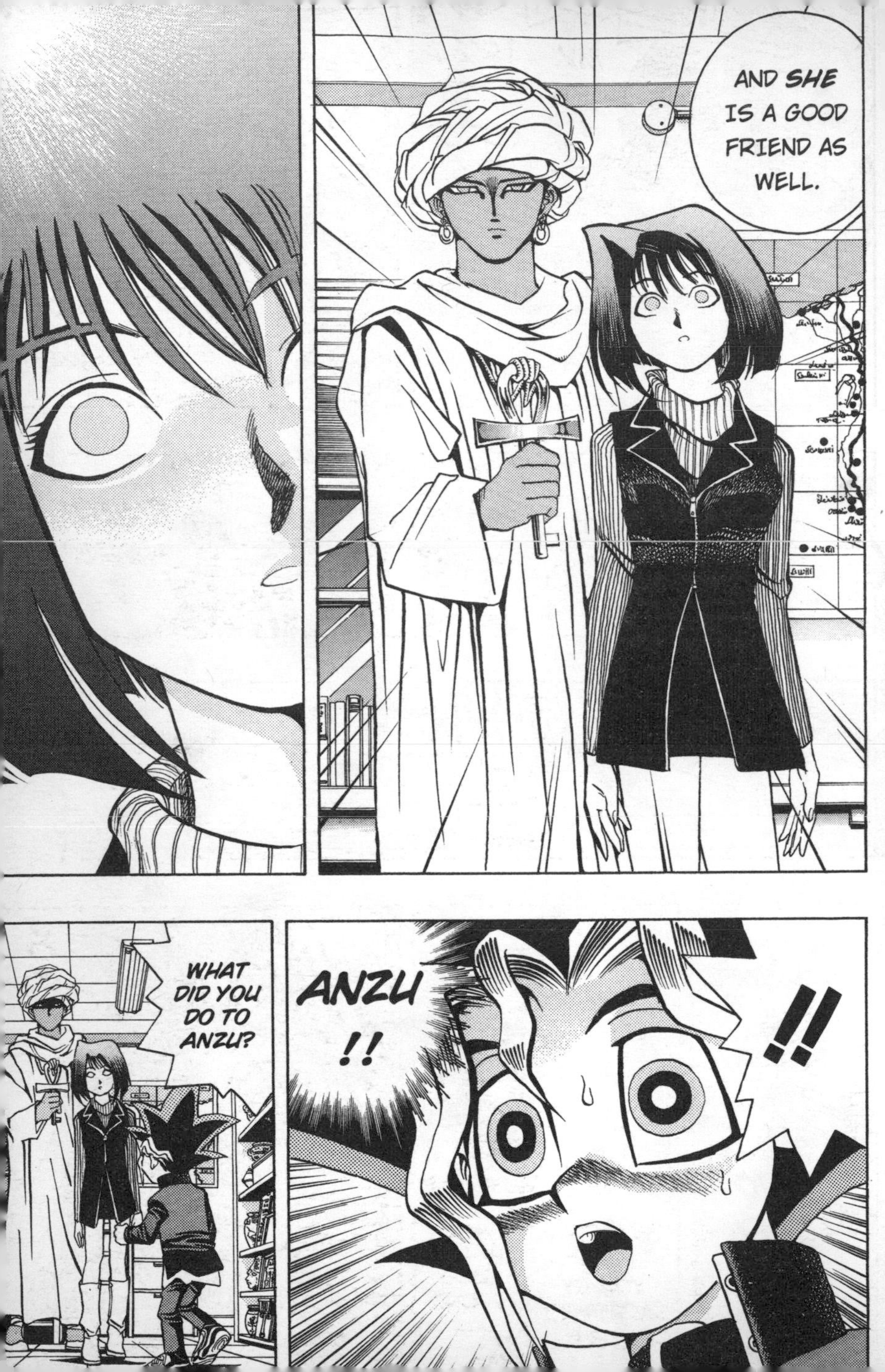
AND SHE IS A GOOD FRIEND AS WELL.
ANZU !!
!!
WHAT DID YOU DO TO ANZU?

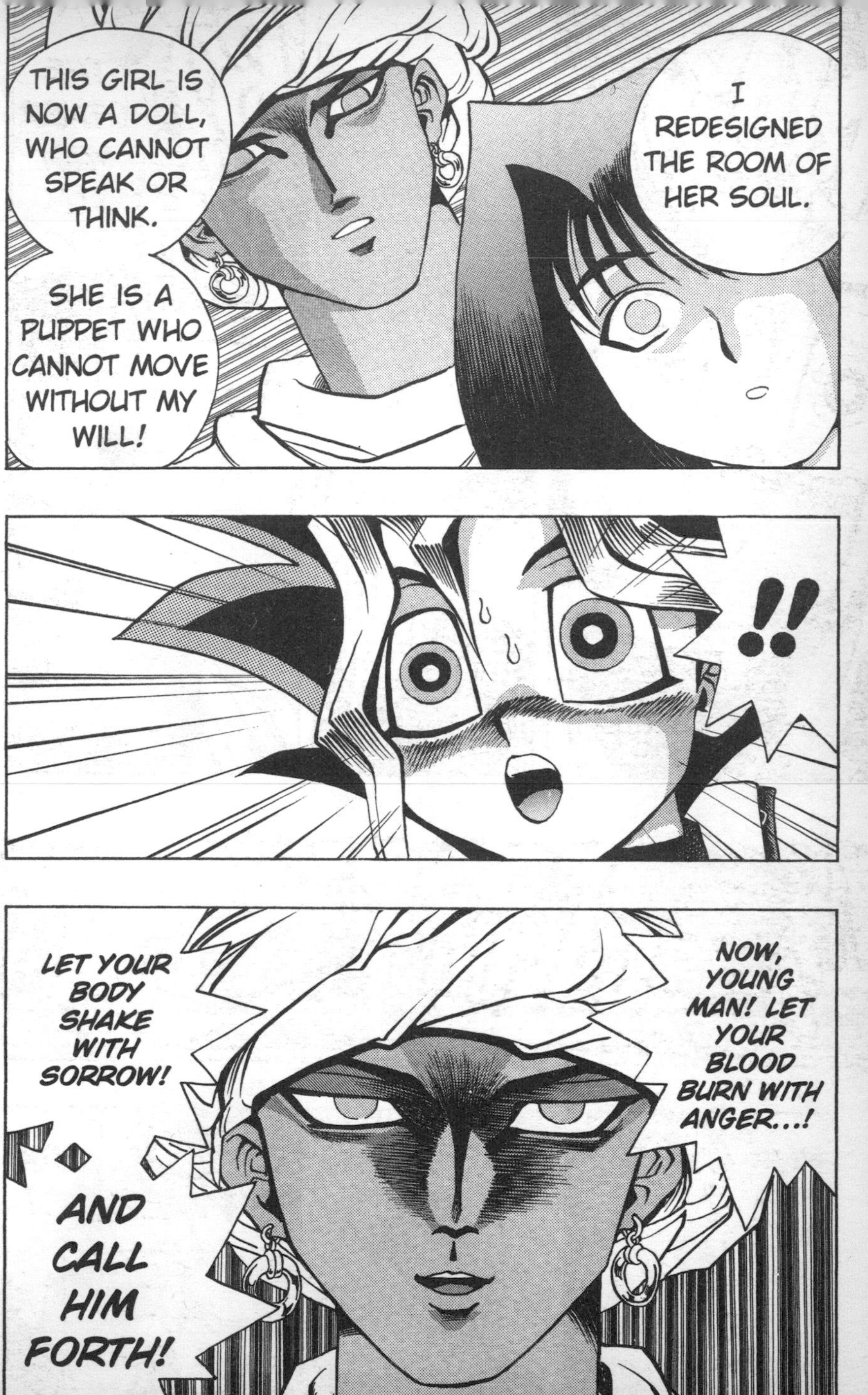
I REDESIGNED THE ROOM OF HER SOUL.
THIS GIRL IS NOW A DOLL, WHO CANNOT SPEAK OR THINK.
SHE IS A PUPPET WHO CANNOT MOVE WITHOUT MY WILL!
!!
NOW, YOUNG MAN! LET YOUR BLOOD BURN WITH ANGER...!
LET YOUR BODY SHAKE WITH SORROW!
AND CALL HIM FORTH!

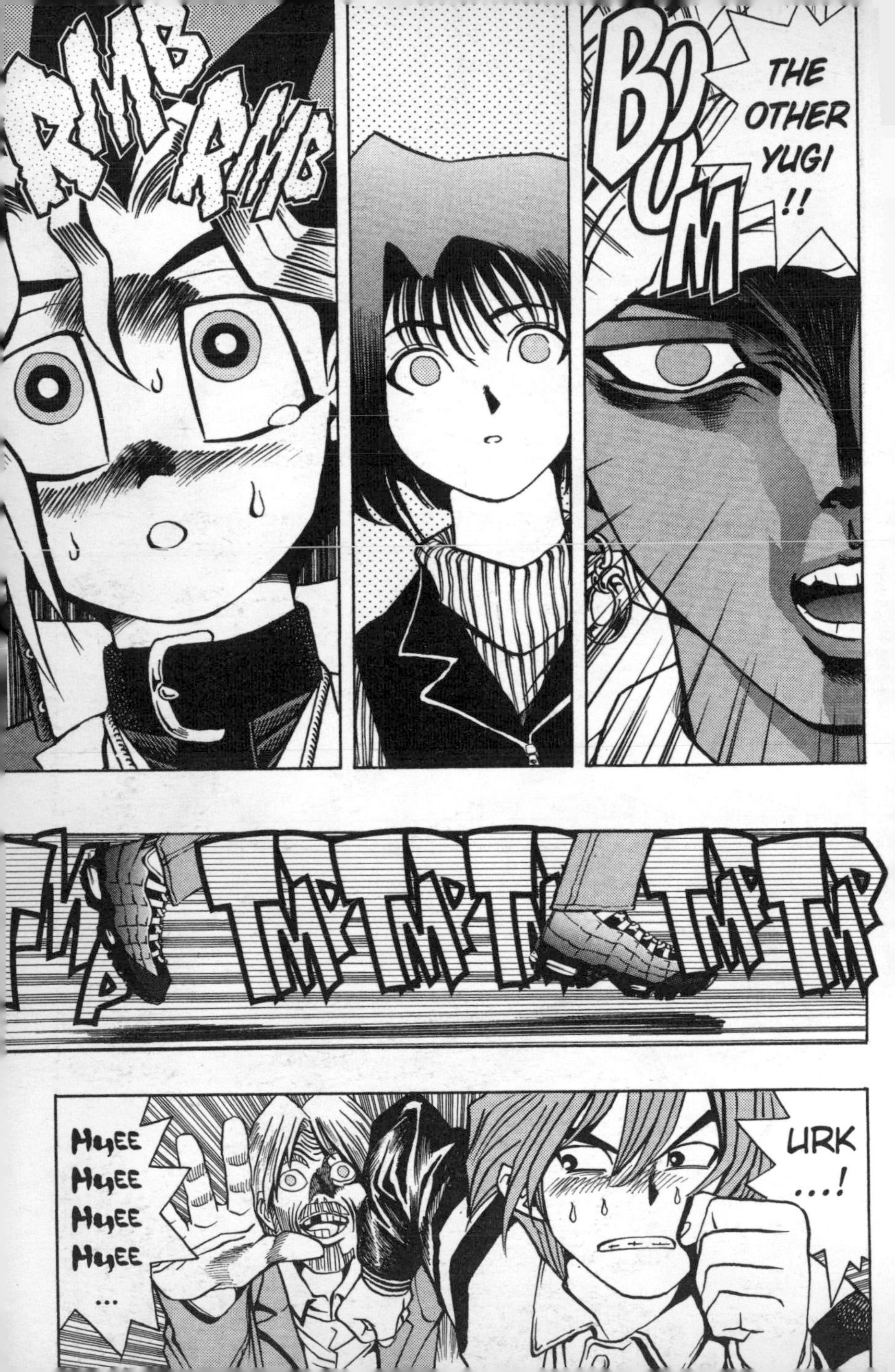
BOOM
THE OTHER YUGI !!
RMB RMB
TMP TMP TMP TMP TMP
URK ...!
HyEE HyEE HyEE HyEE ...

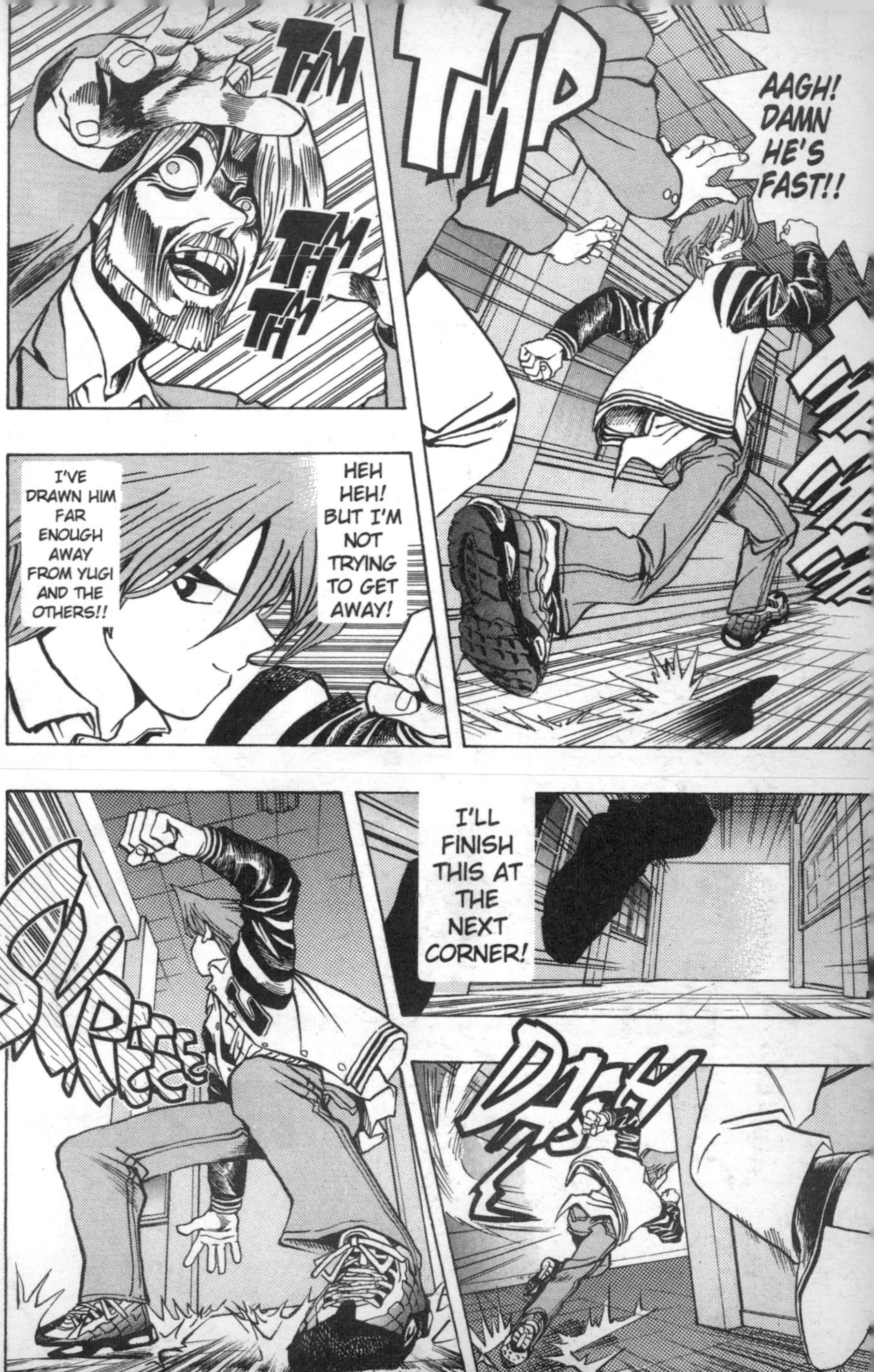
TMP
AAGH! DAMN HE'S FAST!!
THM
THM THM THM
HEH HEH! BUT I'M NOT TRYING TO GET AWAY!
I'VE DRAWN HIM FAR ENOUGH AWAY FROM YUGI AND THE OTHERS!!
I'LL FINISH THIS AT THE NEXT CORNER!

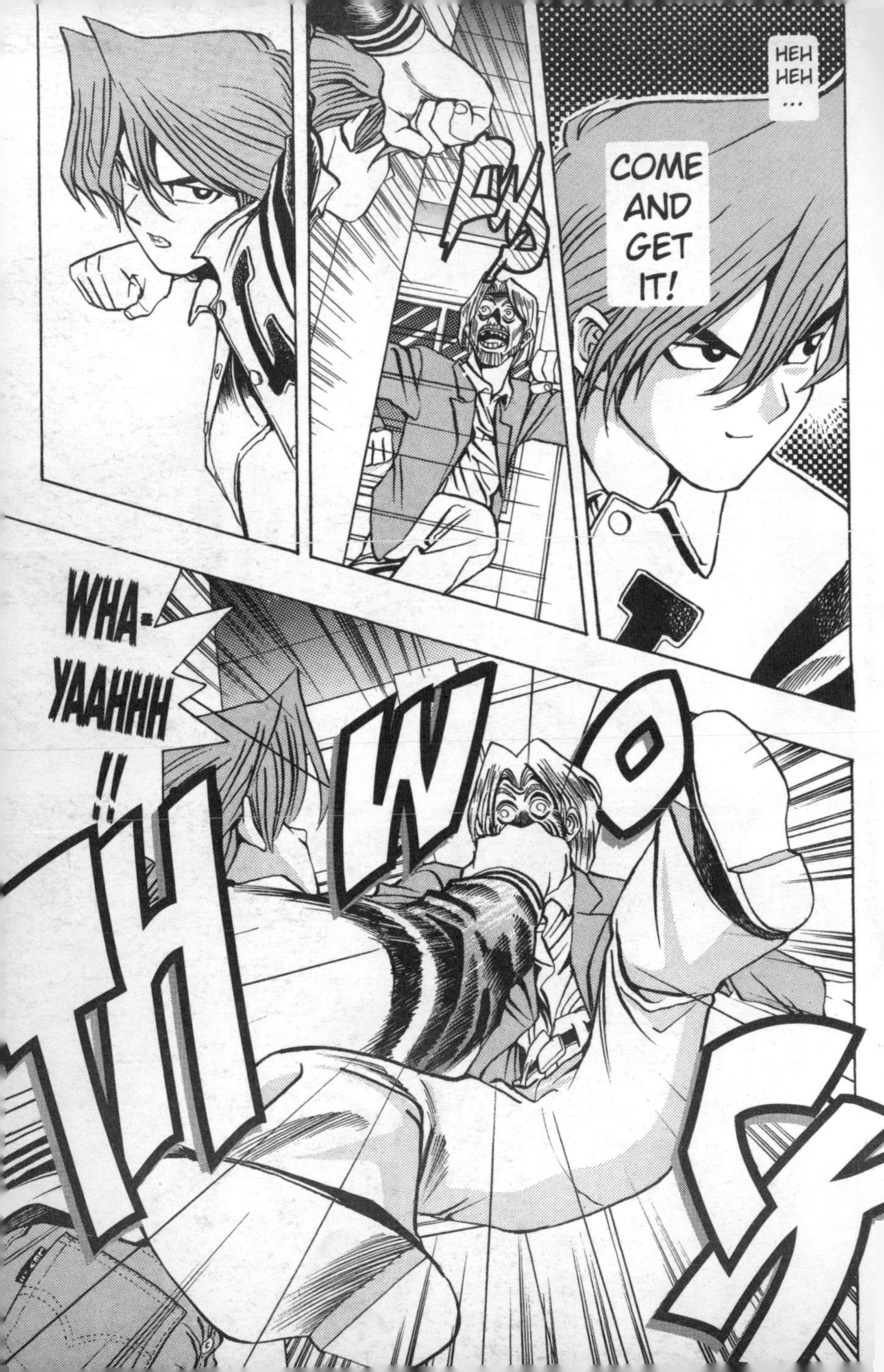
HEH HEH ...
COME AND GET IT!
WHA-YAAHHH!!
THWOK

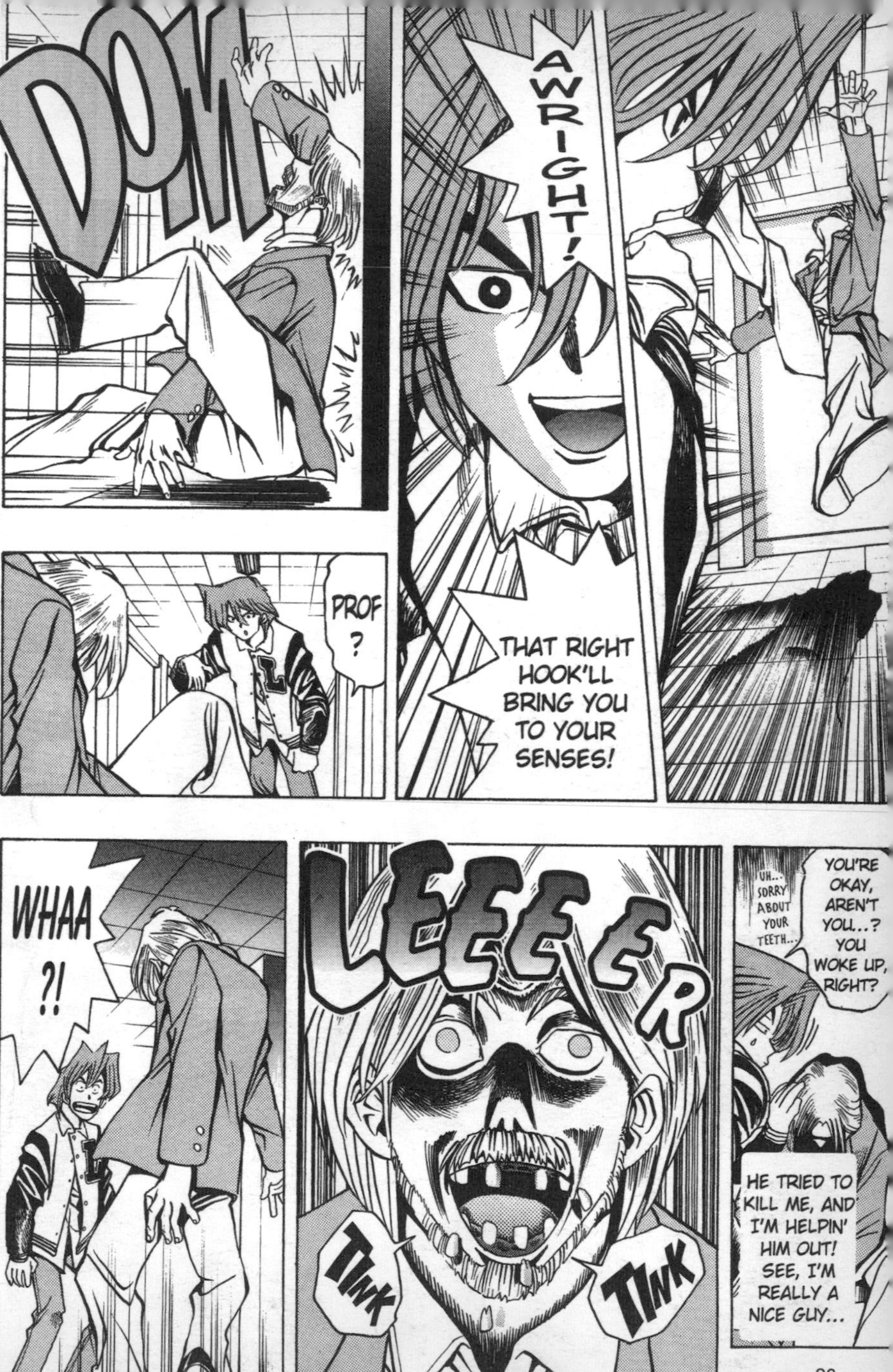

AWRIGHT!
THAT RIGHT HOOK'LL BRING YOU TO YOUR SENSES!
DOM
PROF ?
YOU'RE OKAY, AREN'T YOU...? YOU WOKE UP, RIGHT?
UH... SORRY ABOUT YOUR TEETH...
HE TRIED TO KILL ME, AND I'M HELPIN' HIM OUT! SEE, I'M REALLY A NICE GUY...
LEEEER
TINK
TINK
WHAA ?!

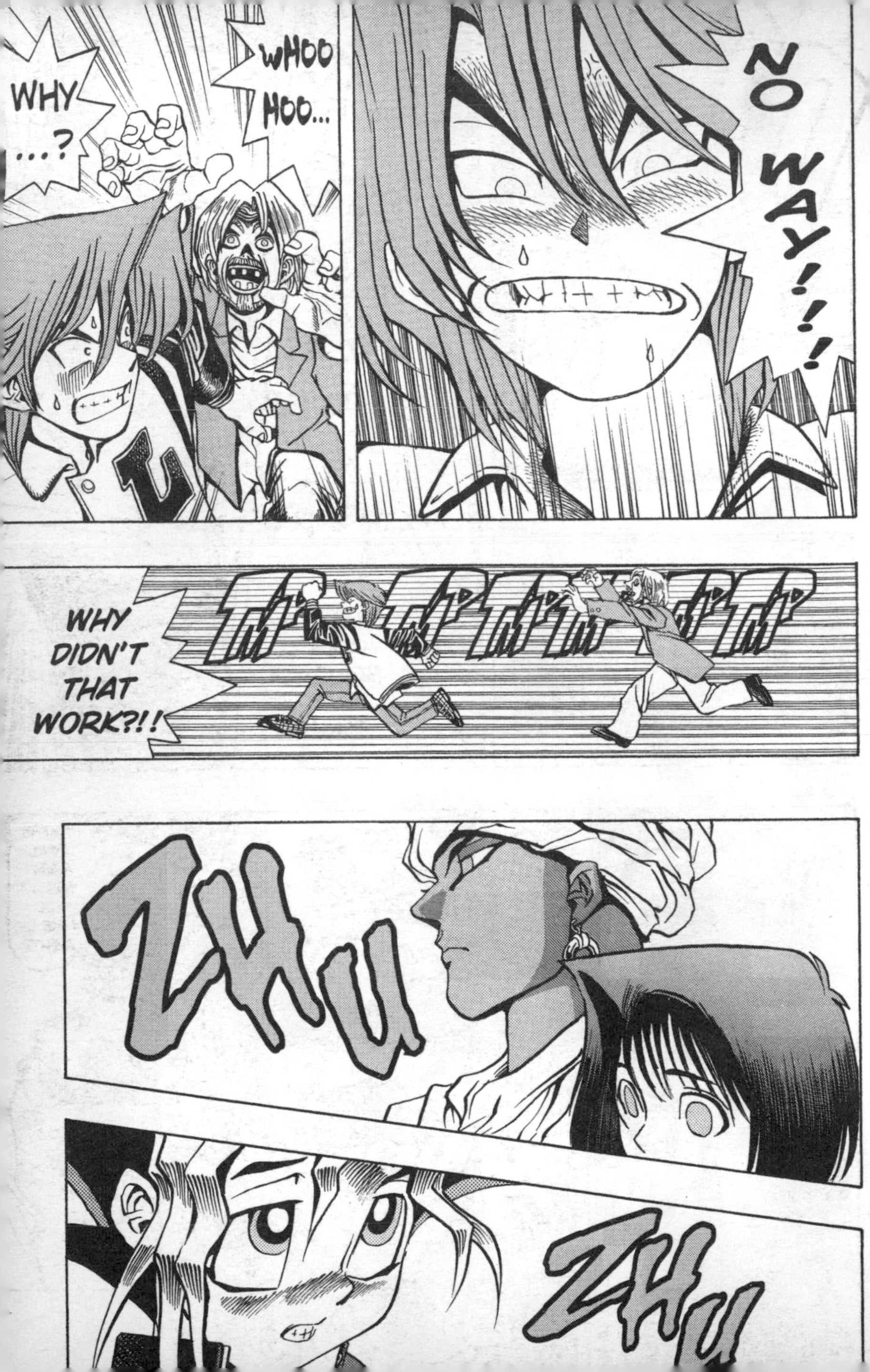
NO WAY!!!
WHOO HOO...
WHY ...?
WHY DIDN'T THAT WORK?!!
ZHU
ZHU

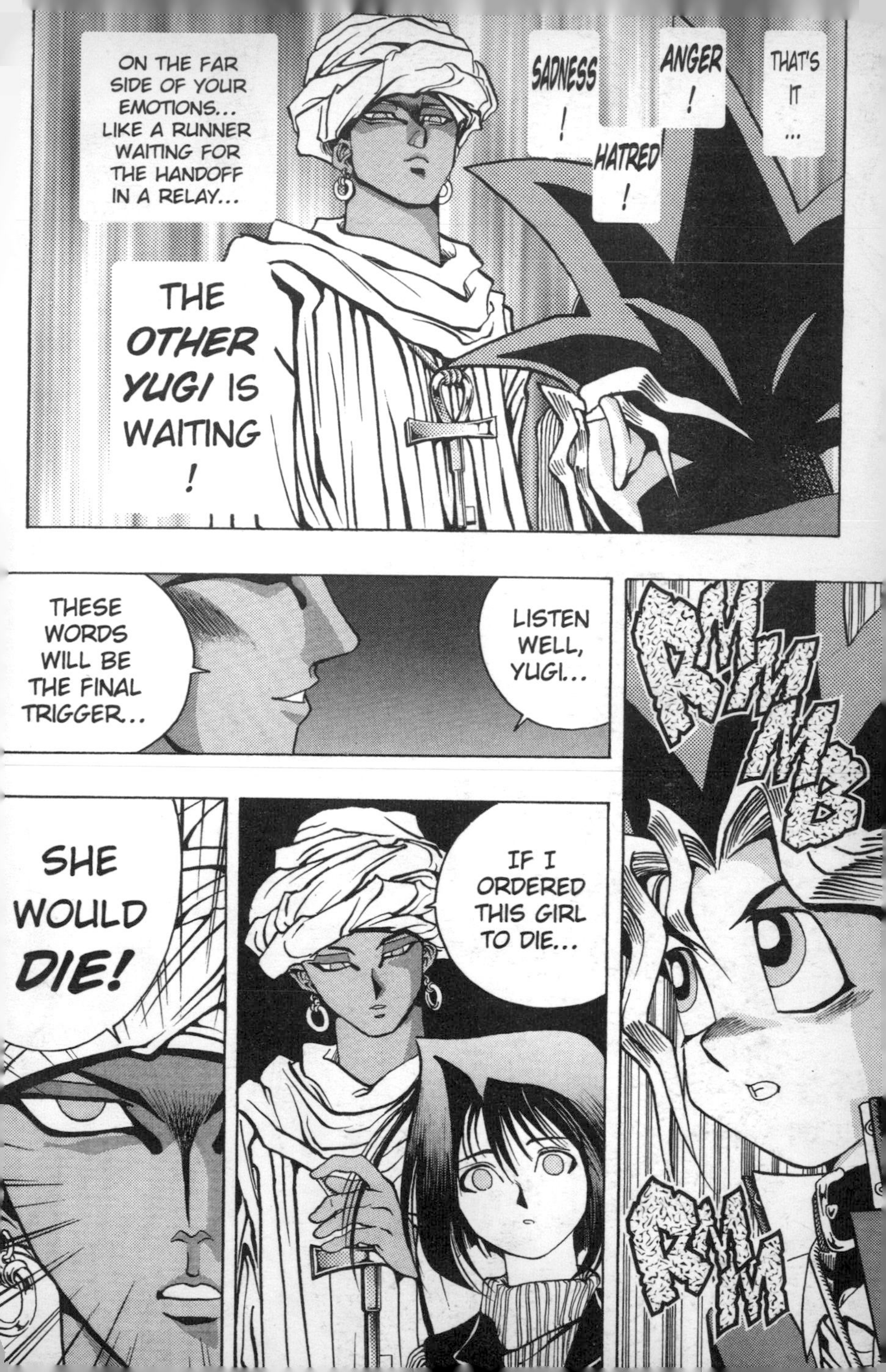
THAT'S IT ...
ANGER !
HATRED !
SADNESS !
ON THE FAR SIDE OF YOUR EMOTIONS... LIKE A RUNNER WAITING FOR THE HANDOFF IN A RELAY...
THE OTHER YUGI IS WAITING !
LISTEN WELL, YUGI...
THESE WORDS WILL BE THE FINAL TRIGGER...
IF I ORDERED THIS GIRL TO DIE...
SHE WOULD DIE!

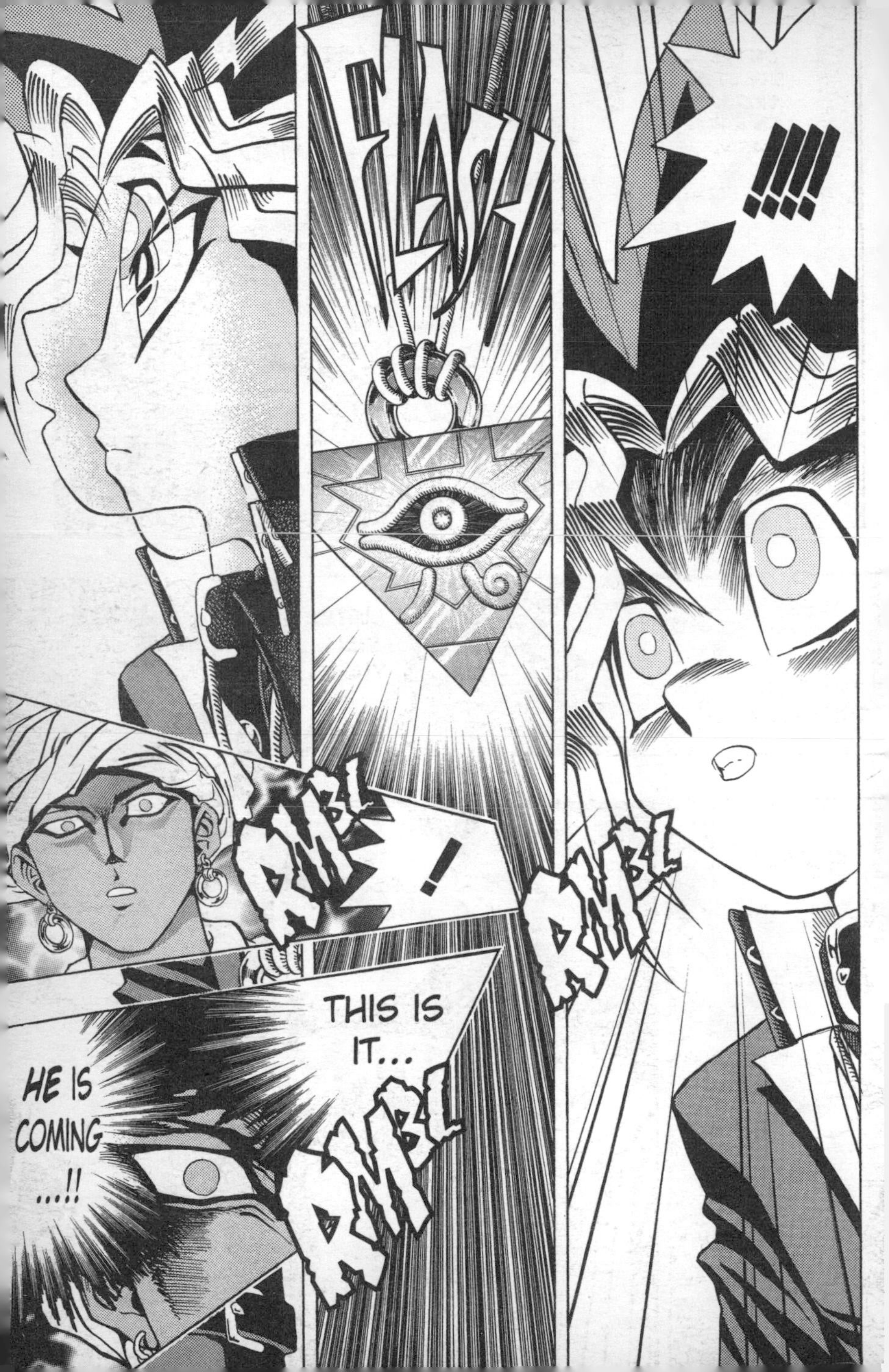
!!!!!
RMBL
FLASH
RMBL
!
THIS IS IT...
HE IS COMING ...!!
RMBL

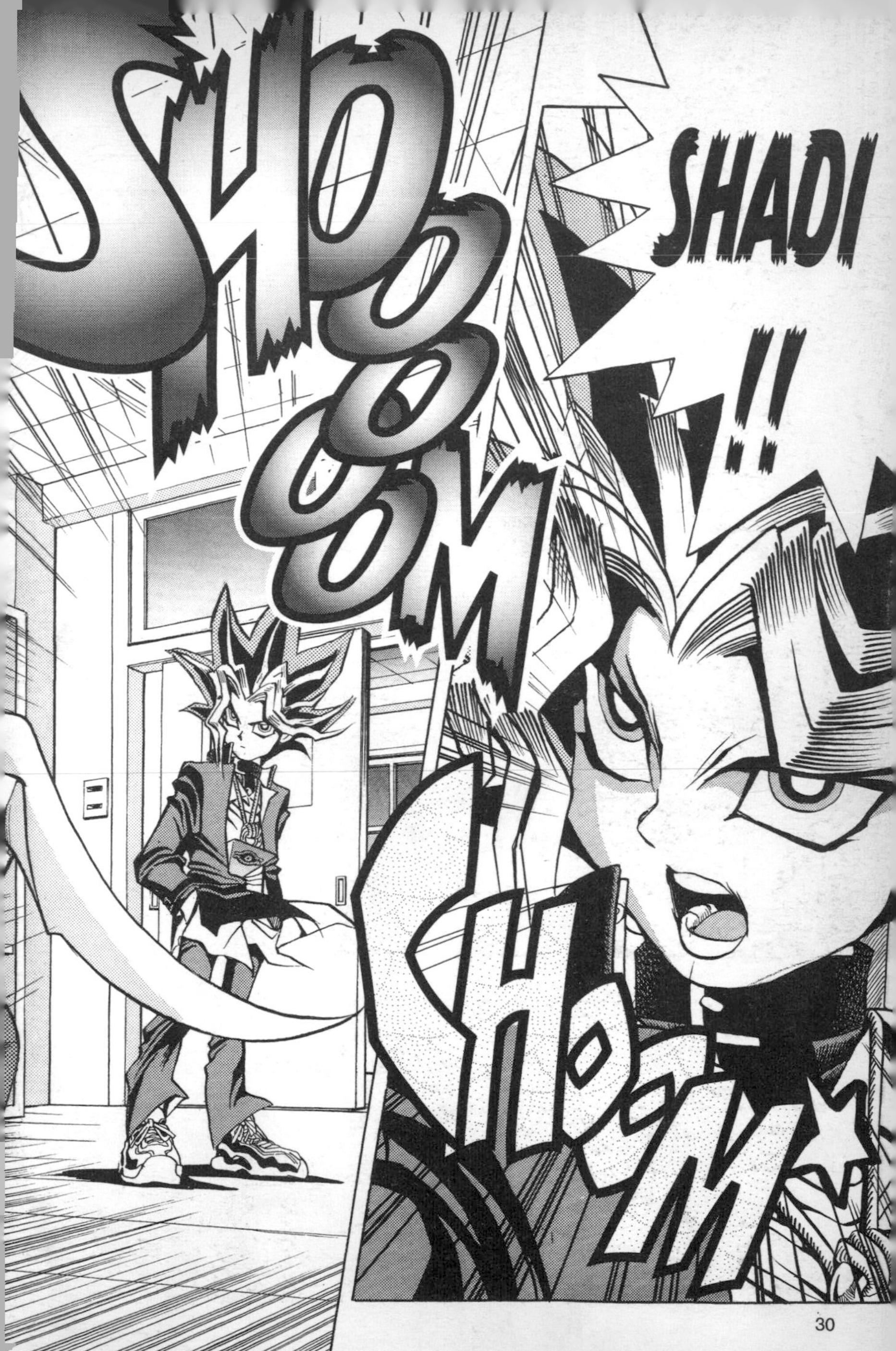
SHADI!!
SHOOOOM
SHOOM

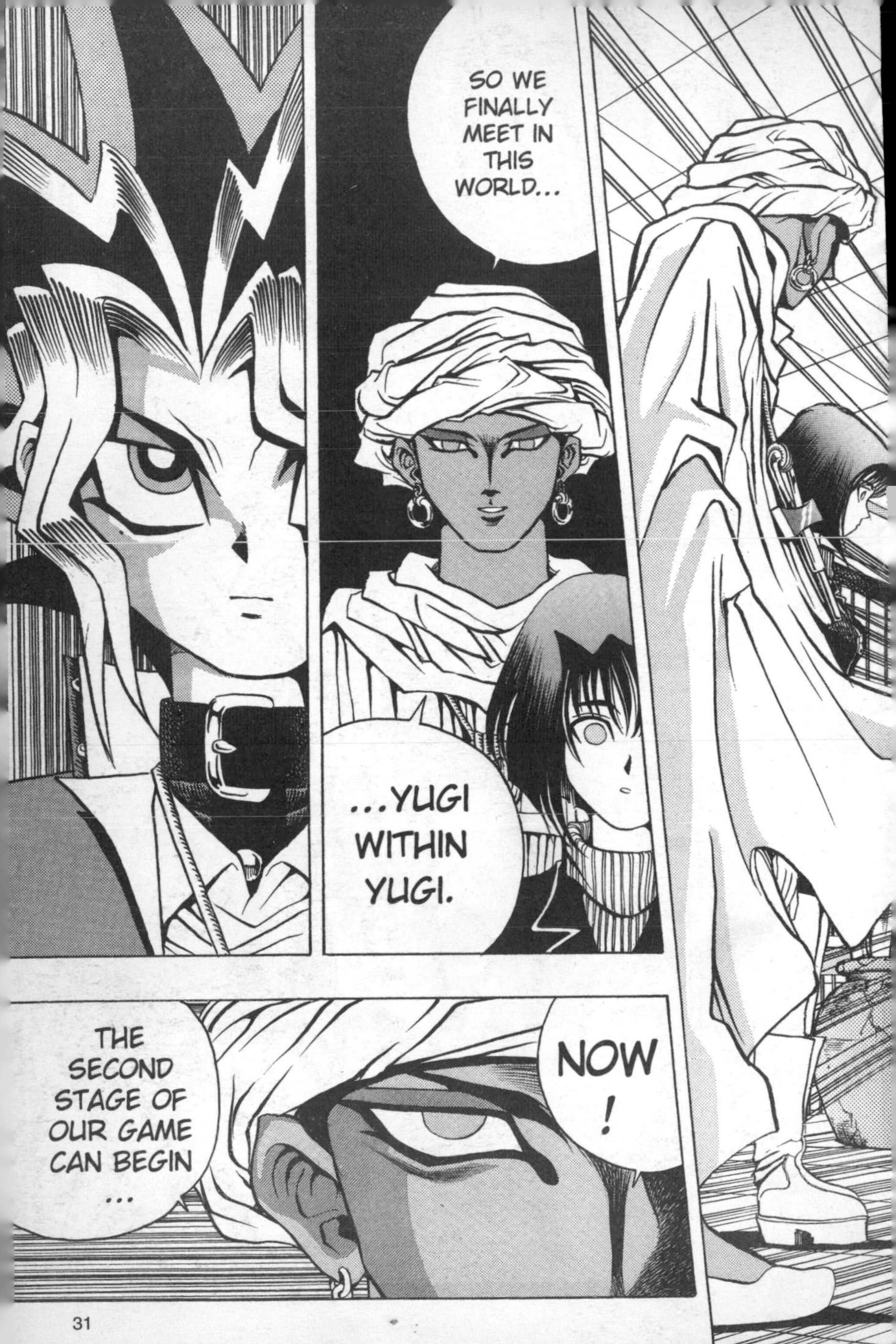
SO WE FINALLY MEET IN THIS WORLD...
...YUGI WITHIN YUGI.
THE SECOND STAGE OF OUR GAME CAN BEGIN ...
NOW !

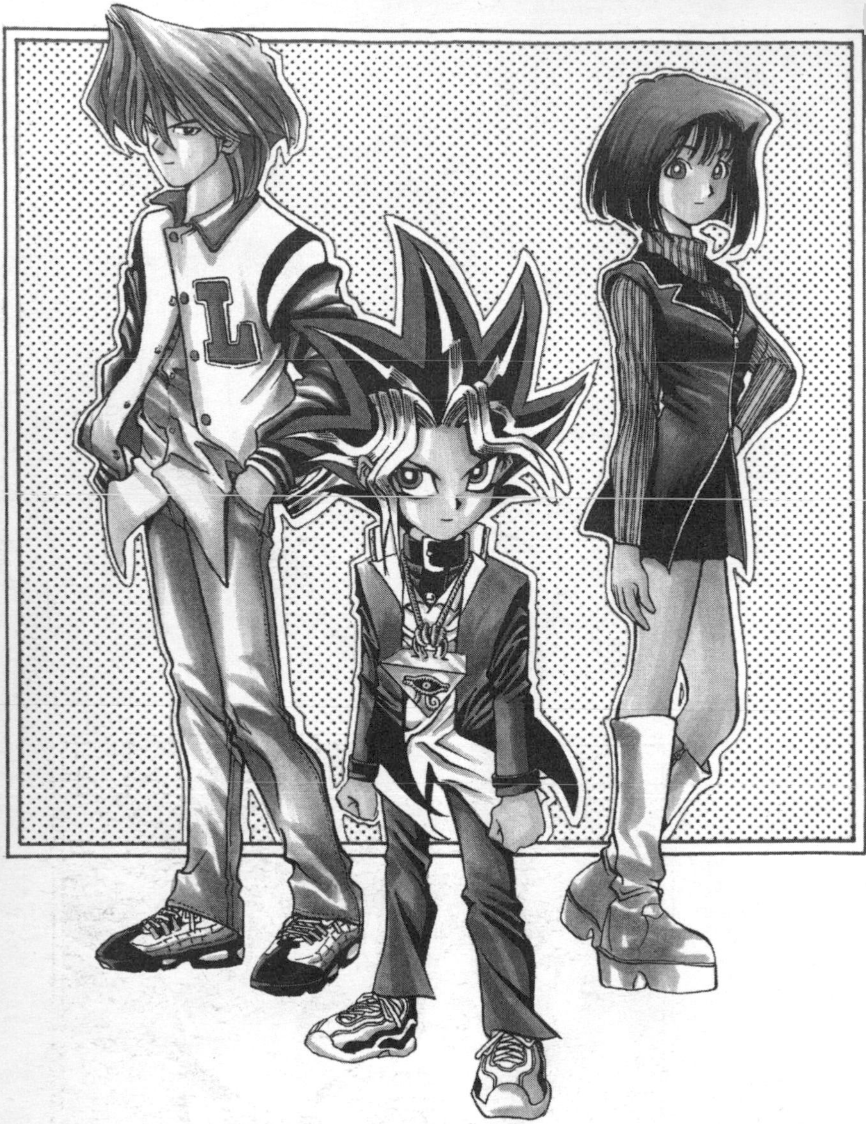

Duel 17: Game Start!

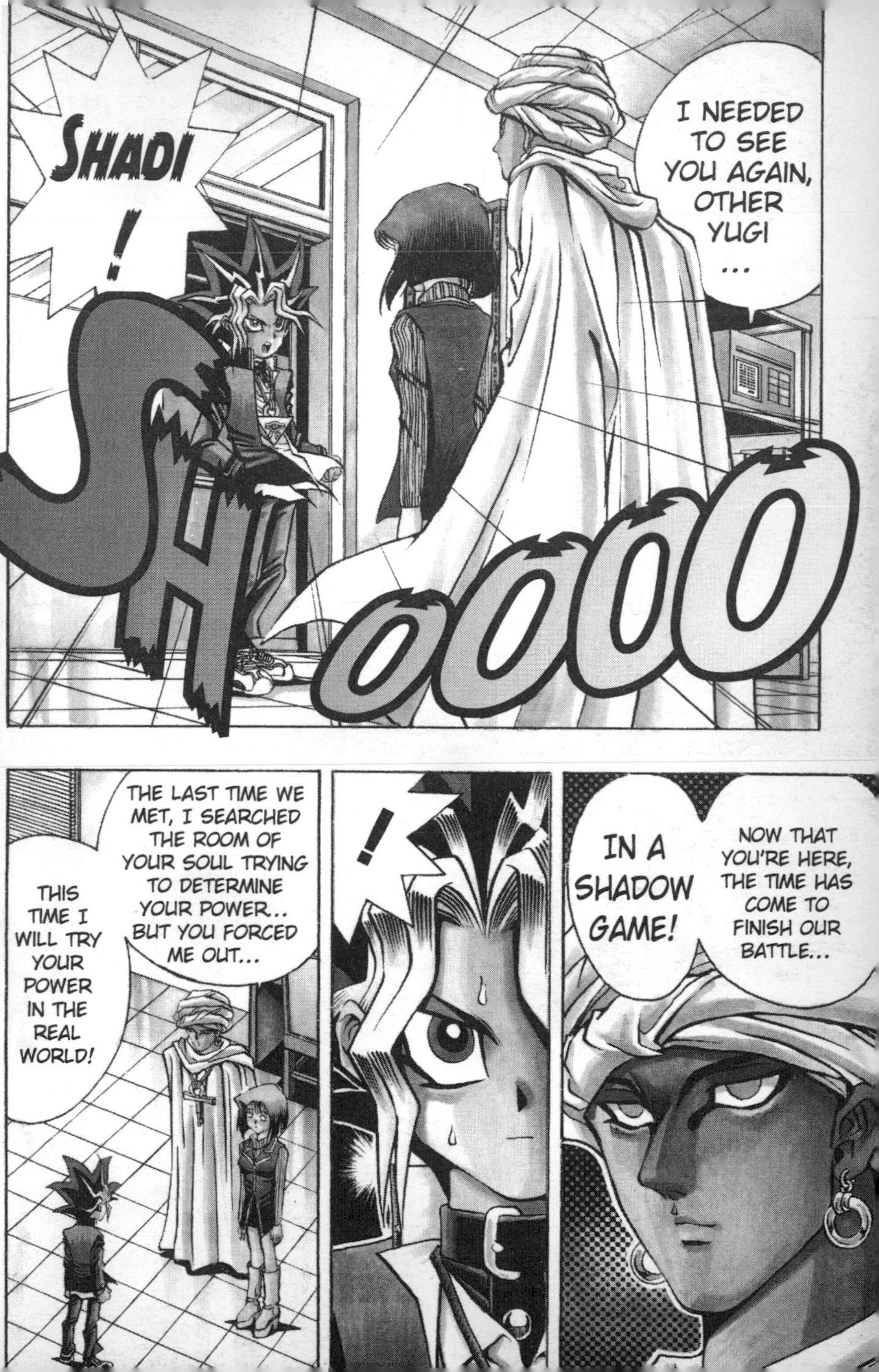
I NEEDED TO SEE YOU AGAIN, OTHER YUGI ...
SHADI !
SHOOOO
NOW THAT YOU'RE HERE, THE TIME HAS COME TO FINISH OUR BATTLE...
IN A SHADOW GAME!
!
THE LAST TIME WE MET, I SEARCHED THE ROOM OF YOUR SOUL TRYING TO DETERMINE YOUR POWER... BUT YOU FORCED ME OUT...
THIS TIME I WILL TRY YOUR POWER IN THE REAL WORLD!

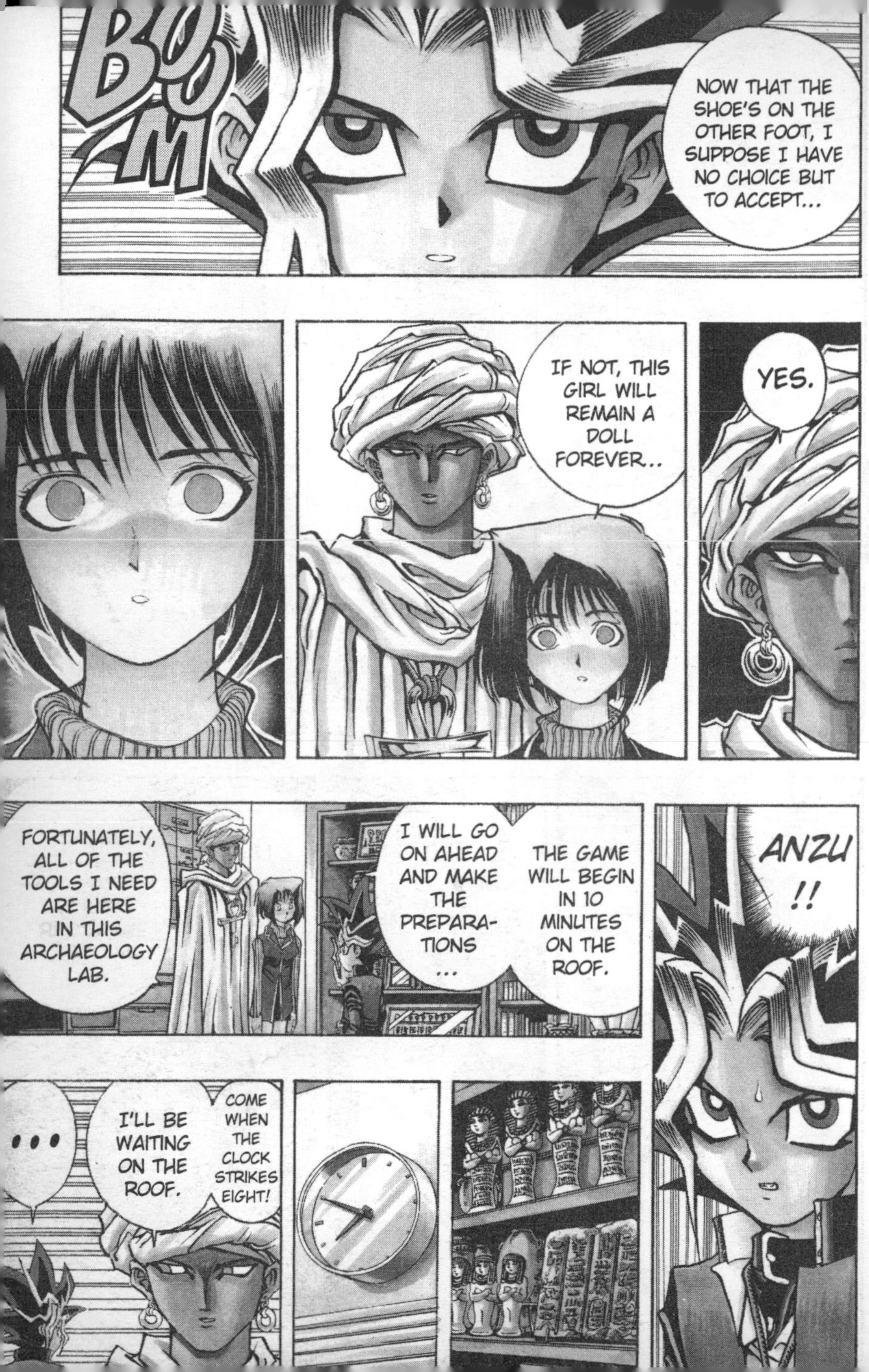
BOOM
NOW THAT THE SHOE'S ON THE OTHER FOOT, I SUPPOSE I HAVE NO CHOICE BUT TO ACCEPT...
YES.
IF NOT, THIS GIRL WILL REMAIN A DOLL FOREVER..
ANZU !!
THE GAME WILL BEGIN IN 10 MINUTES ON THE ROOF.
I WILL GO ON AHEAD AND MAKE THE PREPARATIONS ...
FORTUNATELY, ALL OF THE TOOLS I NEED ARE HERE IN THIS ARCHAEOLOGY LAB.
COME WHEN THE CLOCK STRIKES EIGHT!
I'LL BE WAITING ON THE ROOF.
...

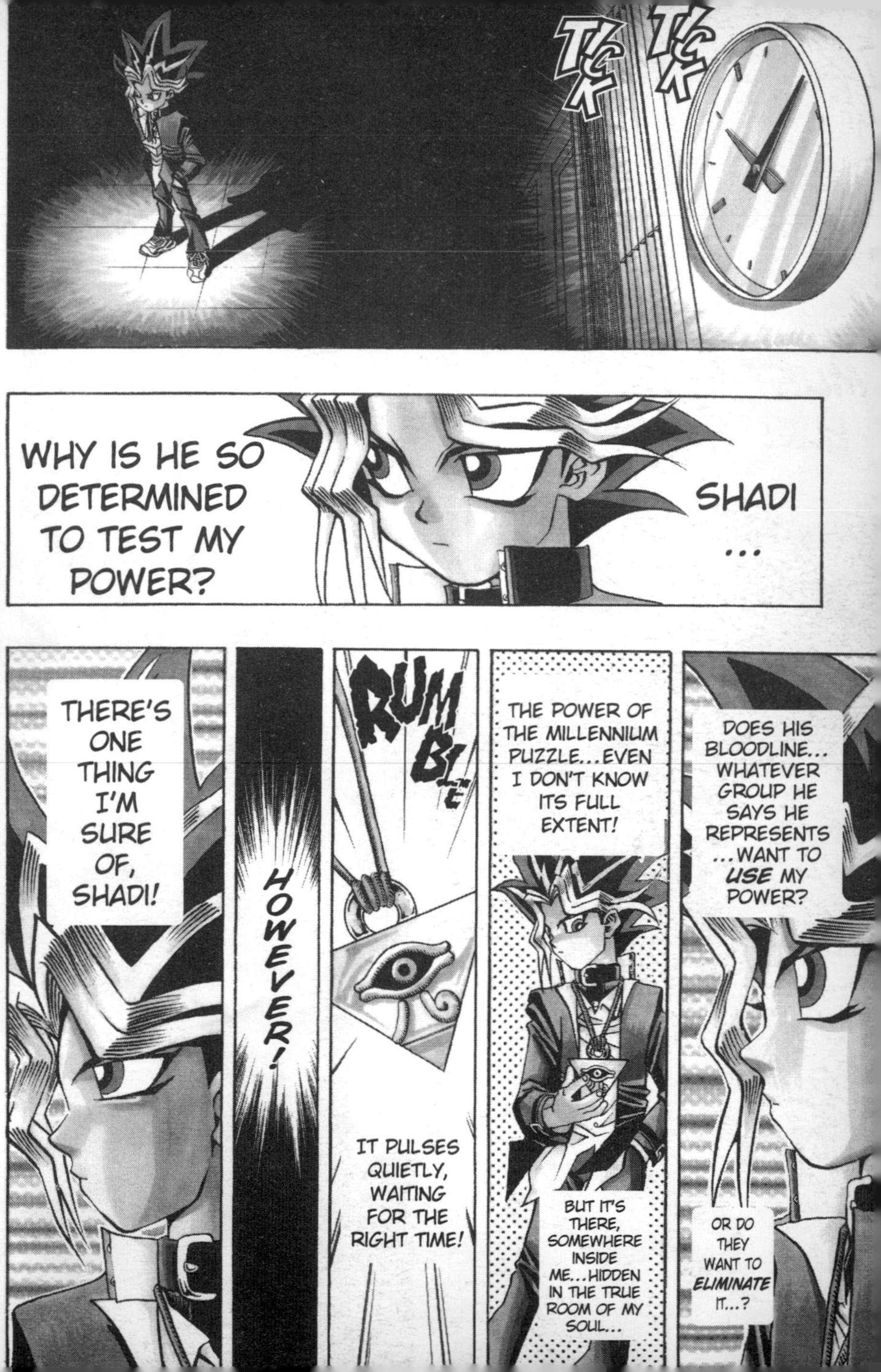
TICK TICK
SHADI...
WHY IS HE SO DETERMINED TO TEST MY POWER?
DOES HIS BLOODLINE... WHATEVER GROUP HE SAYS HE REPRESENTS ...WANT TO USE MY POWER?
OR DO THEY WANT TO ELIMINATE IT...?
THE POWER OF THE MILLENNIUM PUZZLE...EVEN I DON'T KNOW ITS FULL EXTENT!
BUT IT'S THERE, SOMEWHERE INSIDE ME...HIDDEN IN THE TRUE ROOM OF MY SOUL...
RUMBLE
IT PULSES QUIETLY, WAITING FOR THE RIGHT TIME!
HOWEVER!
THERE'S ONE THING I'M SURE OF, SHADI!

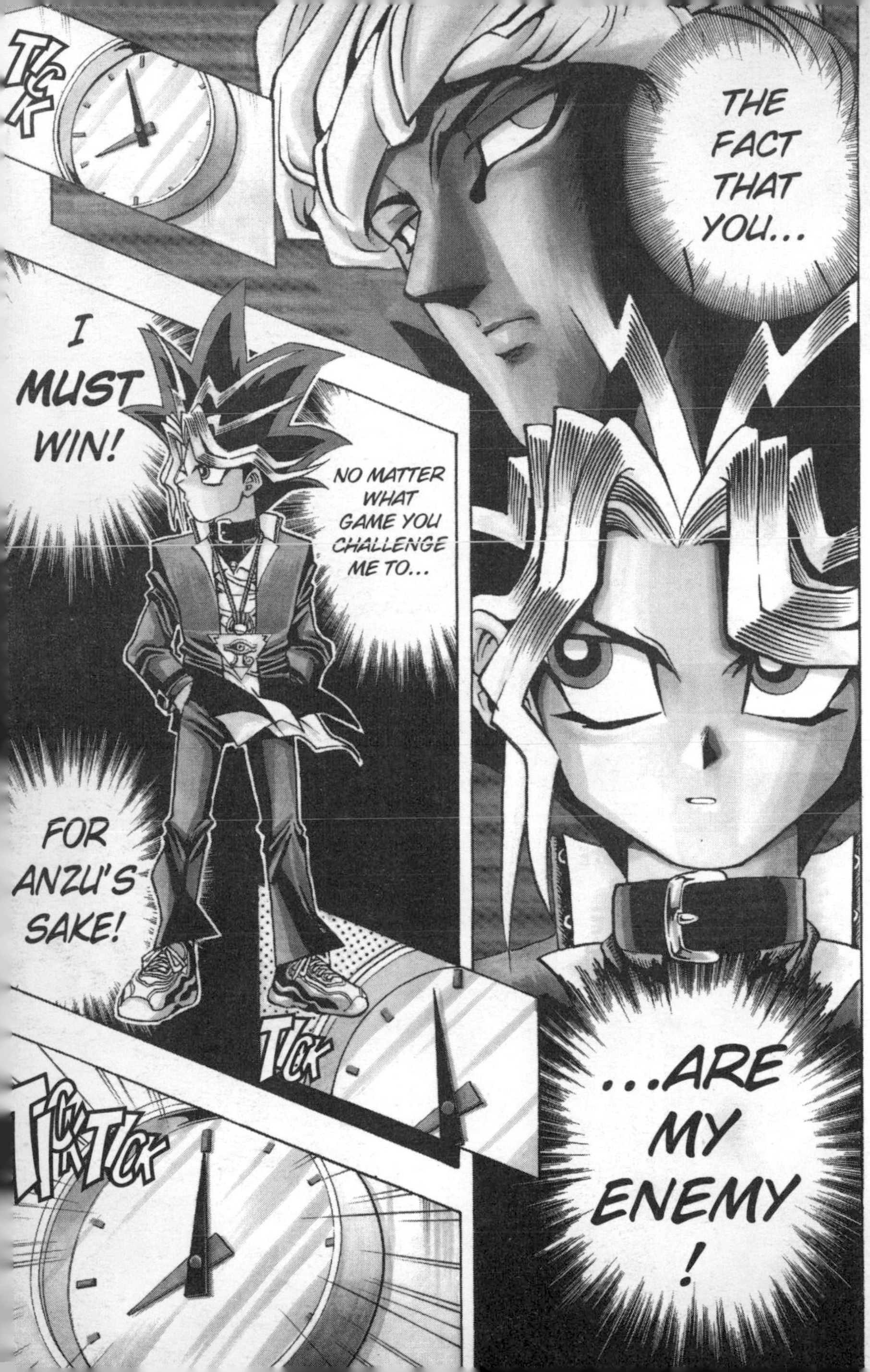
THE FACT THAT YOU...
TICK
...ARE MY ENEMY!
I MUST WIN!
NO MATTER WHAT GAME YOU CHALLENGE ME TO...
FOR ANZU'S SAKE!
TICK
TICK TICK

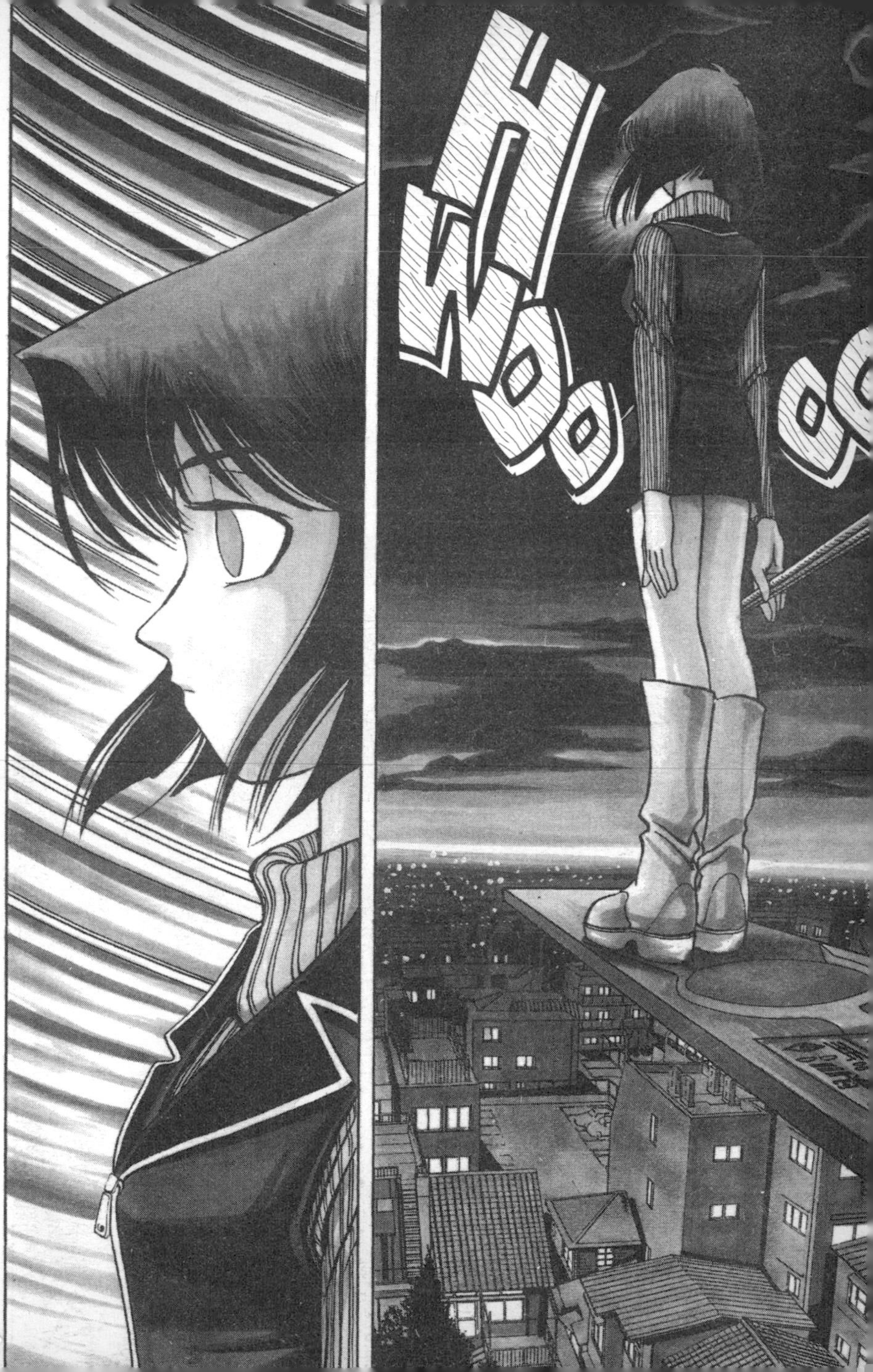
WHOOO
OO

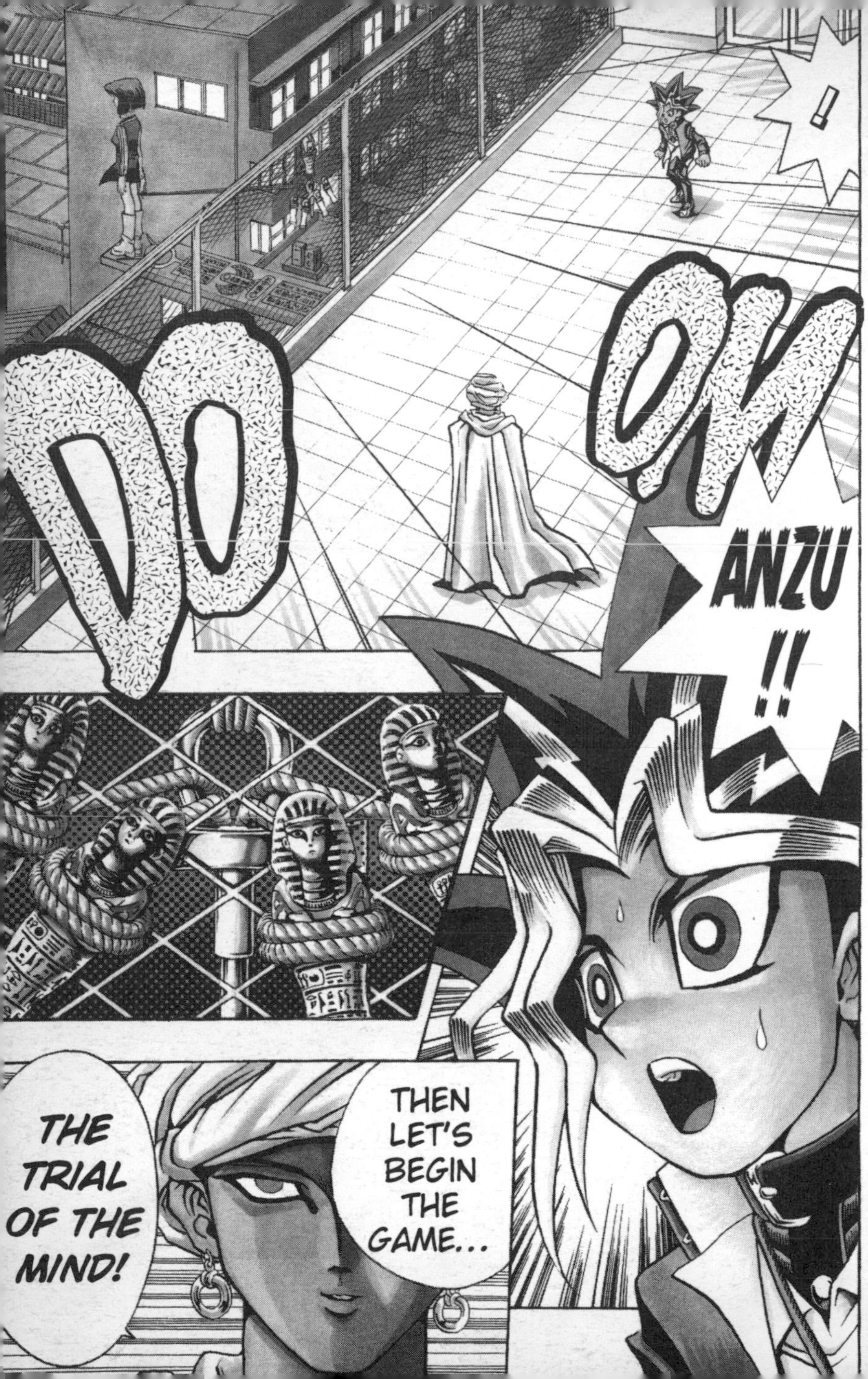
!
DO
OM
ANZU!!
THEN LET'S BEGIN THE GAME...
THE TRIAL OF THE MIND!

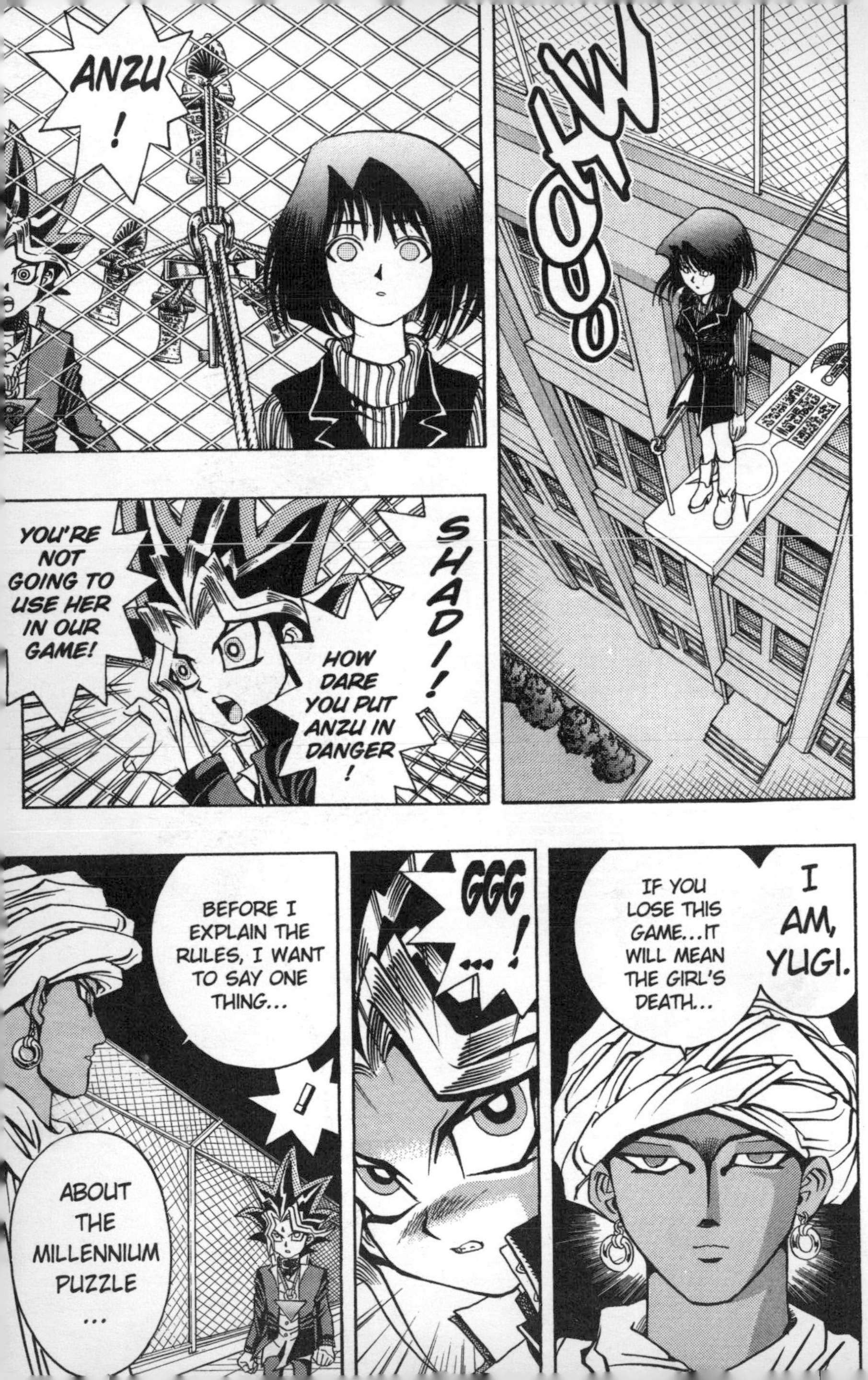
WOOOO
ANZU!
SHADI!!
HOW DARE YOU PUT ANZU IN DANGER!
YOU'RE NOT GOING TO USE HER IN OUR GAME!
I AM, YUGI.
IF YOU LOSE THIS GAME...IT WILL MEAN THE GIRL'S DEATH...
GGG...!
BEFORE I EXPLAIN THE RULES, I WANT TO SAY ONE THING...
!
ABOUT THE MILLENNIUM PUZZLE...

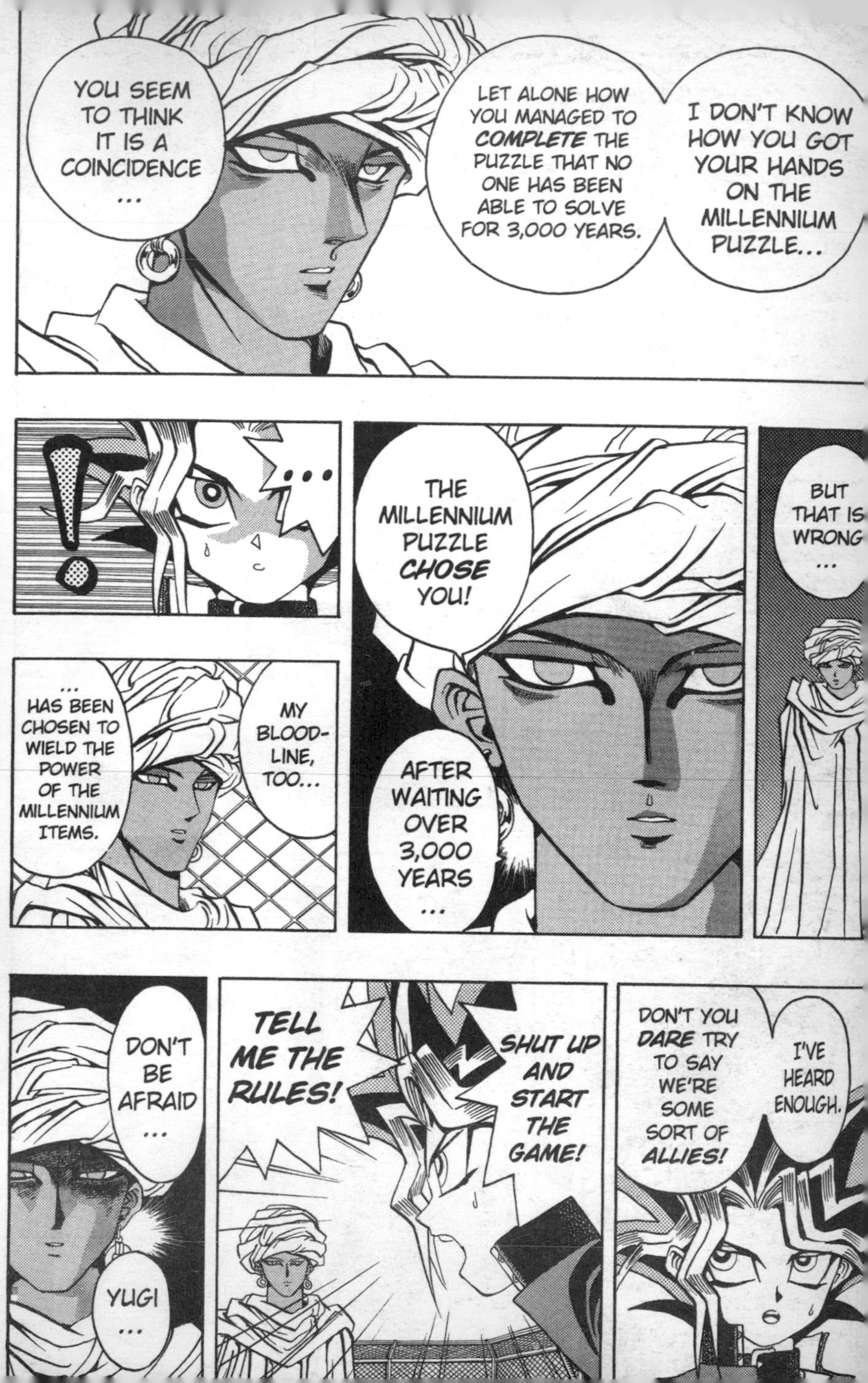
I DON'T KNOW HOW YOU GOT YOUR HANDS ON THE MILLENNIUM PUZZLE...
LET ALONE HOW YOU MANAGED TO **COMPLETE** THE PUZZLE THAT NO ONE HAS BEEN ABLE TO SOLVE FOR 3,000 YEARS.
YOU SEEM TO THINK IT IS A COINCIDENCE ...
BUT THAT IS WRONG ...
THE MILLENNIUM PUZZLE **CHOSE** YOU!
AFTER WAITING OVER 3,000 YEARS ...
!
...
MY BLOOD-LINE, TOO...
... HAS BEEN CHOSEN TO WIELD THE POWER OF THE MILLENNIUM ITEMS.
I'VE HEARD ENOUGH.
DON'T YOU **DARE** TRY TO SAY WE'RE SOME SORT OF **ALLIES!**
SHUT UP AND START THE GAME!
TELL ME THE RULES!
DON'T BE AFRAID ...
YUGI ...

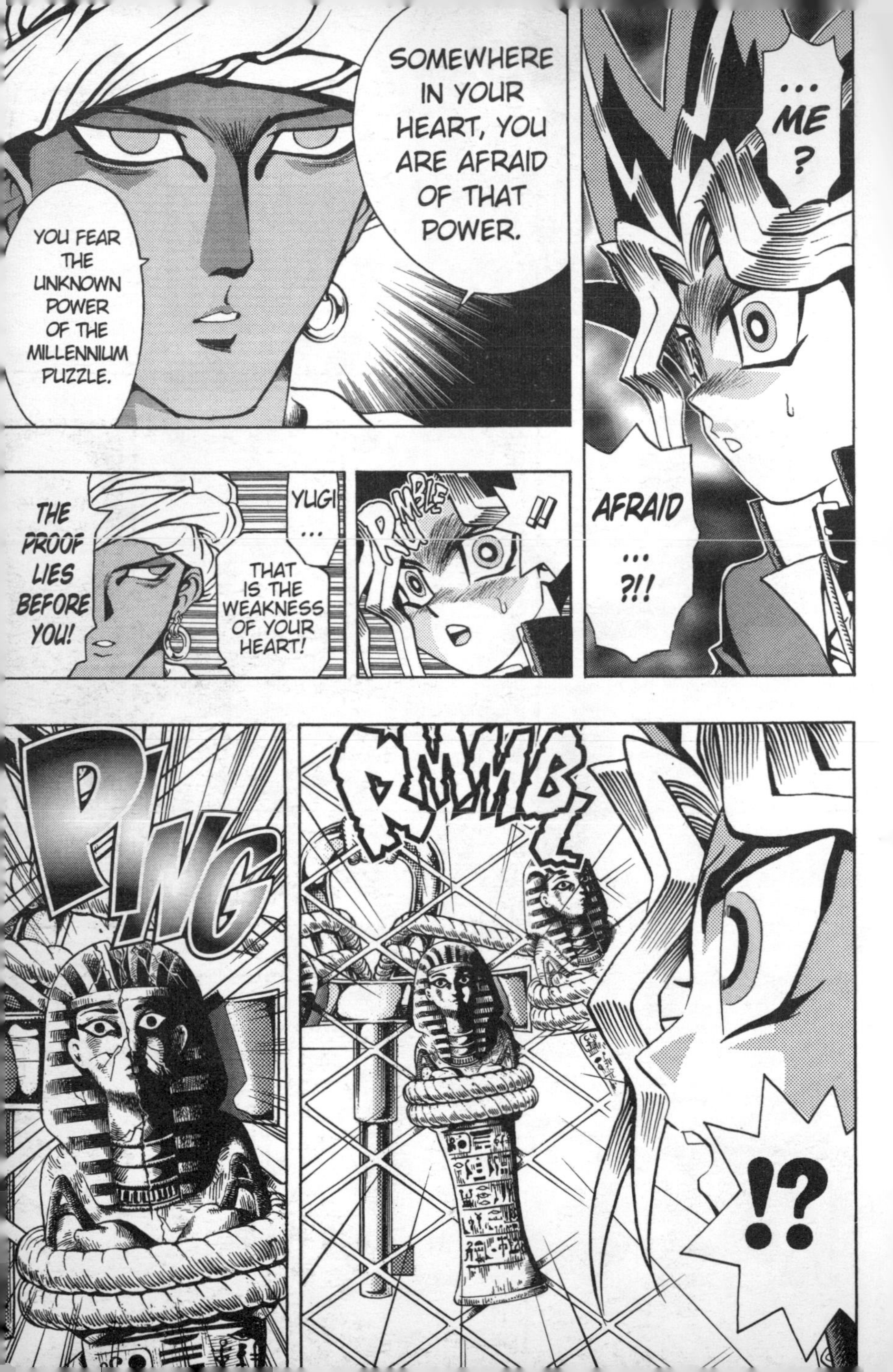
... ME ?
AFRAID ... ?!!
SOMEWHERE IN YOUR HEART, YOU ARE AFRAID OF THAT POWER.
YOU FEAR THE UNKNOWN POWER OF THE MILLENNIUM PUZZLE.
RUMBLE
!!
YUGI ...
THAT IS THE WEAKNESS OF YOUR HEART!
THE PROOF LIES BEFORE YOU!
RMMBL
!?
PING

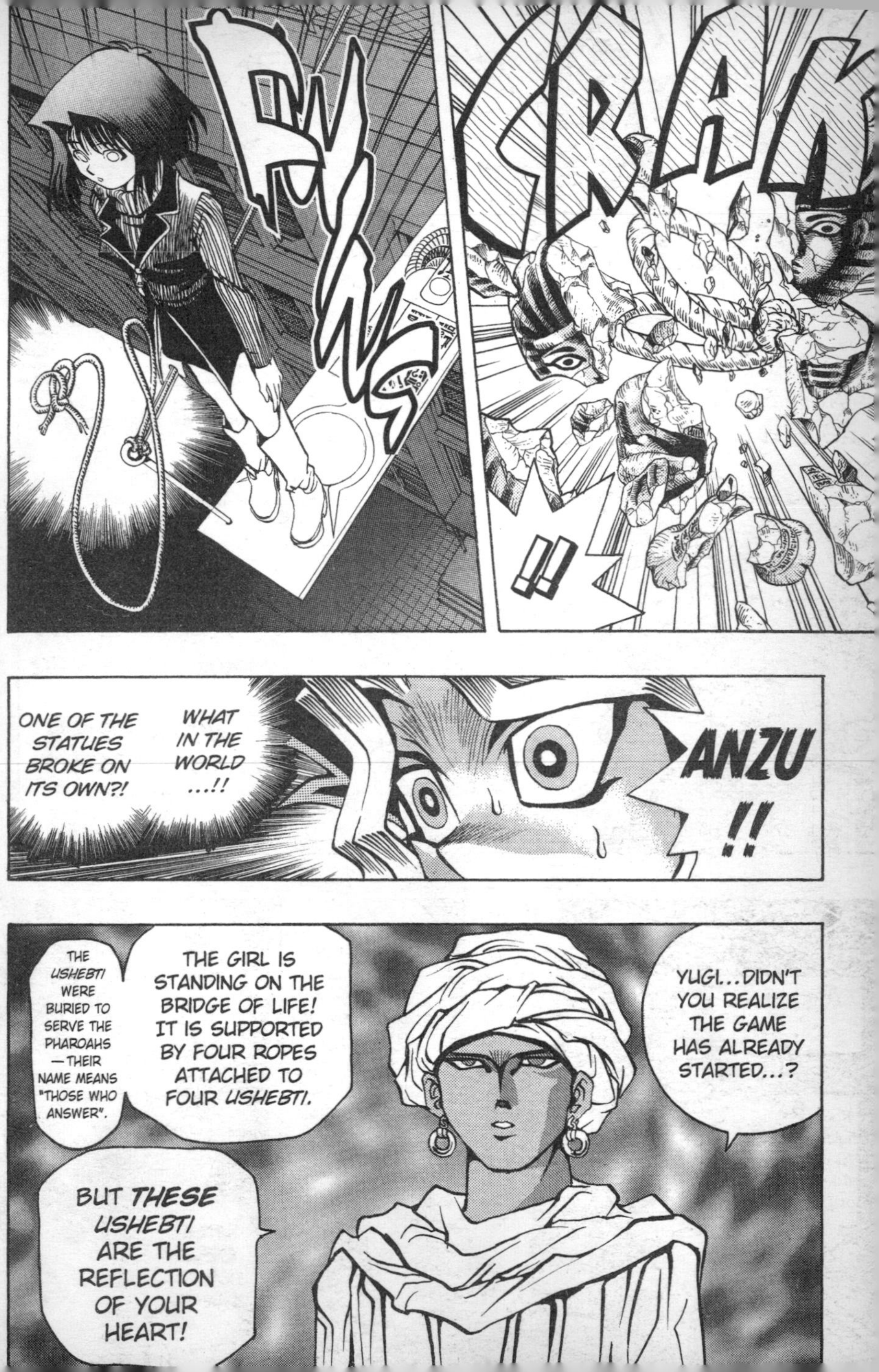
CRAK
!!
ANZU !!
WHAT IN THE WORLD ...!!
ONE OF THE STATUES BROKE ON ITS OWN?!
YUGI...DIDN'T YOU REALIZE THE GAME HAS ALREADY STARTED...?
THE GIRL IS STANDING ON THE BRIDGE OF LIFE! IT IS SUPPORTED BY FOUR ROPES ATTACHED TO FOUR *USHEBTI*.
THE *USHEBTI* WERE BURIED TO SERVE THE PHAROAHS—THEIR NAME MEANS "THOSE WHO ANSWER".
BUT *THESE USHEBTI* ARE THE REFLECTION OF YOUR HEART!

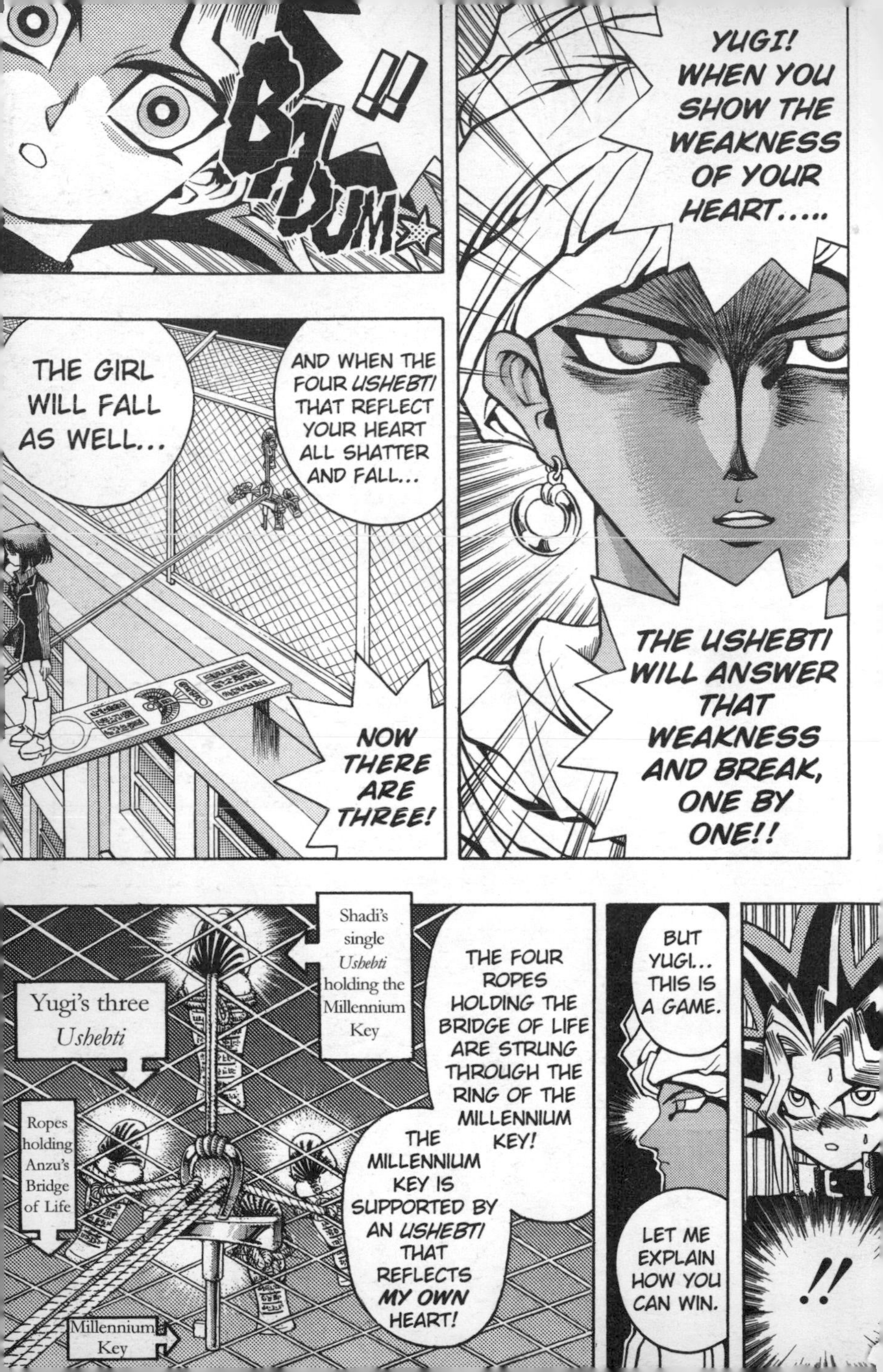
YUGI! WHEN YOU SHOW THE WEAKNESS OF YOUR HEART.....
THE USHEBTI WILL ANSWER THAT WEAKNESS AND BREAK, ONE BY ONE!!
!!
BA-DUM
AND WHEN THE FOUR USHEBTI THAT REFLECT YOUR HEART ALL SHATTER AND FALL...
THE GIRL WILL FALL AS WELL...
NOW THERE ARE THREE!
!!
BUT YUGI... THIS IS A GAME.
LET ME EXPLAIN HOW YOU CAN WIN.
THE FOUR ROPES HOLDING THE BRIDGE OF LIFE ARE STRUNG THROUGH THE RING OF THE MILLENNIUM KEY!
THE MILLENNIUM KEY IS SUPPORTED BY AN USHEBTI THAT REFLECTS MY OWN HEART!
Shadi's single Ushebti holding the Millennium Key
Yugi's three Ushebti
Ropes holding Anzu's Bridge of Life
Millennium Key

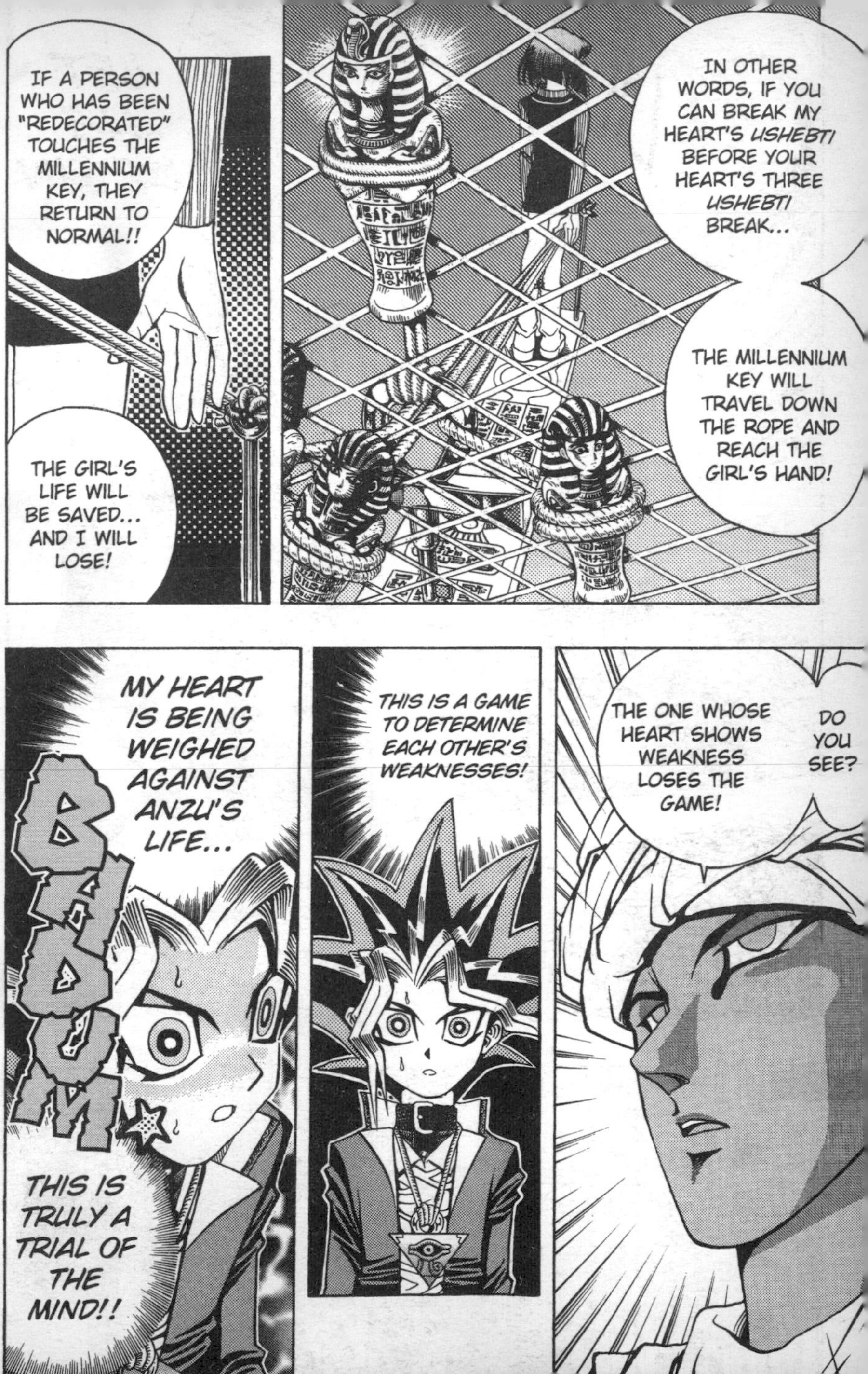
IN OTHER WORDS, IF YOU CAN BREAK MY HEART'S *USHEBTI* BEFORE YOUR HEART'S THREE *USHEBTI* BREAK...
THE MILLENNIUM KEY WILL TRAVEL DOWN THE ROPE AND REACH THE GIRL'S HAND!
IF A PERSON WHO HAS BEEN "REDECORATED" TOUCHES THE MILLENNIUM KEY, THEY RETURN TO NORMAL!!
THE GIRL'S LIFE WILL BE SAVED... AND I WILL LOSE!
DO YOU SEE?
THE ONE WHOSE HEART SHOWS WEAKNESS LOSES THE GAME!
THIS IS A GAME TO DETERMINE EACH OTHER'S WEAKNESSES!
MY HEART IS BEING WEIGHED AGAINST ANZU'S LIFE...
BADUM
THIS IS TRULY A TRIAL OF THE MIND!!

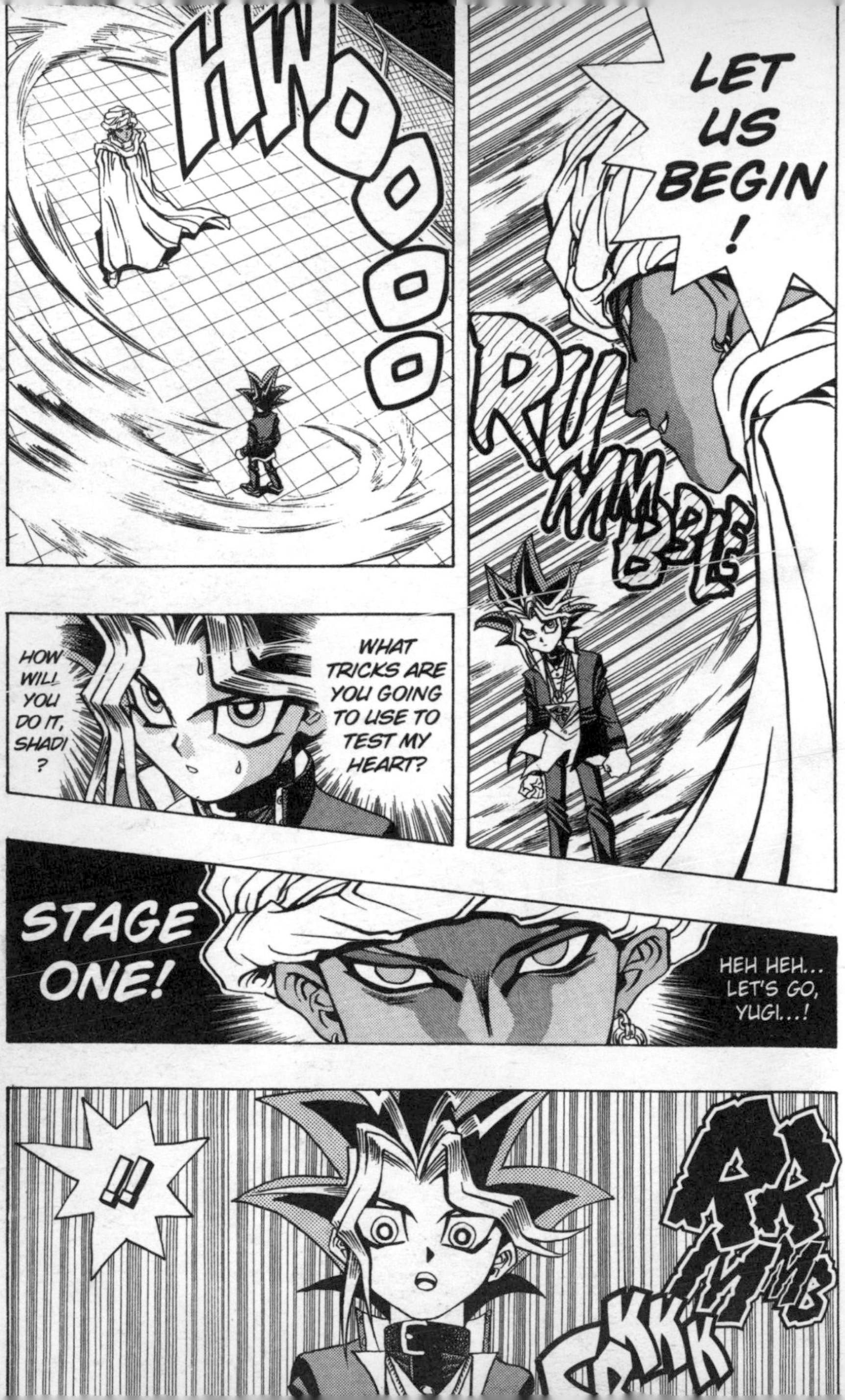
LET US BEGIN!
RUMMBLE
HWOOOOO
WHAT TRICKS ARE YOU GOING TO USE TO TEST MY HEART?
HOW WILL YOU DO IT, SHADI?
HEH HEH... LET'S GO, YUGI...!
STAGE ONE!
!!

READ THIS WAY

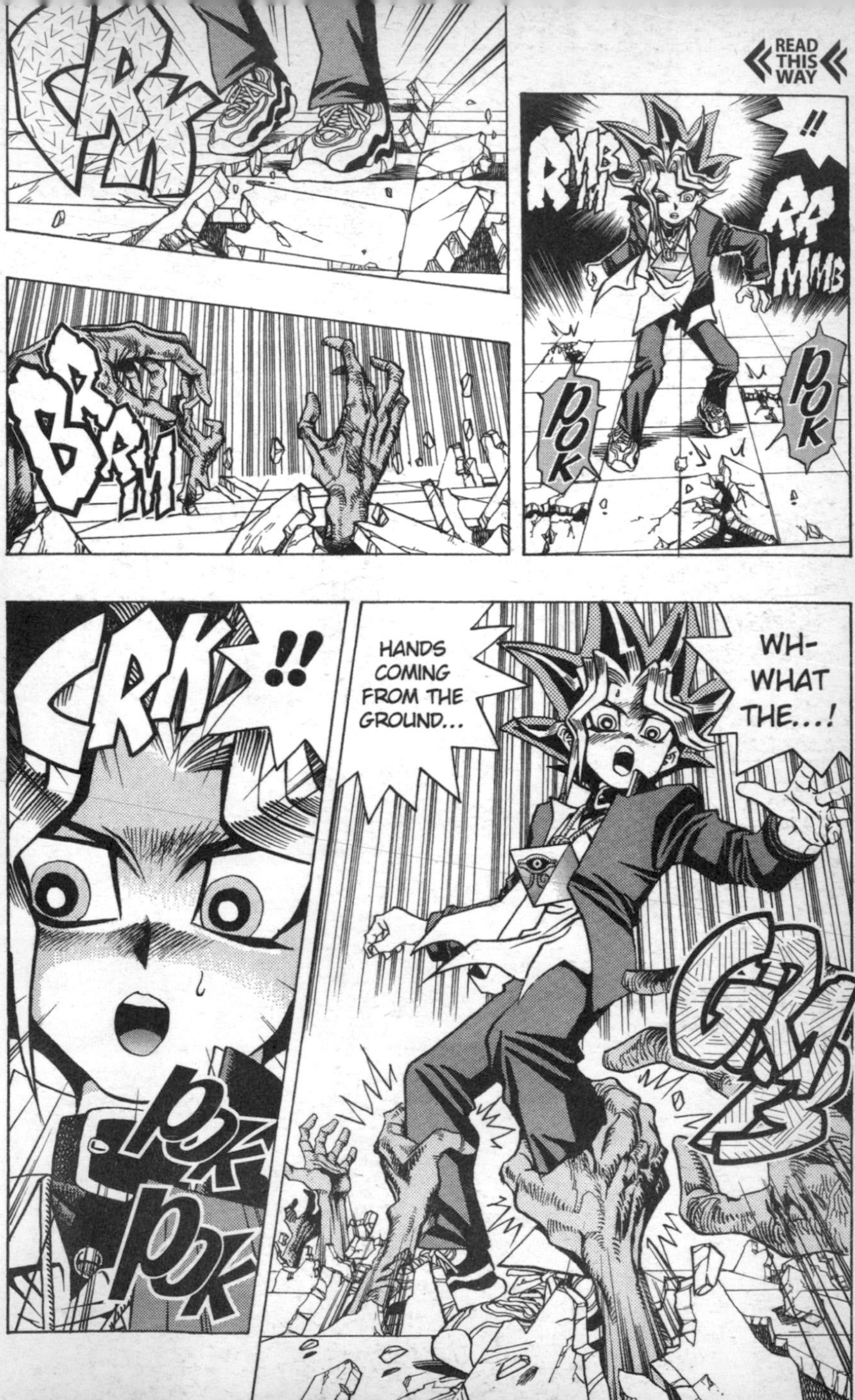
RMB
!!
RR MMB
POK
POK
CRK
BRM
WH- WHAT THE...!
HANDS COMING FROM THE GROUND...
CRK
CRK!!
POK POK
POK POK

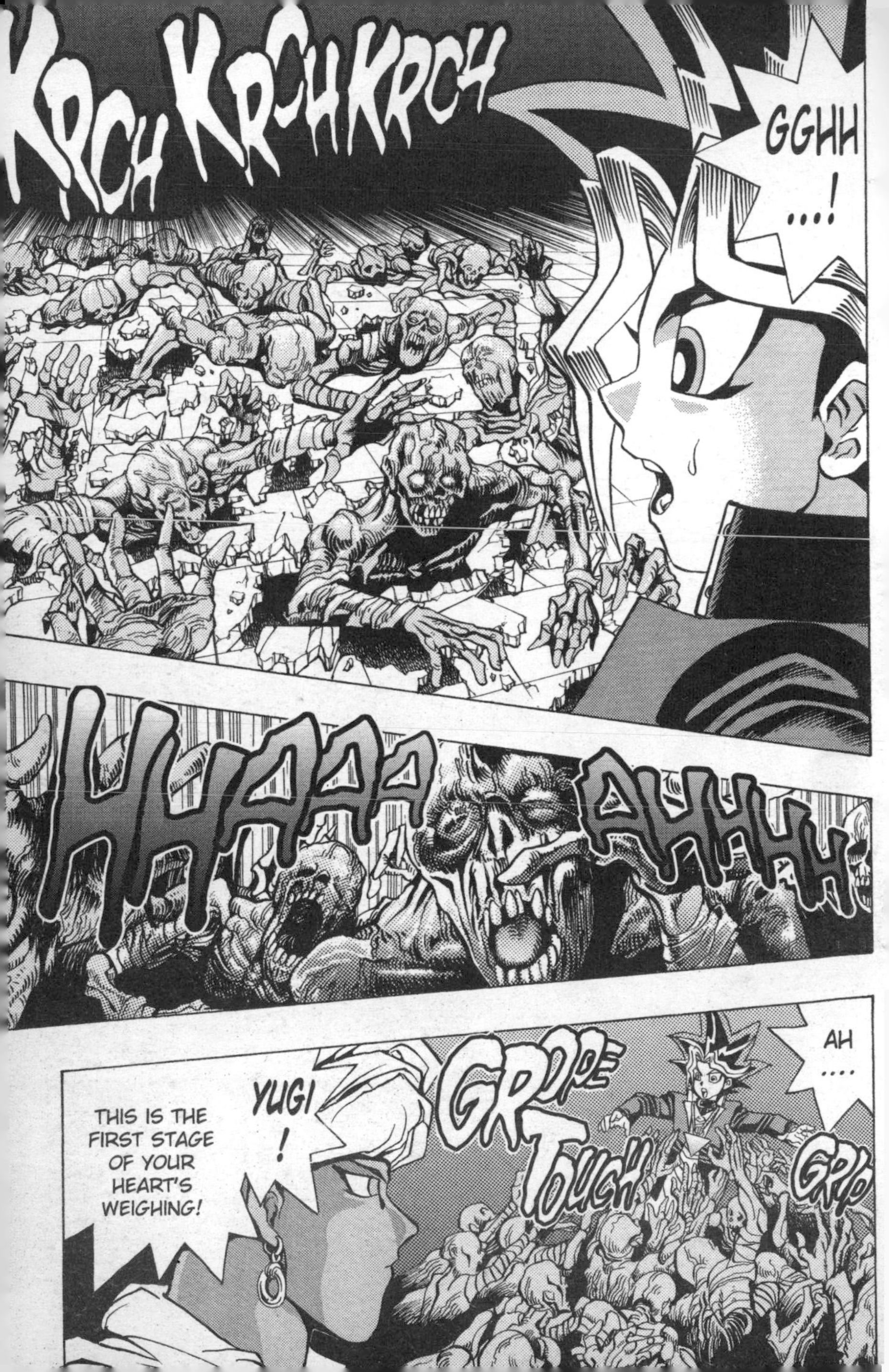
GGHH ...!
KRCH KRCH KRCH
HHAAA AHHHH
AH ....
GRIP
GROPE
TOUCH
YUGI!
THIS IS THE FIRST STAGE OF YOUR HEART'S WEIGHING!

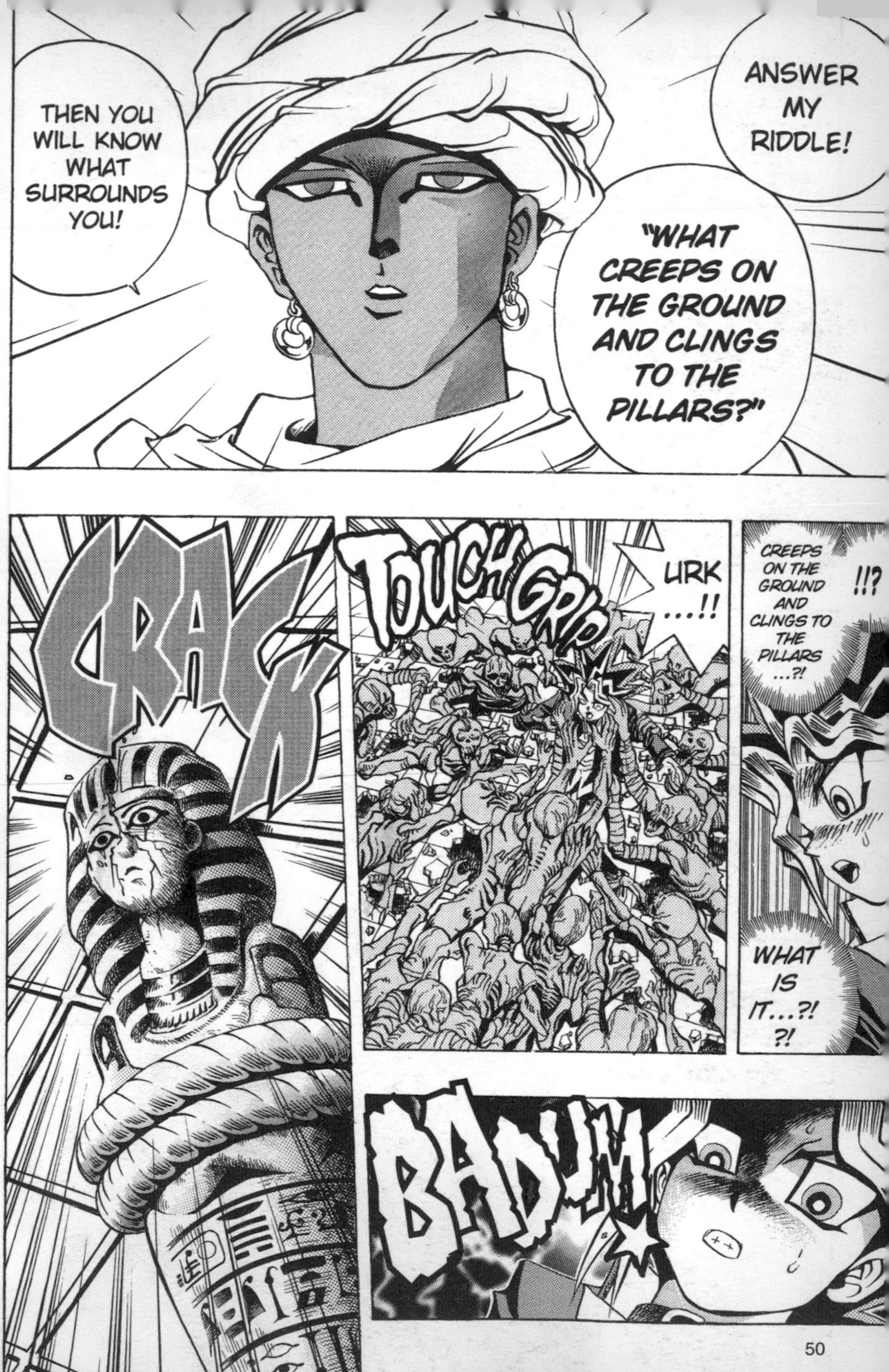
ANSWER MY RIDDLE!
"WHAT CREEPS ON THE GROUND AND CLINGS TO THE PILLARS?"
THEN YOU WILL KNOW WHAT SURROUNDS YOU!
CREEPS ON THE GROUND AND CLINGS TO THE PILLARS ...?!
!!?
WHAT IS IT...?! ?!
TOUCH GRIP
URK ...!!
BADUM
CRACK

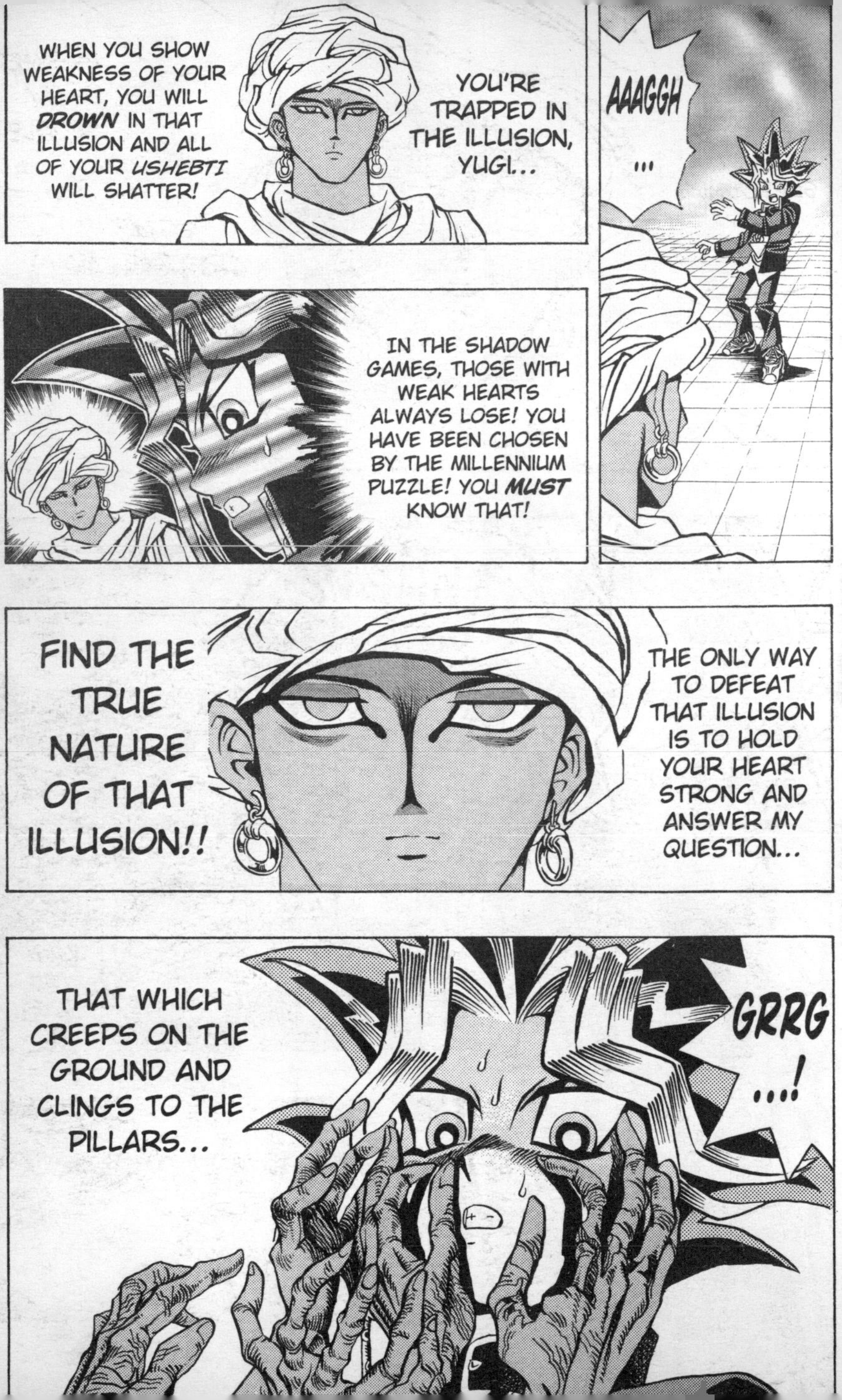
AAAGGH
...
YOU'RE TRAPPED IN THE ILLUSION, YUGI...
WHEN YOU SHOW WEAKNESS OF YOUR HEART, YOU WILL DROWN IN THAT ILLUSION AND ALL OF YOUR USHEBTI WILL SHATTER!
IN THE SHADOW GAMES, THOSE WITH WEAK HEARTS ALWAYS LOSE! YOU HAVE BEEN CHOSEN BY THE MILLENNIUM PUZZLE! YOU MUST KNOW THAT!
THE ONLY WAY TO DEFEAT THAT ILLUSION IS TO HOLD YOUR HEART STRONG AND ANSWER MY QUESTION...
FIND THE TRUE NATURE OF THAT ILLUSION!!
GRRG
...!
THAT WHICH CREEPS ON THE GROUND AND CLINGS TO THE PILLARS...

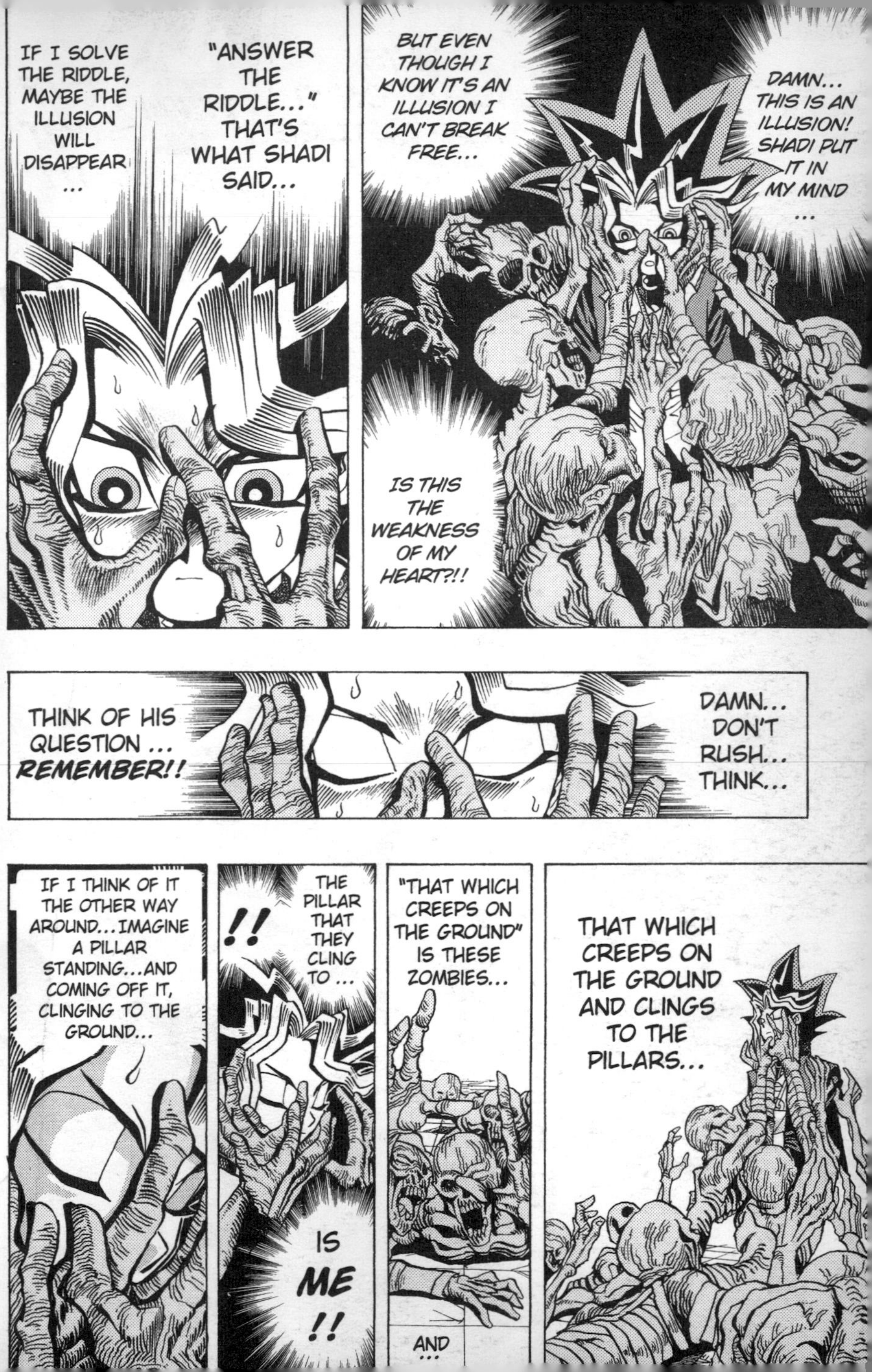
DAMN... THIS IS AN ILLUSION! SHADI PUT IT IN MY MIND ...
BUT EVEN THOUGH I KNOW IT'S AN ILLUSION I CAN'T BREAK FREE...
IS THIS THE WEAKNESS OF MY HEART?!!
"ANSWER THE RIDDLE..." THAT'S WHAT SHADI SAID...
IF I SOLVE THE RIDDLE, MAYBE THE ILLUSION WILL DISAPPEAR ...
DAMN... DON'T RUSH... THINK...
THINK OF HIS QUESTION ... REMEMBER!!
THAT WHICH CREEPS ON THE GROUND AND CLINGS TO THE PILLARS...
"THAT WHICH CREEPS ON THE GROUND" IS THESE ZOMBIES...
AND ...
THE PILLAR THAT THEY CLING TO ...
!!
IS ME !!
IF I THINK OF IT THE OTHER WAY AROUND... IMAGINE A PILLAR STANDING...AND COMING OFF IT, CLINGING TO THE GROUND...

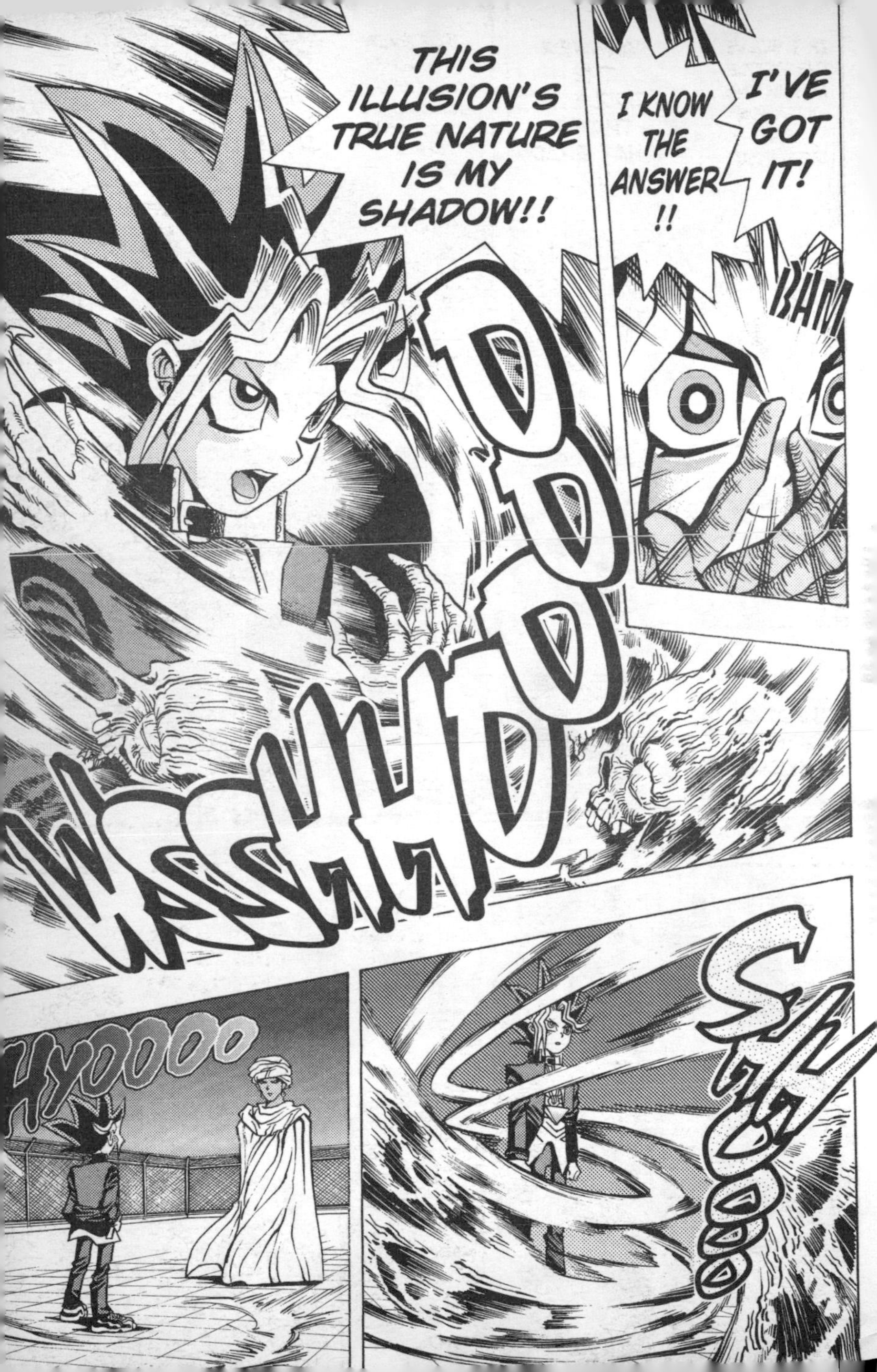
I'VE GOT IT!
I KNOW THE ANSWER!!
BAM
THIS ILLUSION'S TRUE NATURE IS MY SHADOW!!
HYOOOO

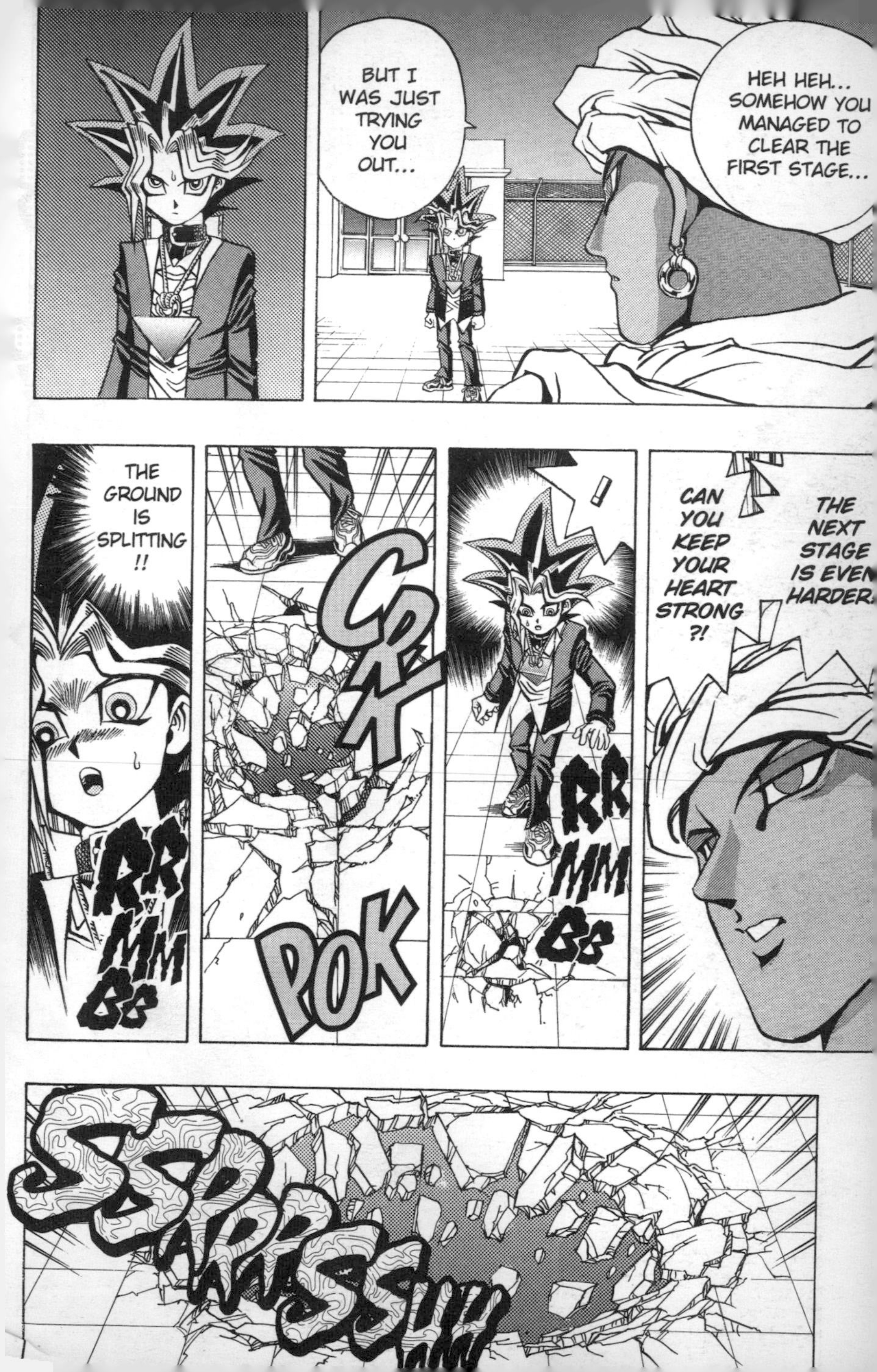
HEH HEH... SOMEHOW YOU MANAGED TO CLEAR THE FIRST STAGE...
BUT I WAS JUST TRYING YOU OUT...
THE NEXT STAGE IS EVEN HARDER...
CAN YOU KEEP YOUR HEART STRONG ?!
!
RRMMBB
CRK
POK
THE GROUND IS SPLITTING !!
RRMMBB

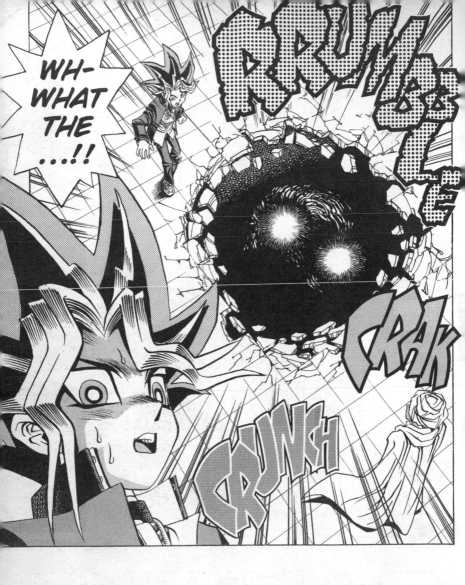

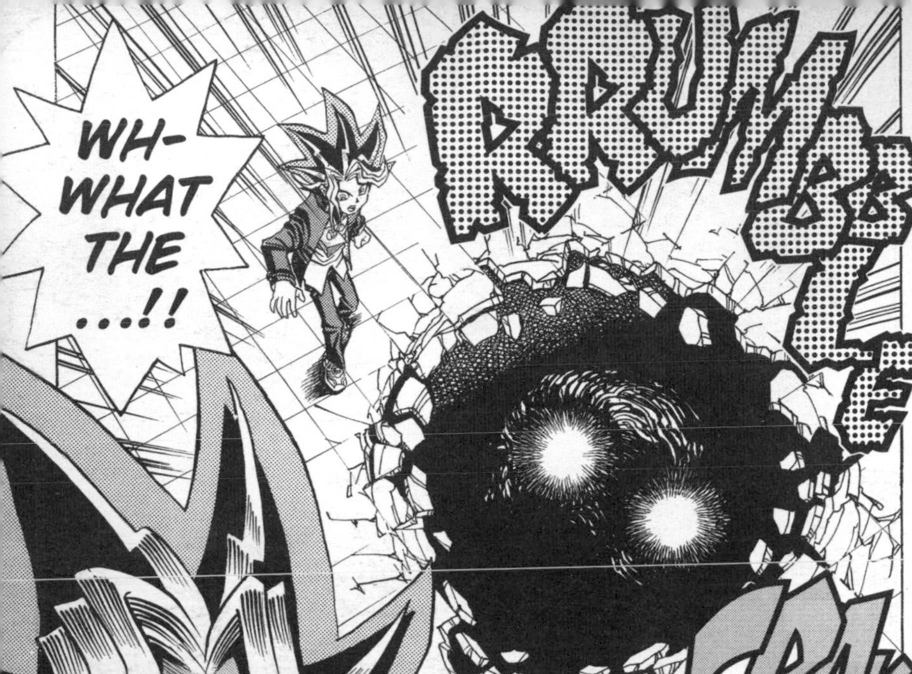
CRUMBLE
WH-
WHAT
THE
...!!
CRAK
CRUNCH

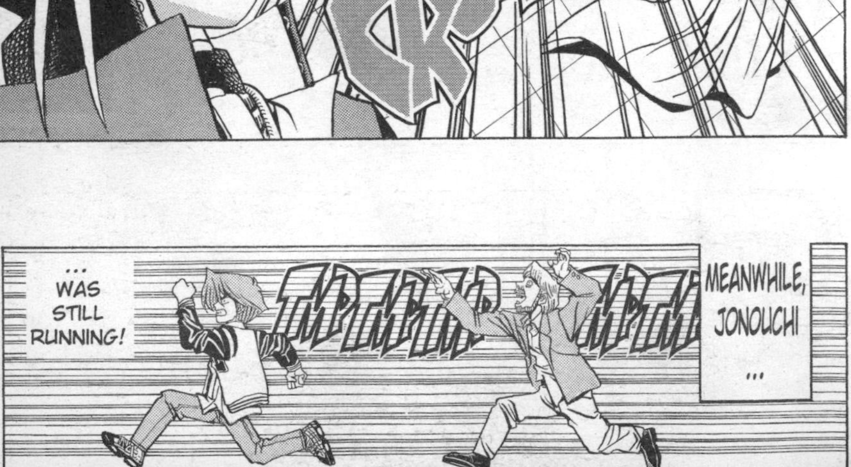
MEANWHILE,
JONOUCHI
...
...
WAS
STILL
RUNNING!

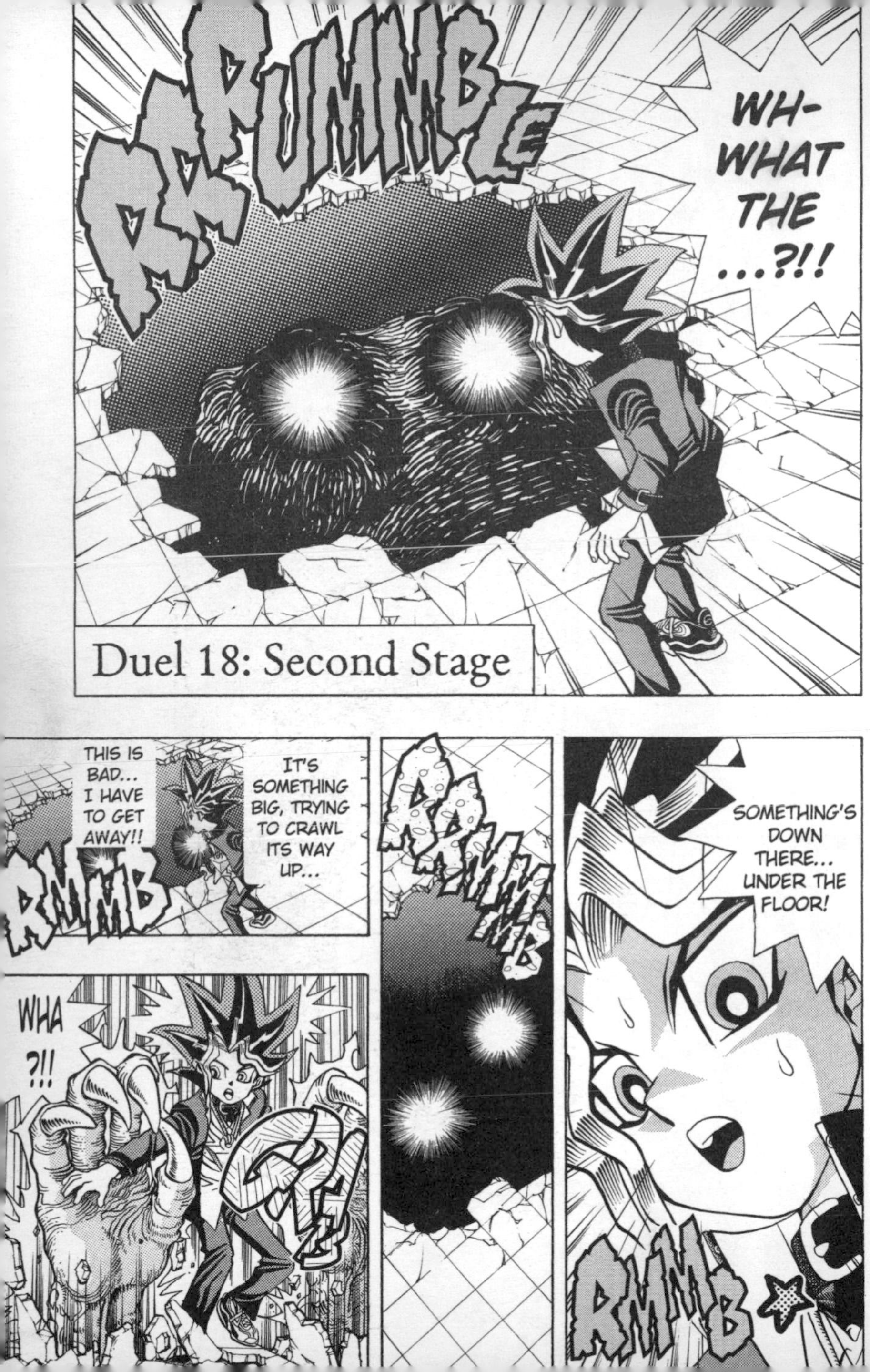
WH- WHAT THE ...?!!
Duel 18: Second Stage
SOMETHING'S DOWN THERE... UNDER THE FLOOR!
RMMB
IT'S SOMETHING BIG, TRYING TO CRAWL ITS WAY UP...
THIS IS BAD... I HAVE TO GET AWAY!!
RMMB
WHA ?!!

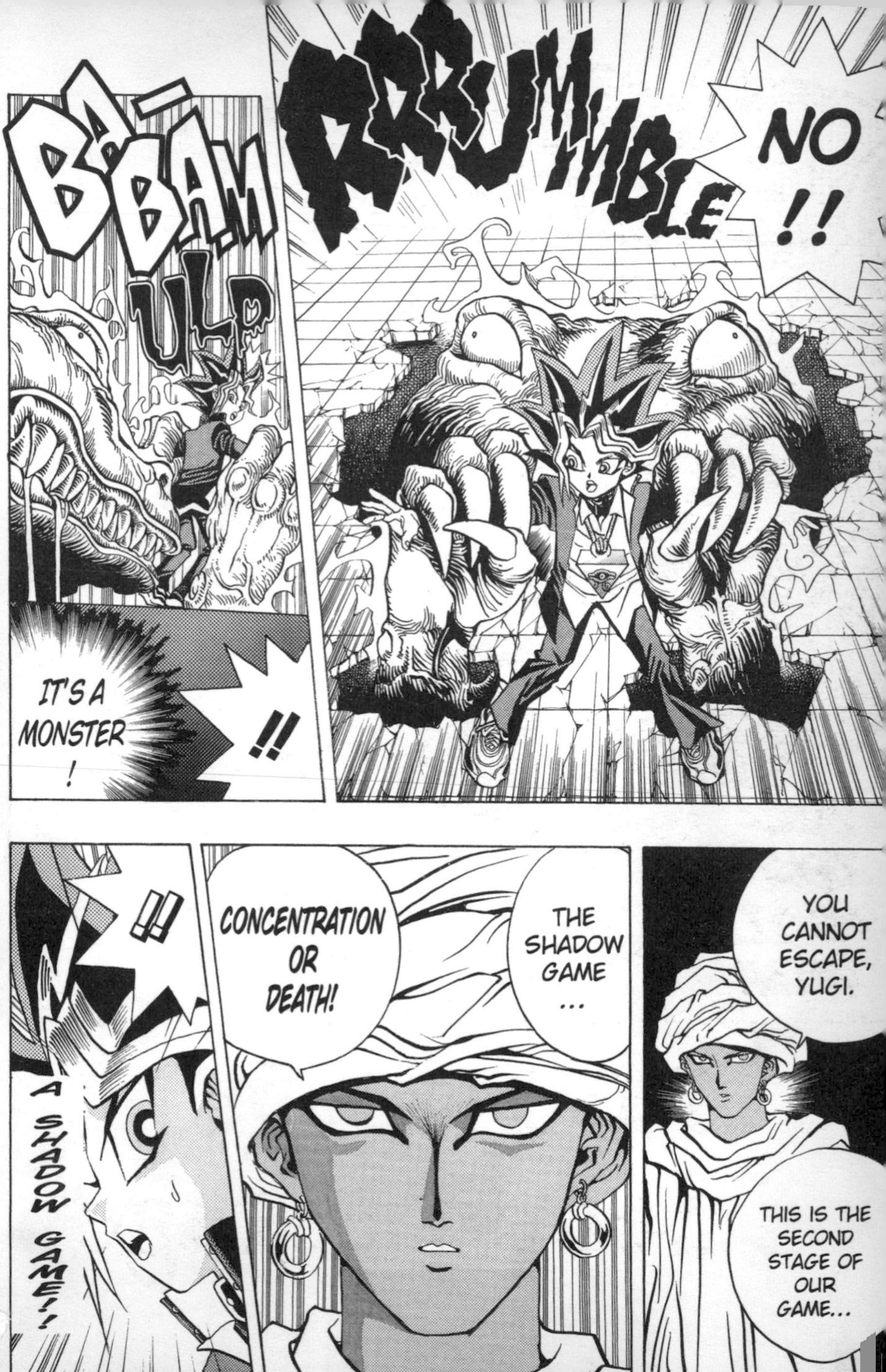
RRRUMMBLE
NO!!
BABAM
ULP
IT'S A MONSTER!
!!
YOU CANNOT ESCAPE, YUGI.
THIS IS THE SECOND STAGE OF OUR GAME...
THE SHADOW GAME...
CONCENTRATION OR DEATH!
!!
A SHADOW GAME!!

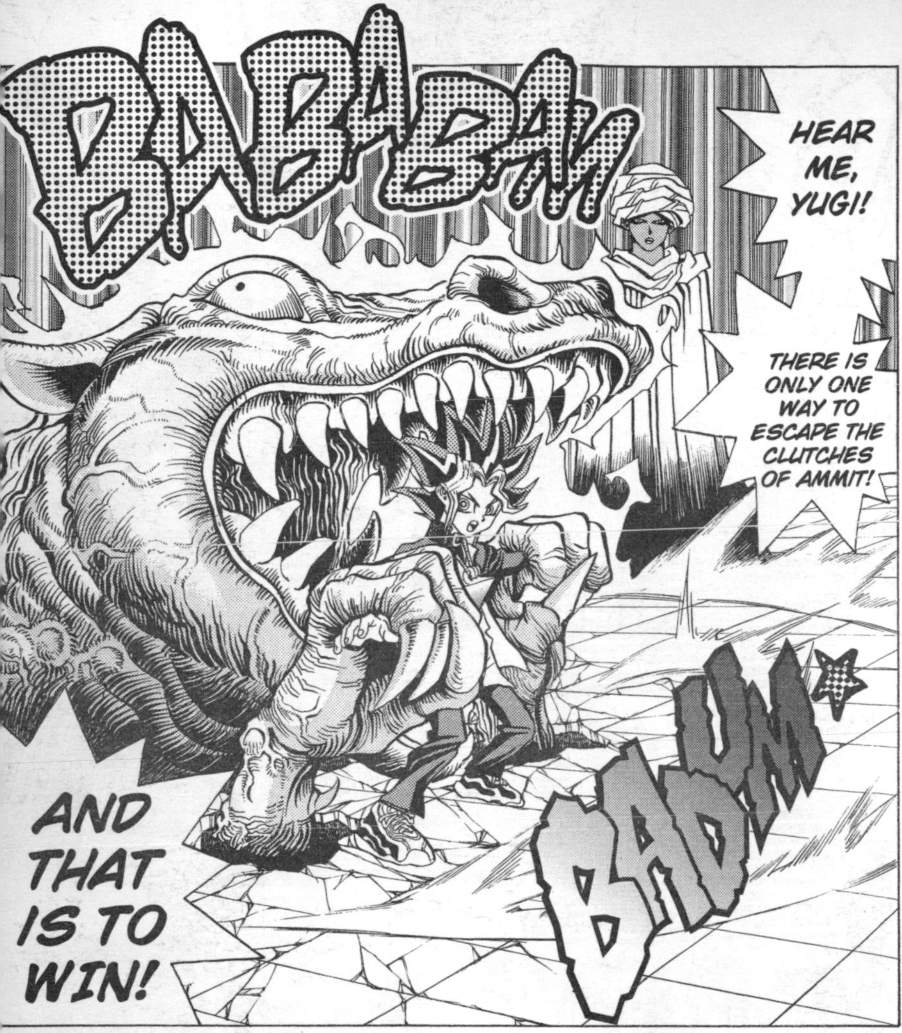
HEAR ME, YUGI!
BABABAM
THERE IS ONLY ONE WAY TO ESCAPE THE CLUTCHES OF AMMIT!
BADUM
AND THAT IS TO WIN!

Duel 18: Second Stage

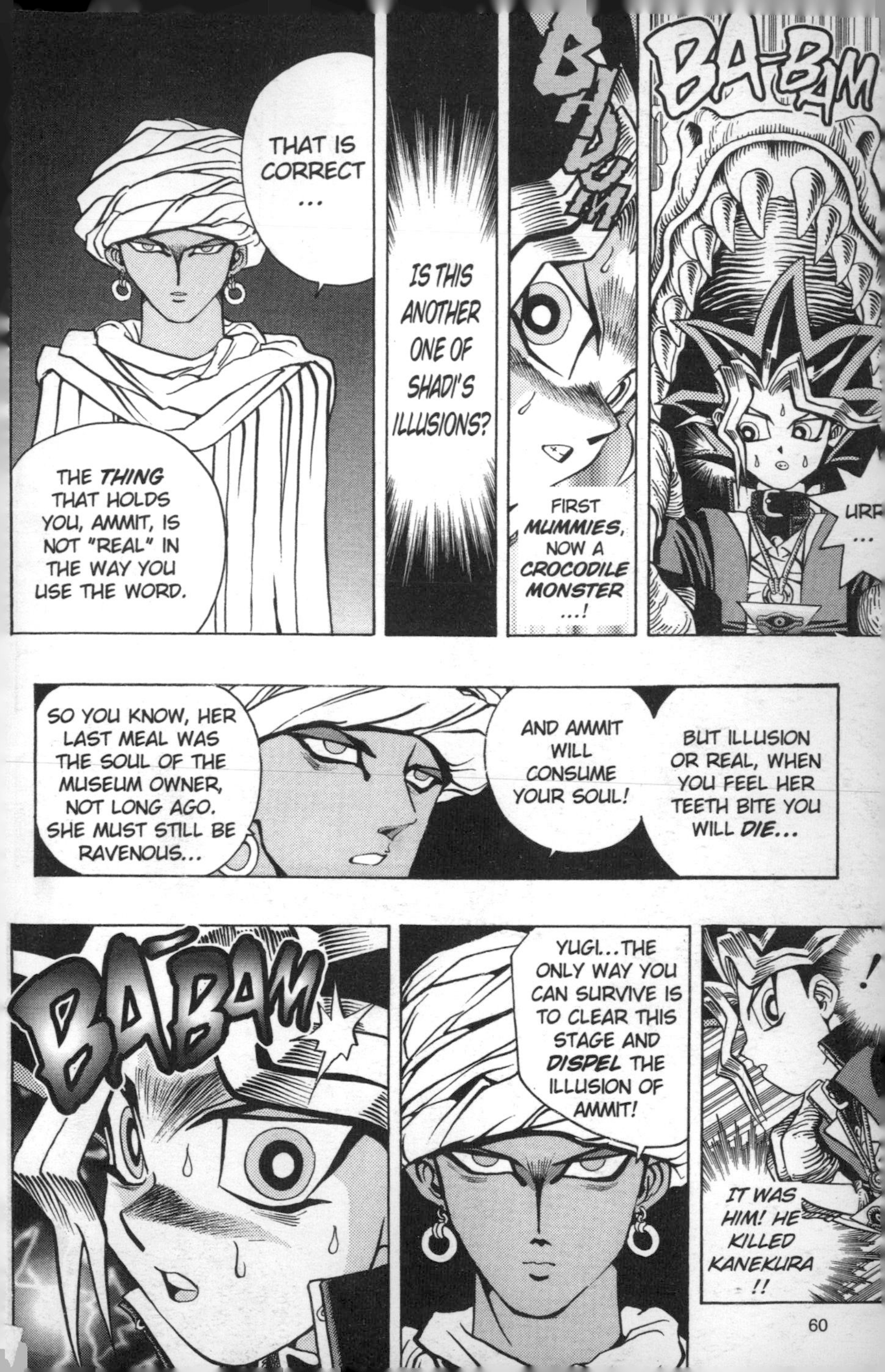
BA-BAM
URR...
BADUM
FIRST MUMMIES, NOW A CROCODILE MONSTER...!
IS THIS ANOTHER ONE OF SHADI'S ILLUSIONS?
THAT IS CORRECT...
THE THING THAT HOLDS YOU, AMMIT, IS NOT "REAL" IN THE WAY YOU USE THE WORD.
BUT ILLUSION OR REAL, WHEN YOU FEEL HER TEETH BITE YOU WILL DIE...
AND AMMIT WILL CONSUME YOUR SOUL!
SO YOU KNOW, HER LAST MEAL WAS THE SOUL OF THE MUSEUM OWNER, NOT LONG AGO. SHE MUST STILL BE RAVENOUS...
!
IT WAS HIM! HE KILLED KANEKURA!!
YUGI...THE ONLY WAY YOU CAN SURVIVE IS TO CLEAR THIS STAGE AND DISPEL THE ILLUSION OF AMMIT!
BA-BAM

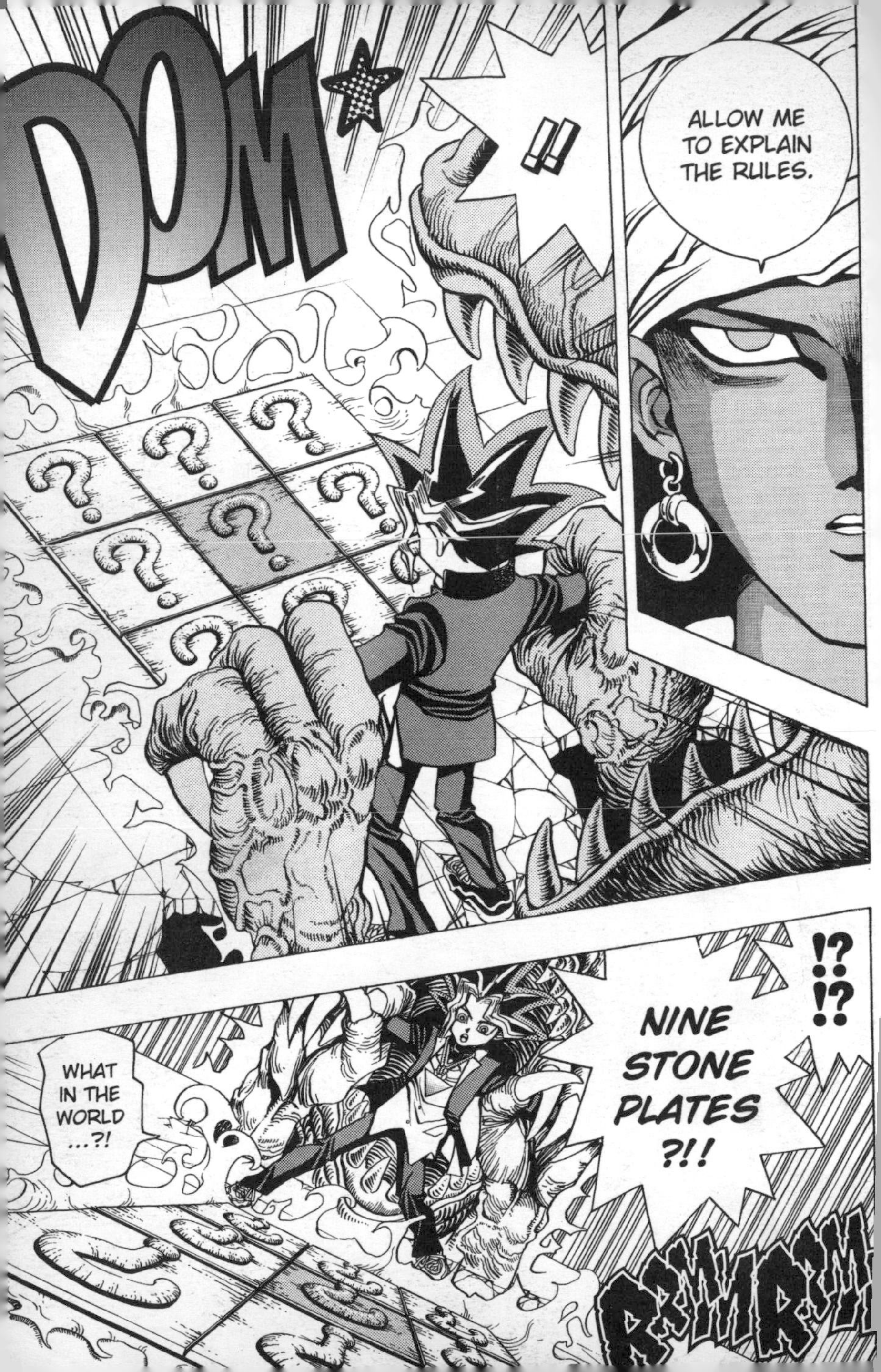
ALLOW ME TO EXPLAIN THE RULES.
DOOM
!!
!? !?
NINE STONE PLATES ?!!
WHAT IN THE WORLD ...?!

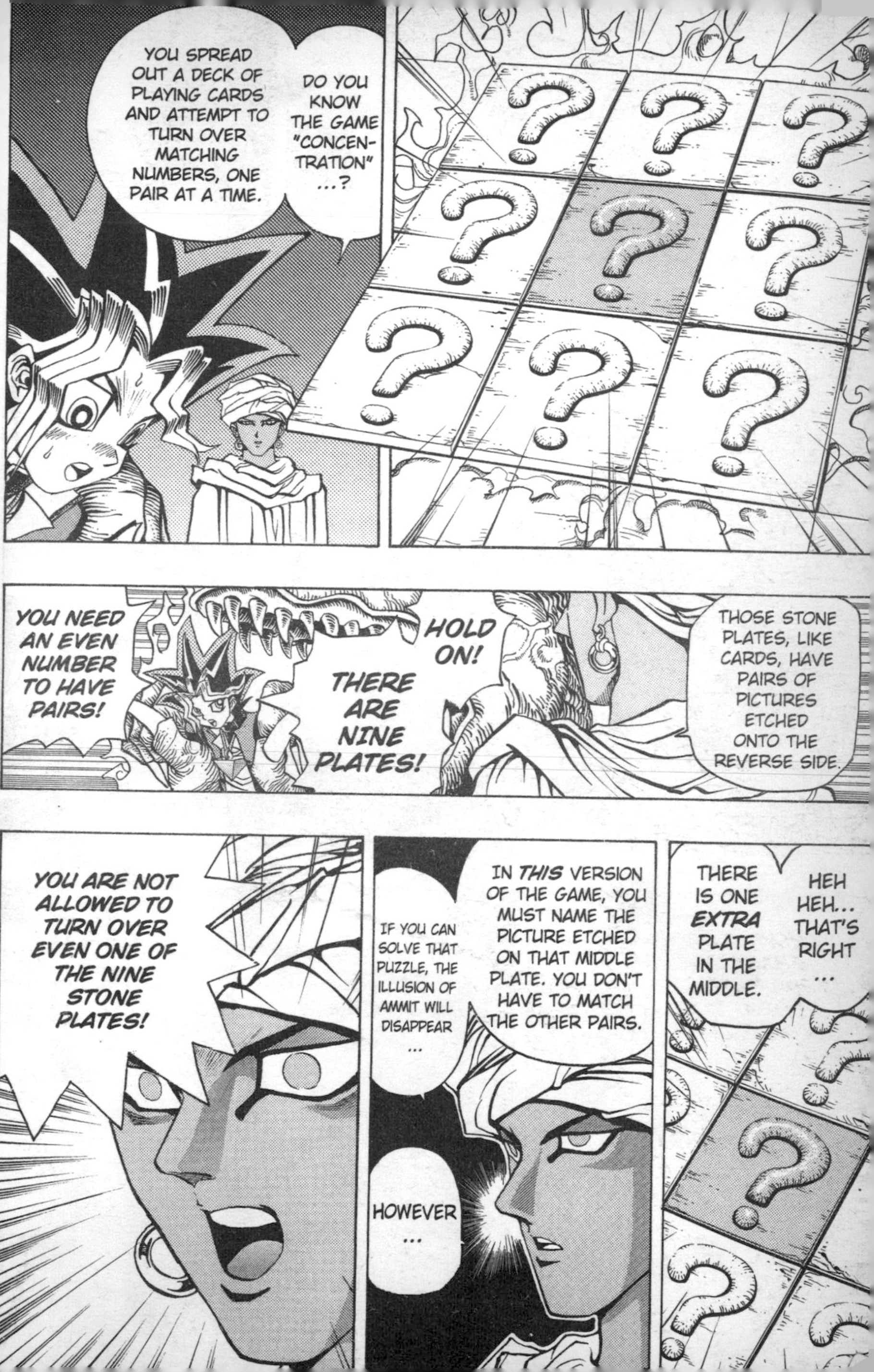
DO YOU KNOW THE GAME "CONCENTRATION" ...?
YOU SPREAD OUT A DECK OF PLAYING CARDS AND ATTEMPT TO TURN OVER MATCHING NUMBERS, ONE PAIR AT A TIME.
THOSE STONE PLATES, LIKE CARDS, HAVE PAIRS OF PICTURES ETCHED ONTO THE REVERSE SIDE.
HOLD ON!
THERE ARE NINE PLATES!
YOU NEED AN EVEN NUMBER TO HAVE PAIRS!
HEH HEH... THAT'S RIGHT ...
THERE IS ONE EXTRA PLATE IN THE MIDDLE.
IN THIS VERSION OF THE GAME, YOU MUST NAME THE PICTURE ETCHED ON THAT MIDDLE PLATE. YOU DON'T HAVE TO MATCH THE OTHER PAIRS.
IF YOU CAN SOLVE THAT PUZZLE, THE ILLUSION OF AMMIT WILL DISAPPEAR ...
HOWEVER ...
YOU ARE NOT ALLOWED TO TURN OVER EVEN ONE OF THE NINE STONE PLATES!

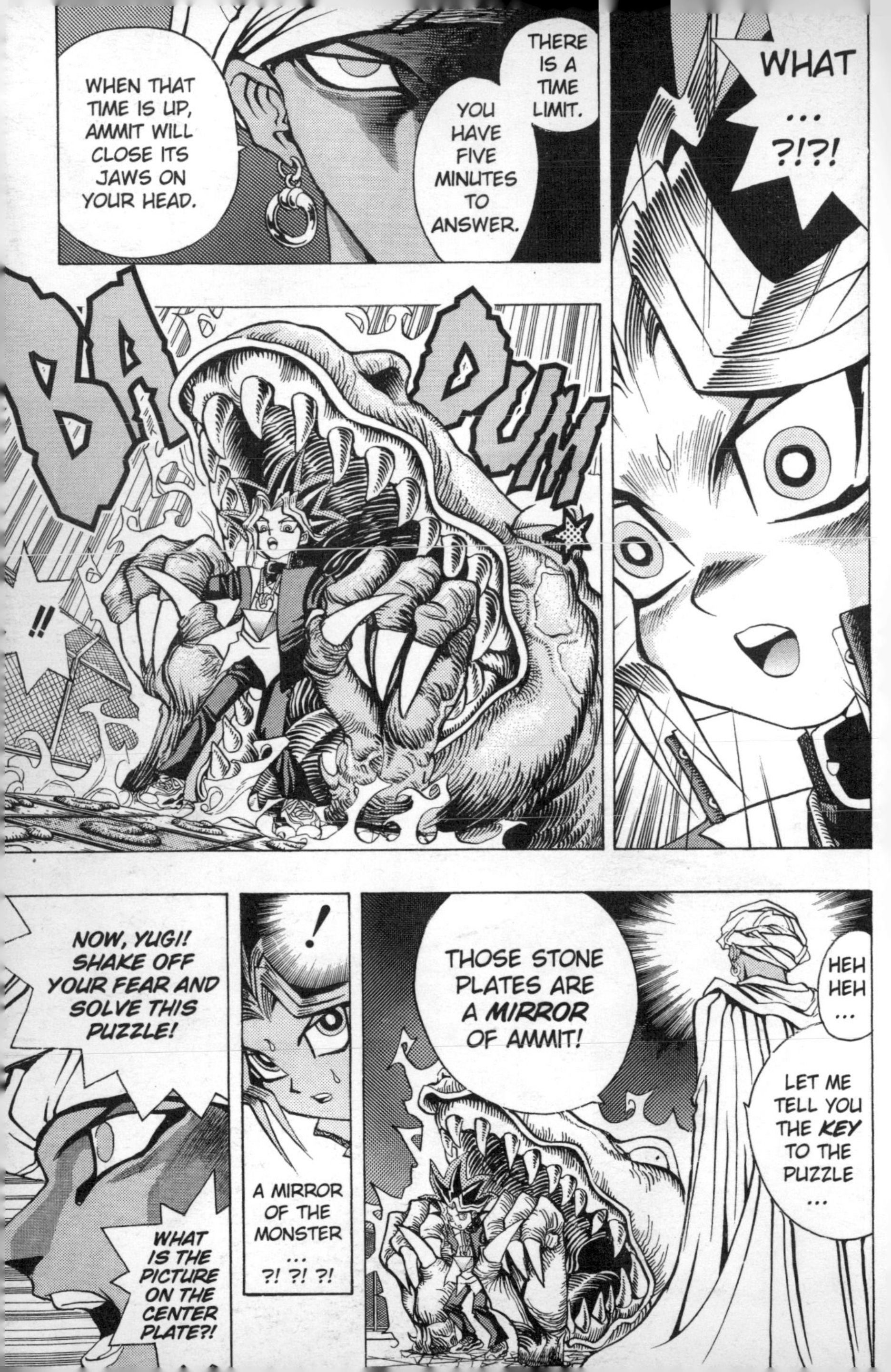
WHAT ... ?!?!
THERE IS A TIME LIMIT.
YOU HAVE FIVE MINUTES TO ANSWER.
WHEN THAT TIME IS UP, AMMIT WILL CLOSE ITS JAWS ON YOUR HEAD.
BA DUM
!!
HEH HEH ...
LET ME TELL YOU THE *KEY* TO THE PUZZLE ...
THOSE STONE PLATES ARE A *MIRROR* OF AMMIT!
!
A MIRROR OF THE MONSTER ... ?! ?! ?!
NOW, YUGI! SHAKE OFF YOUR FEAR AND SOLVE THIS PUZZLE!
WHAT IS THE PICTURE ON THE CENTER PLATE?!

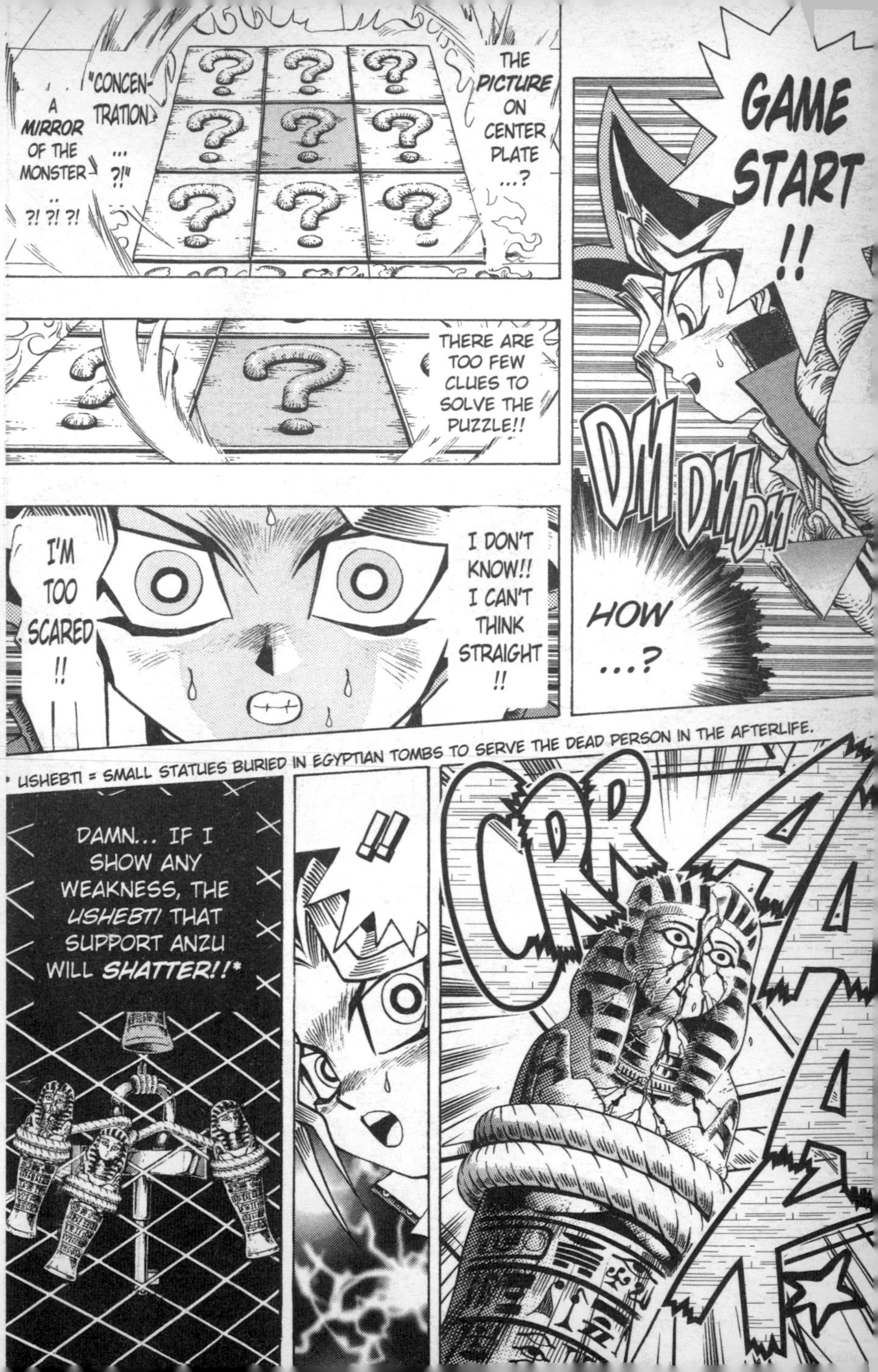
GAME START!!
DM DM DM DM
HOW ...?
THE PICTURE ON CENTER PLATE ...?
"CONCENTRATION" ... ?!"
A MIRROR OF THE MONSTER .. ?! ?! ?!
THERE ARE TOO FEW CLUES TO SOLVE THE PUZZLE!!
I DON'T KNOW!! I CAN'T THINK STRAIGHT!!
I'M TOO SCARED!!
* USHEBTI = SMALL STATUES BURIED IN EGYPTIAN TOMBS TO SERVE THE DEAD PERSON IN THE AFTERLIFE.
CRR
!!
DAMN... IF I SHOW ANY WEAKNESS, THE USHEBTI THAT SUPPORT ANZU WILL SHATTER!!*

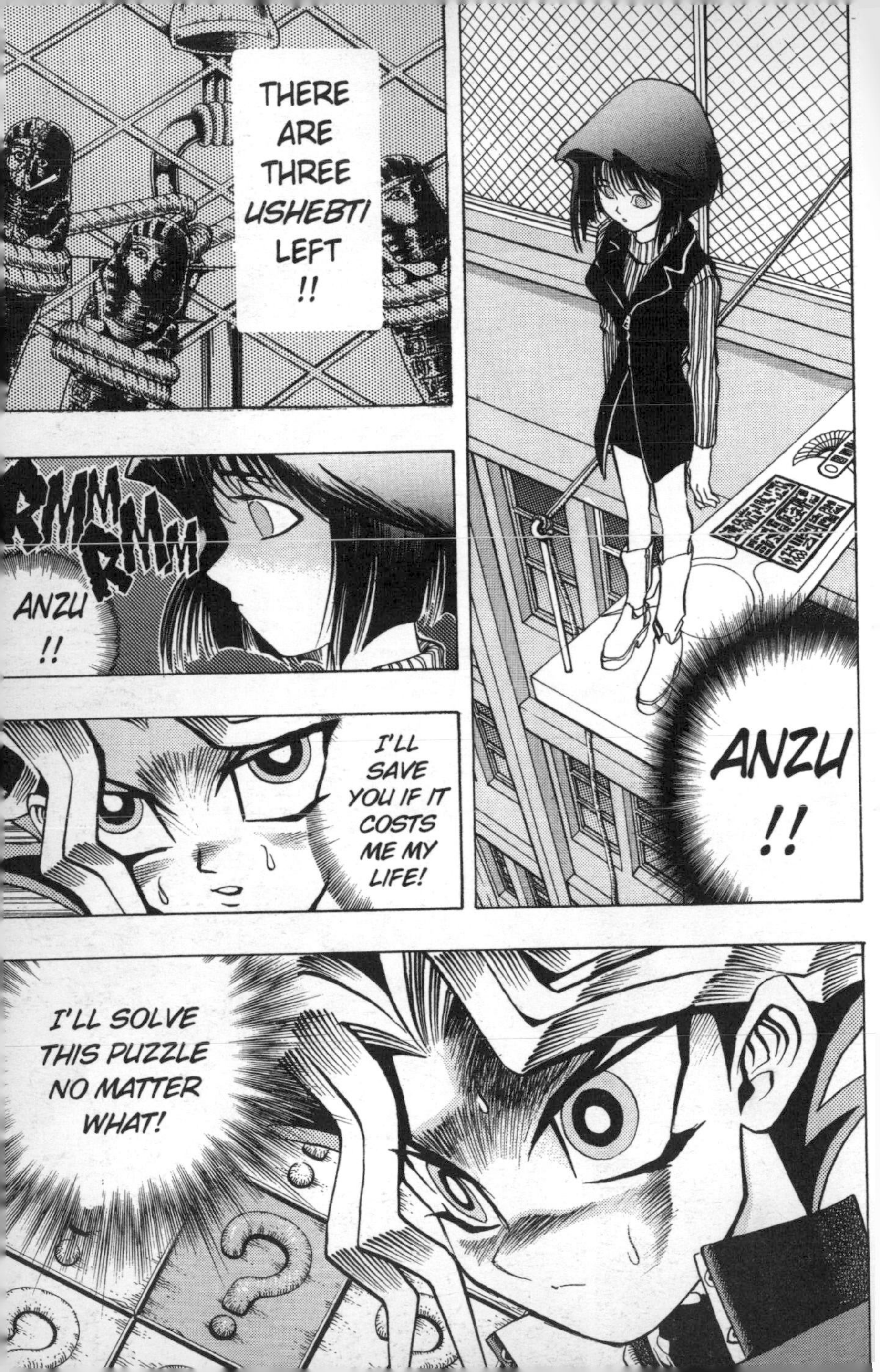
ANZU !!
THERE ARE THREE USHEBTI LEFT !!
RMMM RMM
ANZU !!
I'LL SAVE YOU IF IT COSTS ME MY LIFE!
I'LL SOLVE THIS PUZZLE NO MATTER WHAT!

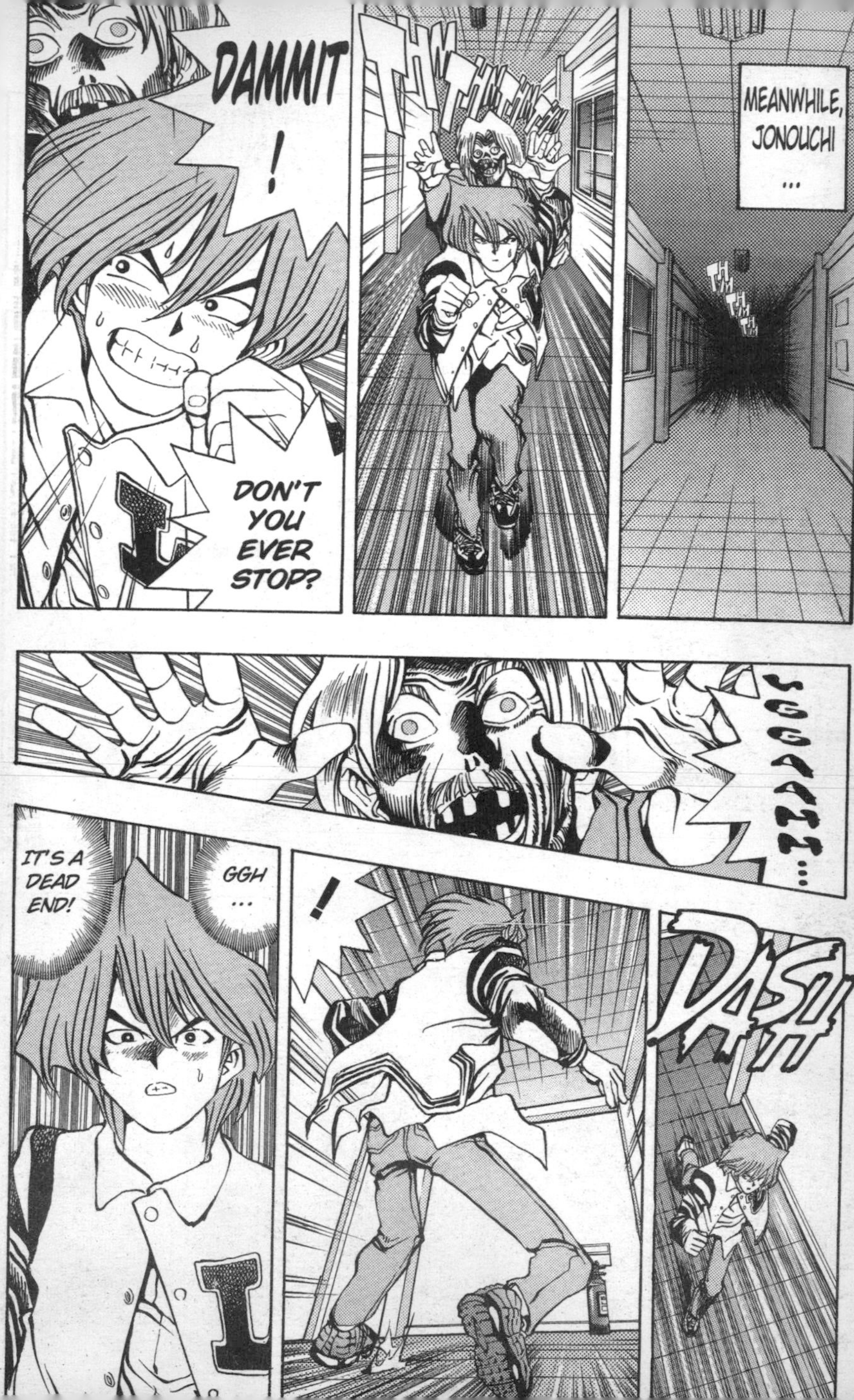
MEANWHILE, JONOUCHI ...
DAMMIT !
DON'T YOU EVER STOP?
UGGAAHH...
DASH
!
GGH ...
IT'S A DEAD END!

READ THIS WAY

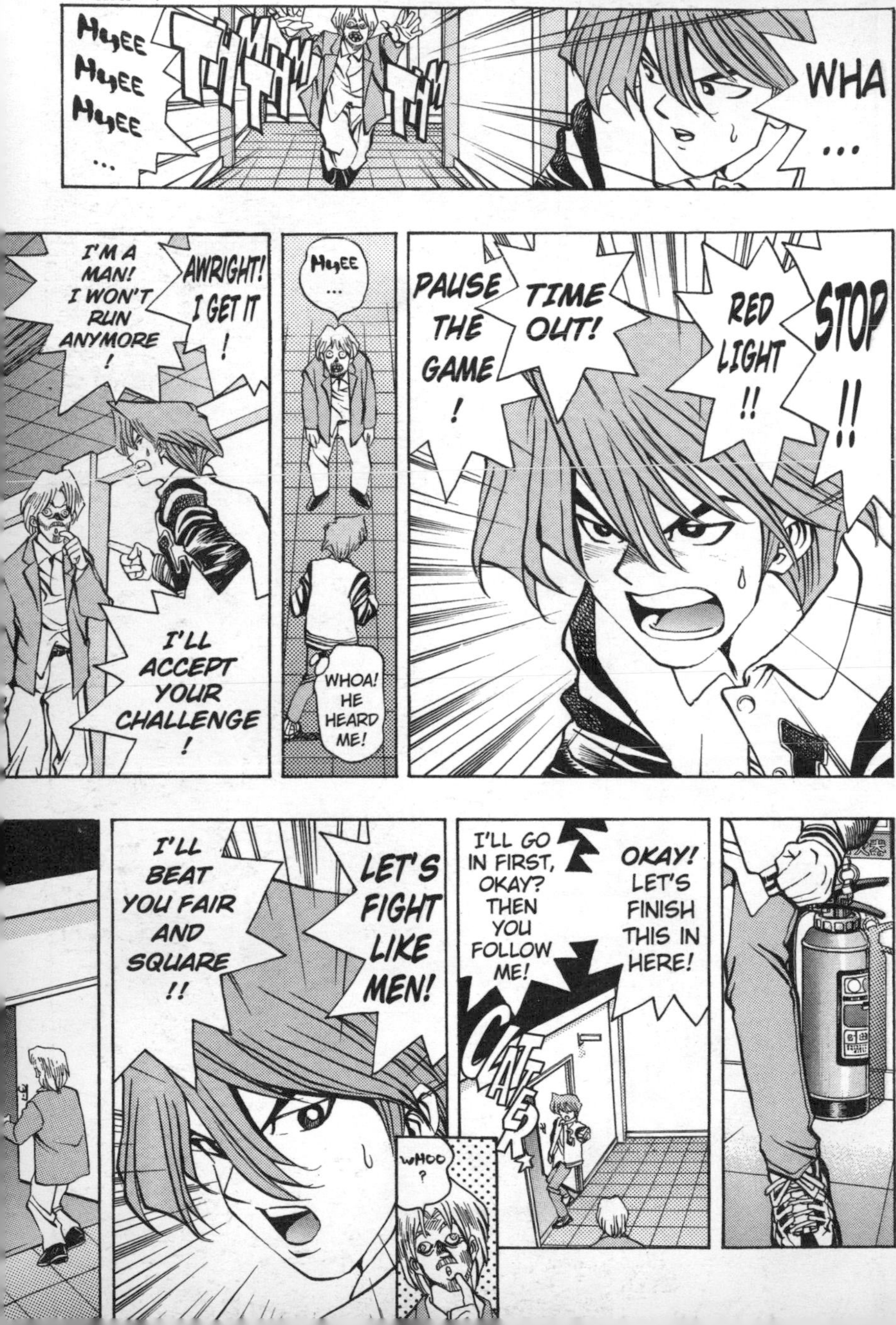
WHA ...
Hyee Hyee Hyee ...
STOP !!
RED LIGHT !!
TIME OUT!
PAUSE THE GAME !
Hyee ...
WHOA! HE HEARD ME!
AWRIGHT! I GET IT !
I'M A MAN! I WON'T RUN ANYMORE !
I'LL ACCEPT YOUR CHALLENGE !
OKAY! LET'S FINISH THIS IN HERE!
I'LL GO IN FIRST, OKAY? THEN YOU FOLLOW ME!
CLATTER
LET'S FIGHT LIKE MEN!
I'LL BEAT YOU FAIR AND SQUARE !!
WHOO ?

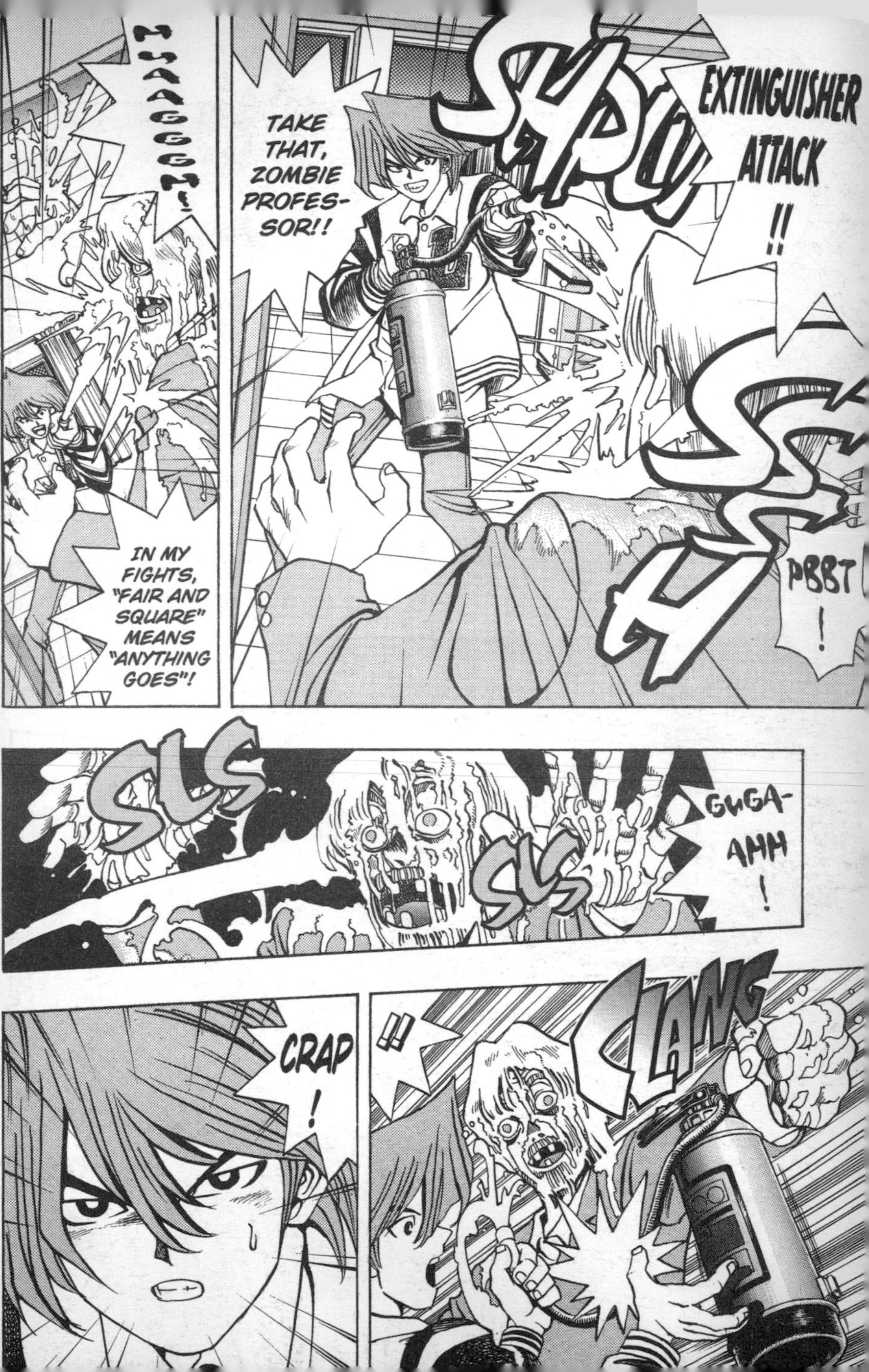
EXTINGUISHER ATTACK!!
SPLUSSH
TAKE THAT, ZOMBIE PROFES-SOR!!
PBBT!
NYAAGGGH!
IN MY FIGHTS, "FAIR AND SQUARE" MEANS "ANYTHING GOES"!
GUGA-AHH!
SLS
SLS
CLANG
!!
CRAP!

READ THIS WAY

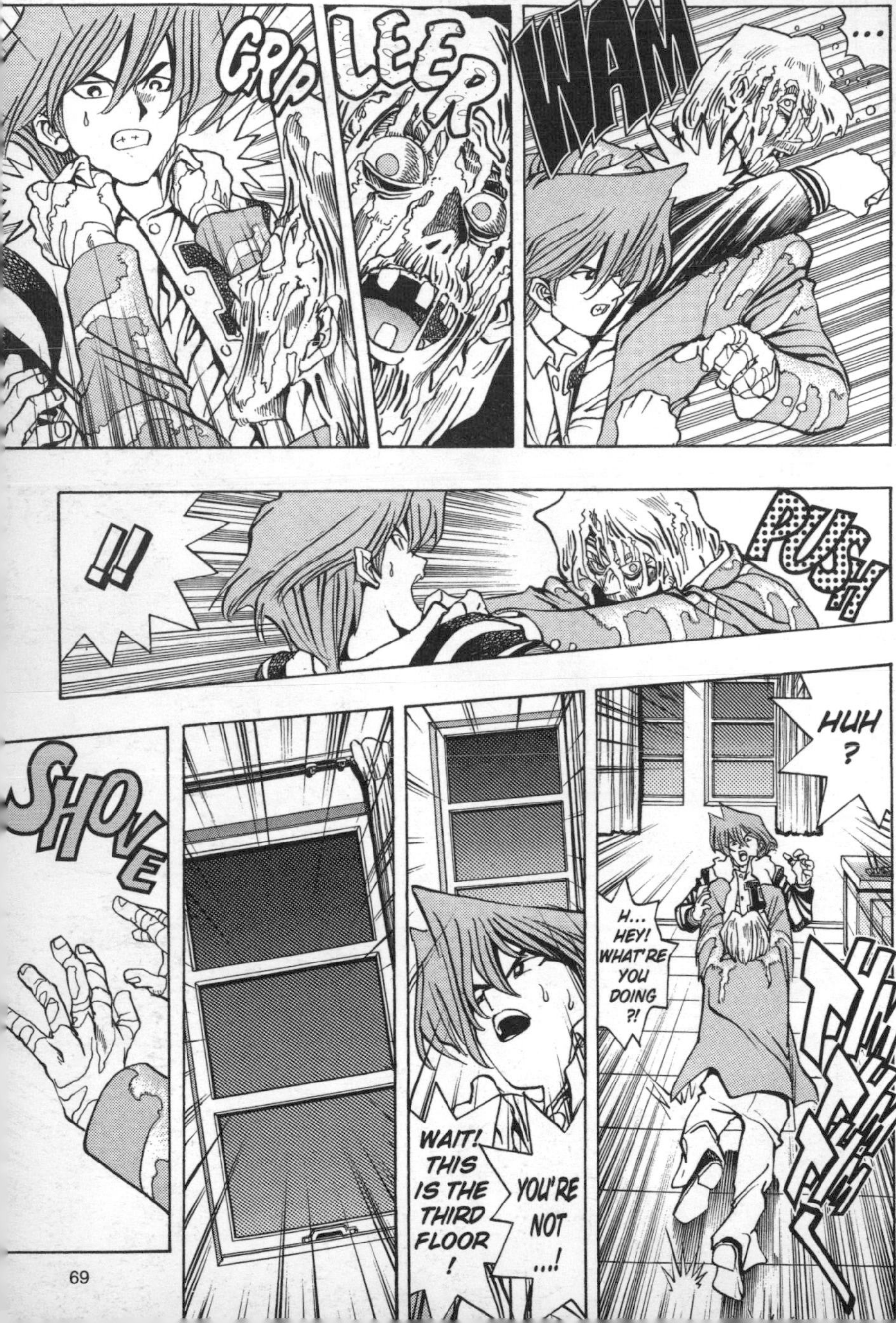

WAM
...
LEEP
GRIP
PUSH
!!
HUH ?
H... HEY! WHAT'RE YOU DOING ?!
WAIT! THIS IS THE THIRD FLOOR !
YOU'RE NOT ...!
SHOVE

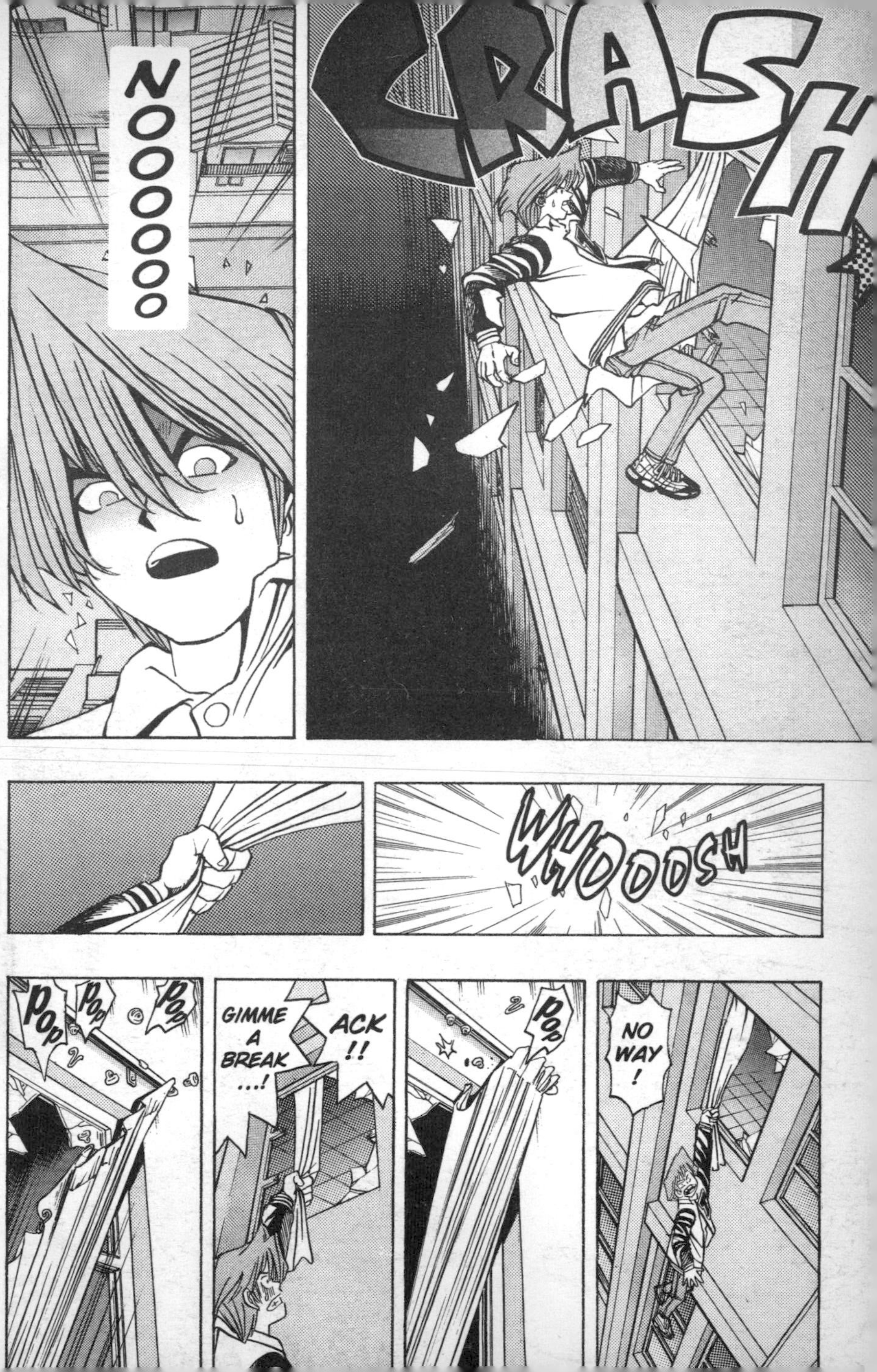
CRASH
NOOOOOOO
WHOOOOSH
NO WAY!
pop
ACK!!
GIMME A BREAK ...!
pop
pop
pop

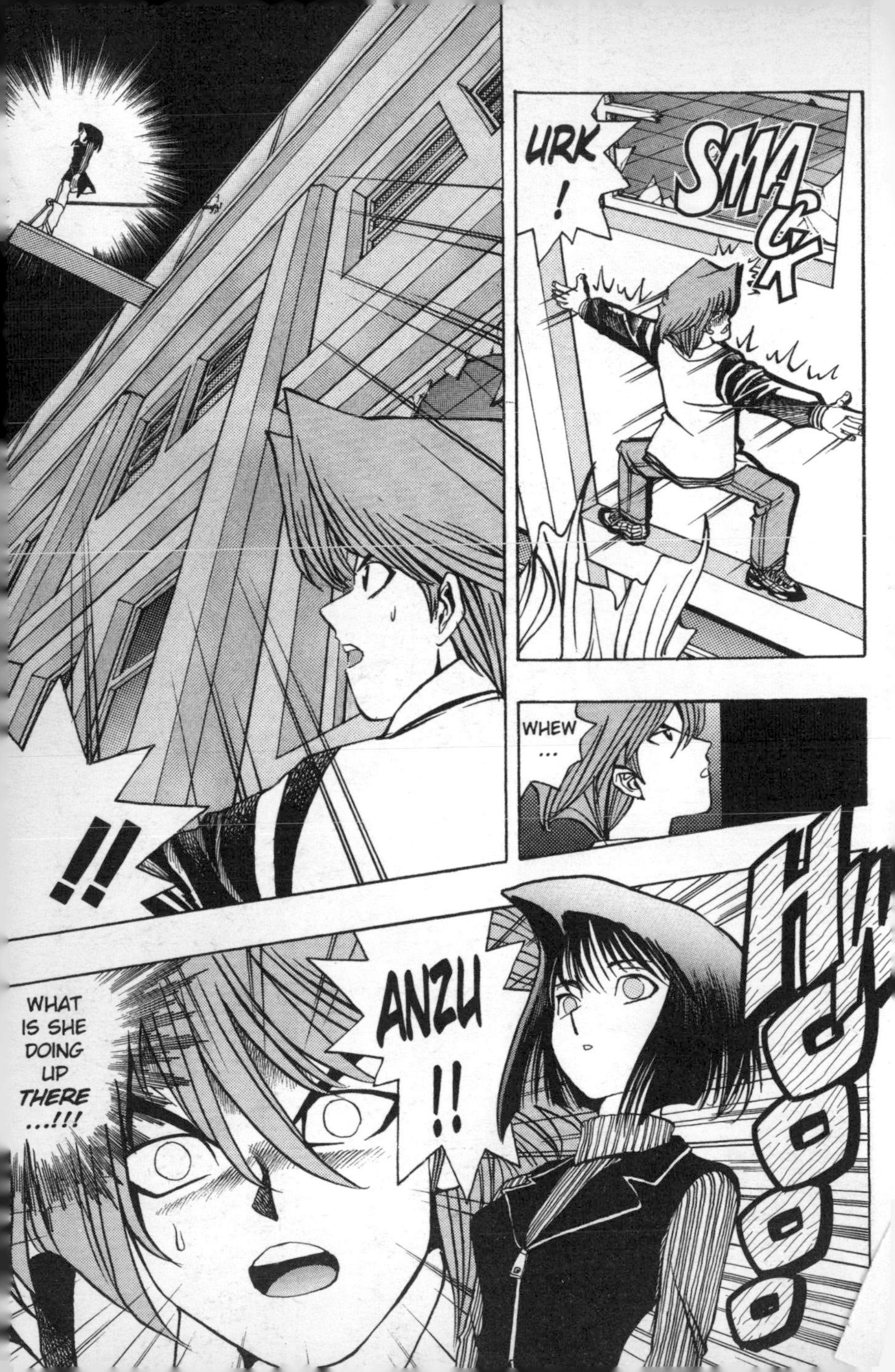
SMACK
URK!
WHEW...
!!
ANZU!!
WHAT IS SHE DOING UP THERE...!!!

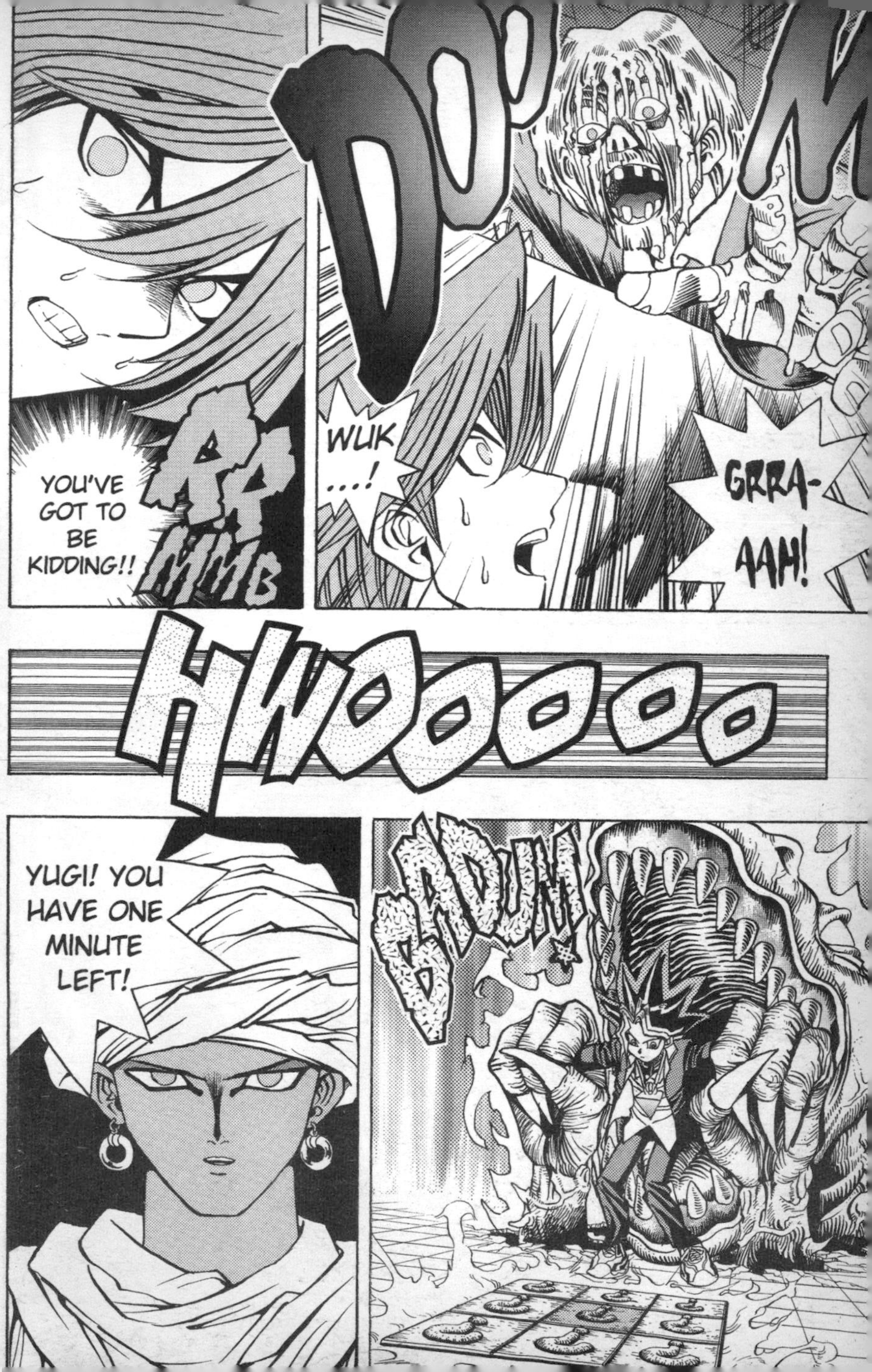
GRRA-AAH!
WUK ...!
YOU'VE GOT TO BE KIDDING!!
HWOOOOO
BADUM
YUGI! YOU HAVE ONE MINUTE LEFT!

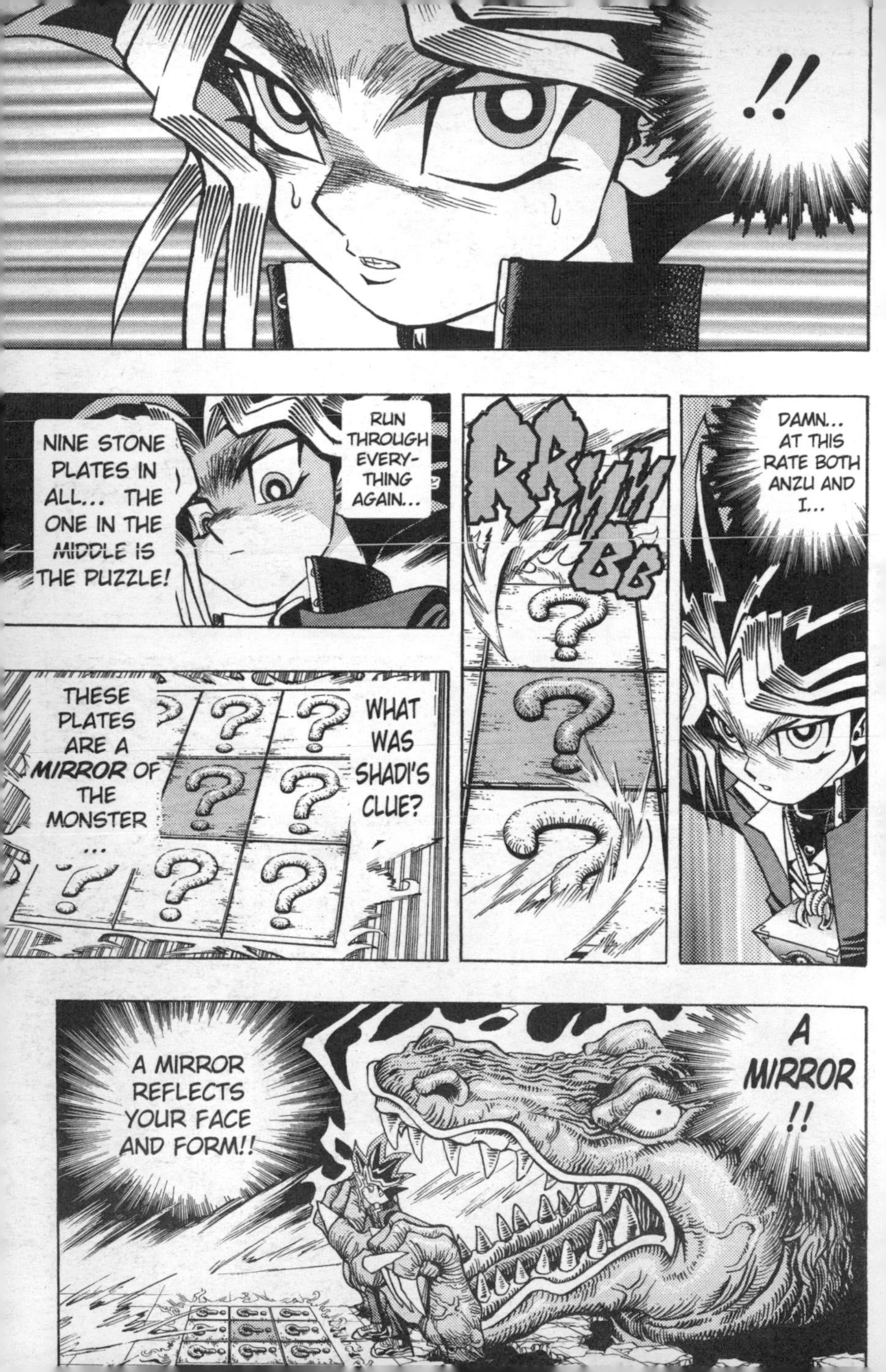
!!
DAMN... AT THIS RATE BOTH ANZU AND I...
RRMMBB
RUN THROUGH EVERY-THING AGAIN...
NINE STONE PLATES IN ALL... THE ONE IN THE MIDDLE IS THE PUZZLE!
WHAT WAS SHADI'S CLUE?
THESE PLATES ARE A MIRROR OF THE MONSTER ...
A MIRROR !!
A MIRROR REFLECTS YOUR FACE AND FORM!!

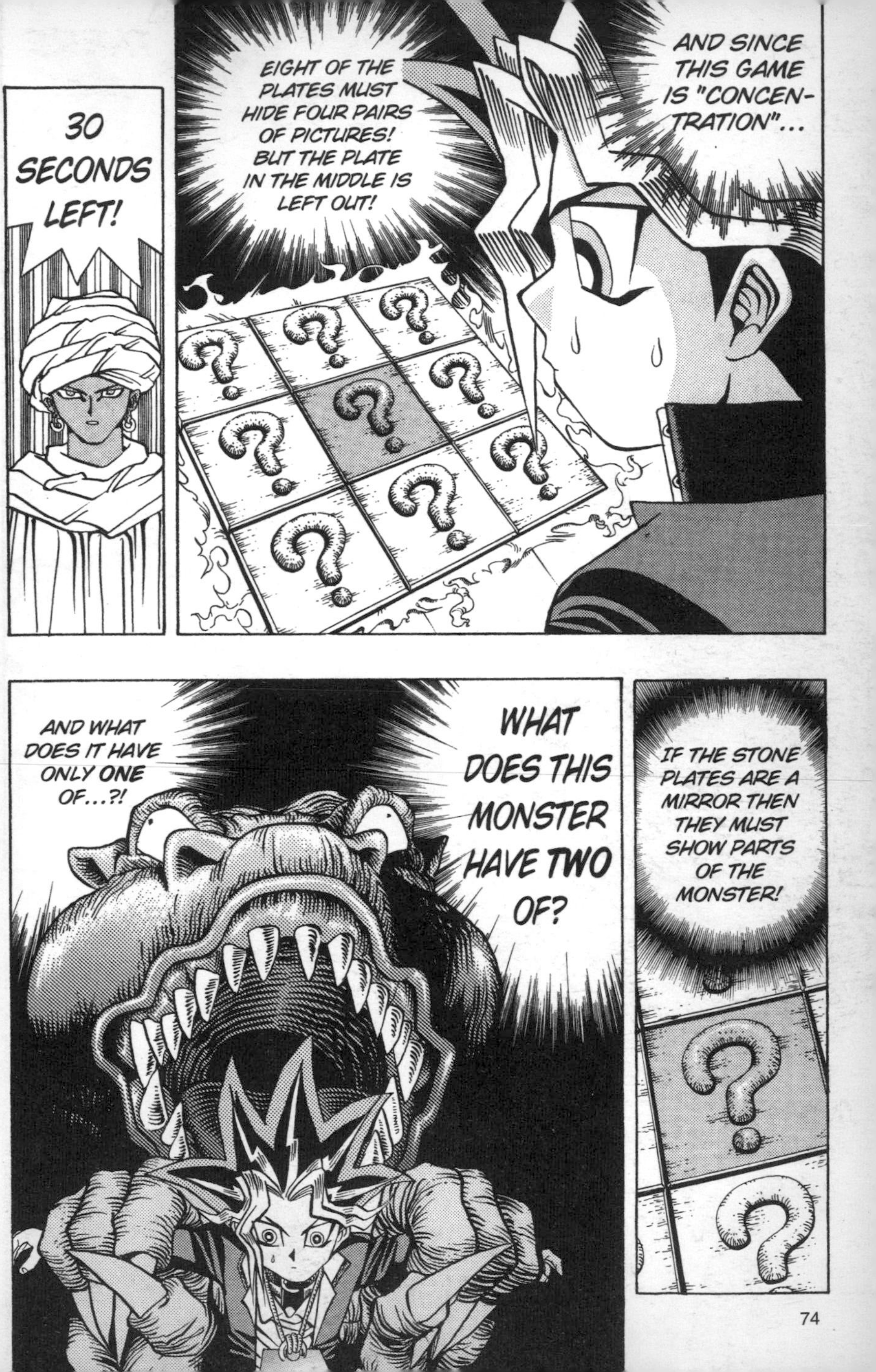

AND SINCE THIS GAME IS "CONCENTRATION"...
EIGHT OF THE PLATES MUST HIDE FOUR PAIRS OF PICTURES! BUT THE PLATE IN THE MIDDLE IS LEFT OUT!
30 SECONDS LEFT!
IF THE STONE PLATES ARE A MIRROR THEN THEY MUST SHOW PARTS OF THE MONSTER!
WHAT DOES THIS MONSTER HAVE **TWO** OF?
AND WHAT DOES IT HAVE ONLY **ONE** OF...?!

READ THIS WAY

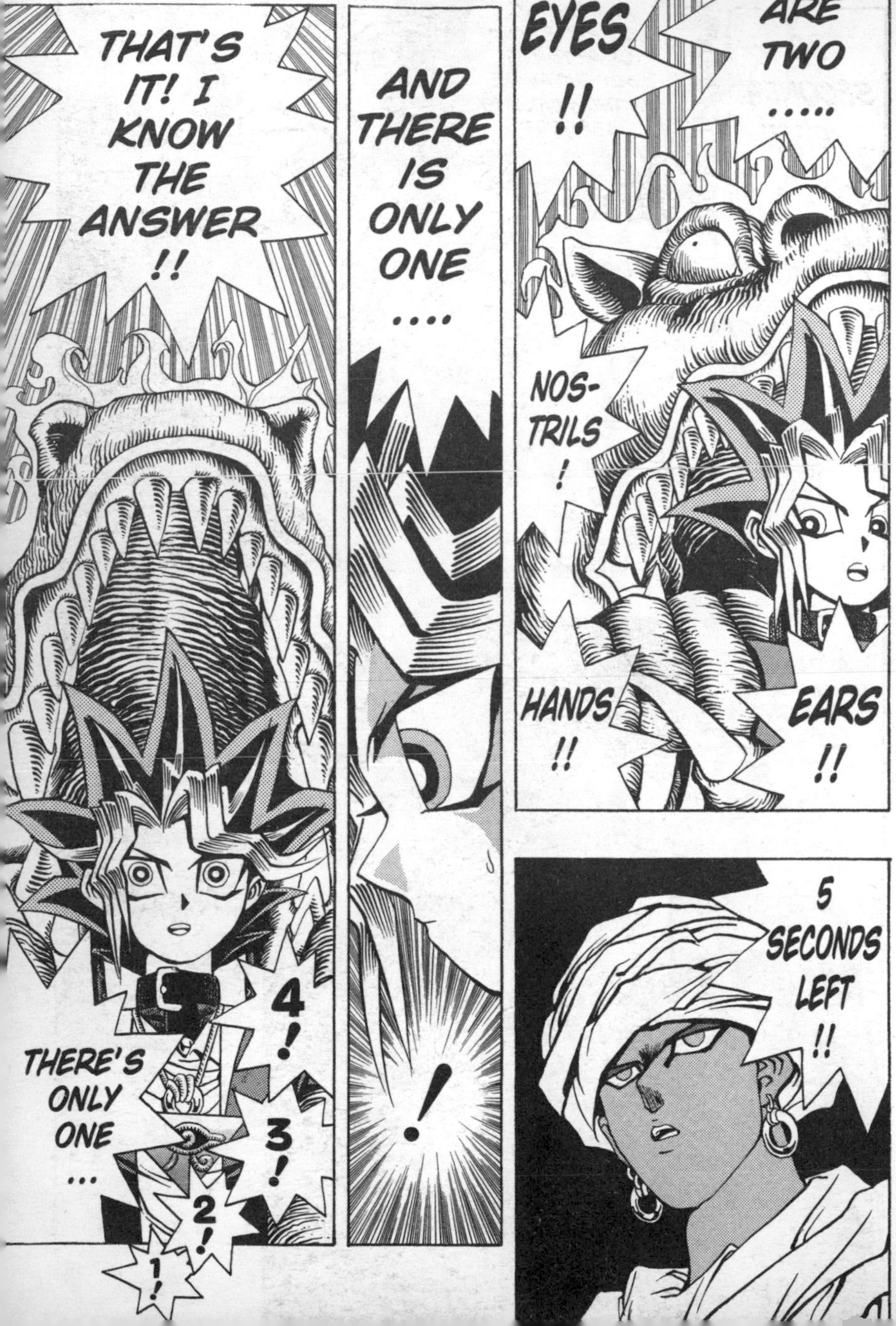
THERE ARE TWO .....
EYES !!
NOS-TRILS !
EARS !!
HANDS !!
5 SECONDS LEFT !!
AND THERE IS ONLY ONE ....
!
THAT'S IT! I KNOW THE ANSWER !!
4 !
3 !
THERE'S ONLY ONE ...
2 !
1 !

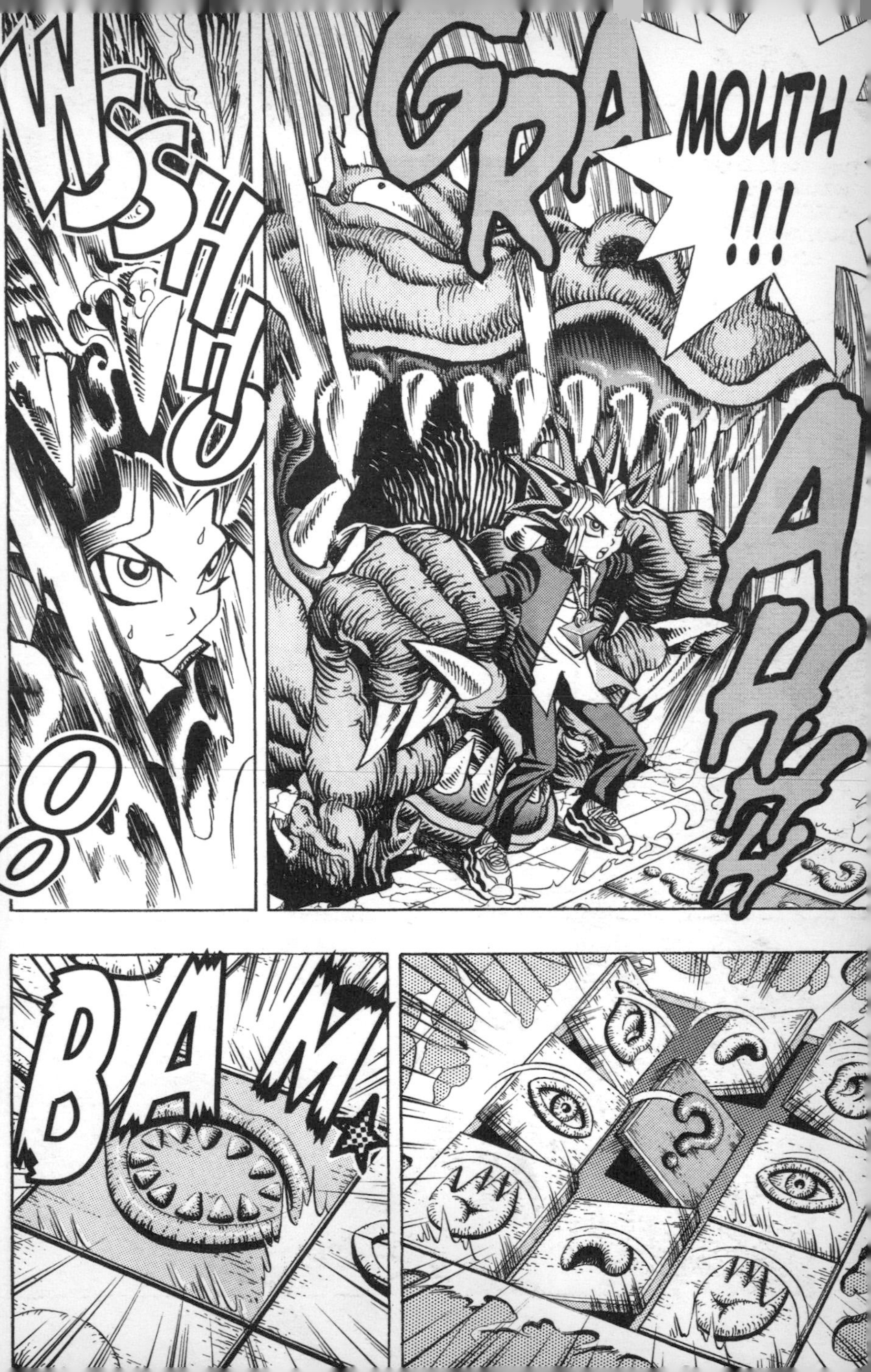
GRA
MOUTH !!!
AH!!
WSHHOOO
BAM

READ THIS WAY

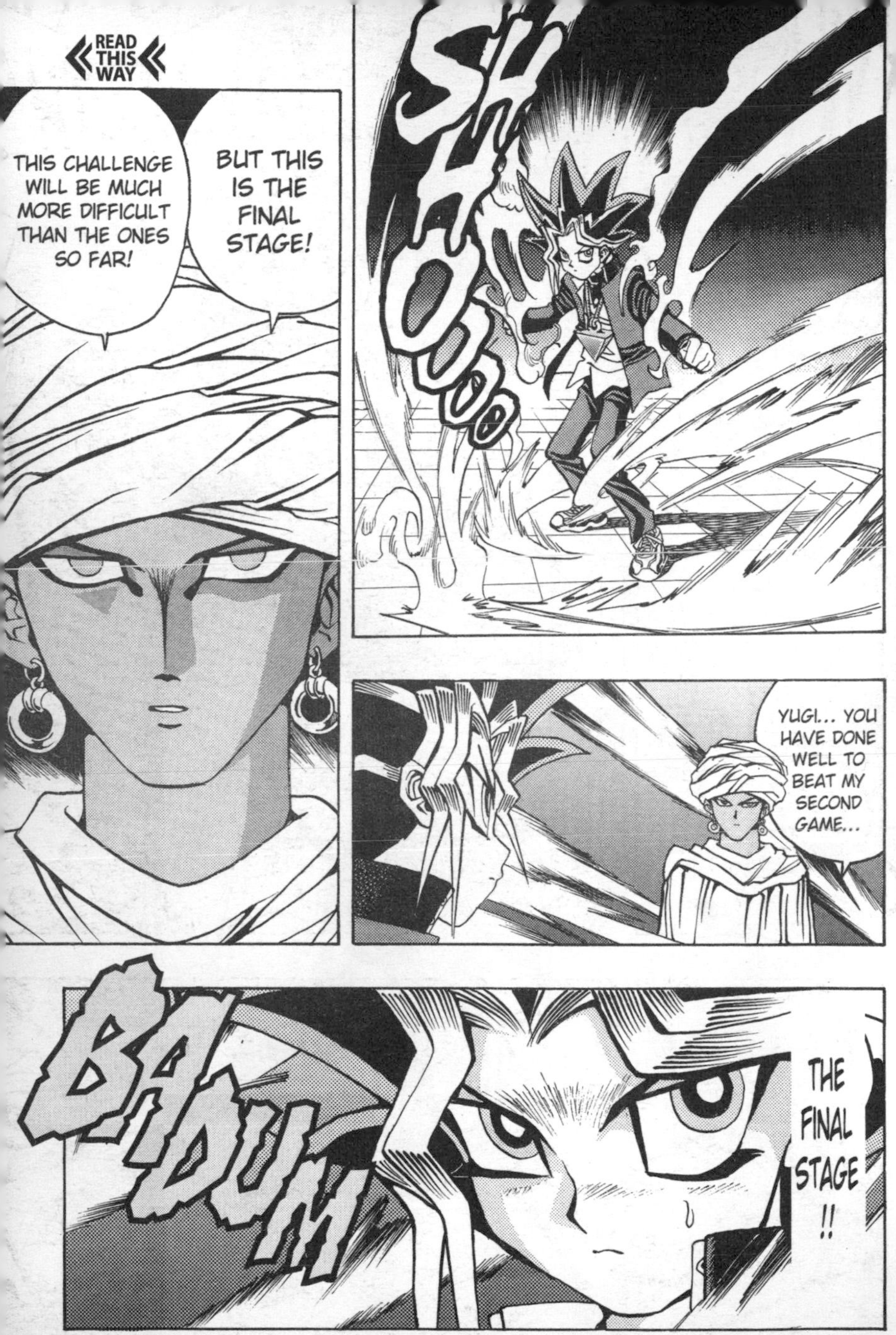
SHHOOOOO
YUGI... YOU HAVE DONE WELL TO BEAT MY SECOND GAME...
BUT THIS IS THE FINAL STAGE!
THIS CHALLENGE WILL BE MUCH MORE DIFFICULT THAN THE ONES SO FAR!
THE FINAL STAGE !!
BA-DUM

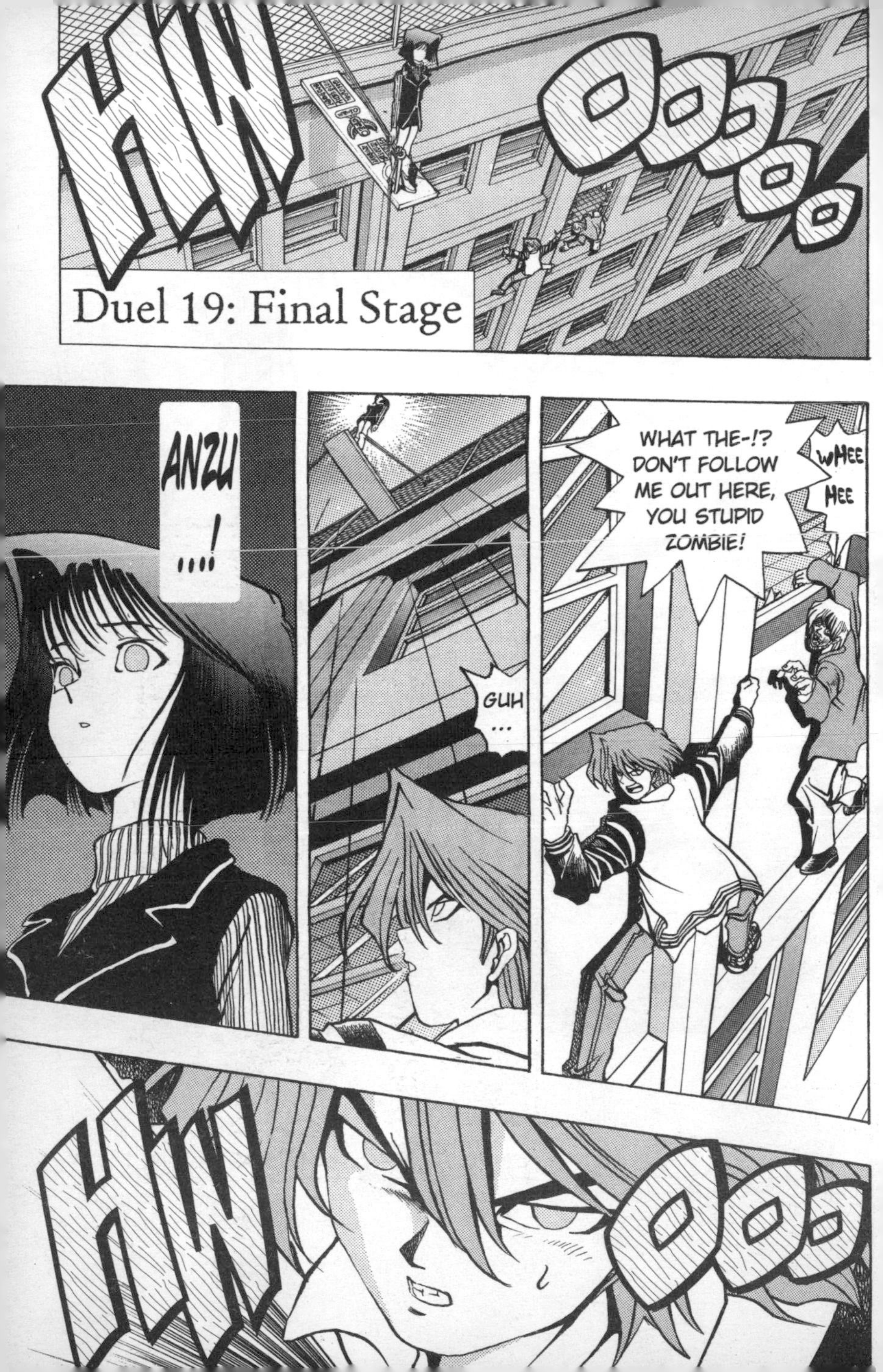
HIN
OOOOO
Duel 19: Final Stage
WHAT THE-!? DON'T FOLLOW ME OUT HERE, YOU STUPID ZOMBIE!
WHEE HEE
GUH ...
ANZU ...!
HIN
OOO

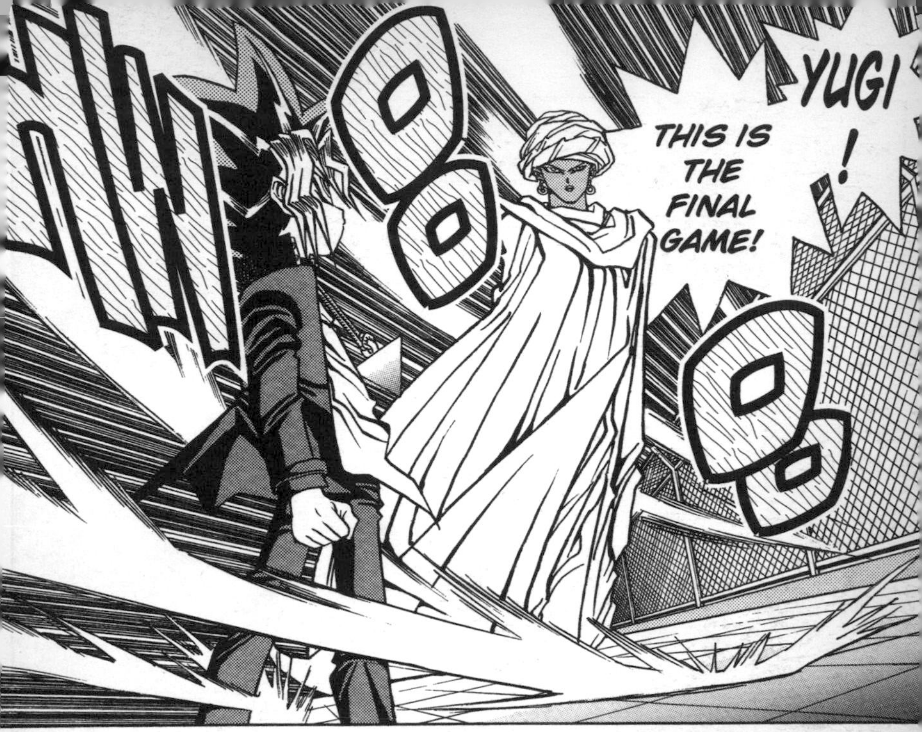
YUGI!
THIS IS THE FINAL GAME!

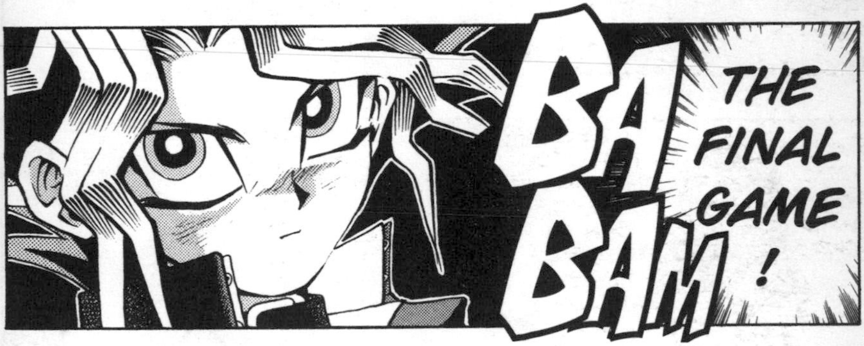
THE FINAL GAME!
BA BAM

Duel 19: Final Stage

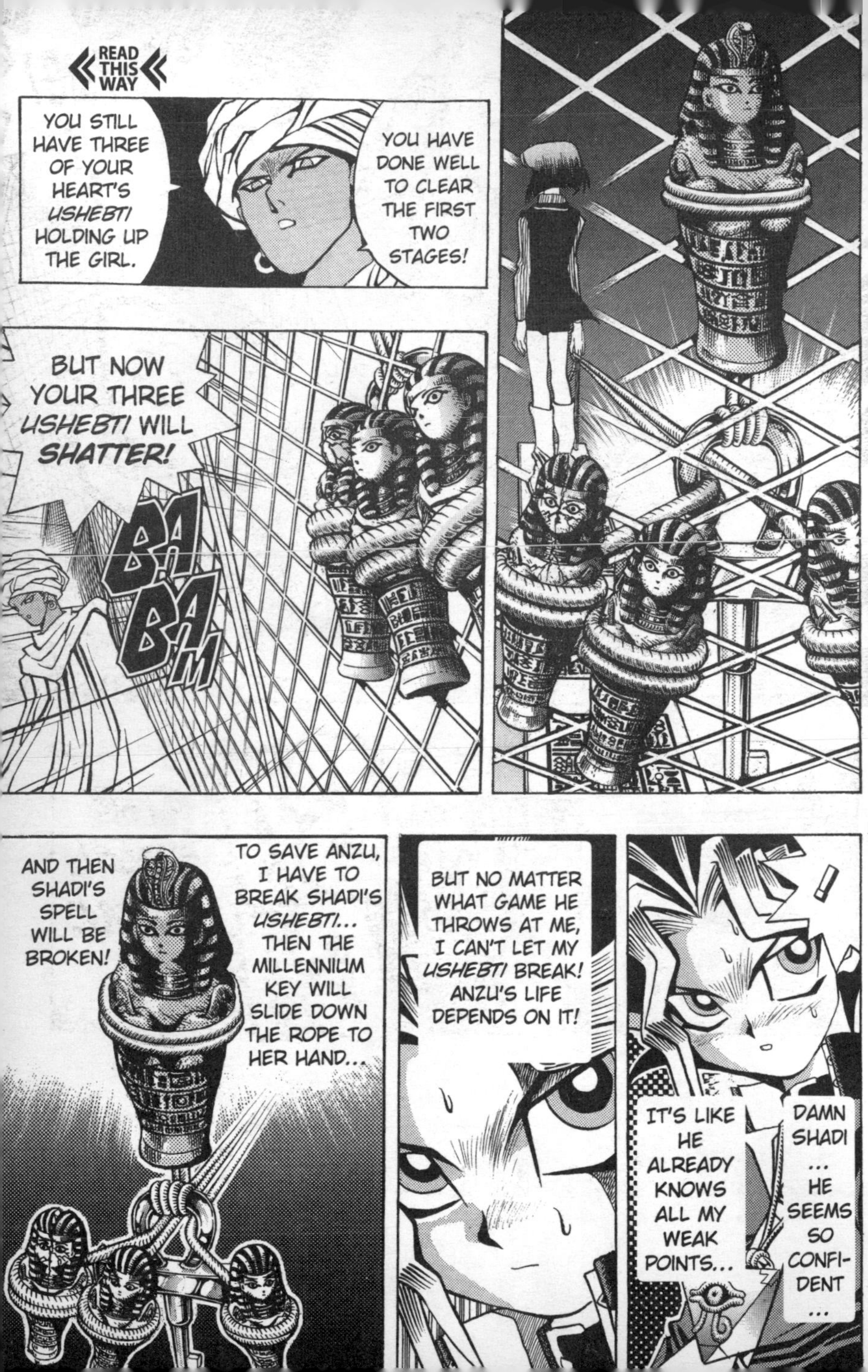
READ THIS WAY
YOU HAVE DONE WELL TO CLEAR THE FIRST TWO STAGES!
YOU STILL HAVE THREE OF YOUR HEART'S *USHEBTI* HOLDING UP THE GIRL.
BUT NOW YOUR THREE *USHEBTI* WILL **SHATTER!**
BA BA BAM
DAMN SHADI ... HE SEEMS SO CONFIDENT ...
IT'S LIKE HE ALREADY KNOWS ALL MY WEAK POINTS...
BUT NO MATTER WHAT GAME HE THROWS AT ME, I CAN'T LET MY *USHEBTI* BREAK! ANZU'S LIFE DEPENDS ON IT!
TO SAVE ANZU, I HAVE TO BREAK SHADI'S *USHEBTI*... THEN THE MILLENNIUM KEY WILL SLIDE DOWN THE ROPE TO HER HAND...
AND THEN SHADI'S SPELL WILL BE BROKEN!

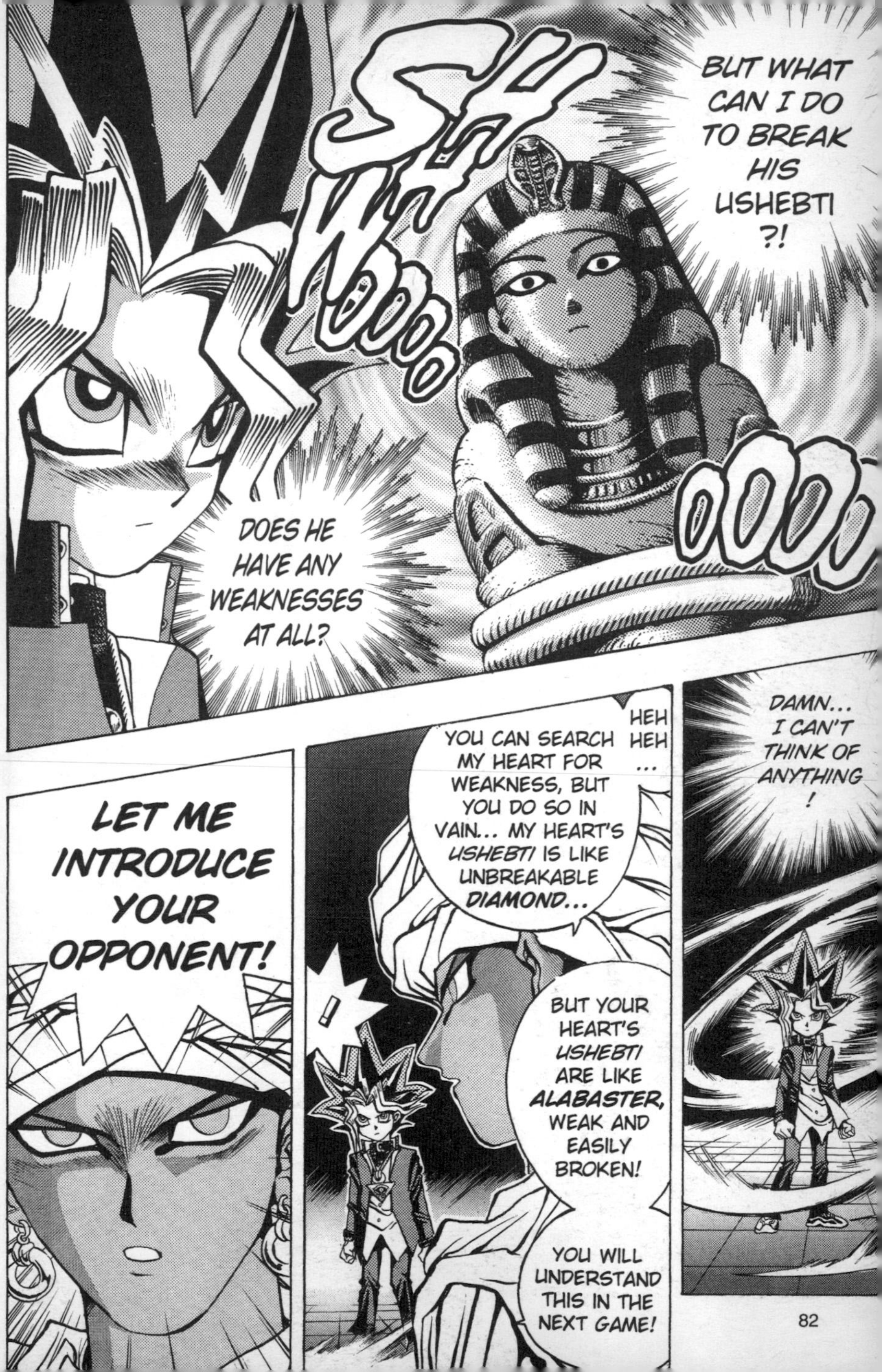
BUT WHAT CAN I DO TO BREAK HIS USHEBTI ?!
SHHOOOOOOOOO
DOES HE HAVE ANY WEAKNESSES AT ALL?
DAMN... I CAN'T THINK OF ANYTHING!
HEH HEH...
YOU CAN SEARCH MY HEART FOR WEAKNESS, BUT YOU DO SO IN VAIN... MY HEART'S USHEBTI IS LIKE UNBREAKABLE DIAMOND...
!
BUT YOUR HEART'S USHEBTI ARE LIKE ALABASTER, WEAK AND EASILY BROKEN!
YOU WILL UNDERSTAND THIS IN THE NEXT GAME!
LET ME INTRODUCE YOUR OPPONENT!

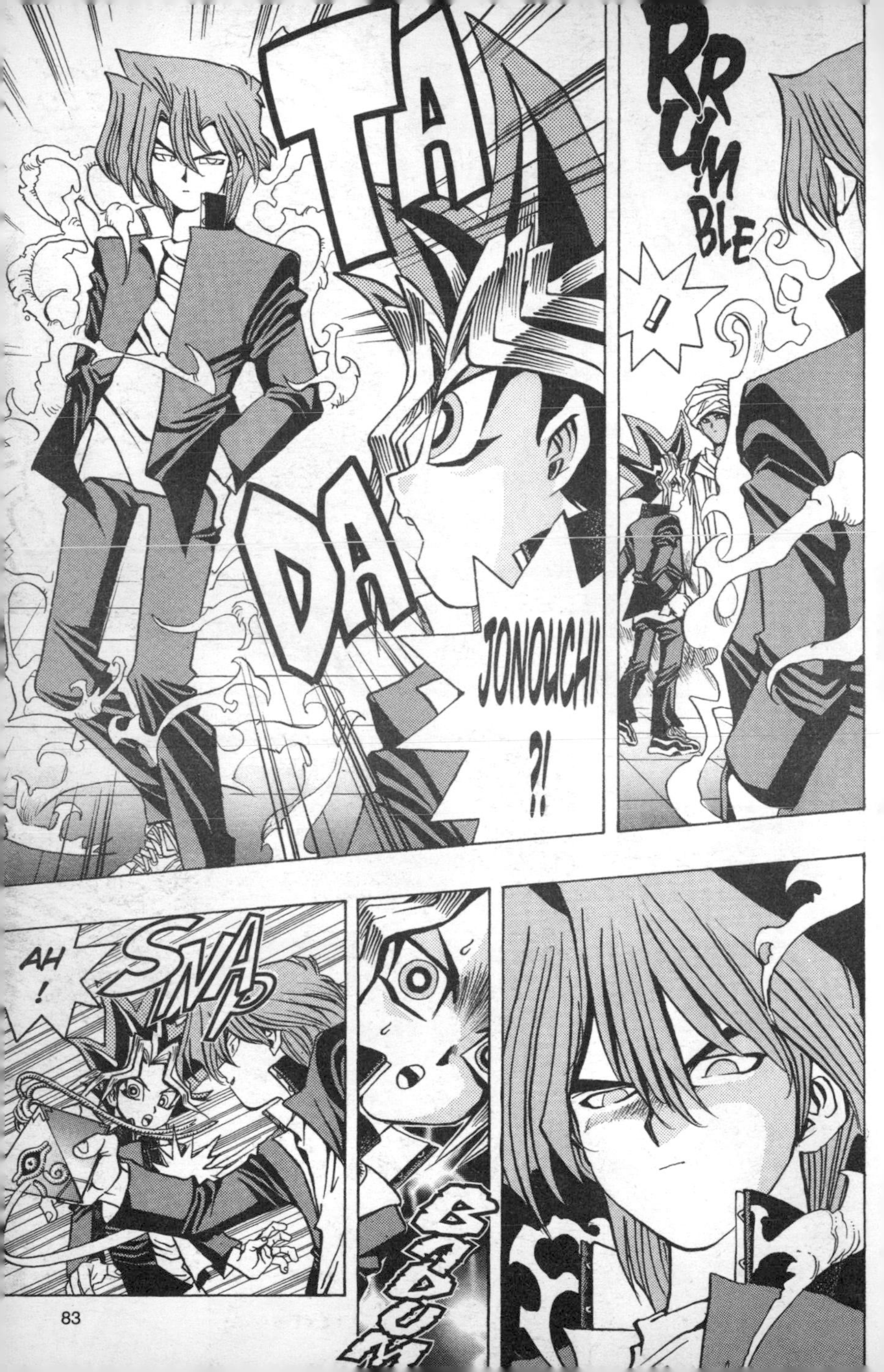

RRUMBLE
!
TA
DA
JONOUCHI ?!
BADUM
AH !
SNA

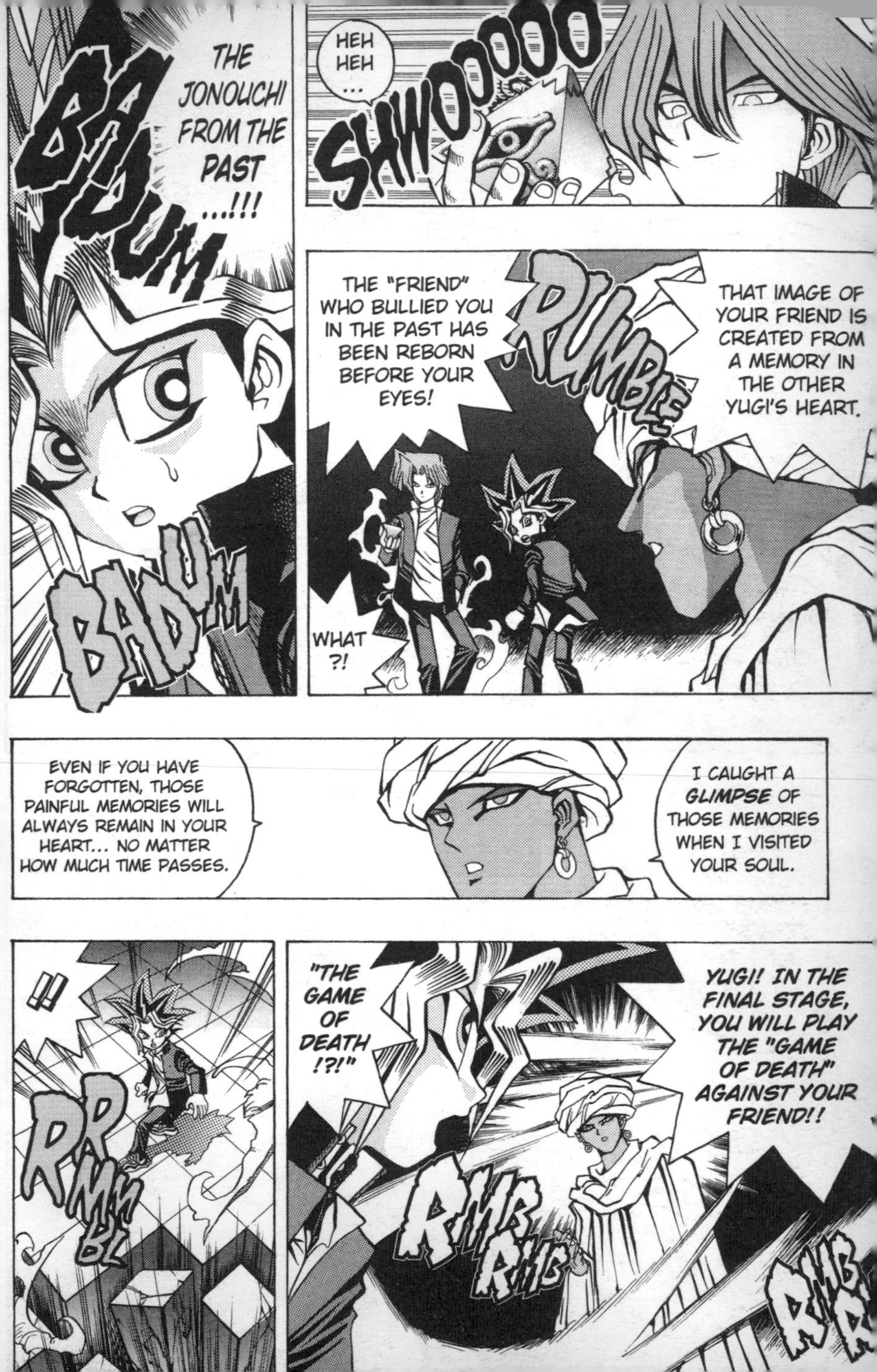
HEH HEH ...
SHWOOOOO
THAT IMAGE OF YOUR FRIEND IS CREATED FROM A MEMORY IN THE OTHER YUGI'S HEART.
RUMBLE
THE "FRIEND" WHO BULLIED YOU IN THE PAST HAS BEEN REBORN BEFORE YOUR EYES!
WHAT ?!
BADUM
THE JONOUCHI FROM THE PAST ...!!!
BADUM
I CAUGHT A GLIMPSE OF THOSE MEMORIES WHEN I VISITED YOUR SOUL.
EVEN IF YOU HAVE FORGOTTEN, THOSE PAINFUL MEMORIES WILL ALWAYS REMAIN IN YOUR HEART... NO MATTER HOW MUCH TIME PASSES.
YUGI! IN THE FINAL STAGE, YOU WILL PLAY THE "GAME OF DEATH" AGAINST YOUR FRIEND!!
"THE GAME OF DEATH !?!"
!!

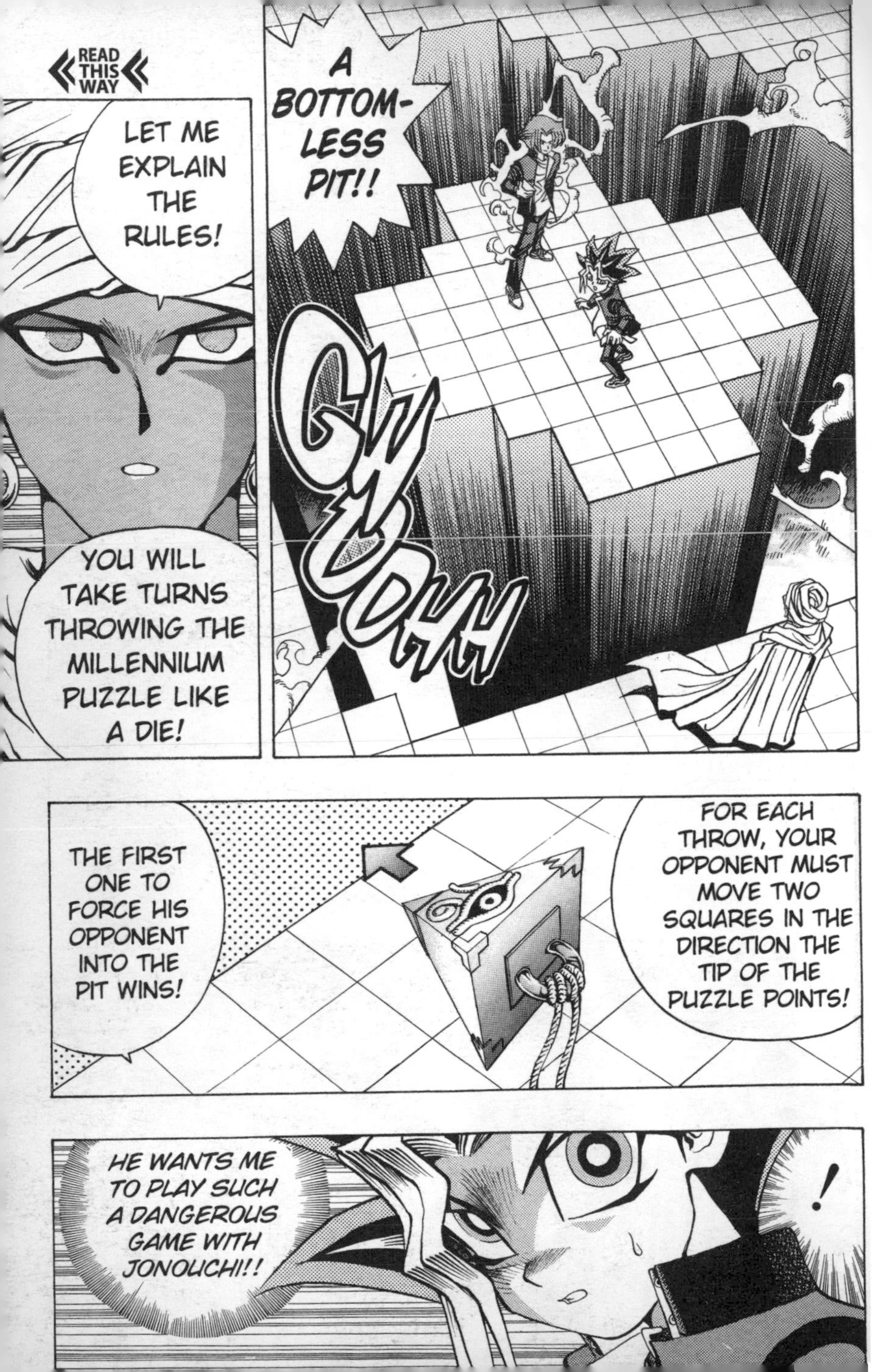
READ THIS WAY
A BOTTOM-LESS PIT!!
LET ME EXPLAIN THE RULES!
YOU WILL TAKE TURNS THROWING THE MILLENNIUM PUZZLE LIKE A DIE!
FOR EACH THROW, YOUR OPPONENT MUST MOVE TWO SQUARES IN THE DIRECTION THE TIP OF THE PUZZLE POINTS!
THE FIRST ONE TO FORCE HIS OPPONENT INTO THE PIT WINS!
!
HE WANTS ME TO PLAY SUCH A DANGEROUS GAME WITH JONOUCHI!!

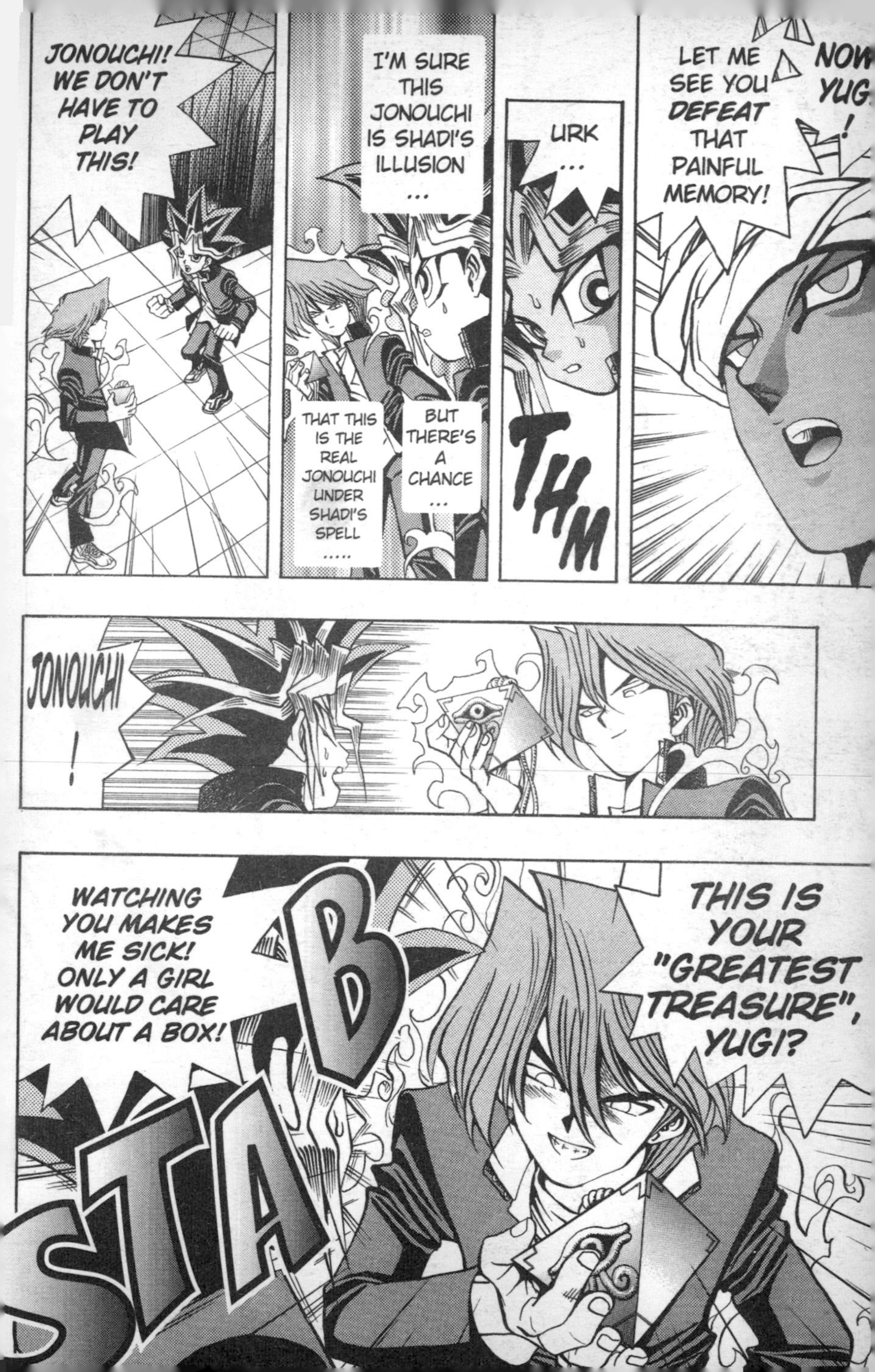
NOW YUG !
LET ME SEE YOU DEFEAT THAT PAINFUL MEMORY!
URK ...
THM
I'M SURE THIS JONOUCHI IS SHADI'S ILLUSION ...
BUT THERE'S A CHANCE ...
THAT THIS IS THE REAL JONOUCHI UNDER SHADI'S SPELL .....
JONOUCHI! WE DON'T HAVE TO PLAY THIS!
JONOUCHI !
THIS IS YOUR "GREATEST TREASURE", YUGI?
STAB
WATCHING YOU MAKES ME SICK! ONLY A GIRL WOULD CARE ABOUT A BOX!

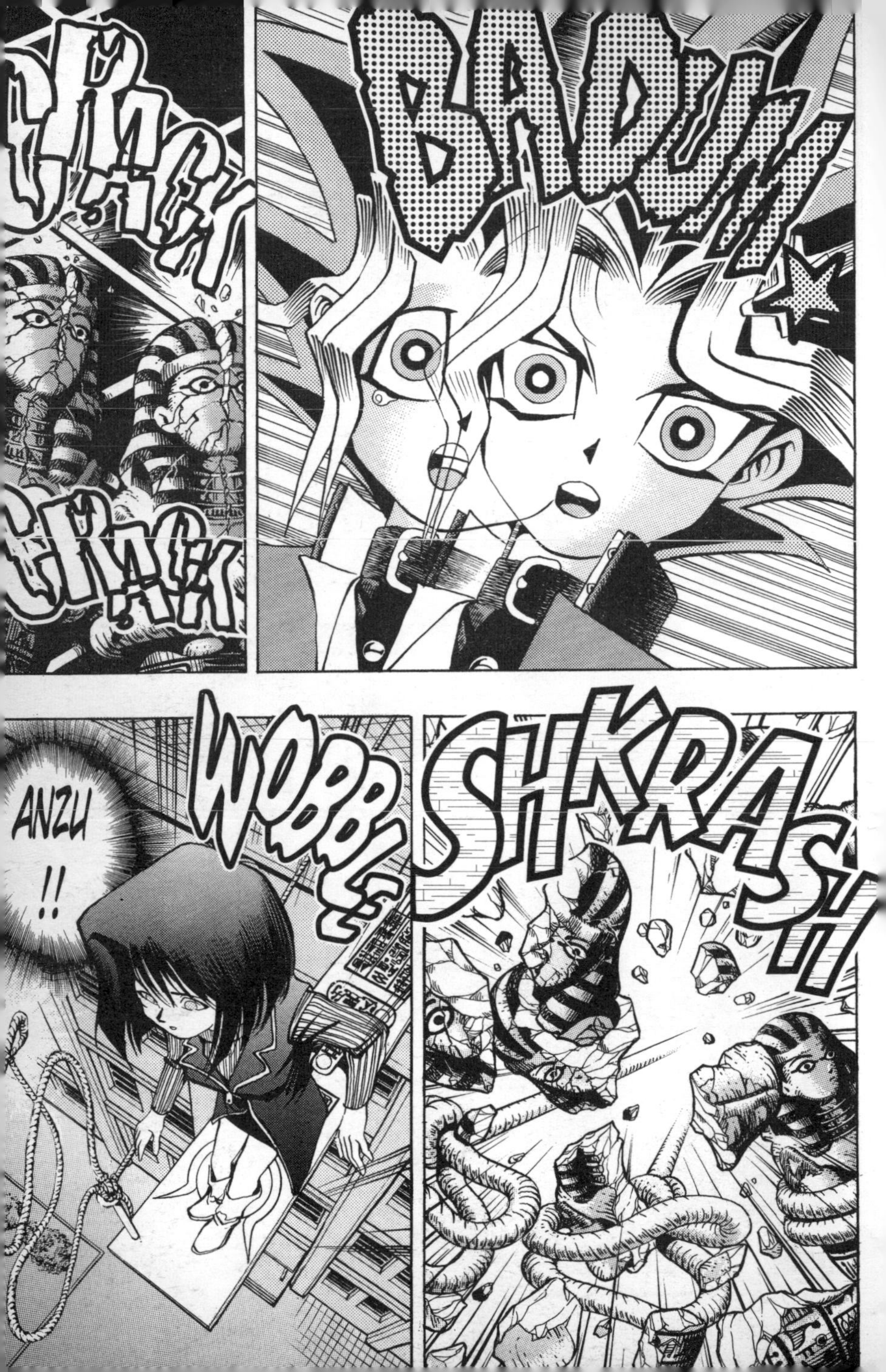
BADUM
CRACK
CRACK
SHKRASH
WOBBLE
ANZU !!

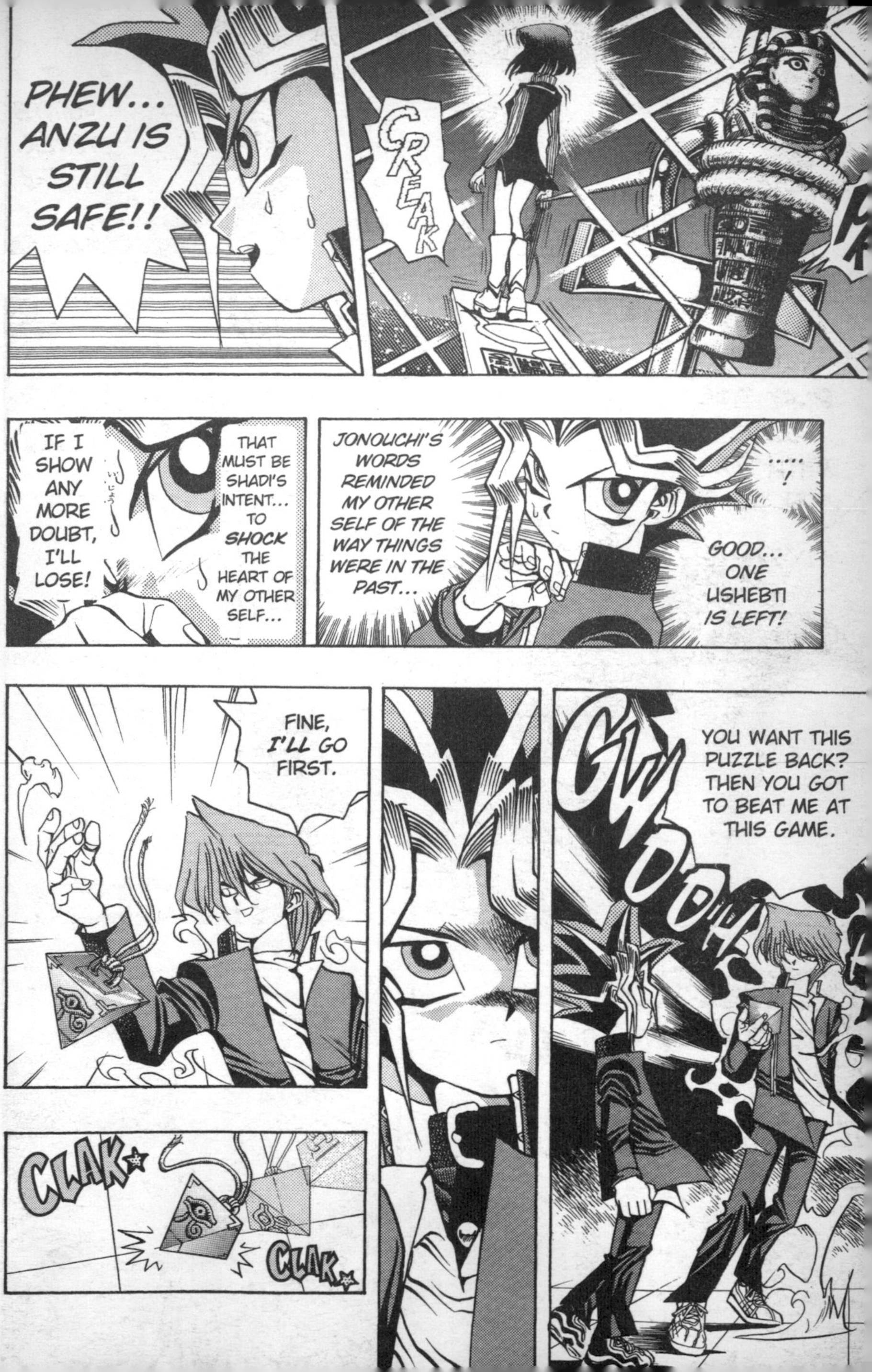
CREAK
PHEW... ANZU IS STILL SAFE!!
......!
GOOD... ONE USHEBTI IS LEFT!
JONOUCHI'S WORDS REMINDED MY OTHER SELF OF THE WAY THINGS WERE IN THE PAST...
THAT MUST BE SHADI'S INTENT... TO SHOCK THE HEART OF MY OTHER SELF...
IF I SHOW ANY MORE DOUBT, I'LL LOSE!
YOU WANT THIS PUZZLE BACK? THEN YOU GOT TO BEAT ME AT THIS GAME.
FINE, I'LL GO FIRST.
CLAK
CLAK

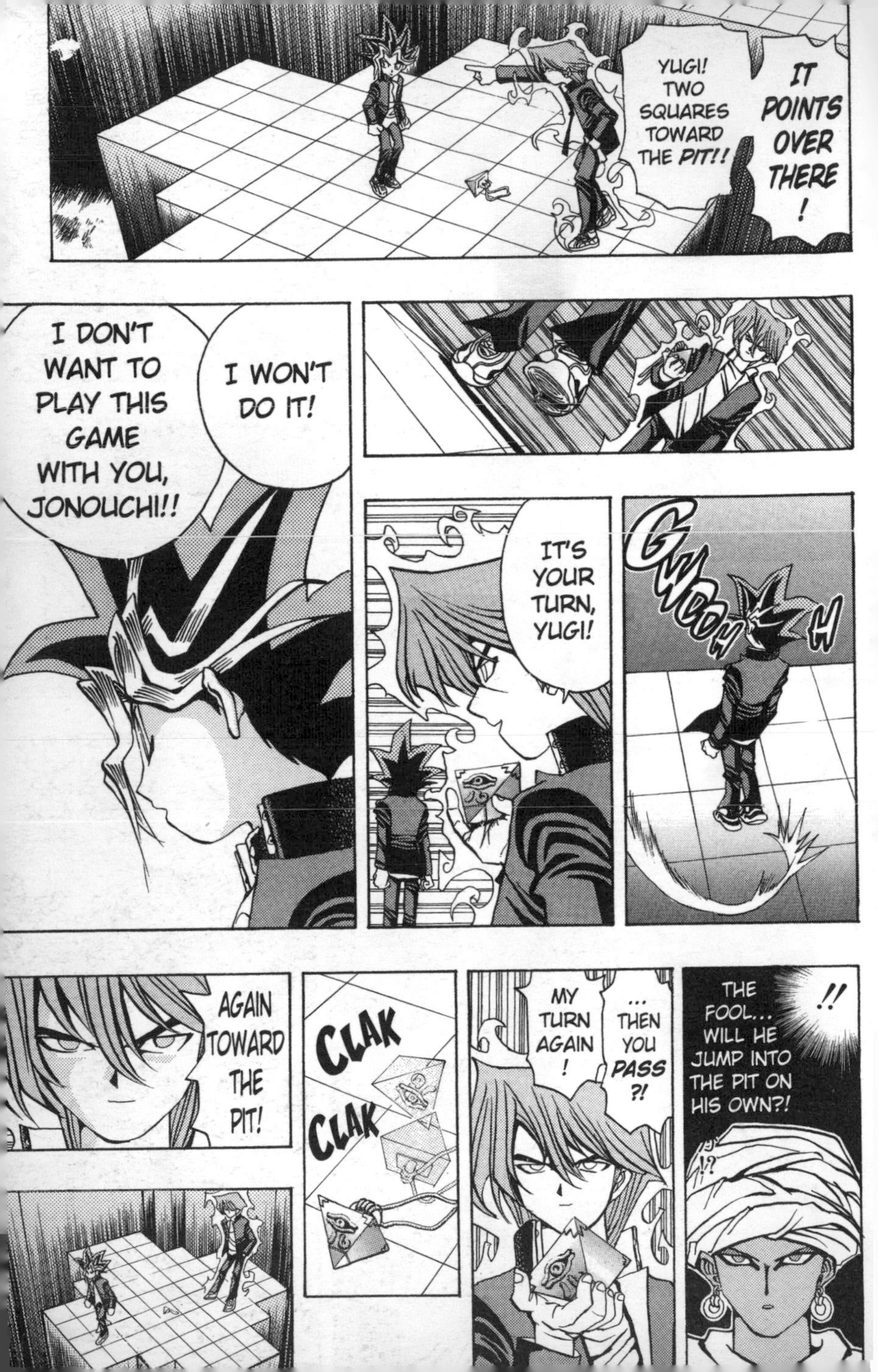
IT POINTS OVER THERE!
YUGI! TWO SQUARES TOWARD THE PIT!!
GWOOOHH
IT'S YOUR TURN, YUGI!
I WON'T DO IT!
I DON'T WANT TO PLAY THIS GAME WITH YOU, JONOUCHI!!
!!
THE FOOL... WILL HE JUMP INTO THE PIT ON HIS OWN?!
!?
... THEN YOU PASS?!
MY TURN AGAIN!
CLAK
CLAK
AGAIN TOWARD THE PIT!

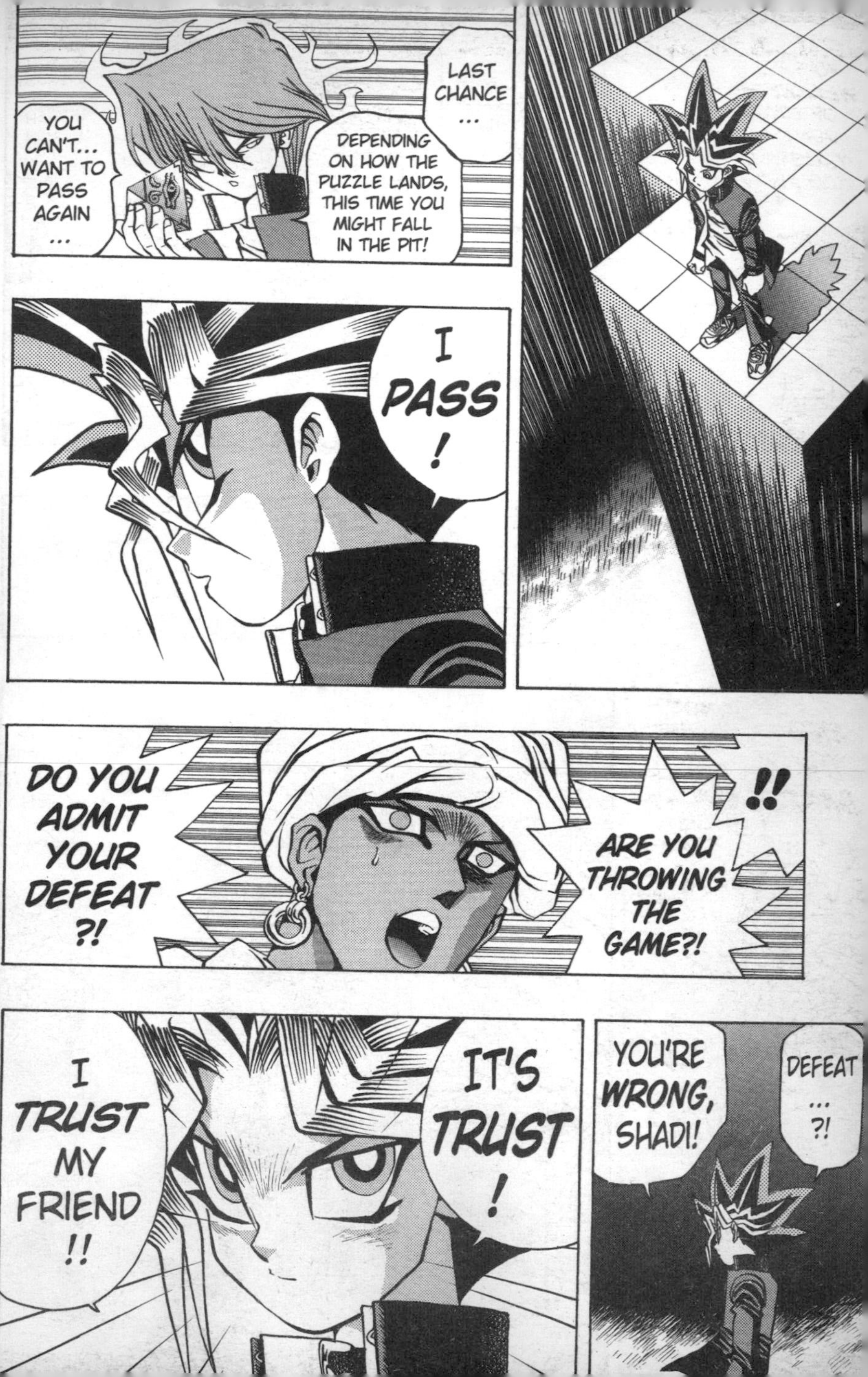

LAST CHANCE ...
DEPENDING ON HOW THE PUZZLE LANDS, THIS TIME YOU MIGHT FALL IN THE PIT!
YOU CAN'T... WANT TO PASS AGAIN ...
I PASS !
!!
ARE YOU THROWING THE GAME?!
DO YOU ADMIT YOUR DEFEAT ?!
DEFEAT ... ?!
YOU'RE WRONG, SHADI!
IT'S TRUST !
I TRUST MY FRIEND !!

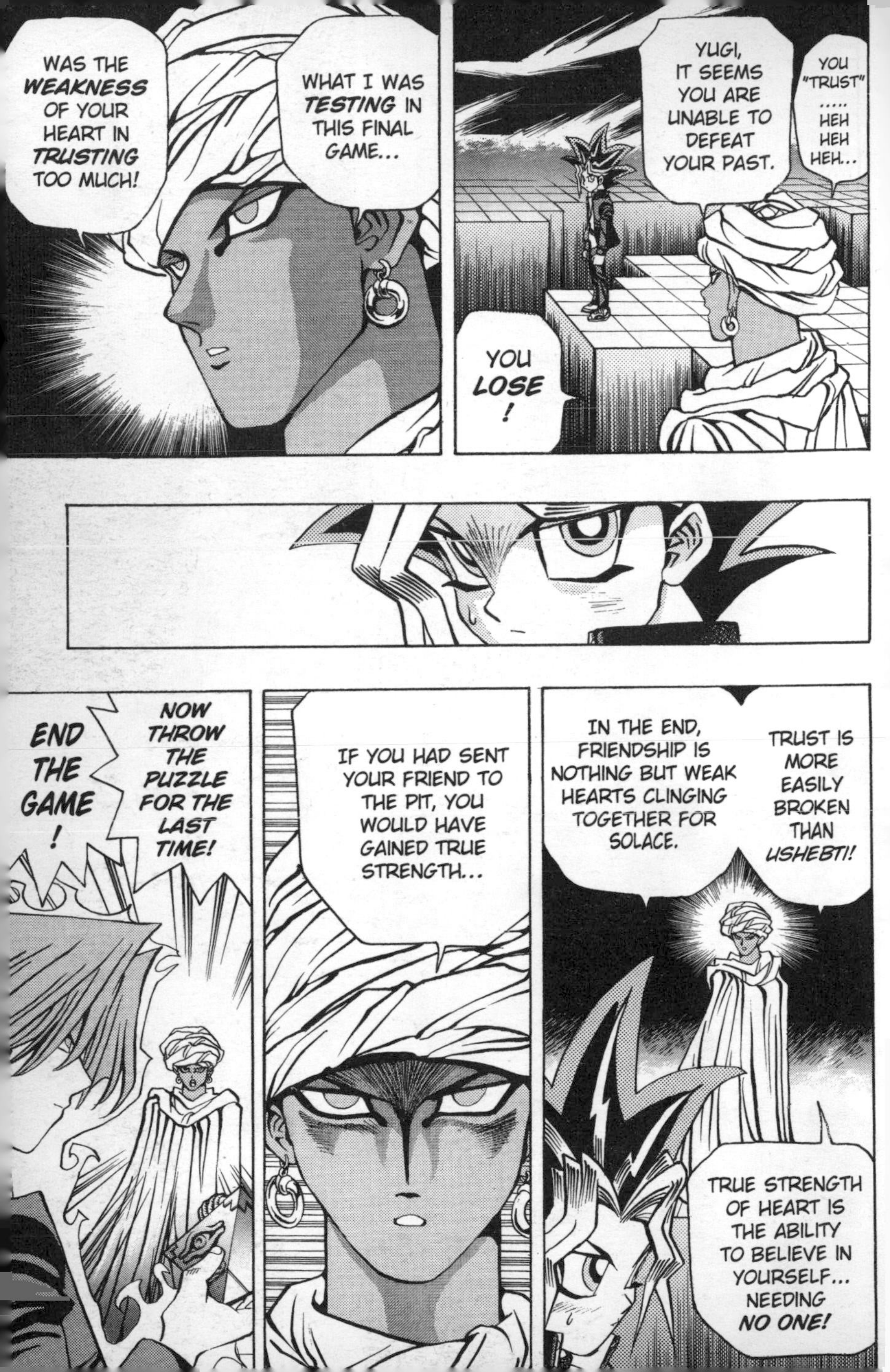
YOU "TRUST" ..... HEH HEH HEH...
YUGI, IT SEEMS YOU ARE UNABLE TO DEFEAT YOUR PAST.
YOU LOSE!
WHAT I WAS TESTING IN THIS FINAL GAME...
WAS THE WEAKNESS OF YOUR HEART IN TRUSTING TOO MUCH!
TRUST IS MORE EASILY BROKEN THAN USHEBTI!
IN THE END, FRIENDSHIP IS NOTHING BUT WEAK HEARTS CLINGING TOGETHER FOR SOLACE.
TRUE STRENGTH OF HEART IS THE ABILITY TO BELIEVE IN YOURSELF... NEEDING NO ONE!
IF YOU HAD SENT YOUR FRIEND TO THE PIT, YOU WOULD HAVE GAINED TRUE STRENGTH...
NOW THROW THE PUZZLE FOR THE LAST TIME!
END THE GAME!

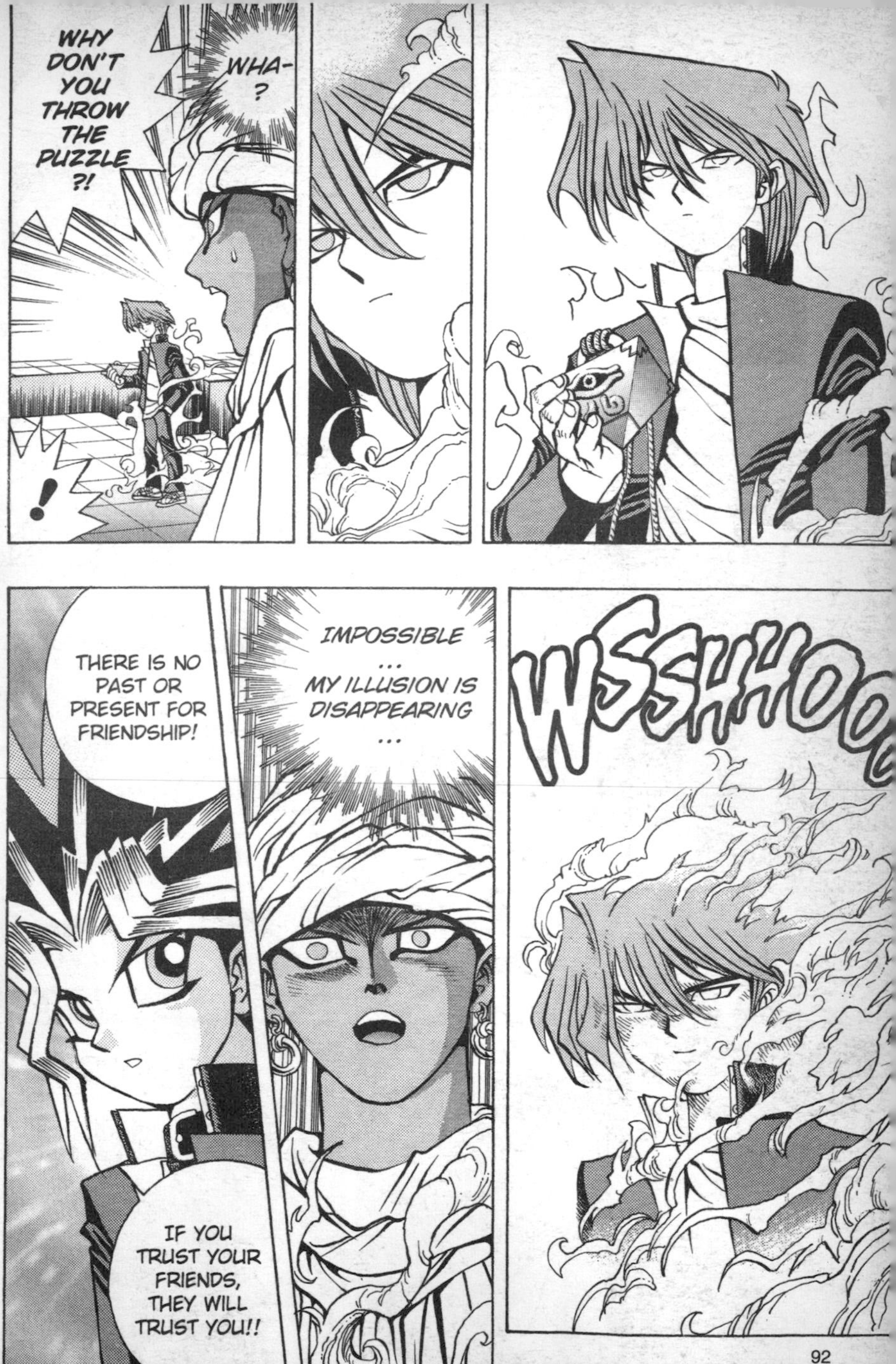
WHA-?
WHY DON'T YOU THROW THE PUZZLE?!
!
WSSHHOOO
IMPOSSIBLE ... MY ILLUSION IS DISAPPEARING ...
THERE IS NO PAST OR PRESENT FOR FRIENDSHIP!
IF YOU TRUST YOUR FRIENDS, THEY WILL TRUST YOU!!

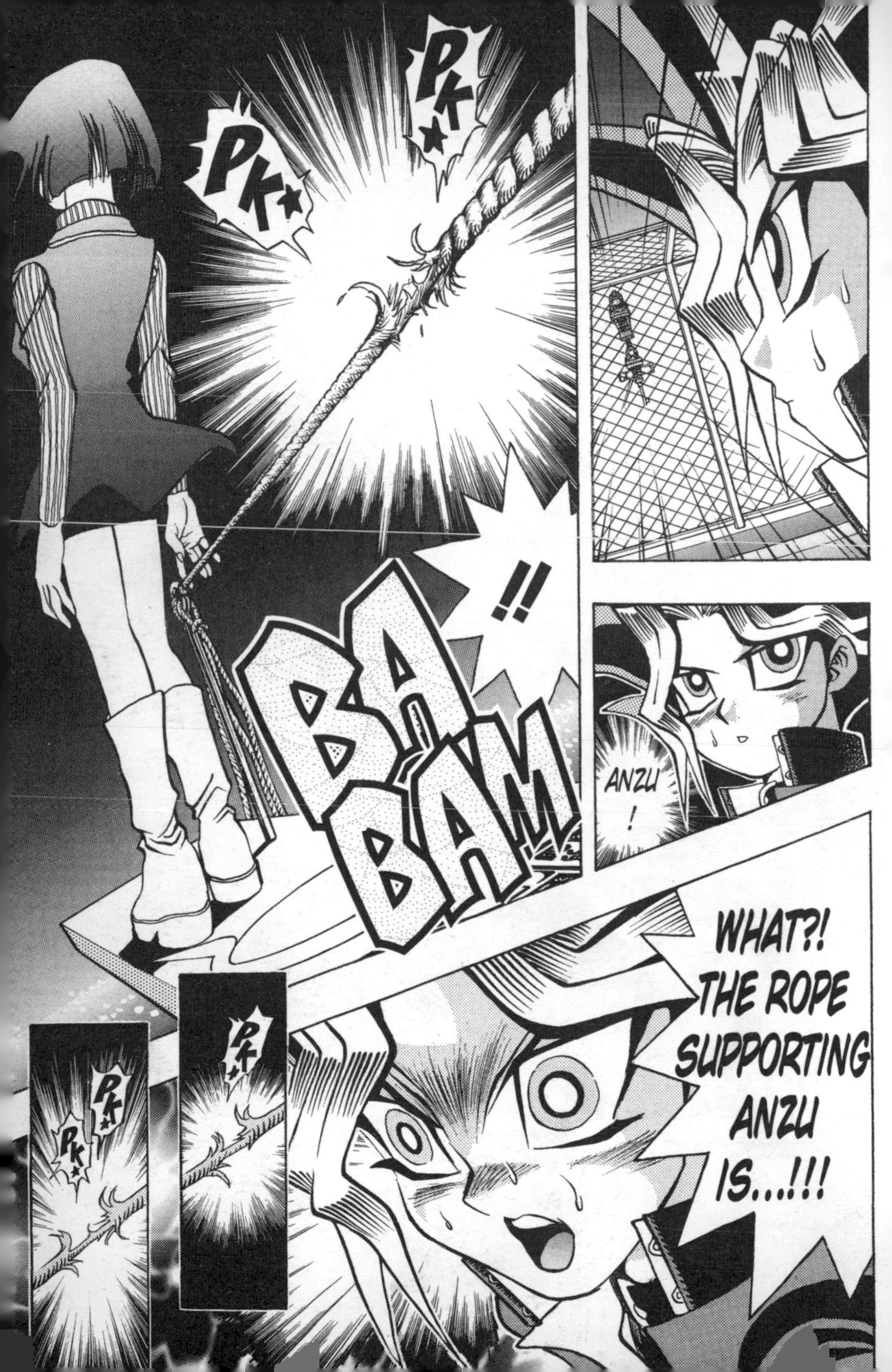
ANZU!
WHAT?! THE ROPE SUPPORTING ANZU IS...!!!
PK★
PK★
!!
BA BAM
PK★
PK★
PK★

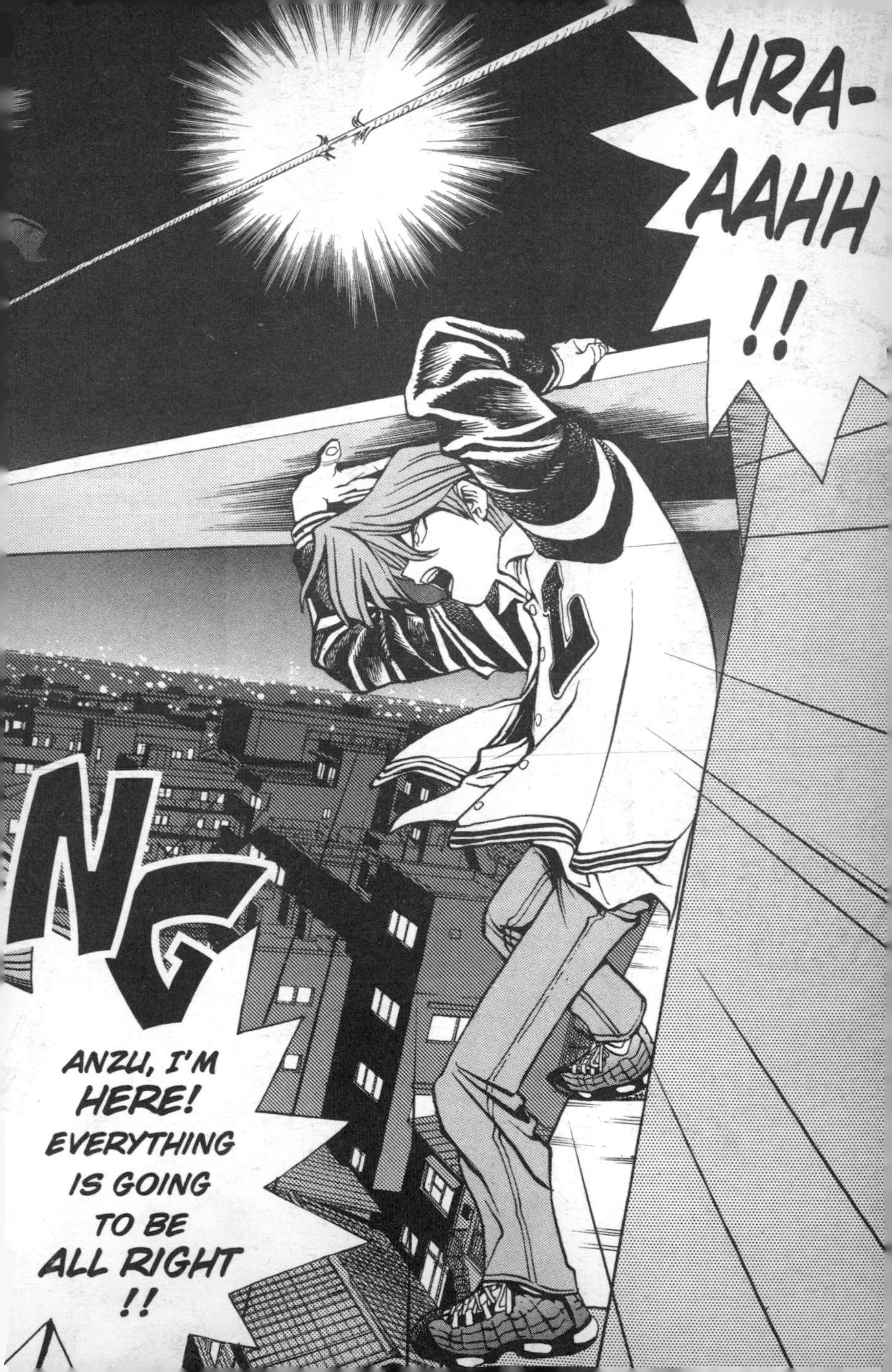
URA-AAHH!!
NG
ANZU, I'M HERE! EVERYTHING IS GOING TO BE ALL RIGHT!!

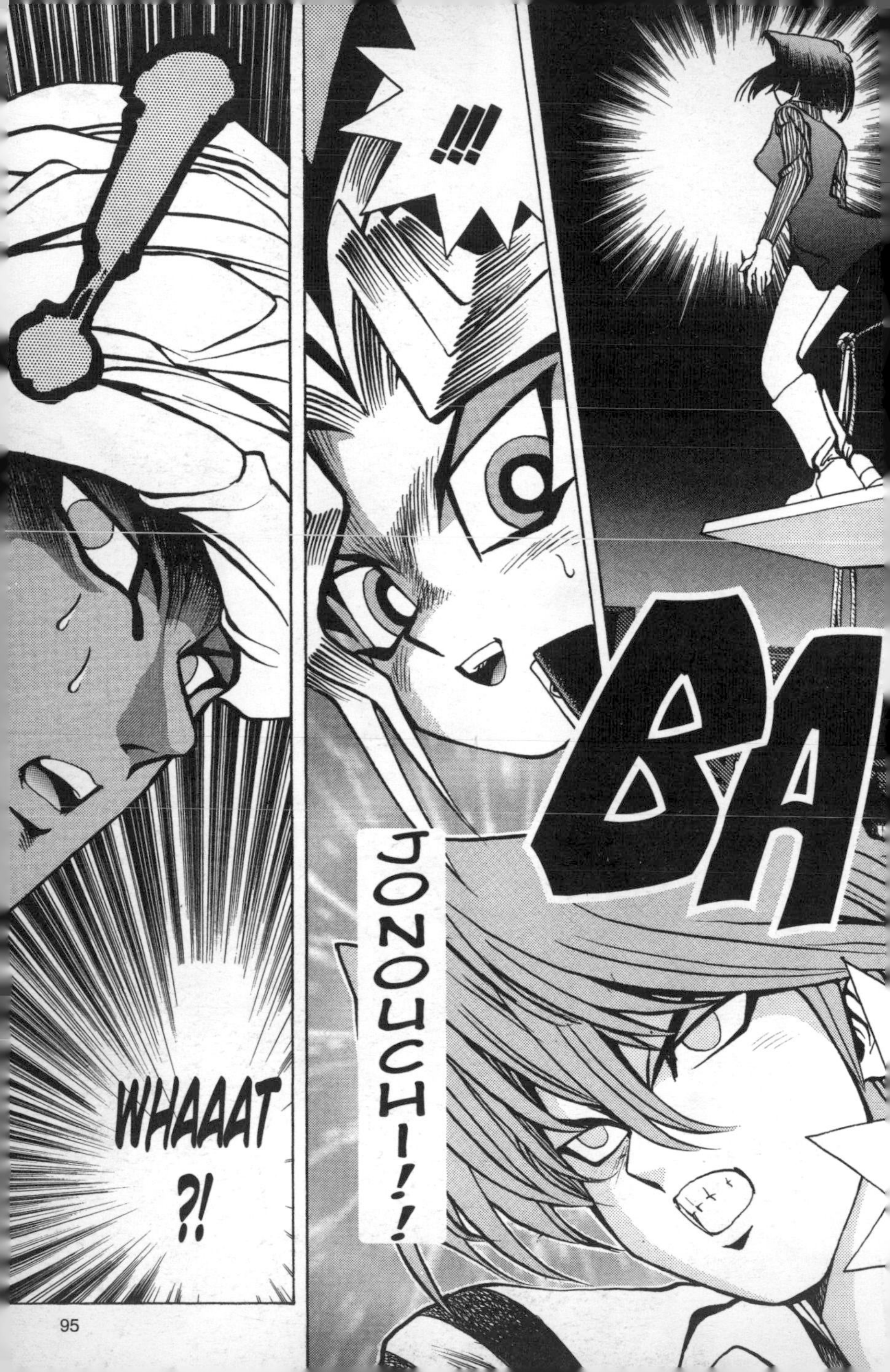
BA
!!!!
JONOUCHI!!
!
WHAAAT ?!

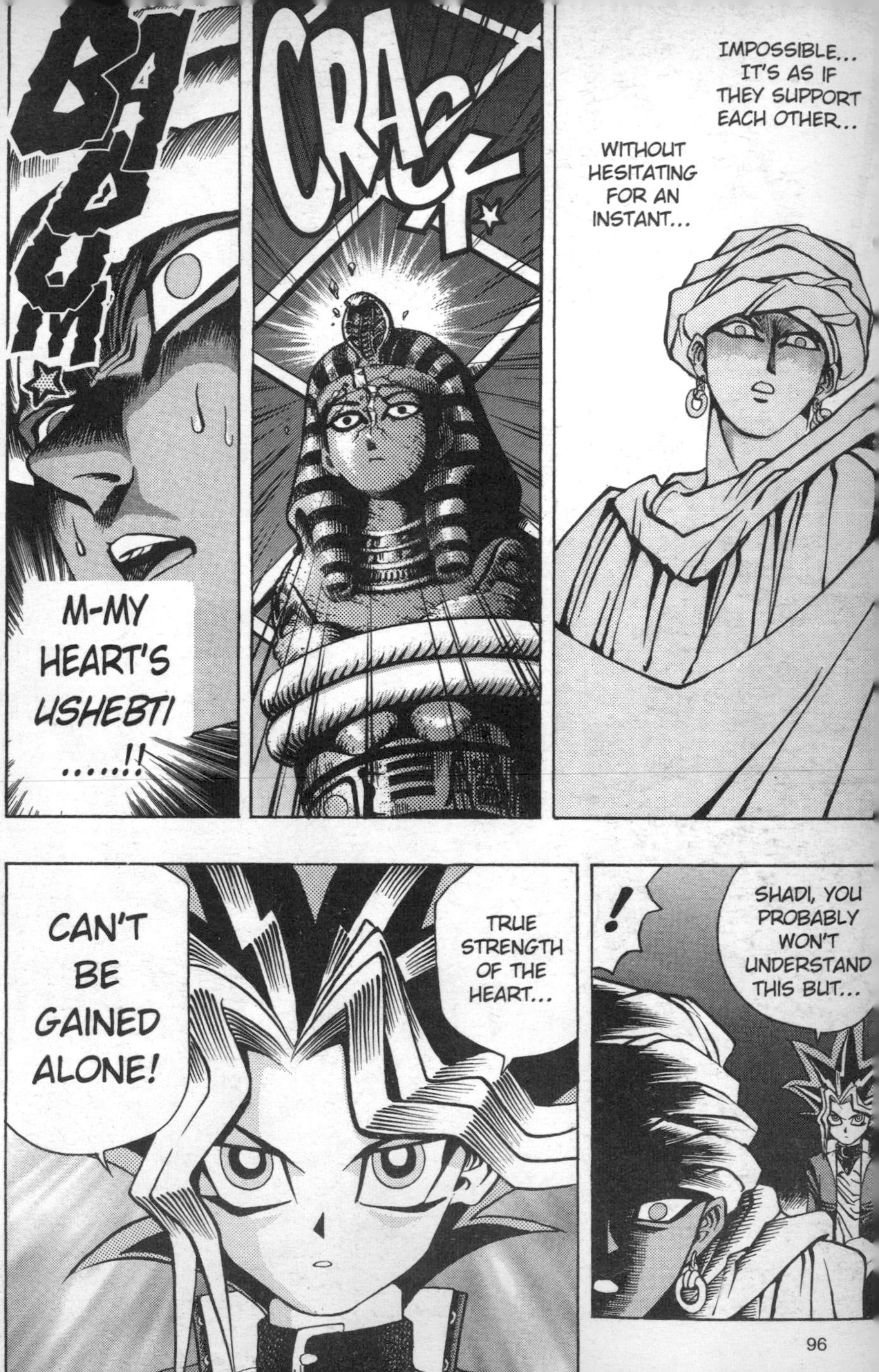
IMPOSSIBLE... IT'S AS IF THEY SUPPORT EACH OTHER...
WITHOUT HESITATING FOR AN INSTANT...
CRACK
BADUM!!
M-MY HEART'S USHEBTI .....!!
!
SHADI, YOU PROBABLY WON'T UNDERSTAND THIS BUT...
TRUE STRENGTH OF THE HEART...
CAN'T BE GAINED ALONE!

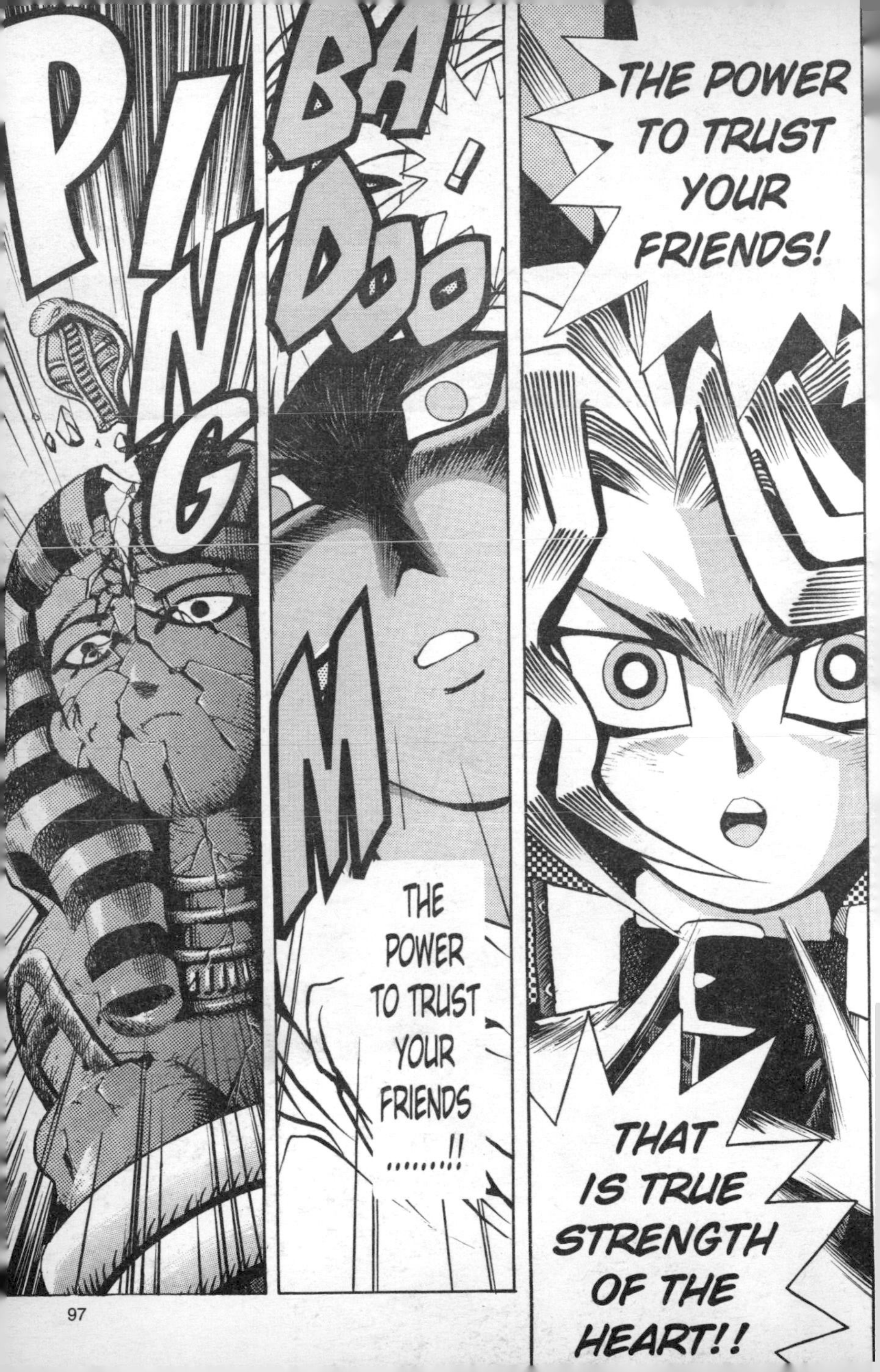
THE POWER TO TRUST YOUR FRIENDS!
THAT IS TRUE STRENGTH OF THE HEART!!
BA!
DOOOM
THE POWER TO TRUST YOUR FRIENDS ....!!
PING

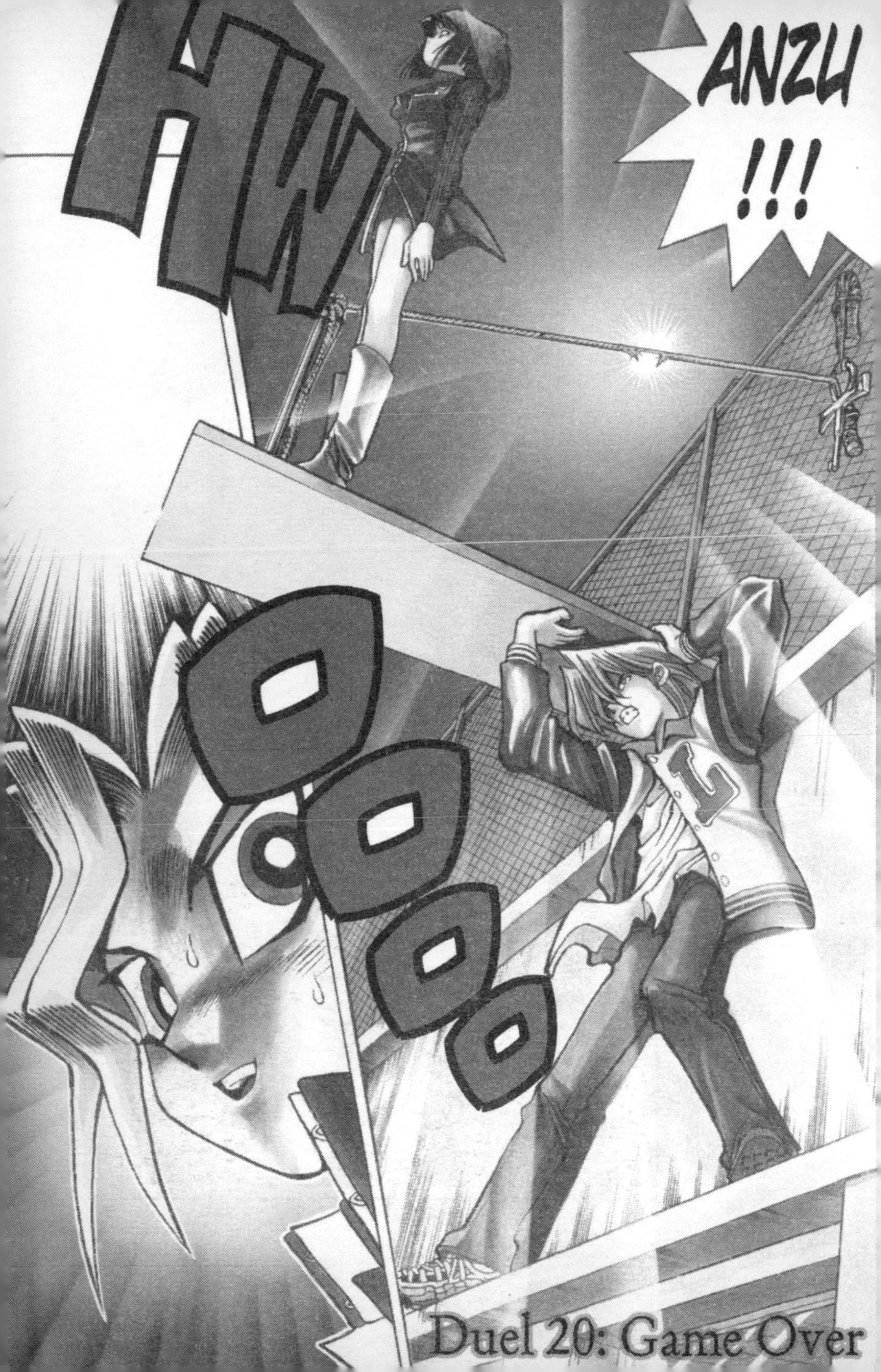
ANZU !!!

Duel 20: Game Over

Duel 20: Game Over

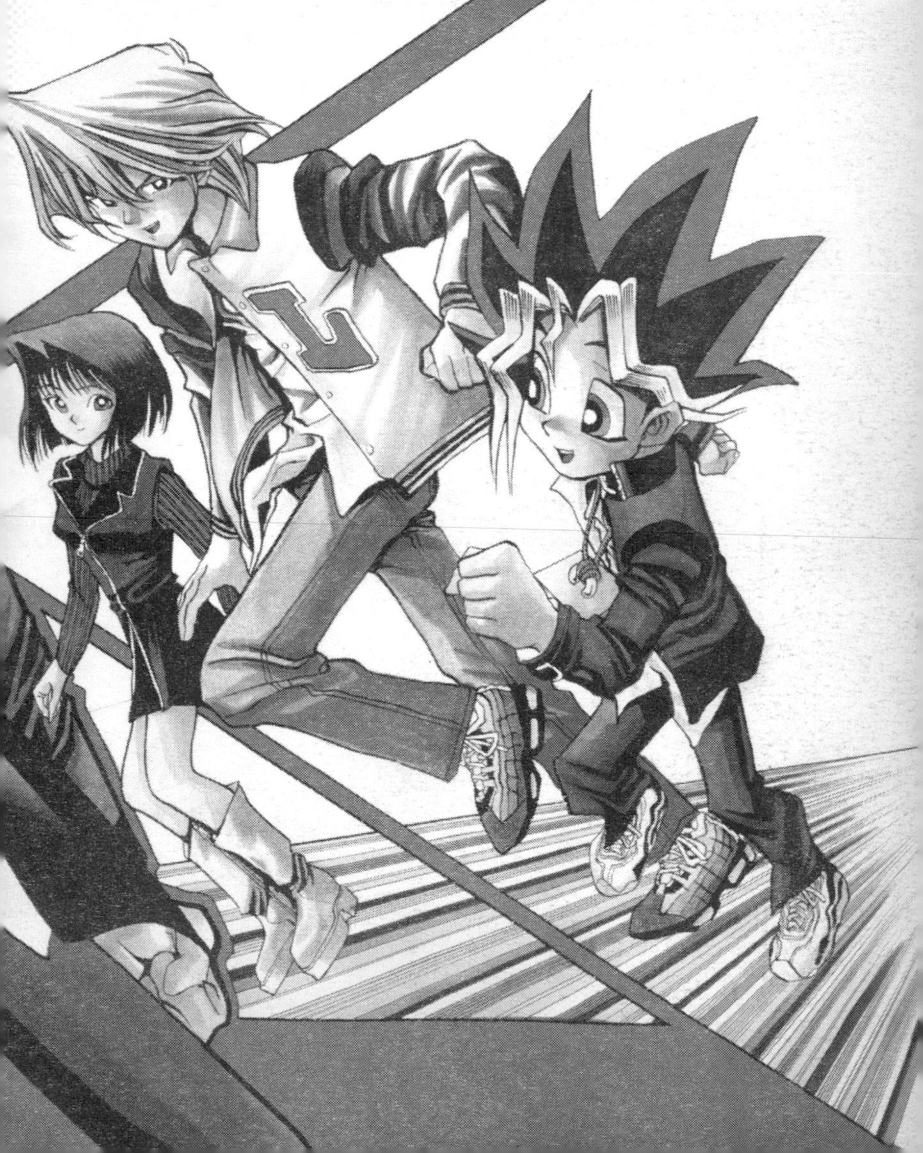

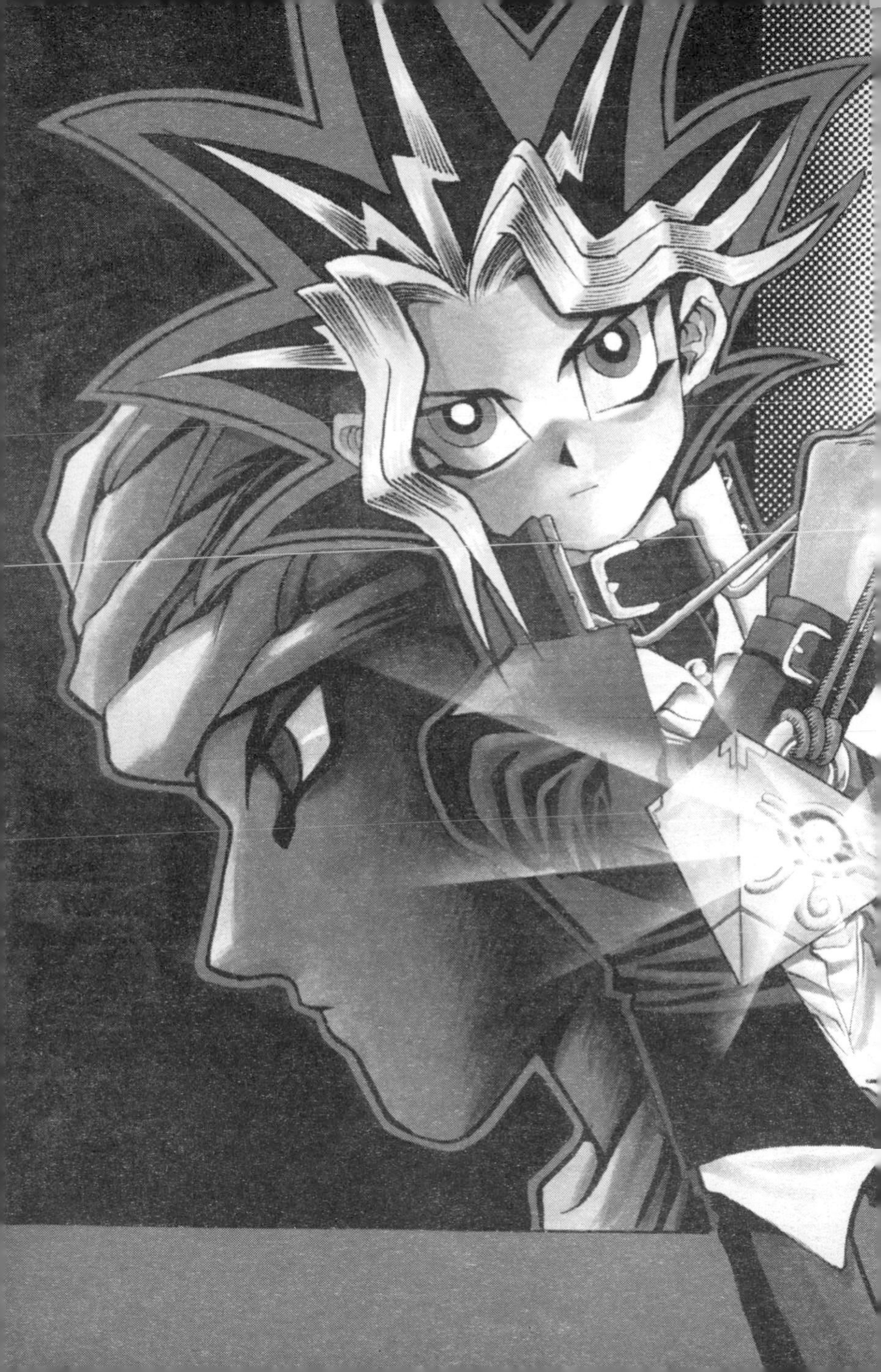

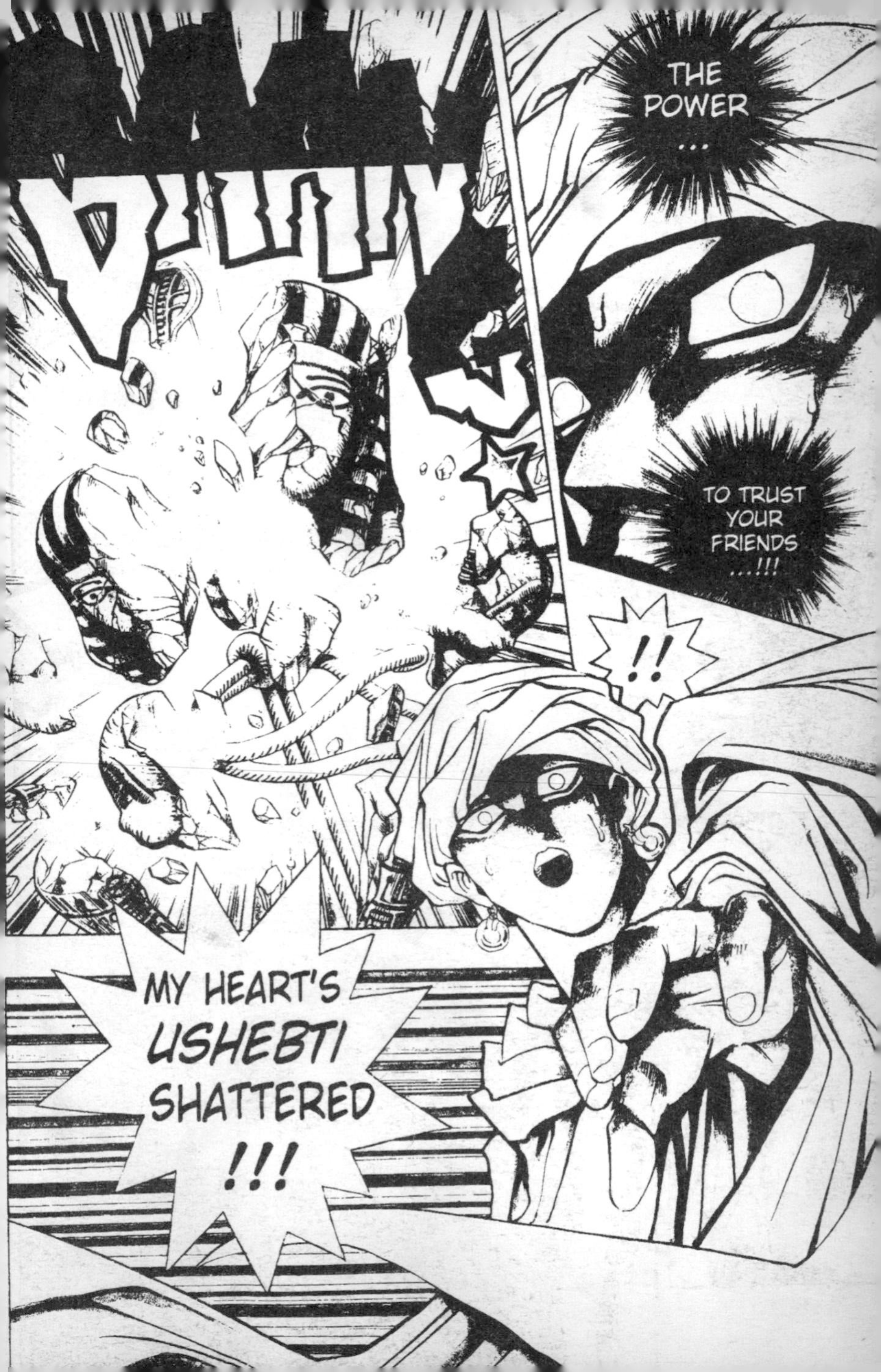
THE POWER ...
TO TRUST YOUR FRIENDS ...!!!
!!
MY HEART'S USHEBTI SHATTERED !!!

SHADI'S STATUE HAS BROKEN!!

THE MILLENNIUM KEY WILL SLIDE DOWN THE ROPE TO ANZU'S HAND!

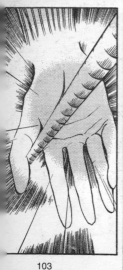

103

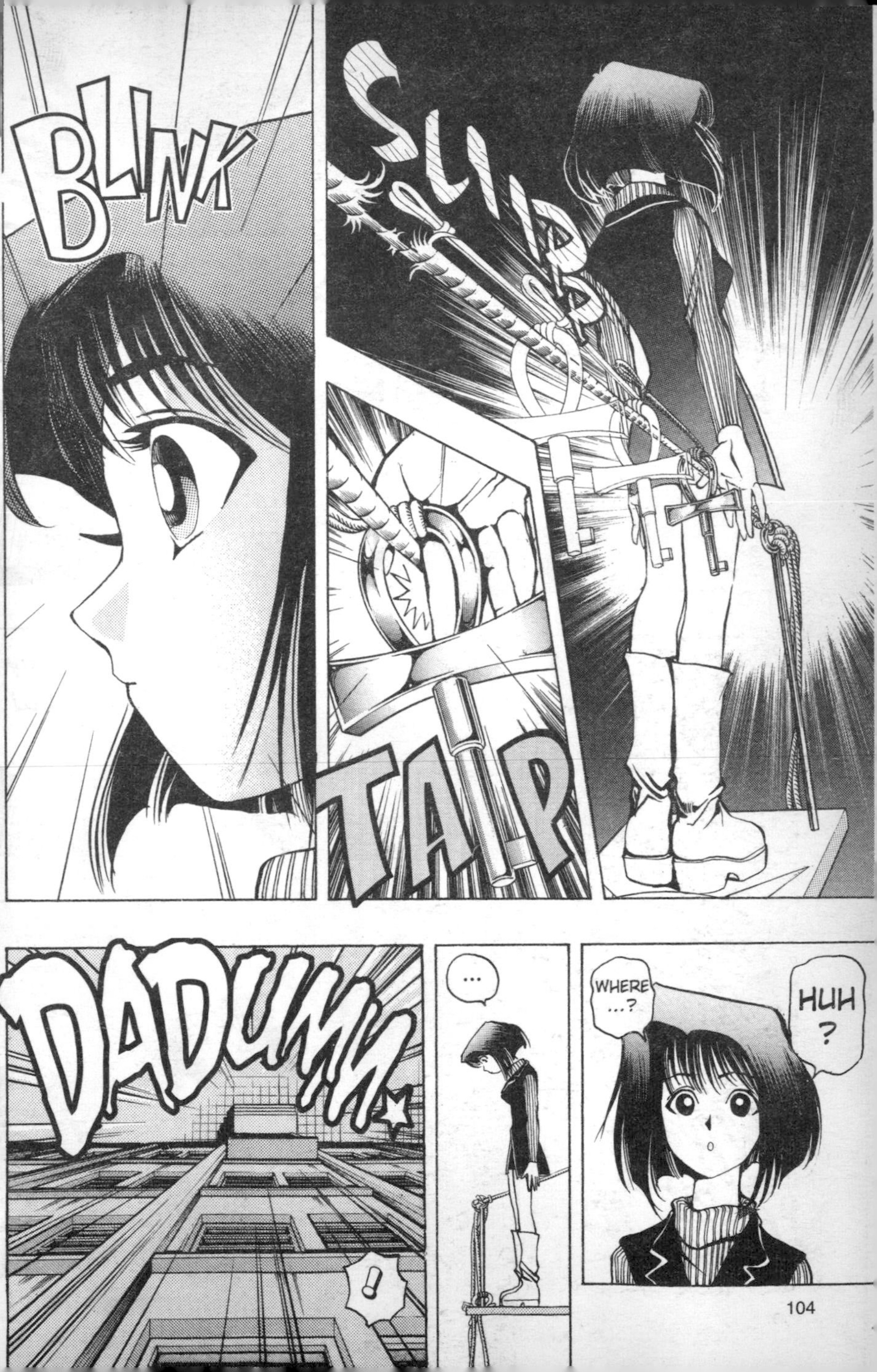
SLIDD
TAP
BLINK
HUH ?
WHERE ...?
...
DADUMM
!

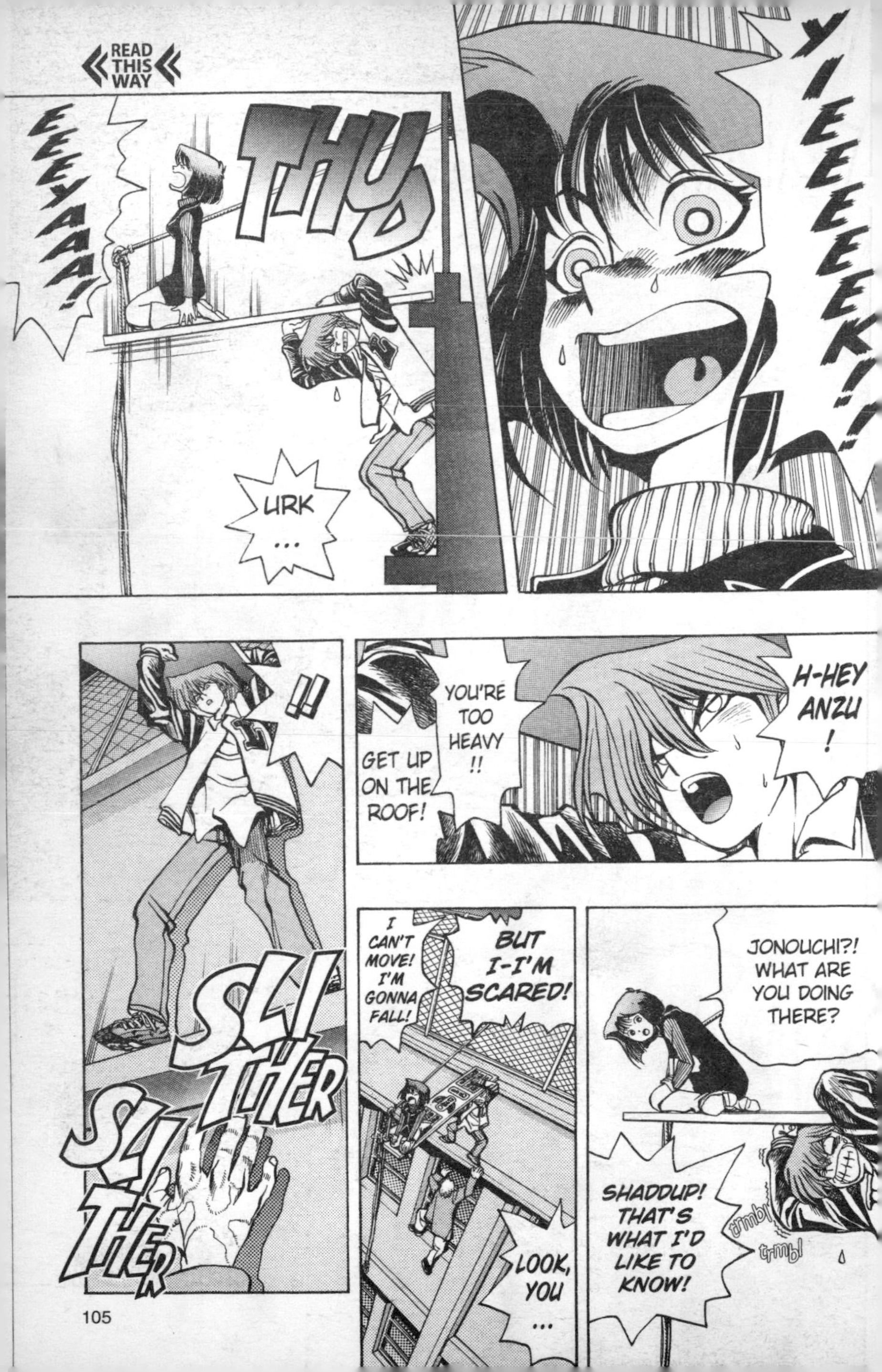
READ THIS WAY
YIEEEEEK!!!
EEEYAAA!
THUD
URK ...
H-HEY ANZU!
YOU'RE TOO HEAVY!!
GET UP ON THE ROOF!
JONOUCHI?! WHAT ARE YOU DOING THERE?
SHADDUP! THAT'S WHAT I'D LIKE TO KNOW!
trmbl
trmbl
BUT I-I'M SCARED!
I CAN'T MOVE! I'M GONNA FALL!
LOOK, YOU ...
!!
SLITHER
SLITHER

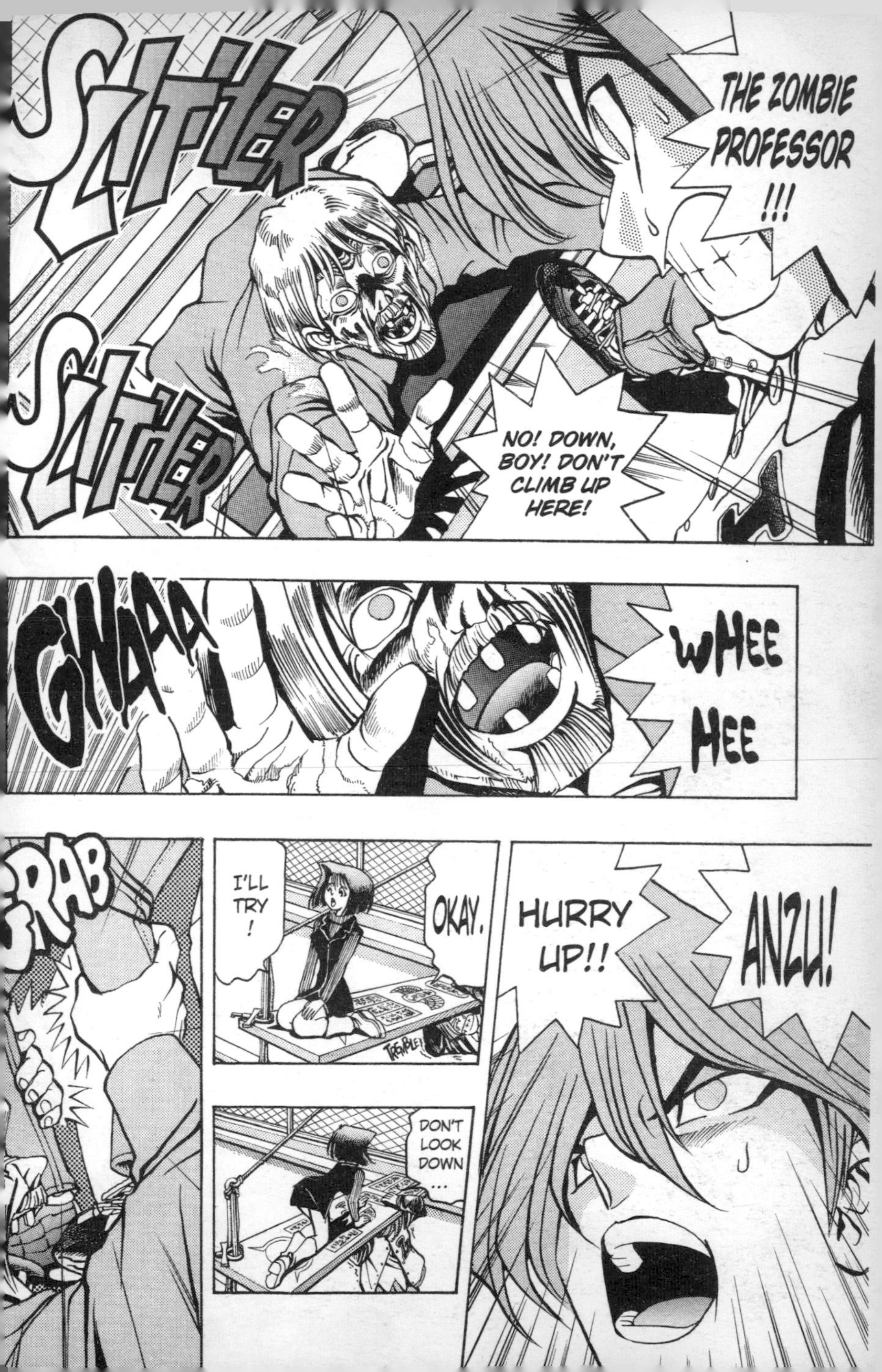
THE ZOMBIE PROFESSOR !!!
SLITHER
NO! DOWN, BOY! DON'T CLIMB UP HERE!
SLITHER
WHEE HEE
GNAAA
ANZU!
HURRY UP!!
OKAY.
I'LL TRY!
TREMBLE!
DON'T LOOK DOWN ...
GRAB

READ THIS WAY

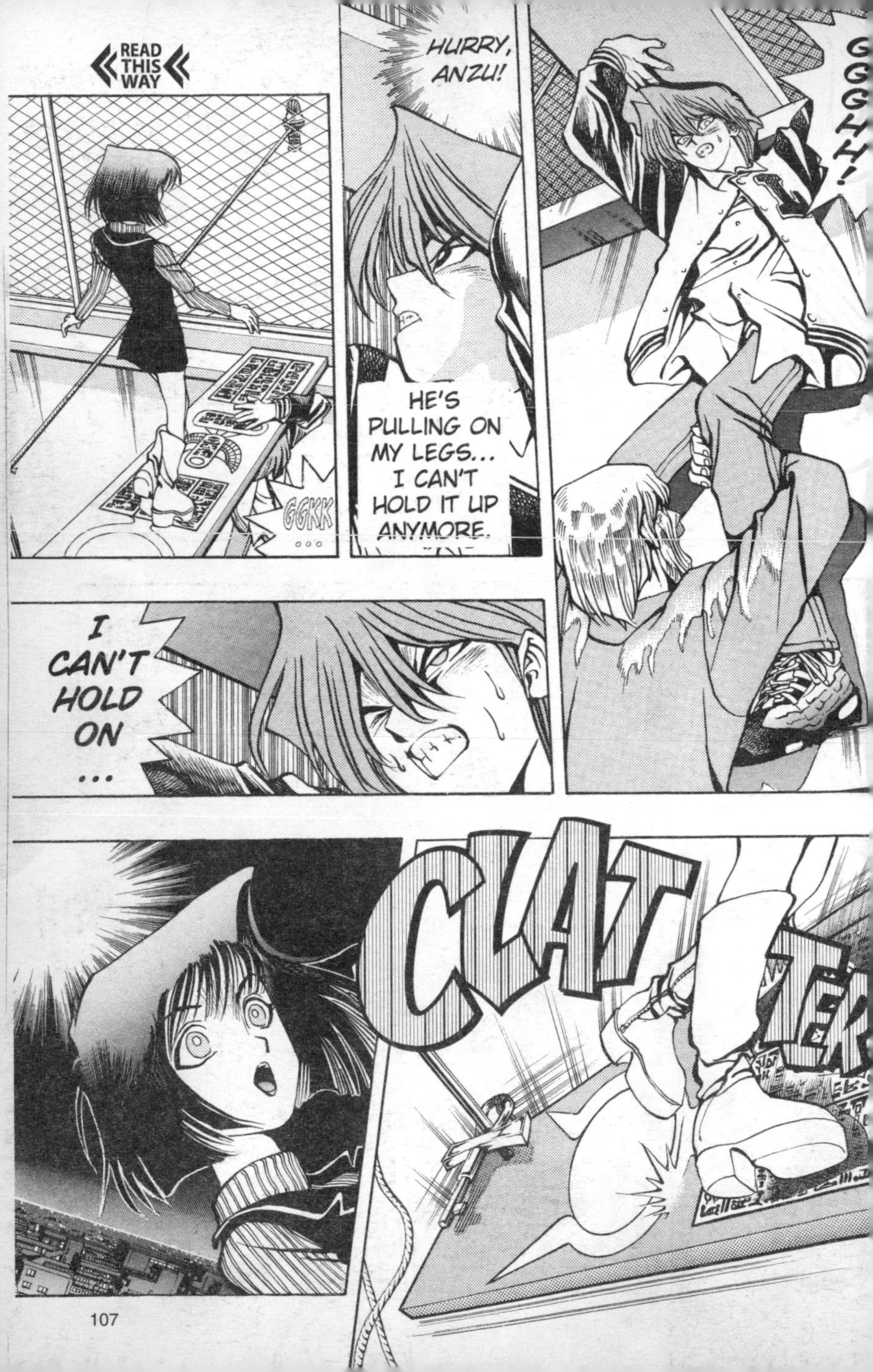
GGGHH!
HURRY, ANZU!
HE'S PULLING ON MY LEGS... I CAN'T HOLD IT UP ANYMORE.
GGKK
...
I CAN'T HOLD ON...
CLAT
TEK

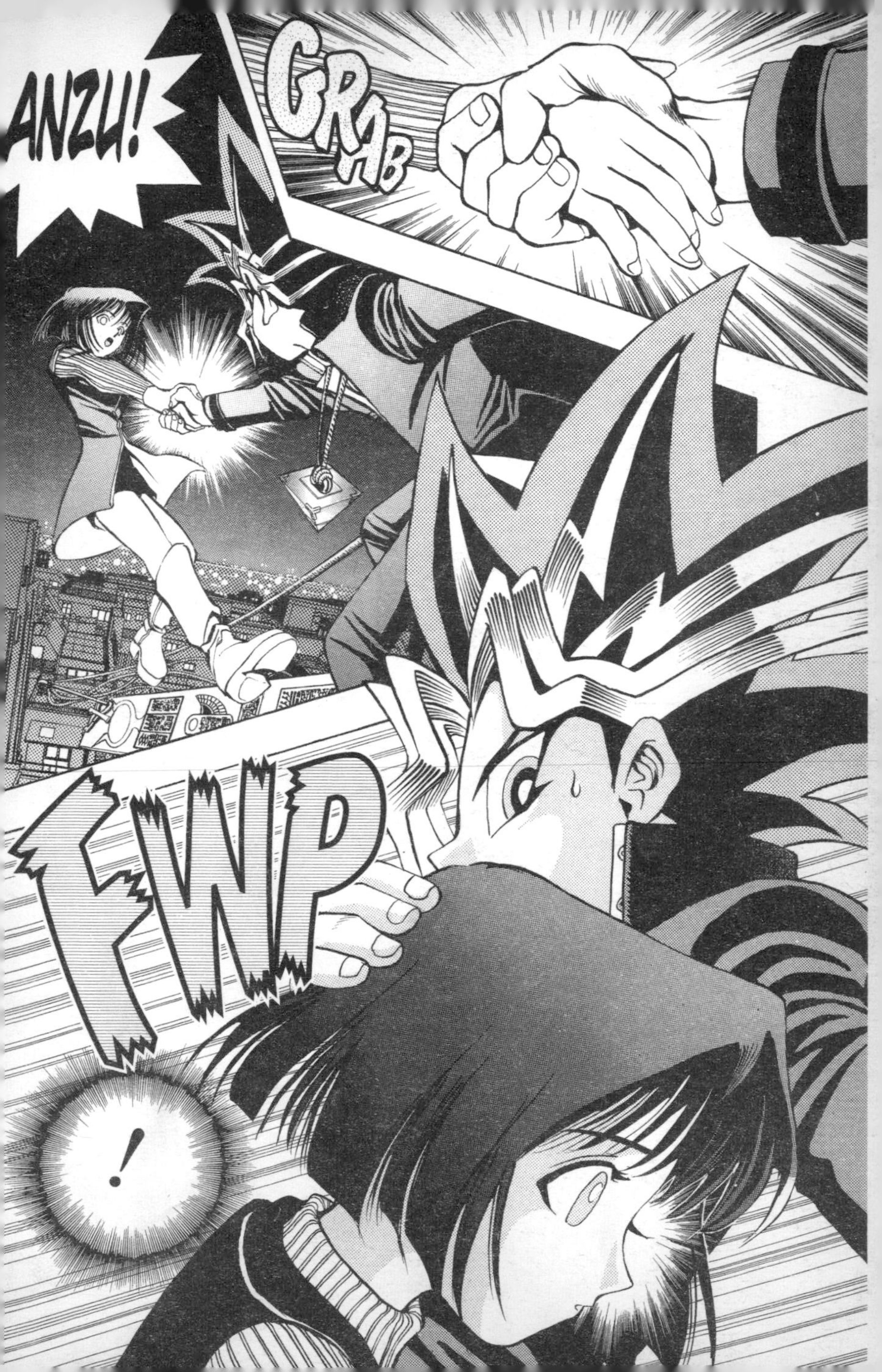
GRAB
ANZU!
FWP
!

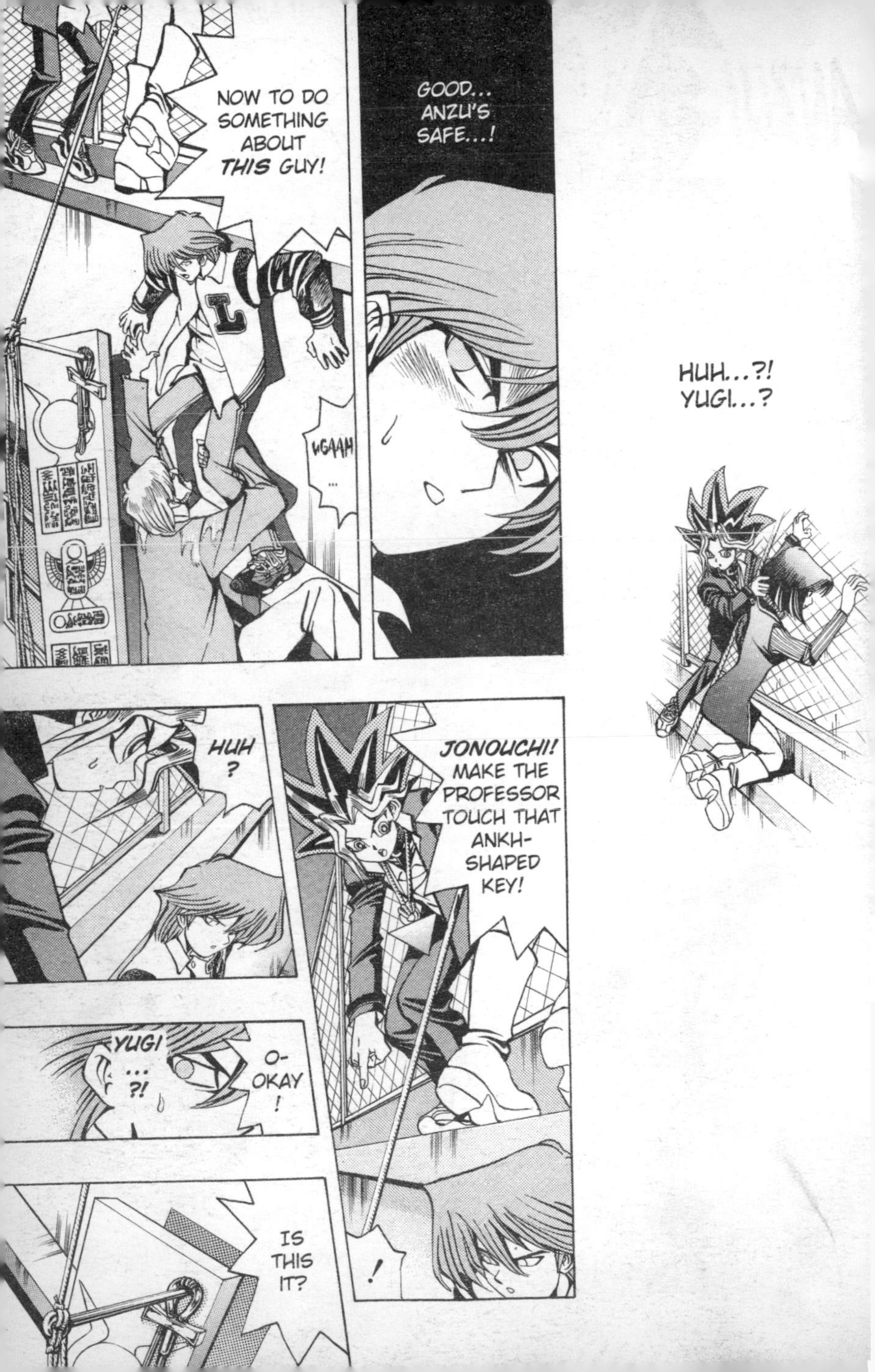
HUH...?! YUGI...?
GOOD... ANZU'S SAFE...!
NOW TO DO SOMETHING ABOUT THIS GUY!
UGAAH...
JONOUCHI! MAKE THE PROFESSOR TOUCH THAT ANKH-SHAPED KEY!
!
HUH?
YUGI...?!
O-OKAY!
IS THIS IT?

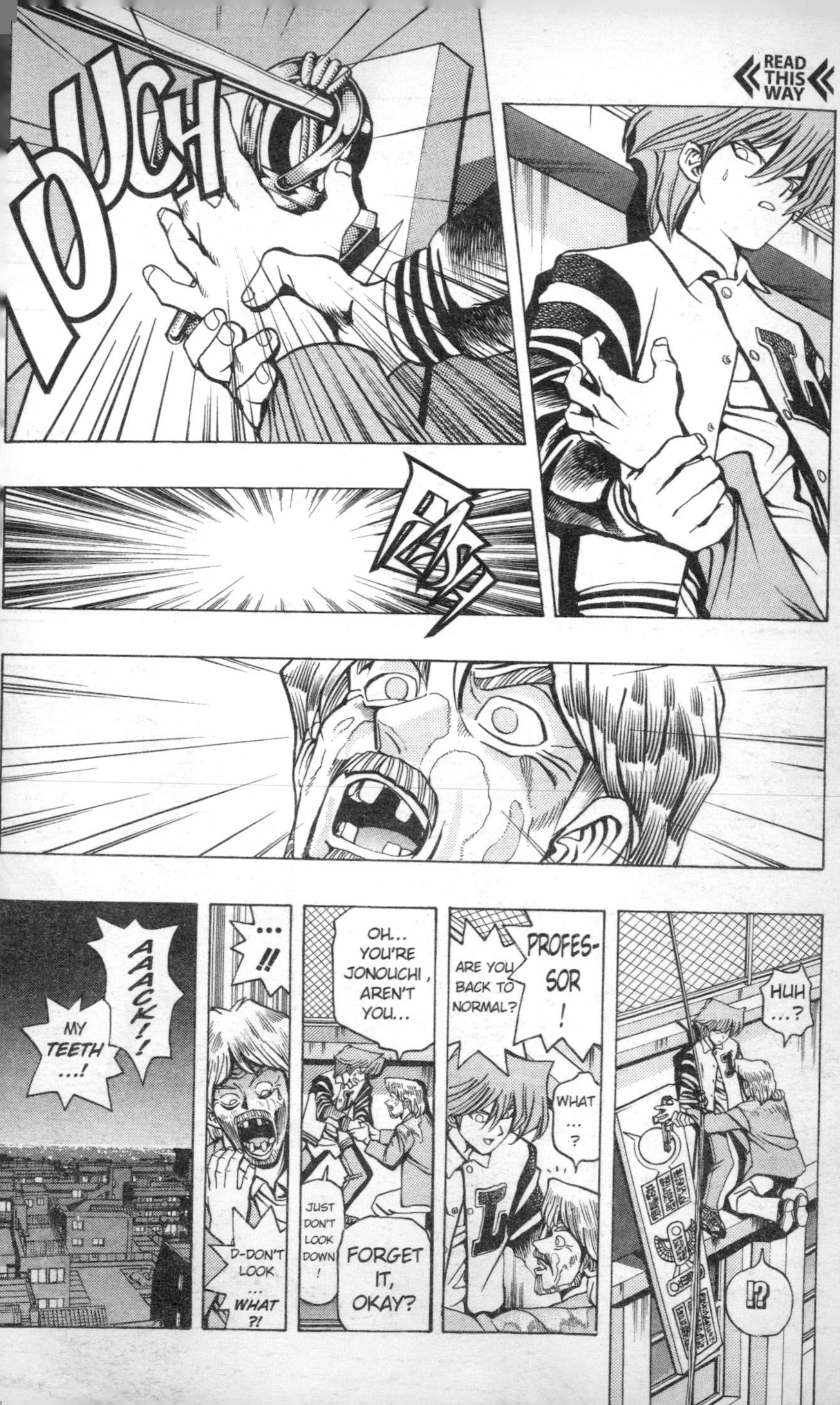
READ THIS WAY
OUCH
FLASH
HUH ...?
!?
PROFES-SOR !
ARE YOU BACK TO NORMAL?
WHAT ...?
OH... YOU'RE JONOUCHI, AREN'T YOU...
FORGET IT, OKAY?
JUST DON'T LOOK DOWN!
...!!
D-DON'T LOOK ... WHAT ?!
AAACK!!
MY TEETH ...!

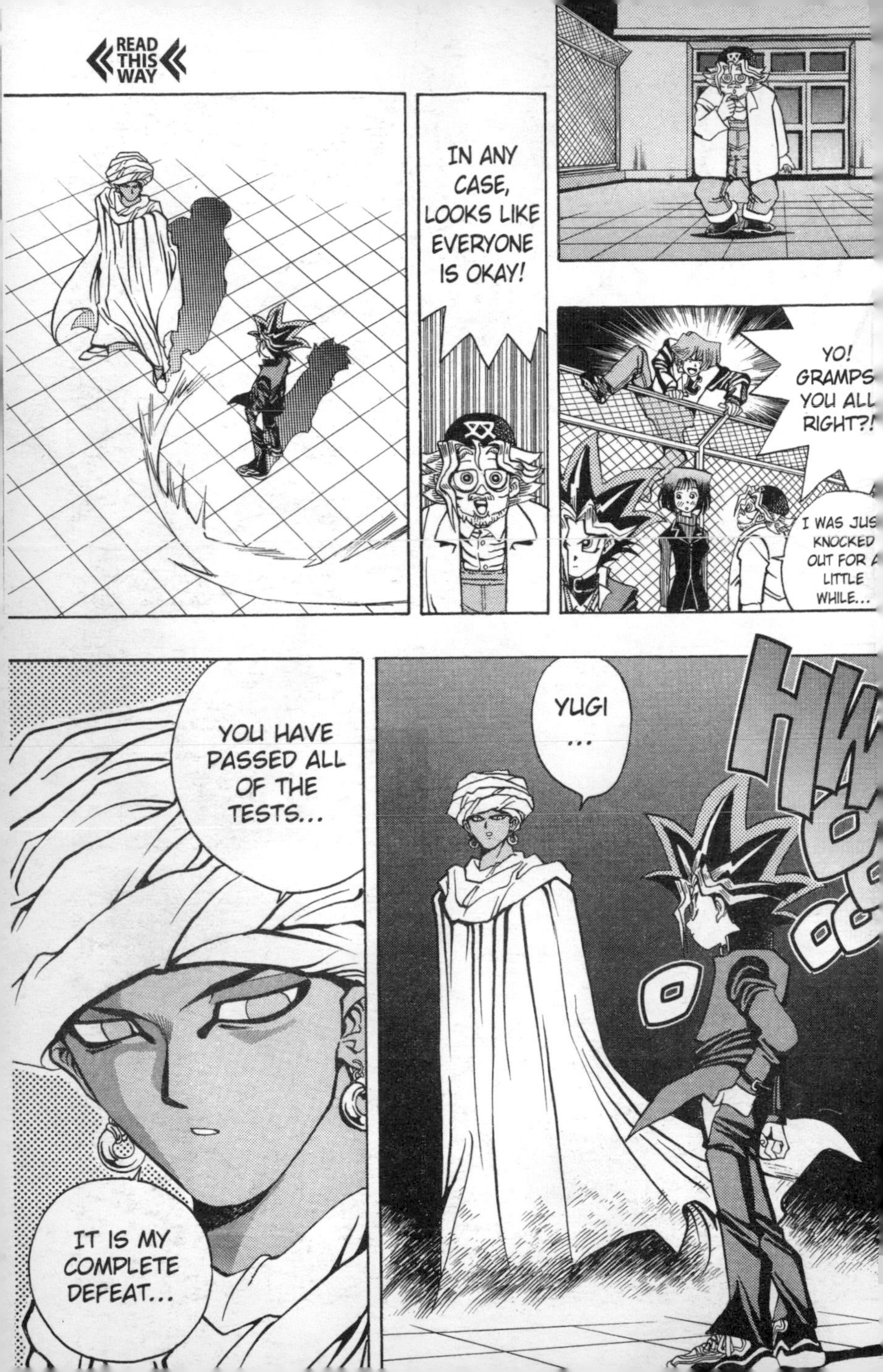
READ THIS WAY
YO! GRAMPS YOU ALL RIGHT?!
I WAS JUS KNOCKED OUT FOR A LITTLE WHILE...
IN ANY CASE, LOOKS LIKE EVERYONE IS OKAY!
YUGI ...
HW
YOU HAVE PASSED ALL OF THE TESTS...
IT IS MY COMPLETE DEFEAT...

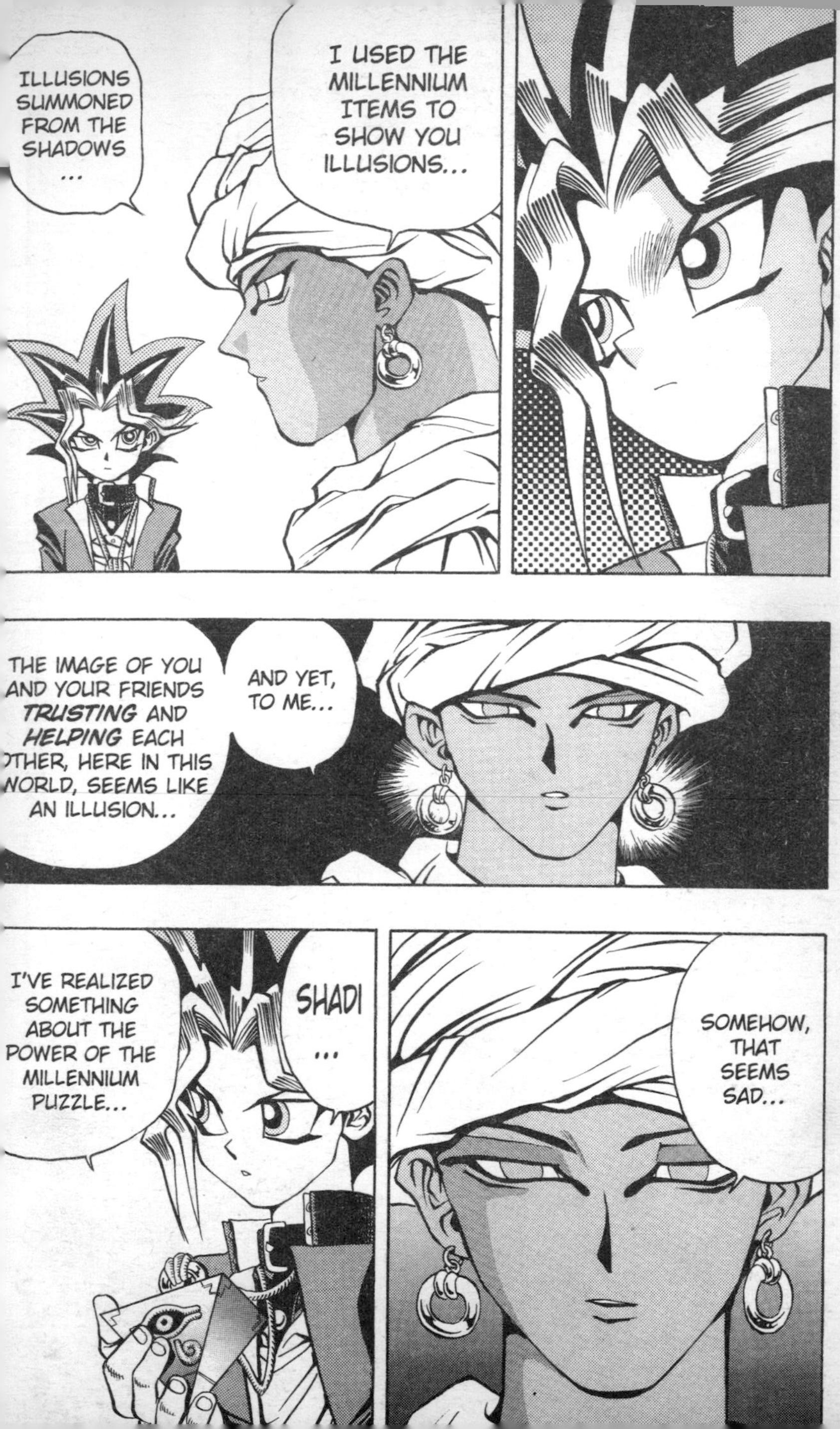
I USED THE MILLENNIUM ITEMS TO SHOW YOU ILLUSIONS...
ILLUSIONS SUMMONED FROM THE SHADOWS ...
AND YET, TO ME...
THE IMAGE OF YOU AND YOUR FRIENDS *TRUSTING* AND *HELPING* EACH OTHER, HERE IN THIS WORLD, SEEMS LIKE AN ILLUSION...
SOMEHOW, THAT SEEMS SAD...
SHADI ...
I'VE REALIZED SOMETHING ABOUT THE POWER OF THE MILLENNIUM PUZZLE...

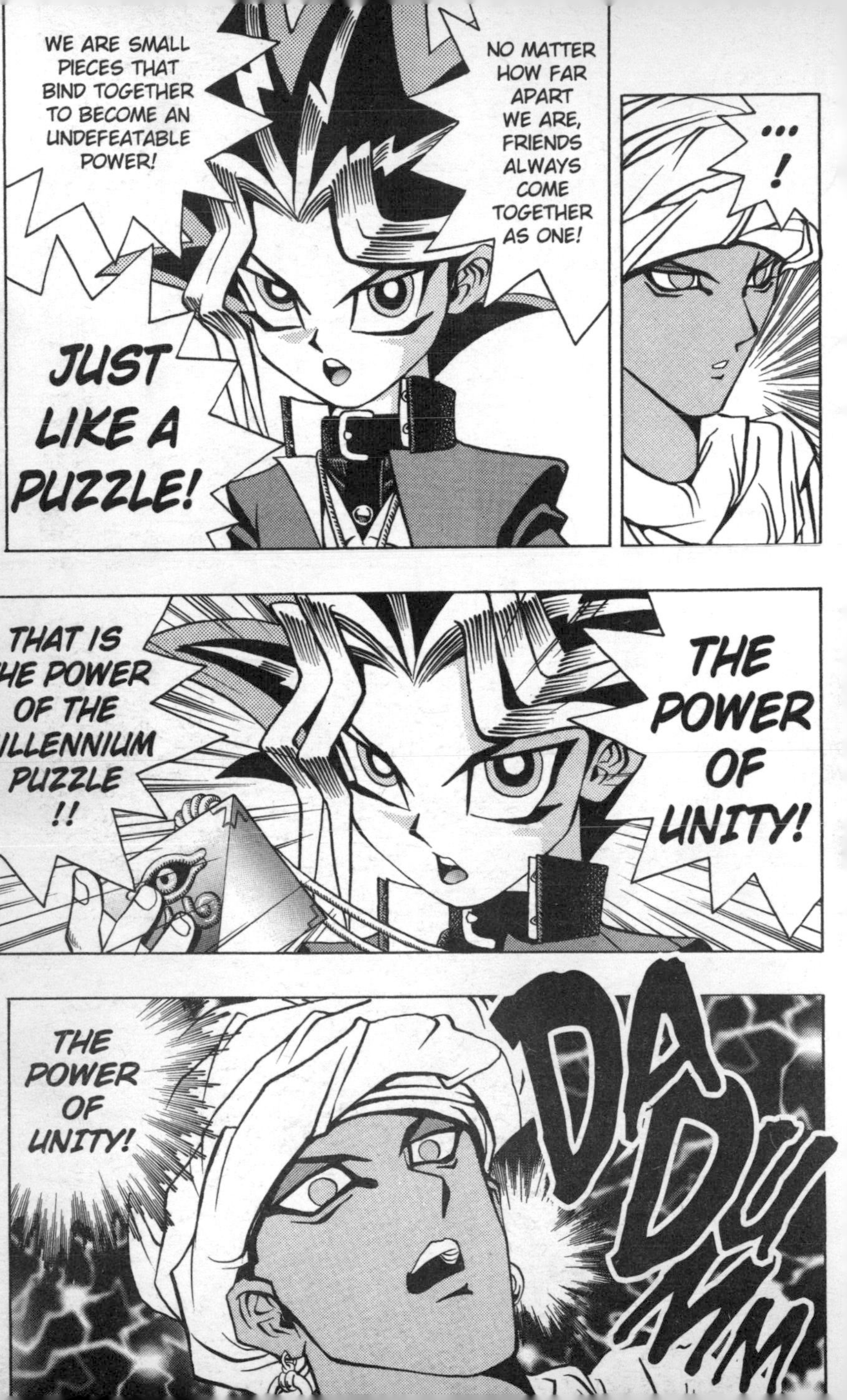
...!
NO MATTER HOW FAR APART WE ARE, FRIENDS ALWAYS COME TOGETHER AS ONE!
WE ARE SMALL PIECES THAT BIND TOGETHER TO BECOME AN UNDEFEATABLE POWER!
JUST LIKE A PUZZLE!
THE POWER OF UNITY!
THAT IS THE POWER OF THE MILLENNIUM PUZZLE !!
DADUMM
THE POWER OF UNITY!

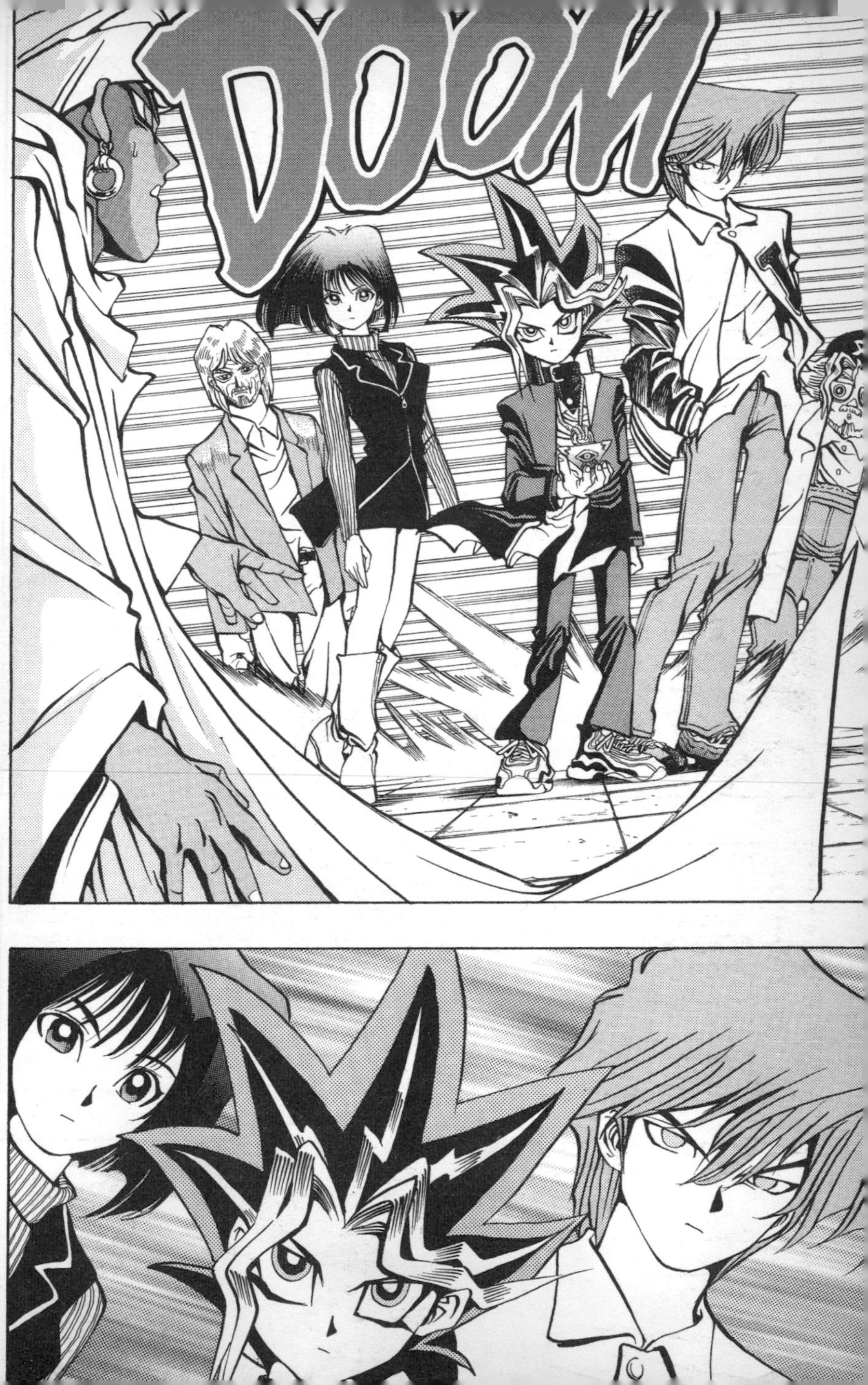
DOOM

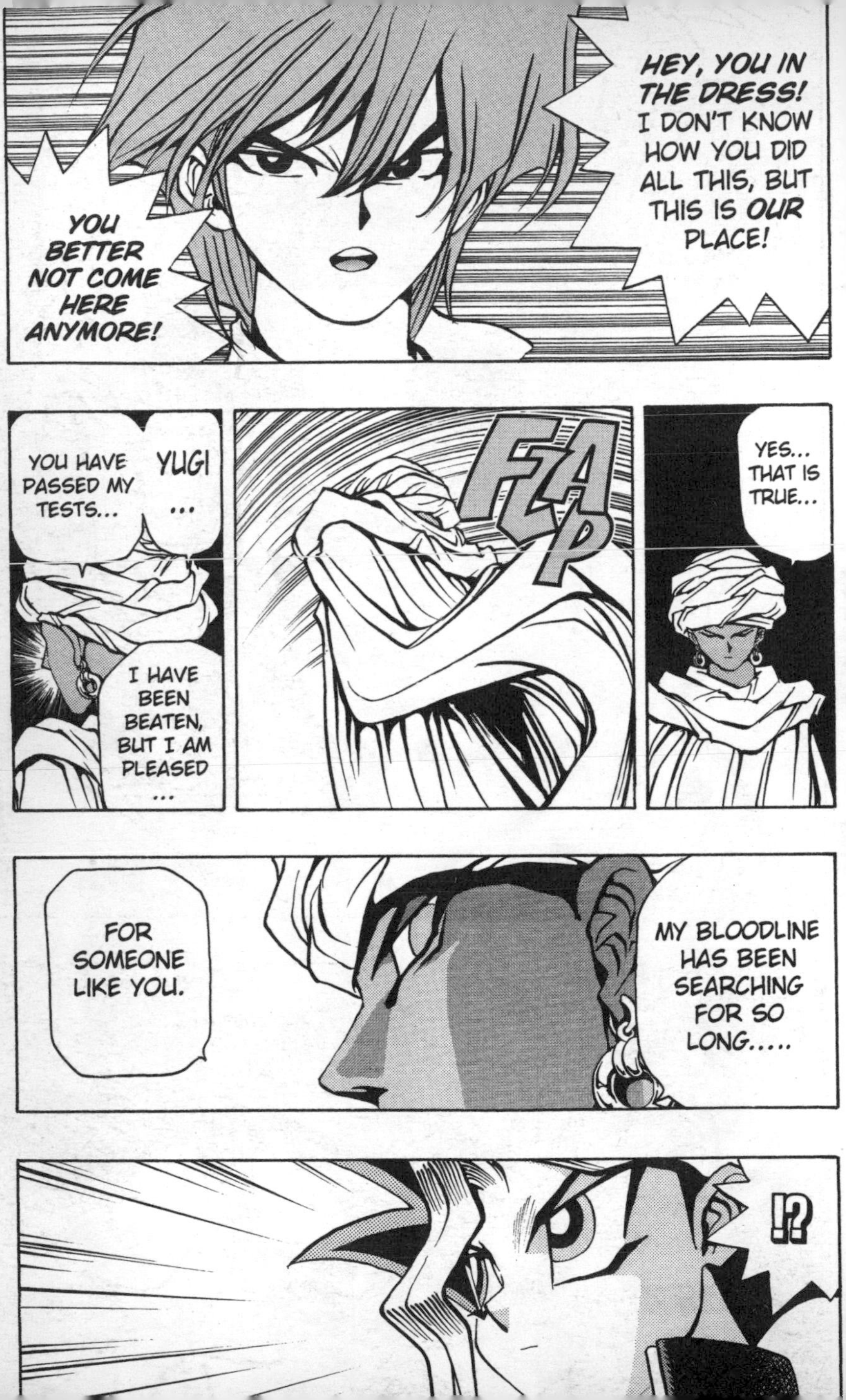
HEY, YOU IN THE DRESS! I DON'T KNOW HOW YOU DID ALL THIS, BUT THIS IS OUR PLACE!
YOU BETTER NOT COME HERE ANYMORE!
YES... THAT IS TRUE...
FZAP
YUGI ...
YOU HAVE PASSED MY TESTS...
I HAVE BEEN BEATEN, BUT I AM PLEASED ...
MY BLOODLINE HAS BEEN SEARCHING FOR SO LONG.....
FOR SOMEONE LIKE YOU.
!?

READ THIS WAY

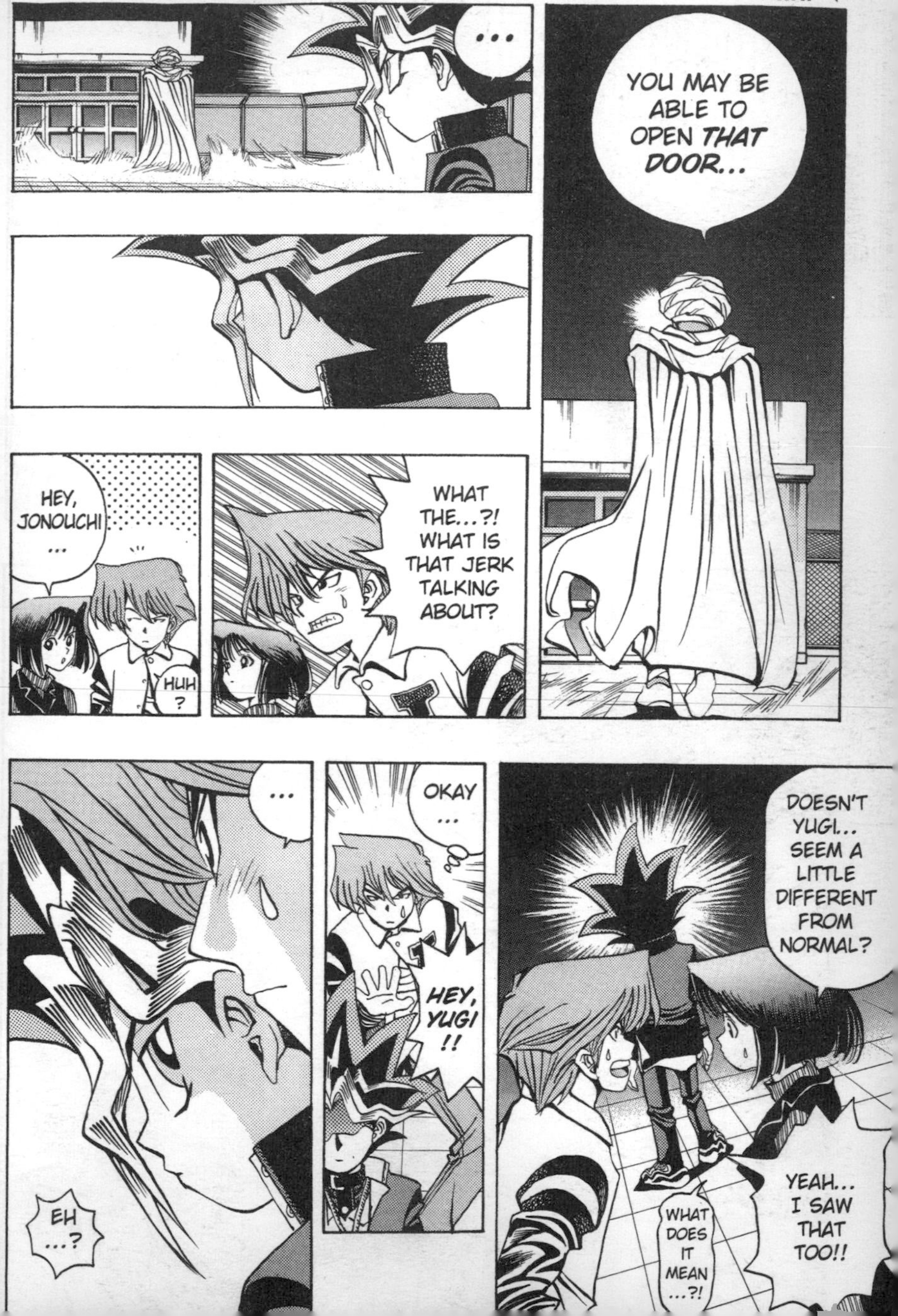
YOU MAY BE ABLE TO OPEN *THAT DOOR*...
...
WHAT THE...?! WHAT IS THAT JERK TALKING ABOUT?
HEY, JONOUCHI ...
HUH ?
DOESN'T YUGI... SEEM A LITTLE DIFFERENT FROM NORMAL?
YEAH... I SAW THAT TOO!!
WHAT DOES IT MEAN ...?!
OKAY ...
HEY, YUGI !!
...
EH ...?

READ THIS WAY

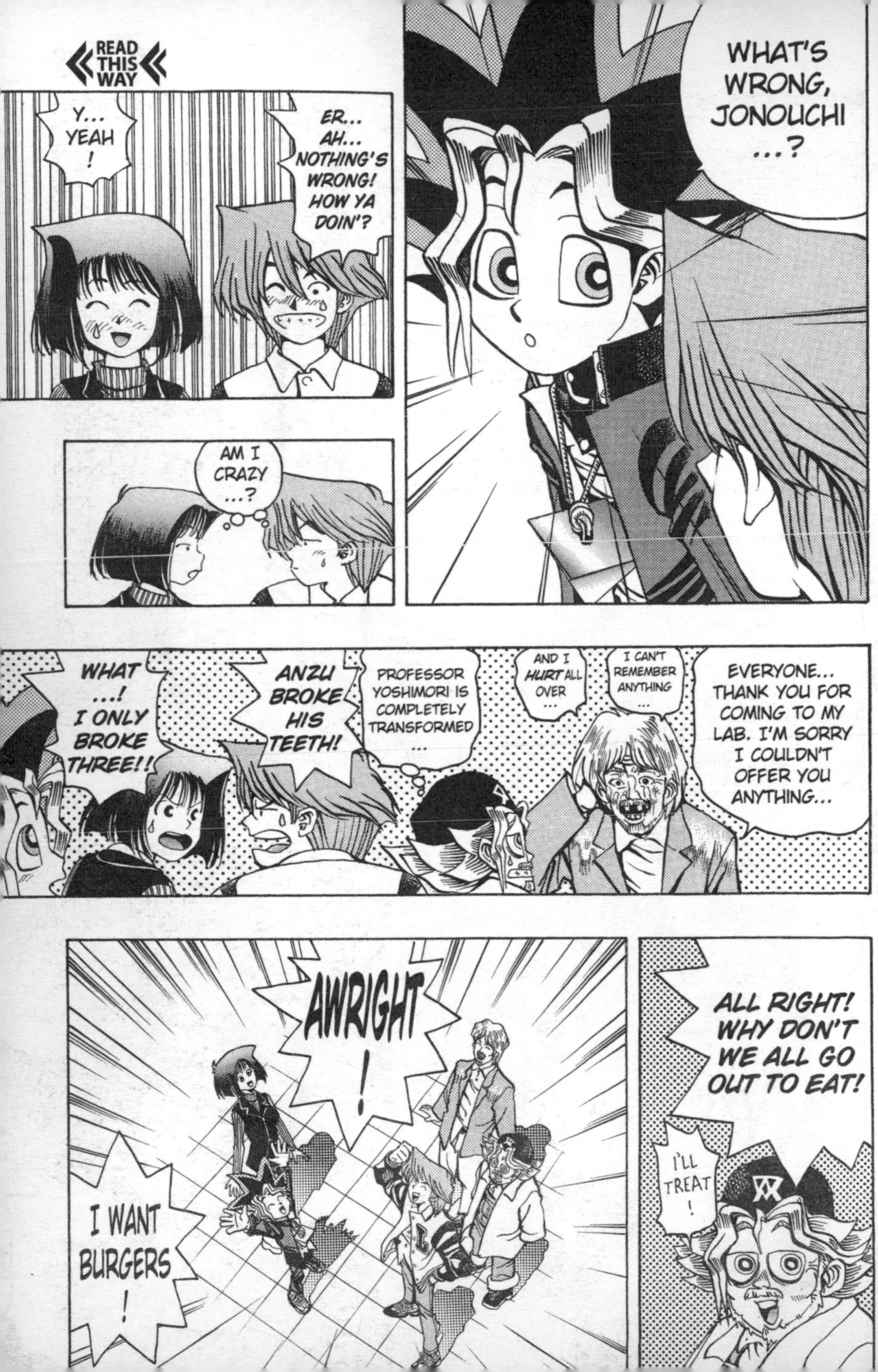

WHAT'S WRONG, JONOUCHI ...?
ER... AH... NOTHING'S WRONG! HOW YA DOIN'?
Y... YEAH !
AM I CRAZY ...?
EVERYONE... THANK YOU FOR COMING TO MY LAB. I'M SORRY I COULDN'T OFFER YOU ANYTHING...
I CAN'T REMEMBER ANYTHING ...
AND I HURT ALL OVER ...
PROFESSOR YOSHIMORI IS COMPLETELY TRANSFORMED ...
ANZU BROKE HIS TEETH!
WHAT ...! I ONLY BROKE THREE!!
ALL RIGHT! WHY DON'T WE ALL GO OUT TO EAT!
I'LL TREAT !
AWRIGHT !
I WANT BURGERS !

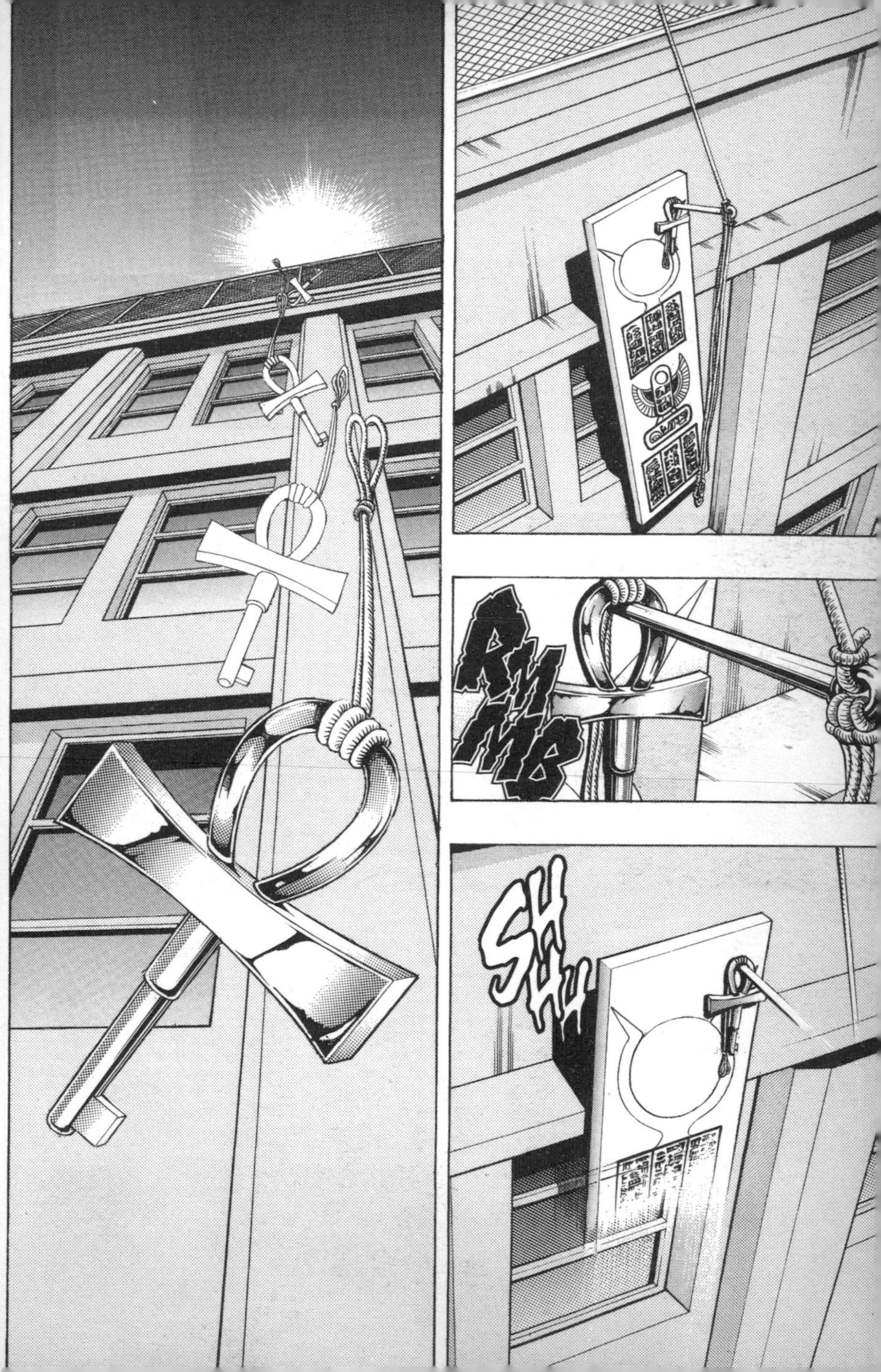
RUMB
SHU

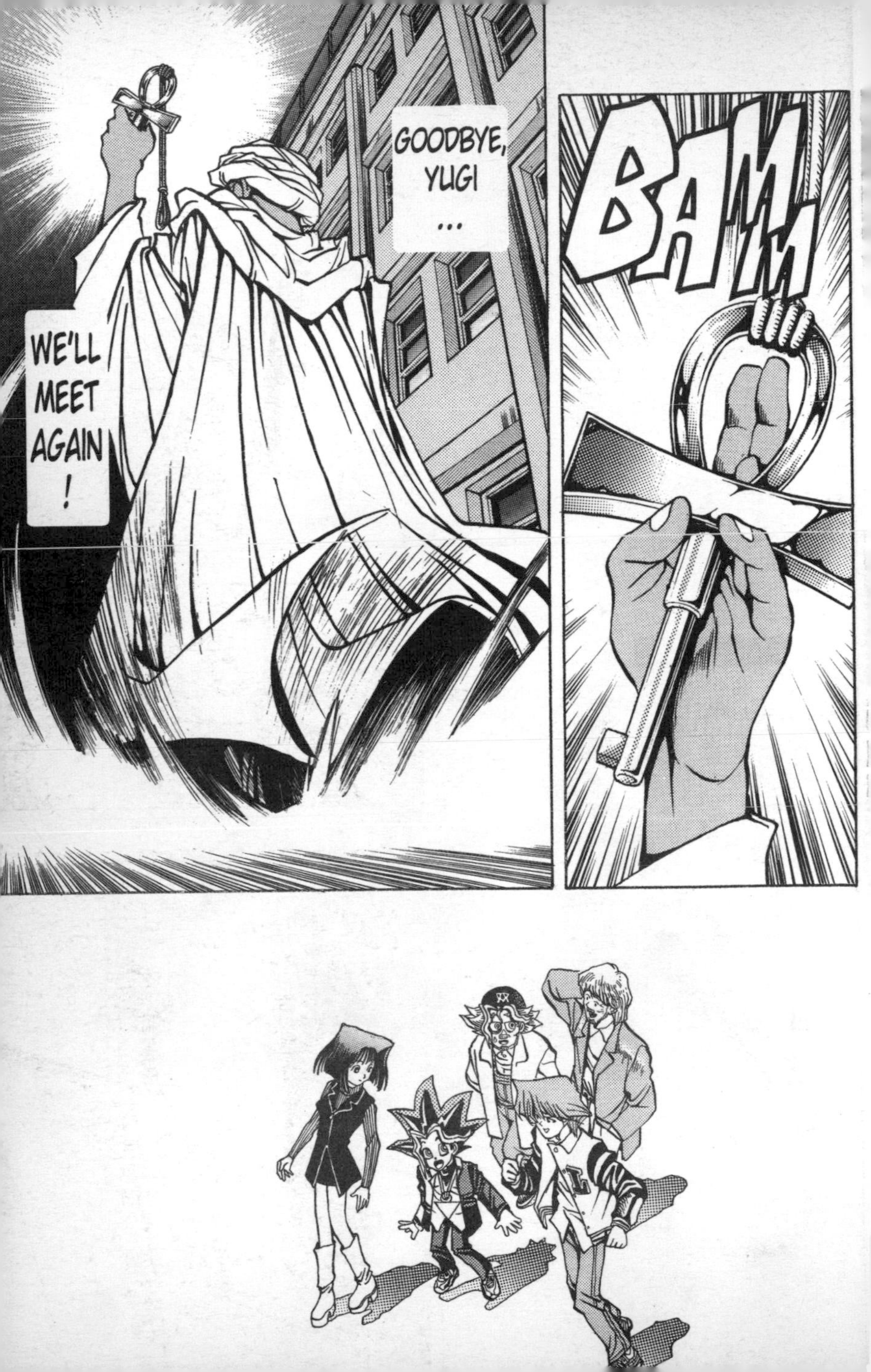
BAM
GOODBYE, YUGI ...
WE'LL MEET AGAIN !

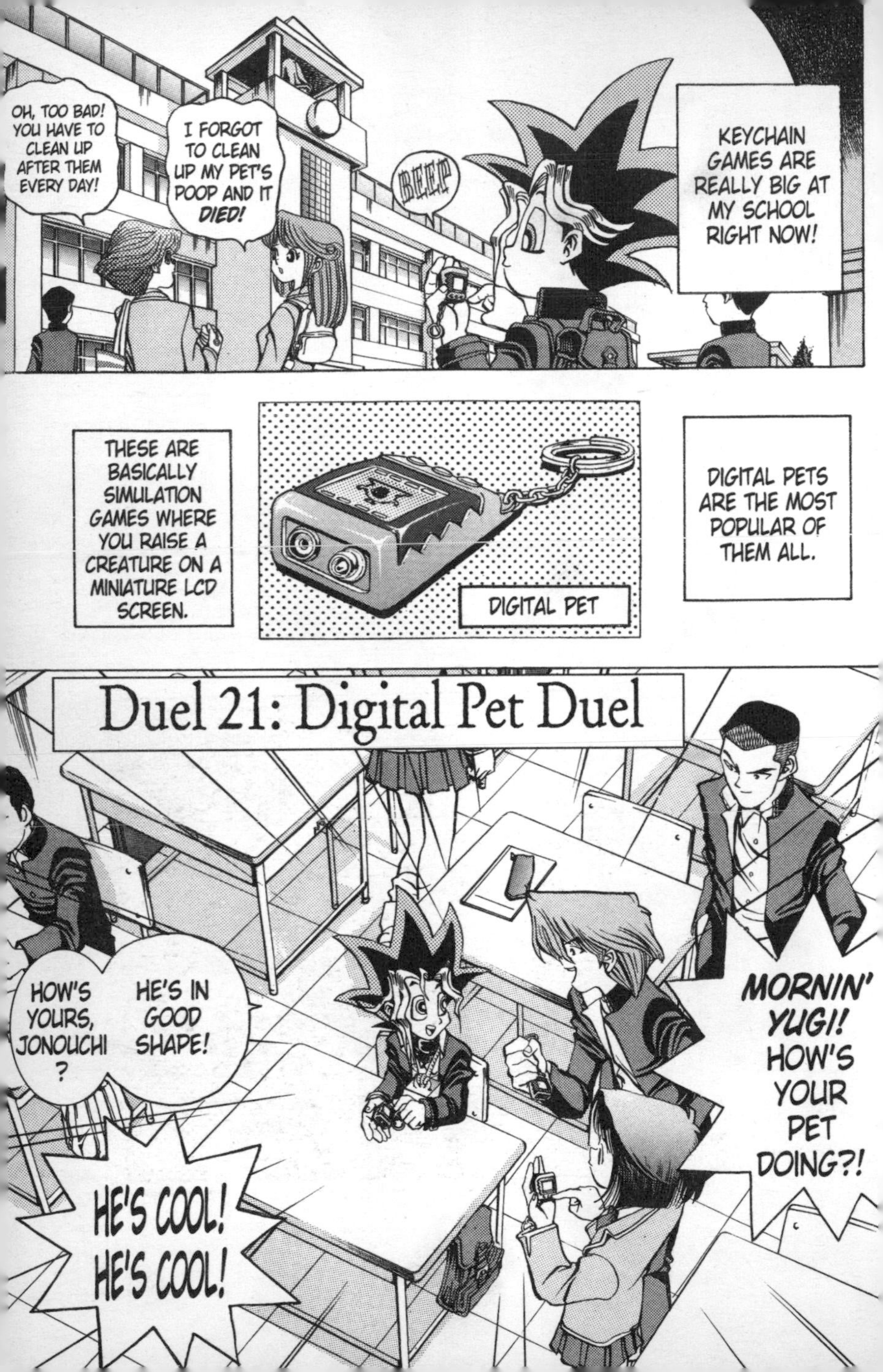
KEYCHAIN GAMES ARE REALLY BIG AT MY SCHOOL RIGHT NOW!
BEEP
I FORGOT TO CLEAN UP MY PET'S POOP AND IT DIED!
OH, TOO BAD! YOU HAVE TO CLEAN UP AFTER THEM EVERY DAY!
DIGITAL PETS ARE THE MOST POPULAR OF THEM ALL.
DIGITAL PET
THESE ARE BASICALLY SIMULATION GAMES WHERE YOU RAISE A CREATURE ON A MINIATURE LCD SCREEN.
Duel 21: Digital Pet Duel
MORNIN' YUGI! HOW'S YOUR PET DOING?!
HE'S IN GOOD SHAPE!
HOW'S YOURS, JONOUCHI?
HE'S COOL! HE'S COOL!

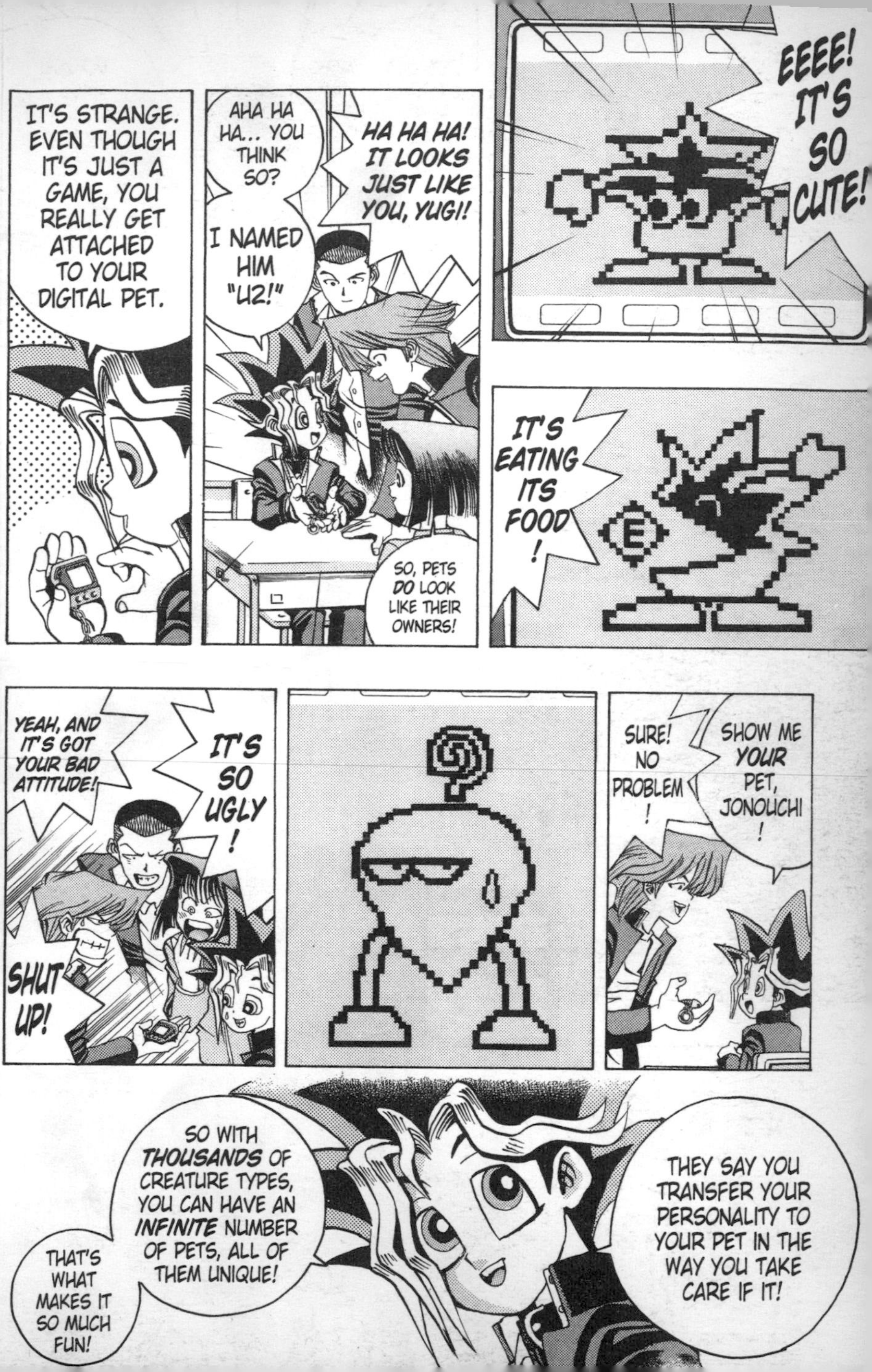

EEEE! IT'S SO CUTE!
IT'S EATING ITS FOOD!
HA HA HA! IT LOOKS JUST LIKE YOU, YUGI!
AHA HA HA... YOU THINK SO?
I NAMED HIM "U2!"
SO, PETS DO LOOK LIKE THEIR OWNERS!
IT'S STRANGE. EVEN THOUGH IT'S JUST A GAME, YOU REALLY GET ATTACHED TO YOUR DIGITAL PET.
SHOW ME YOUR PET, JONOUCHI!
SURE! NO PROBLEM!
IT'S SO UGLY!
YEAH, AND IT'S GOT YOUR BAD ATTITUDE!
SHUT UP!
THEY SAY YOU TRANSFER YOUR PERSONALITY TO YOUR PET IN THE WAY YOU TAKE CARE IF IT!
SO WITH THOUSANDS OF CREATURE TYPES, YOU CAN HAVE AN INFINITE NUMBER OF PETS, ALL OF THEM UNIQUE!
THAT'S WHAT MAKES IT SO MUCH FUN!

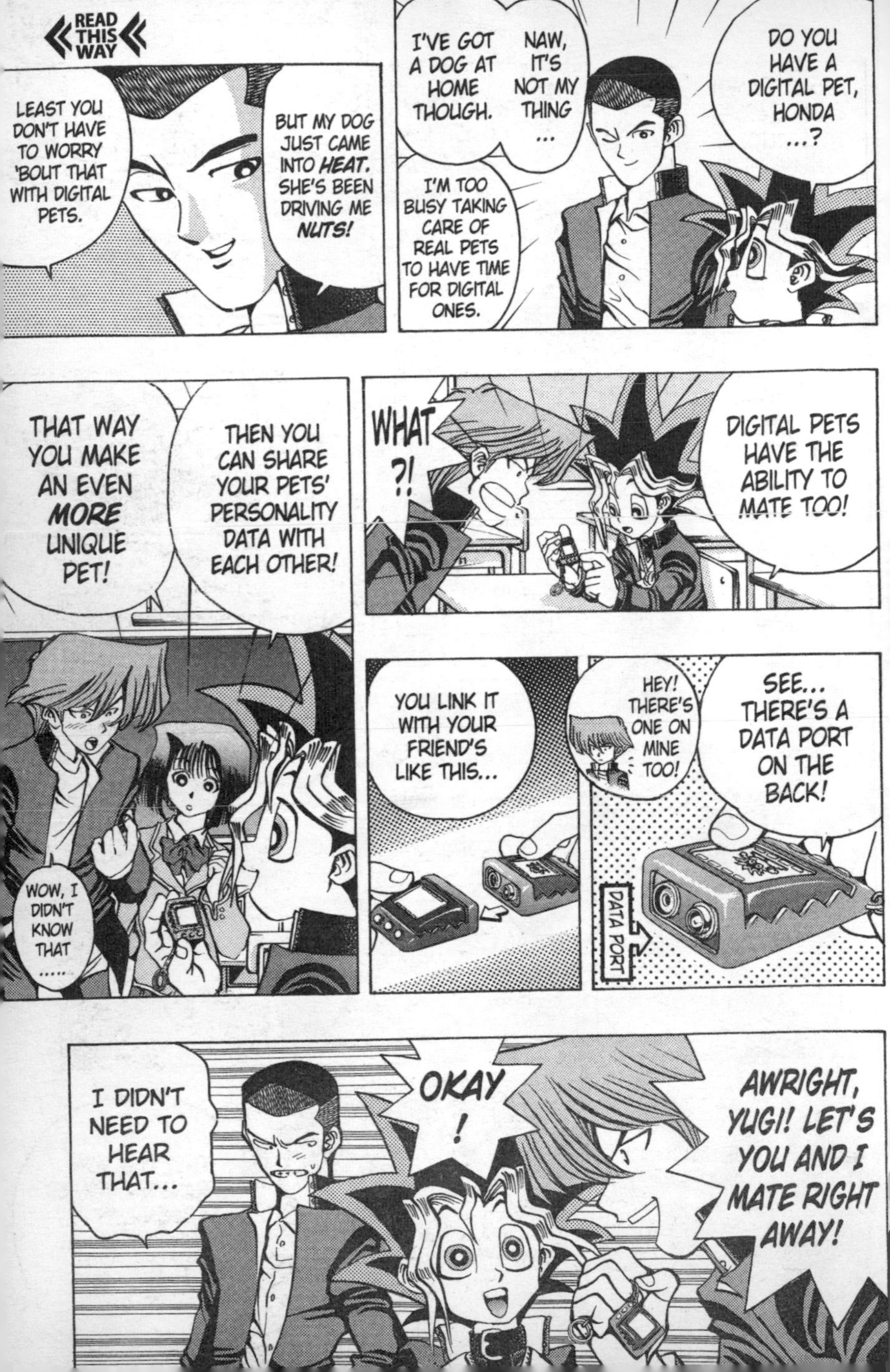
READ THIS WAY
DO YOU HAVE A DIGITAL PET, HONDA ...?
NAW, IT'S NOT MY THING ...
I'VE GOT A DOG AT HOME THOUGH.
I'M TOO BUSY TAKING CARE OF REAL PETS TO HAVE TIME FOR DIGITAL ONES.
BUT MY DOG JUST CAME INTO HEAT. SHE'S BEEN DRIVING ME NUTS!
LEAST YOU DON'T HAVE TO WORRY 'BOUT THAT WITH DIGITAL PETS.
DIGITAL PETS HAVE THE ABILITY TO MATE TOO!
WHAT ?!
SEE... THERE'S A DATA PORT ON THE BACK!
HEY! THERE'S ONE ON MINE TOO!
DATA PORT
YOU LINK IT WITH YOUR FRIEND'S LIKE THIS...
THEN YOU CAN SHARE YOUR PETS' PERSONALITY DATA WITH EACH OTHER!
THAT WAY YOU MAKE AN EVEN MORE UNIQUE PET!
WOW, I DIDN'T KNOW THAT .....
AWRIGHT, YUGI! LET'S YOU AND I MATE RIGHT AWAY!
OKAY !
I DIDN'T NEED TO HEAR THAT...

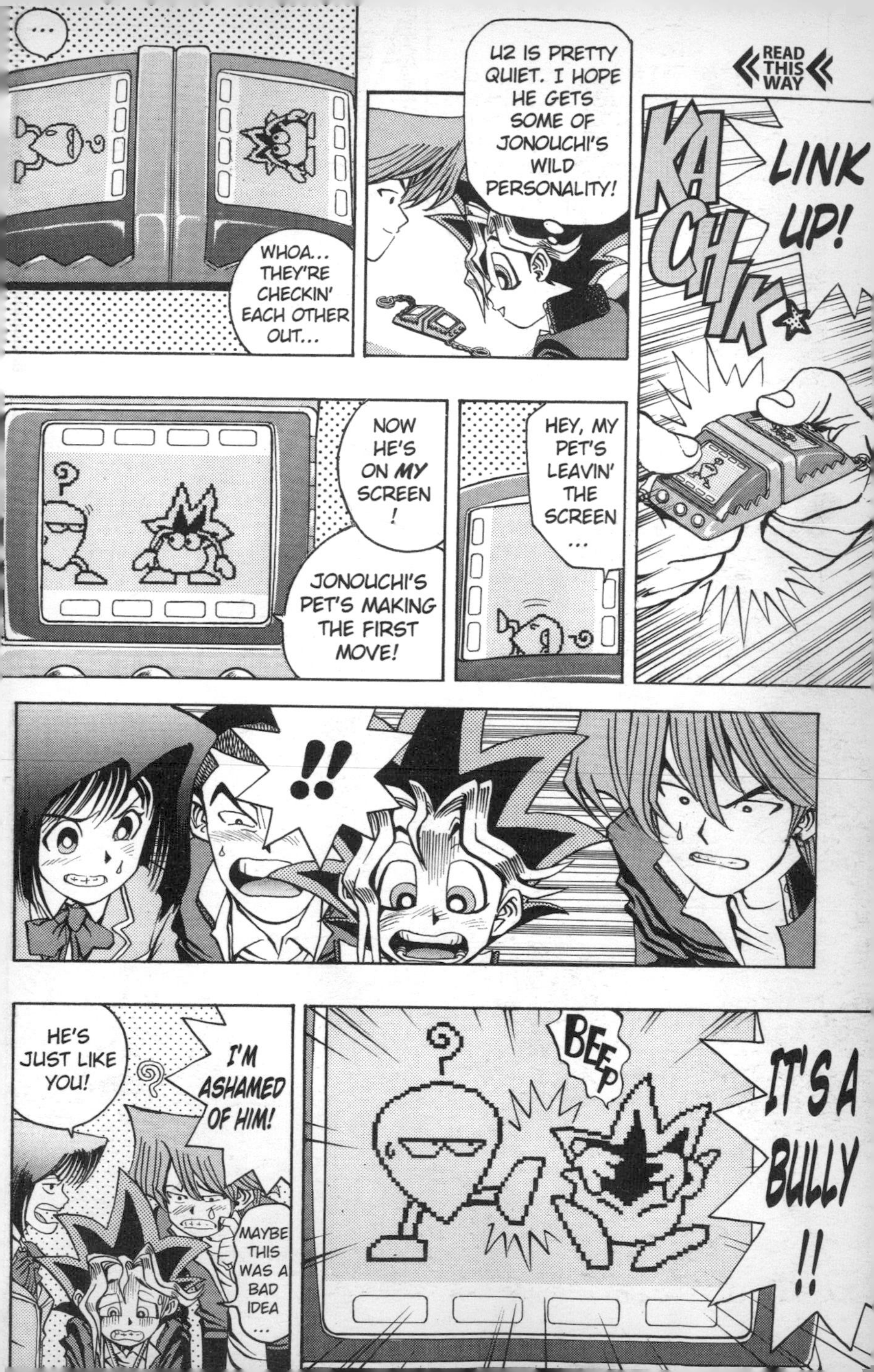
READ THIS WAY
KA CHIK
LINK UP!
U2 IS PRETTY QUIET. I HOPE HE GETS SOME OF JONOUCHI'S WILD PERSONALITY!
...
WHOA... THEY'RE CHECKIN' EACH OTHER OUT...
HEY, MY PET'S LEAVIN' THE SCREEN...
NOW HE'S ON *MY* SCREEN!
JONOUCHI'S PET'S MAKING THE FIRST MOVE!
!!
BEEP
IT'S A BULLY!!
HE'S JUST LIKE YOU!
I'M ASHAMED OF HIM!
MAYBE THIS WAS A BAD IDEA...

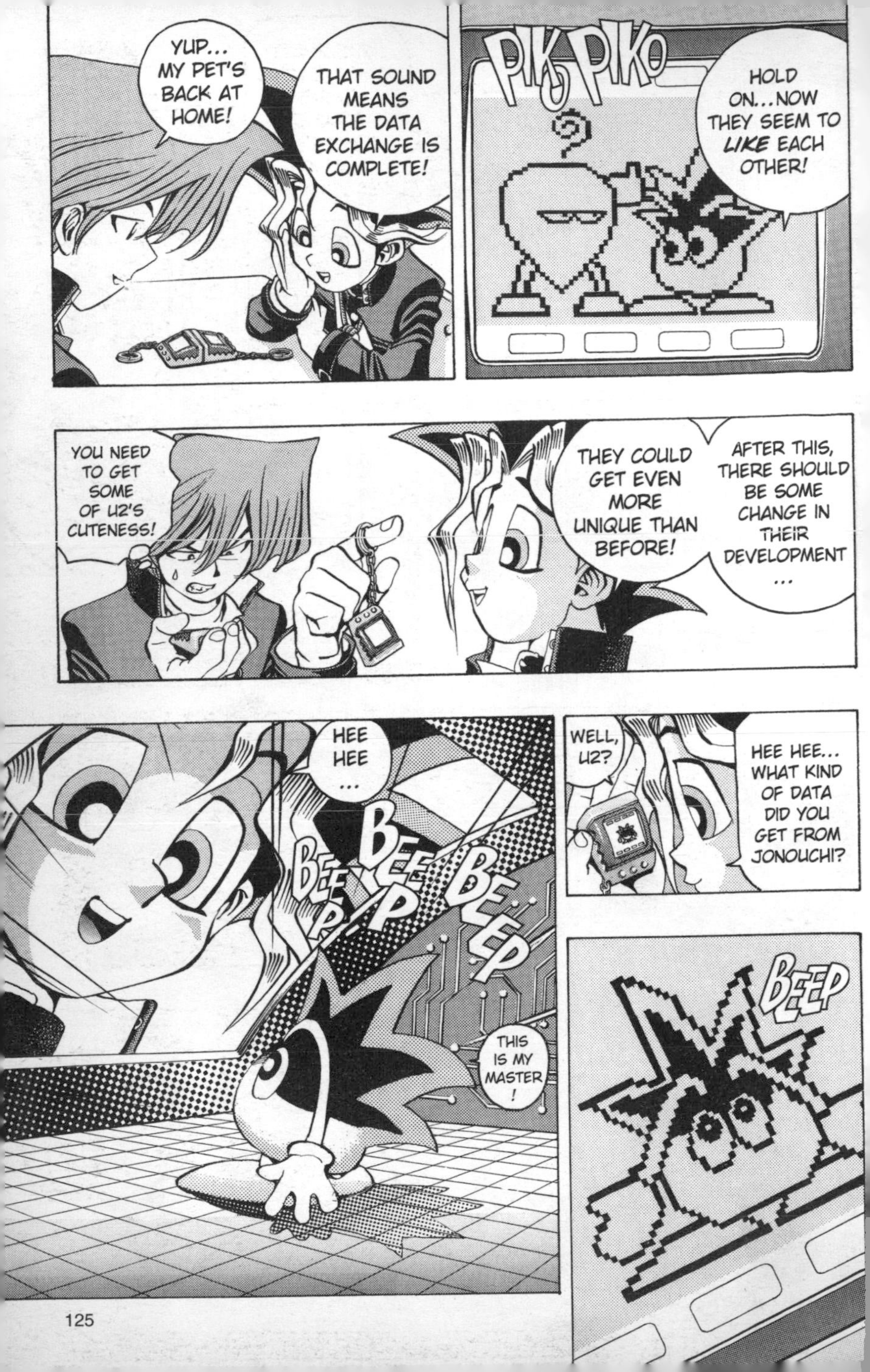
PIKOPIKO
HOLD ON...NOW THEY SEEM TO LIKE EACH OTHER!
THAT SOUND MEANS THE DATA EXCHANGE IS COMPLETE!
YUP... MY PET'S BACK AT HOME!
AFTER THIS, THERE SHOULD BE SOME CHANGE IN THEIR DEVELOPMENT ...
THEY COULD GET EVEN MORE UNIQUE THAN BEFORE!
YOU NEED TO GET SOME OF U2'S CUTENESS!
HEE HEE... WHAT KIND OF DATA DID YOU GET FROM JONOUCHI?
WELL, U2?
BEEP
HEE HEE ...
BEEP BEEP BEEP
THIS IS MY MASTER!

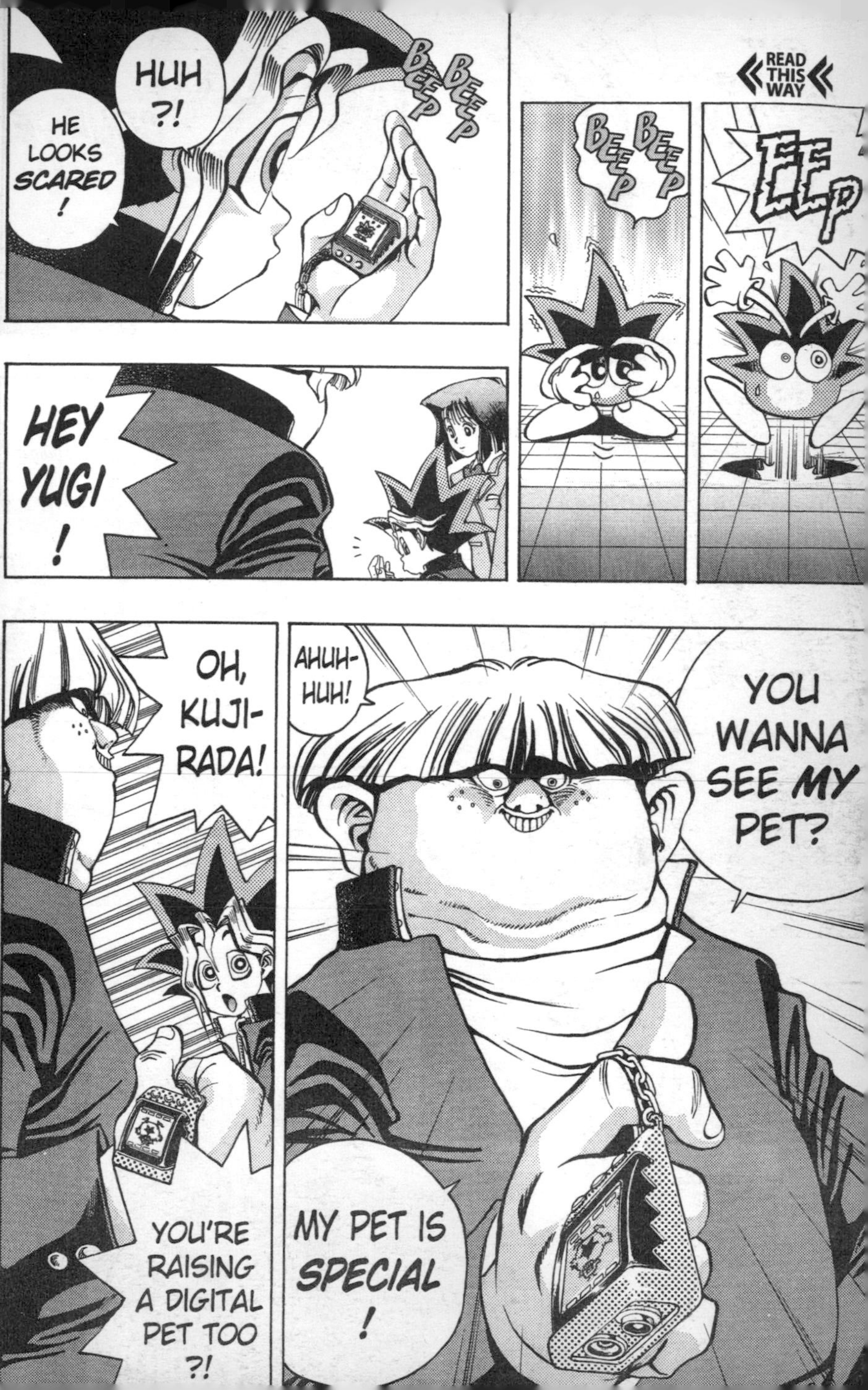
READ THIS WAY
EEP
BEEP BEEP
BEEP BEEP
HUH ?!
HE LOOKS SCARED !
HEY YUGI !
YOU WANNA SEE MY PET?
AHUH-HUH!
MY PET IS SPECIAL !
OH, KUJI-RADA!
YOU'RE RAISING A DIGITAL PET TOO ?!

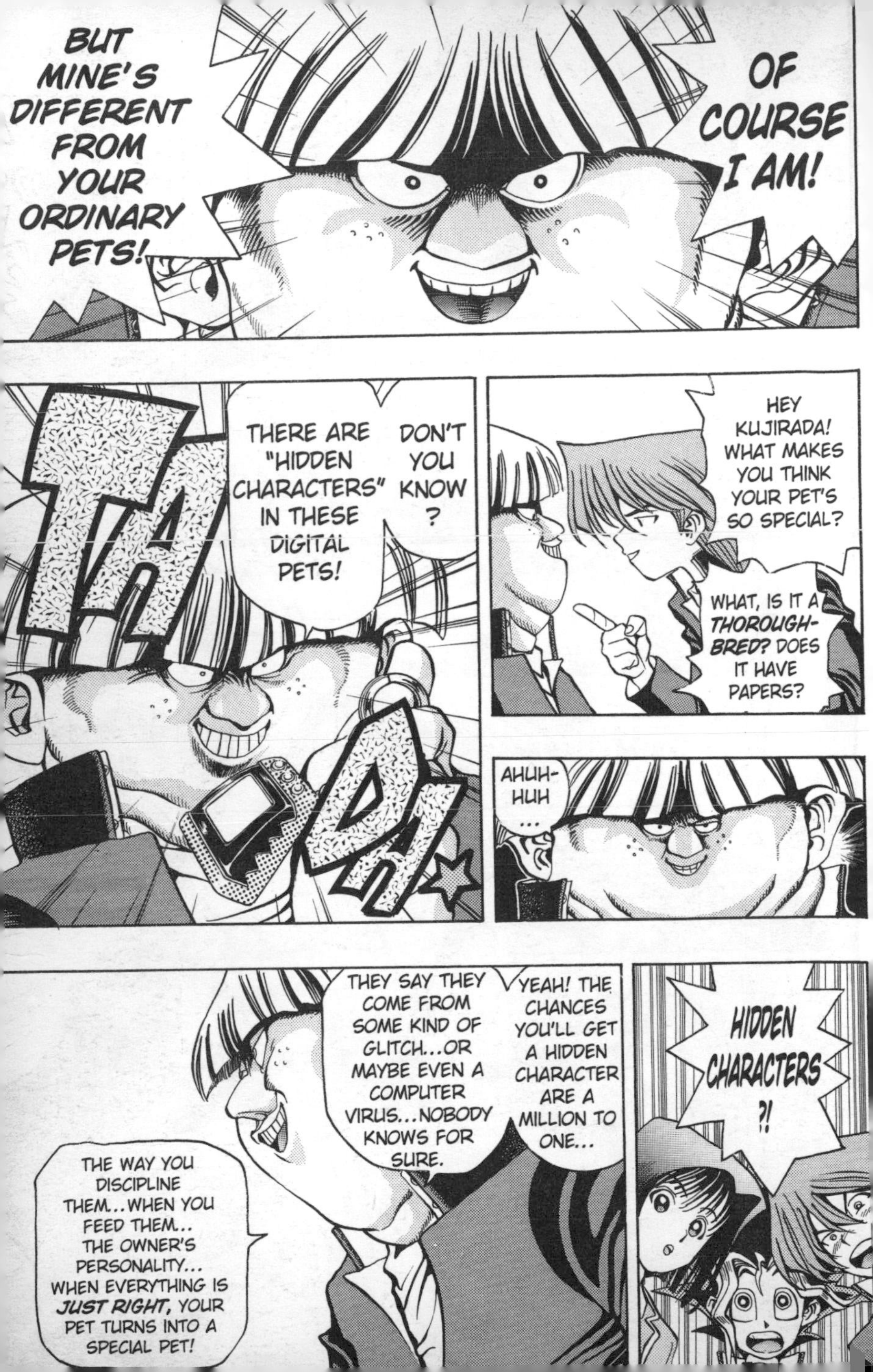
OF COURSE I AM!
BUT MINE'S DIFFERENT FROM YOUR ORDINARY PETS!
HEY KUJIRADA! WHAT MAKES YOU THINK YOUR PET'S SO SPECIAL?
WHAT, IS IT A *THOROUGHBRED?* DOES IT HAVE PAPERS?
AHUH-HUH ...
DON'T YOU KNOW ?
THERE ARE "HIDDEN CHARACTERS" IN THESE DIGITAL PETS!
TA
DA
HIDDEN CHARACTERS ?!
YEAH! THE CHANCES YOU'LL GET A HIDDEN CHARACTER ARE A MILLION TO ONE...
THEY SAY THEY COME FROM SOME KIND OF GLITCH...OR MAYBE EVEN A COMPUTER VIRUS...NOBODY KNOWS FOR SURE.
THE WAY YOU DISCIPLINE THEM...WHEN YOU FEED THEM... THE OWNER'S PERSONALITY... WHEN EVERYTHING IS *JUST RIGHT*, YOUR PET TURNS INTO A SPECIAL PET!

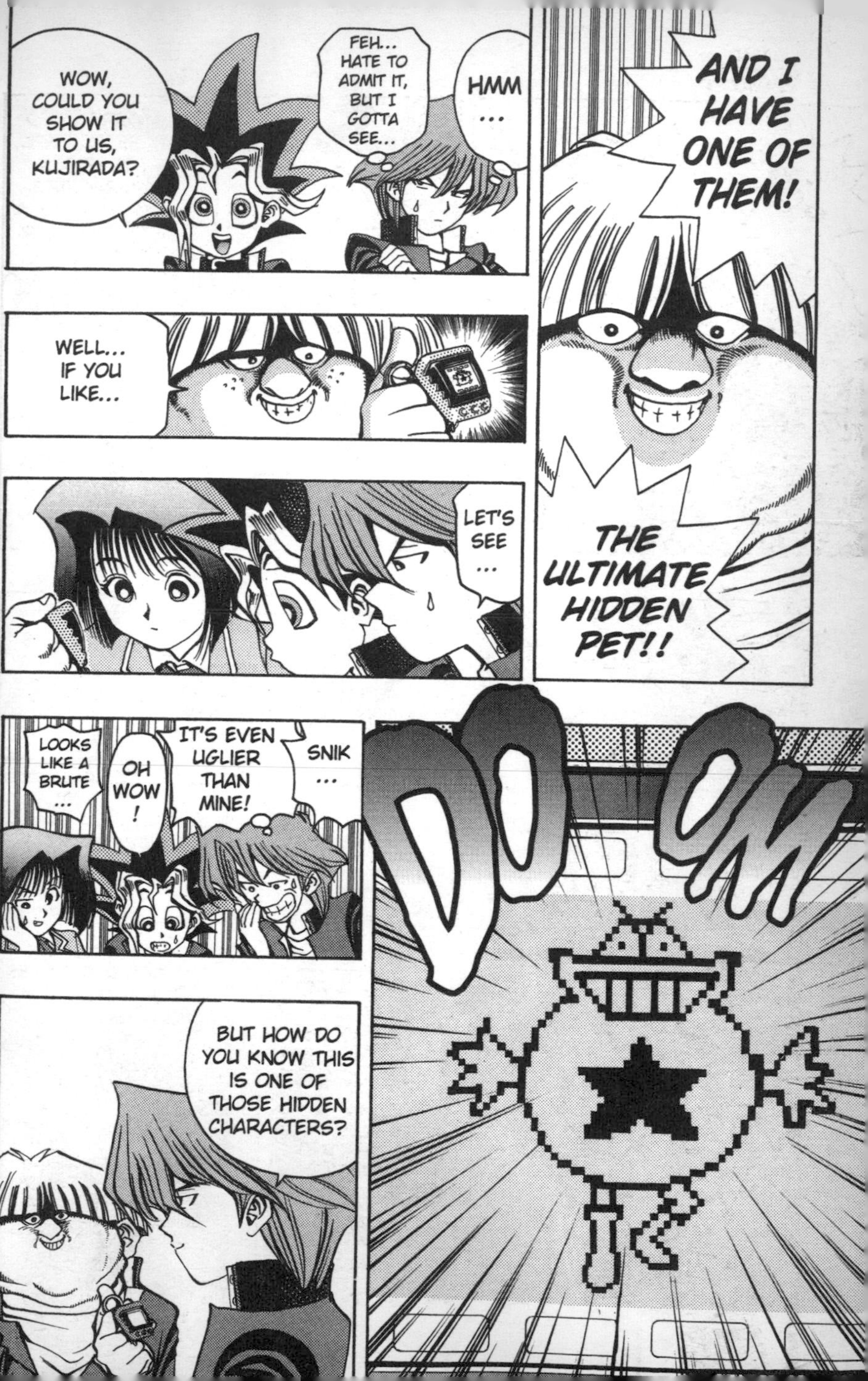
AND I HAVE ONE OF THEM!
THE ULTIMATE HIDDEN PET!!
HMM ...
FEH... HATE TO ADMIT IT, BUT I GOTTA SEE...
WOW, COULD YOU SHOW IT TO US, KUJIRADA?
WELL... IF YOU LIKE...
LET'S SEE ...
DOOM
SNIK ...
IT'S EVEN UGLIER THAN MINE!
OH WOW !
LOOKS LIKE A BRUTE ...
BUT HOW DO YOU KNOW THIS IS ONE OF THOSE HIDDEN CHARACTERS?

READ THIS WAY

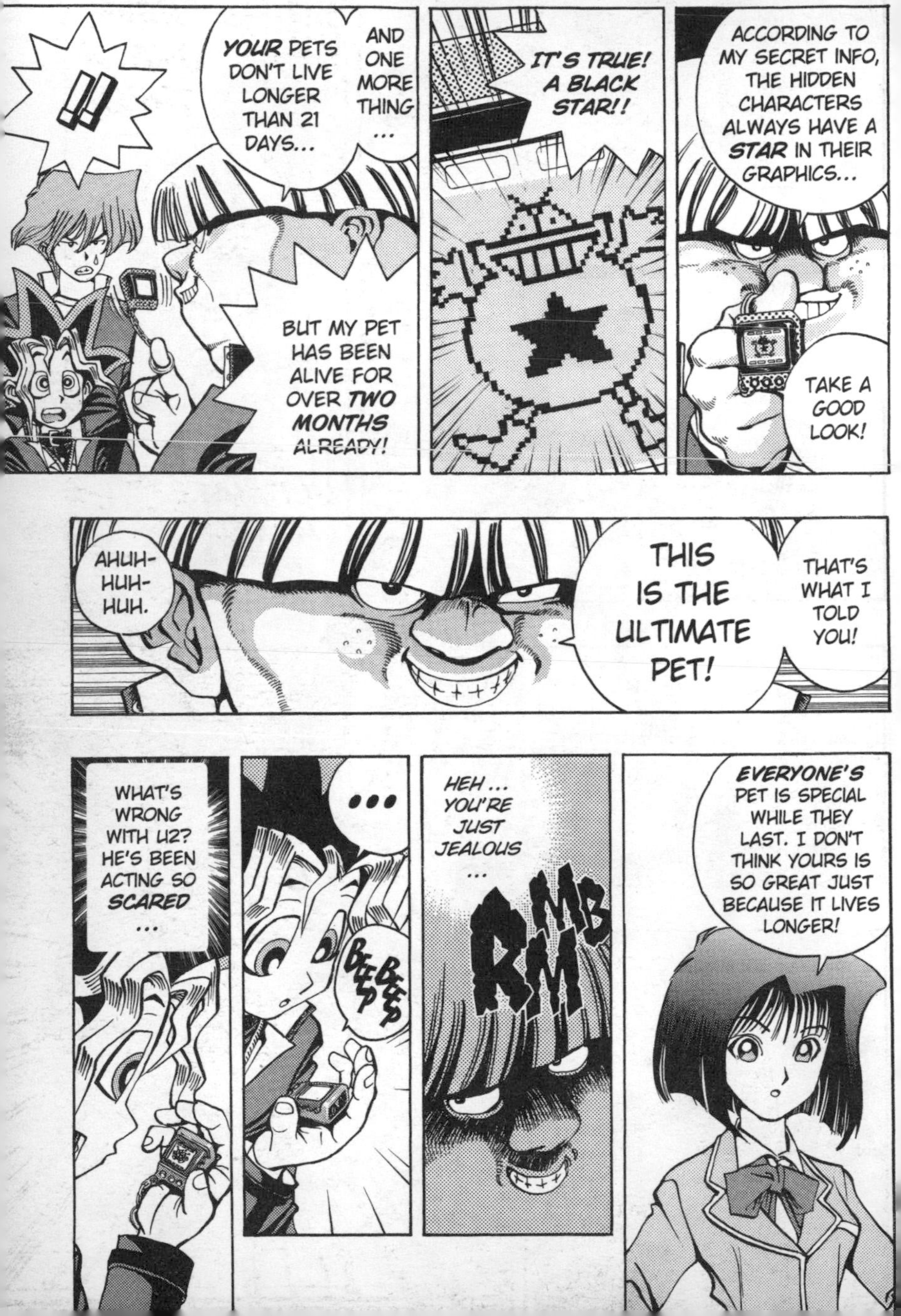
ACCORDING TO MY SECRET INFO, THE HIDDEN CHARACTERS ALWAYS HAVE A *STAR* IN THEIR GRAPHICS...
TAKE A GOOD LOOK!
IT'S TRUE! A BLACK STAR!!
AND ONE MORE THING ...
YOUR PETS DON'T LIVE LONGER THAN 21 DAYS...
BUT MY PET HAS BEEN ALIVE FOR OVER *TWO MONTHS* ALREADY!
!!
THAT'S WHAT I TOLD YOU!
THIS IS THE ULTIMATE PET!
AHUH-HUH-HUH.
EVERYONE'S PET IS SPECIAL WHILE THEY LAST. I DON'T THINK YOURS IS SO GREAT JUST BECAUSE IT LIVES LONGER!
HEH ... YOU'RE JUST JEALOUS ...
RMB RMB
...
BEEP BEEP
WHAT'S WRONG WITH U2? HE'S BEEN ACTING SO *SCARED* ...

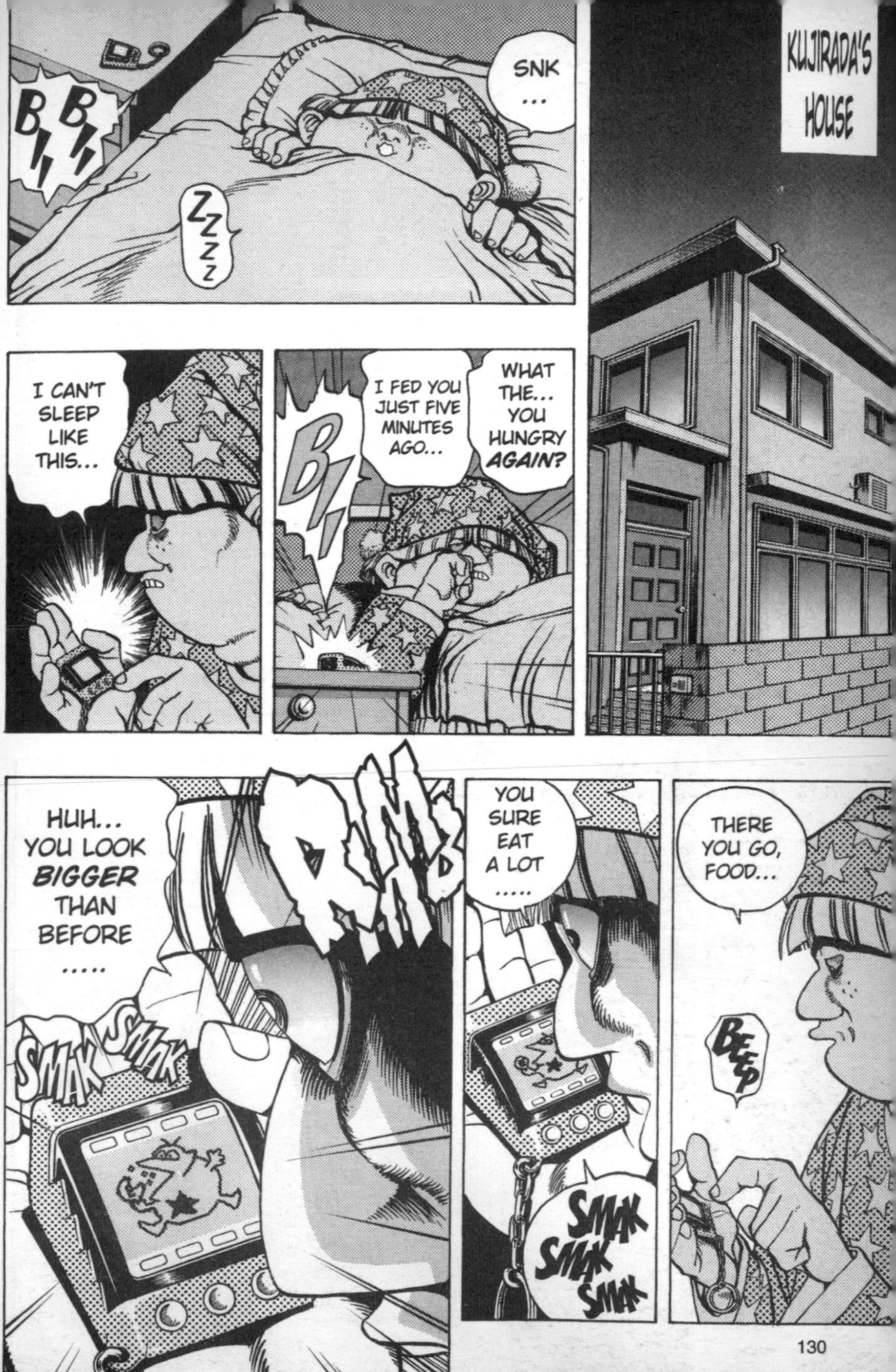
KUJIRADA'S HOUSE
SNK ...
B B
ZZZZ
WHAT THE... YOU HUNGRY AGAIN?
I FED YOU JUST FIVE MINUTES AGO...
B
I CAN'T SLEEP LIKE THIS...
THERE YOU GO, FOOD...
BEEP
YOU SURE EAT A LOT .....
SMAK SMAK SMAK
HUH... YOU LOOK BIGGER THAN BEFORE .....
SMAK SMAK

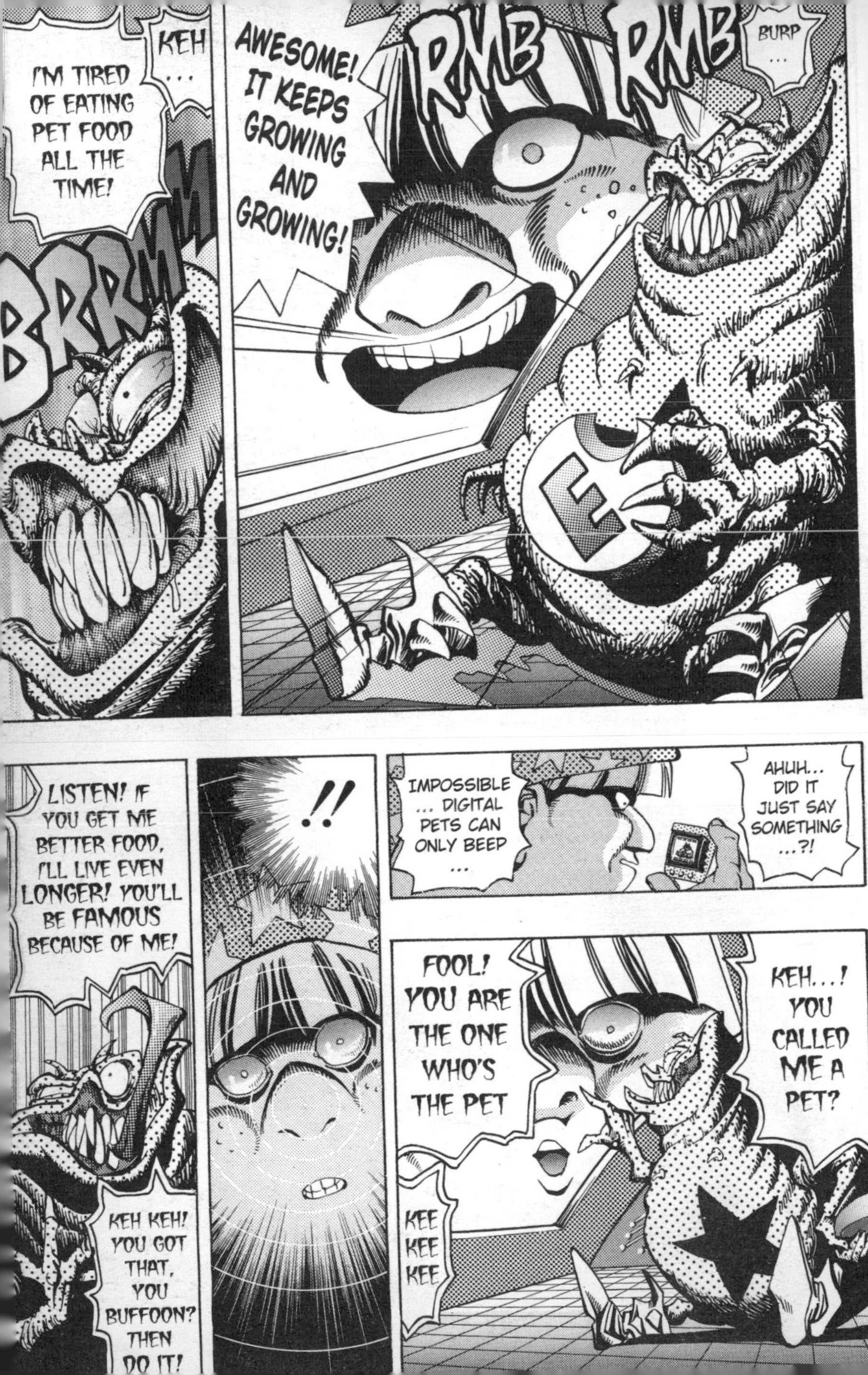
BURP ...
RMB RMB
AWESOME! IT KEEPS GROWING AND GROWING!
KEH ...
I'M TIRED OF EATING PET FOOD ALL THE TIME!
BRRMM
AHUH... DID IT JUST SAY SOMETHING ...?!
IMPOSSIBLE ... DIGITAL PETS CAN ONLY BEEP ...
KEH...! YOU CALLED ME A PET?
FOOL! YOU ARE THE ONE WHO'S THE PET
KEE KEE KEE
!!
LISTEN! IF YOU GET ME BETTER FOOD, I'LL LIVE EVEN LONGER! YOU'LL BE FAMOUS BECAUSE OF ME!
KEH KEH! YOU GOT THAT, YOU BUFFOON? THEN DO IT!

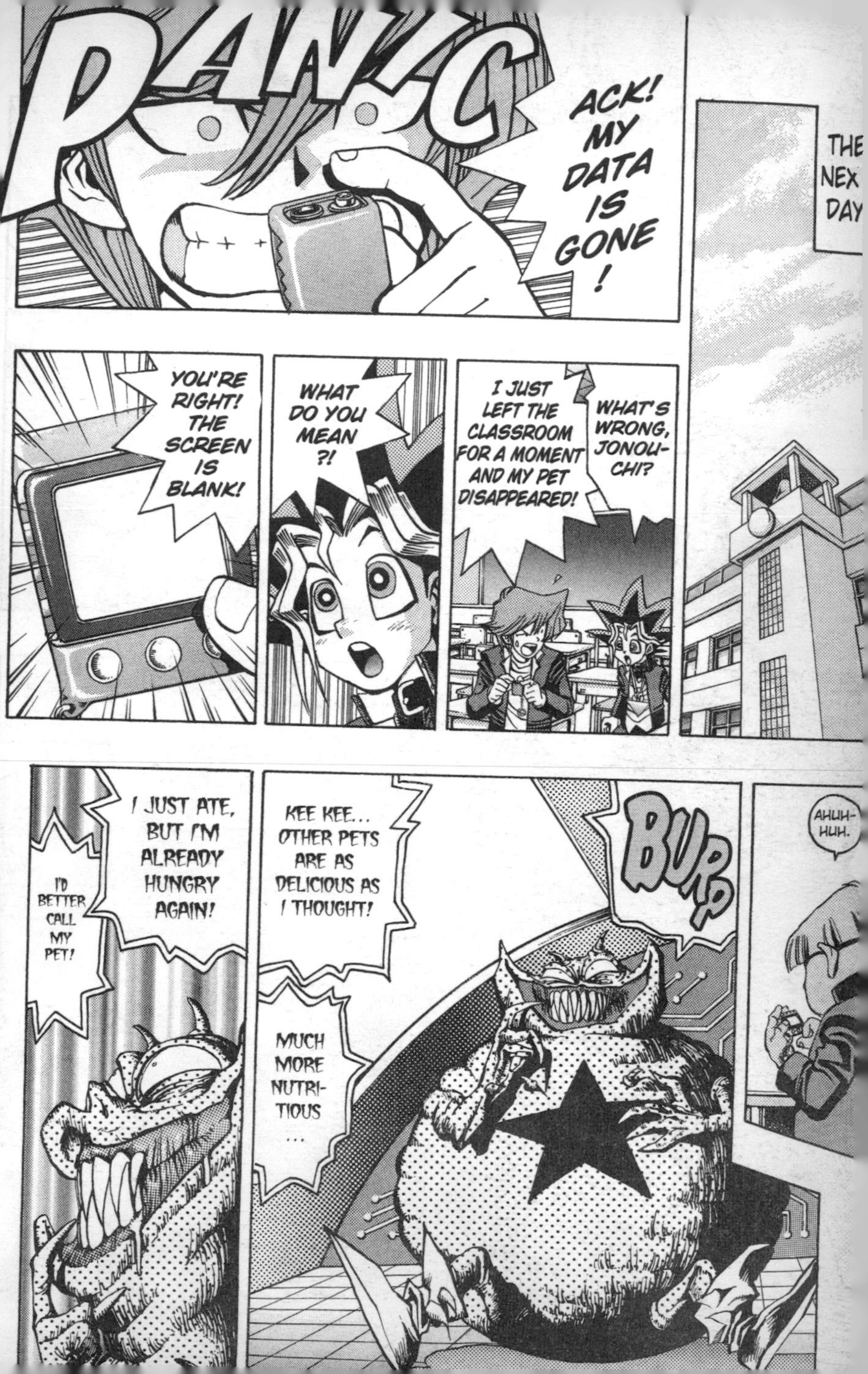
THE NEX DAY
PANIC
ACK! MY DATA IS GONE!
WHAT'S WRONG, JONOUCHI?
I JUST LEFT THE CLASSROOM FOR A MOMENT AND MY PET DISAPPEARED!
WHAT DO YOU MEAN?!
YOU'RE RIGHT! THE SCREEN IS BLANK!
AHUH-HUH.
BURP
KEE KEE... OTHER PETS ARE AS DELICIOUS AS I THOUGHT!
MUCH MORE NUTRITIOUS...
I JUST ATE, BUT I'M ALREADY HUNGRY AGAIN!
I'D BETTER CALL MY PET!

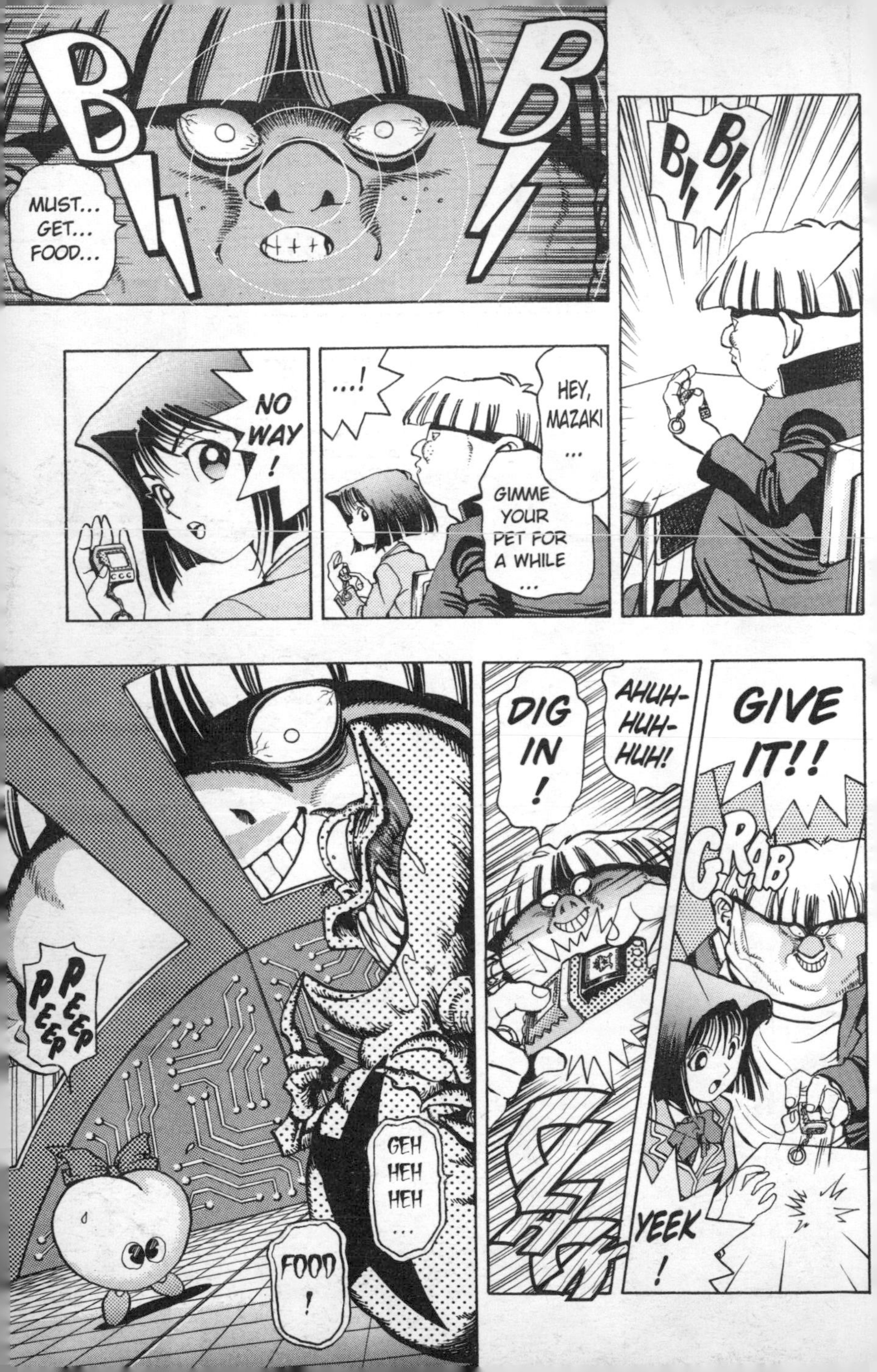
B B
MUST... GET... FOOD...
BI BI
HEY, MAZAKI ...
GIMME YOUR PET FOR A WHILE ...
...!
NO WAY !
GIVE IT!!
GRAB
YEEK !
AHUH-HUH-HUH!
DIG IN !
PEEP PEEP
GEH HEH HEH ...
FOOD !

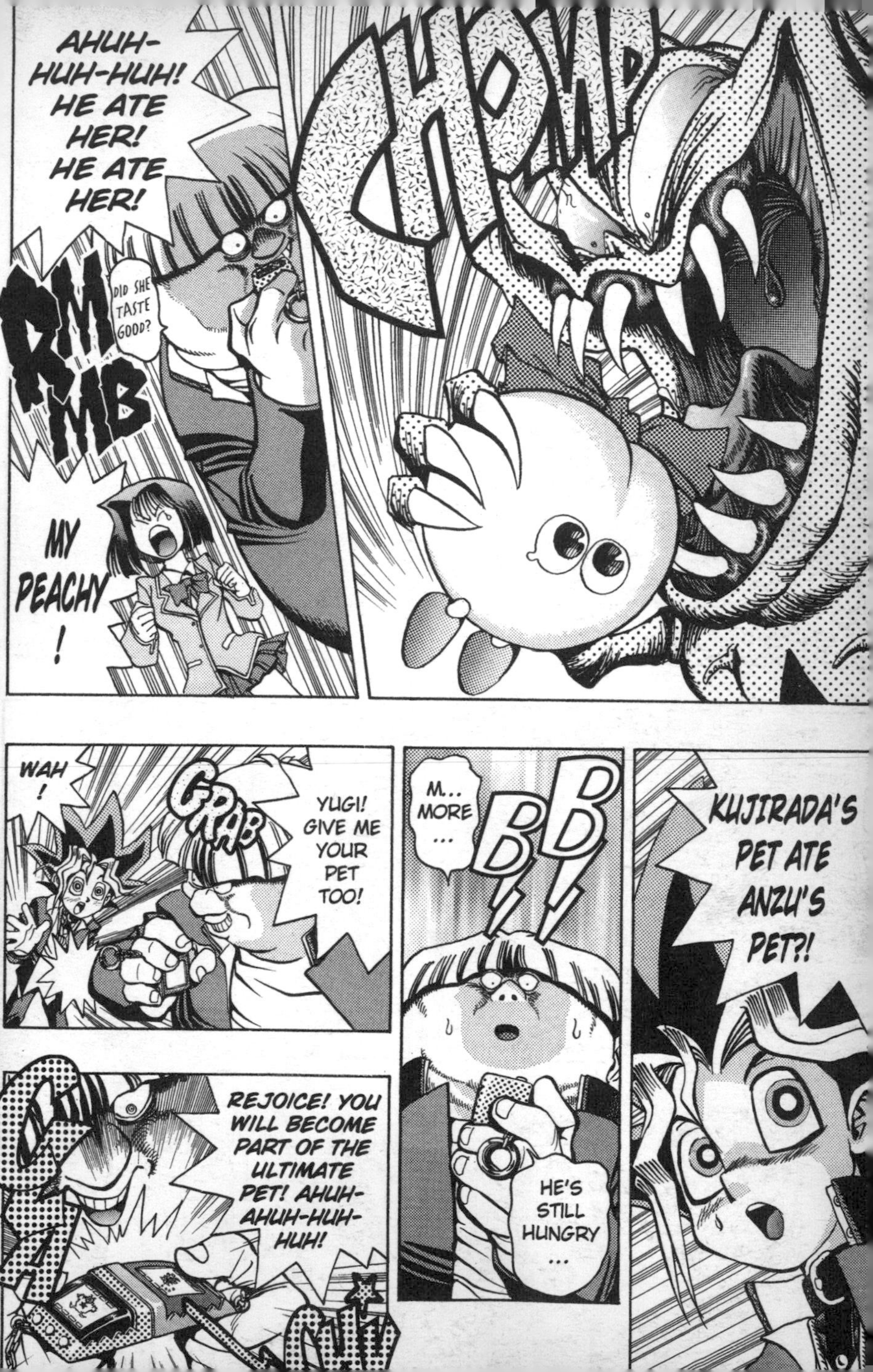
CHOMP
AHUH-HUH-HUH! HE ATE HER! HE ATE HER!
DID SHE TASTE GOOD?
RMMB
MY PEACHY!
KUJIRADA'S PET ATE ANZU'S PET?!
M... MORE ...
BB
HE'S STILL HUNGRY ...
YUGI! GIVE ME YOUR PET TOO!
GRAB
WAH!
REJOICE! YOU WILL BECOME PART OF THE ULTIMATE PET! AHUH-AHUH-HUH-HUH!

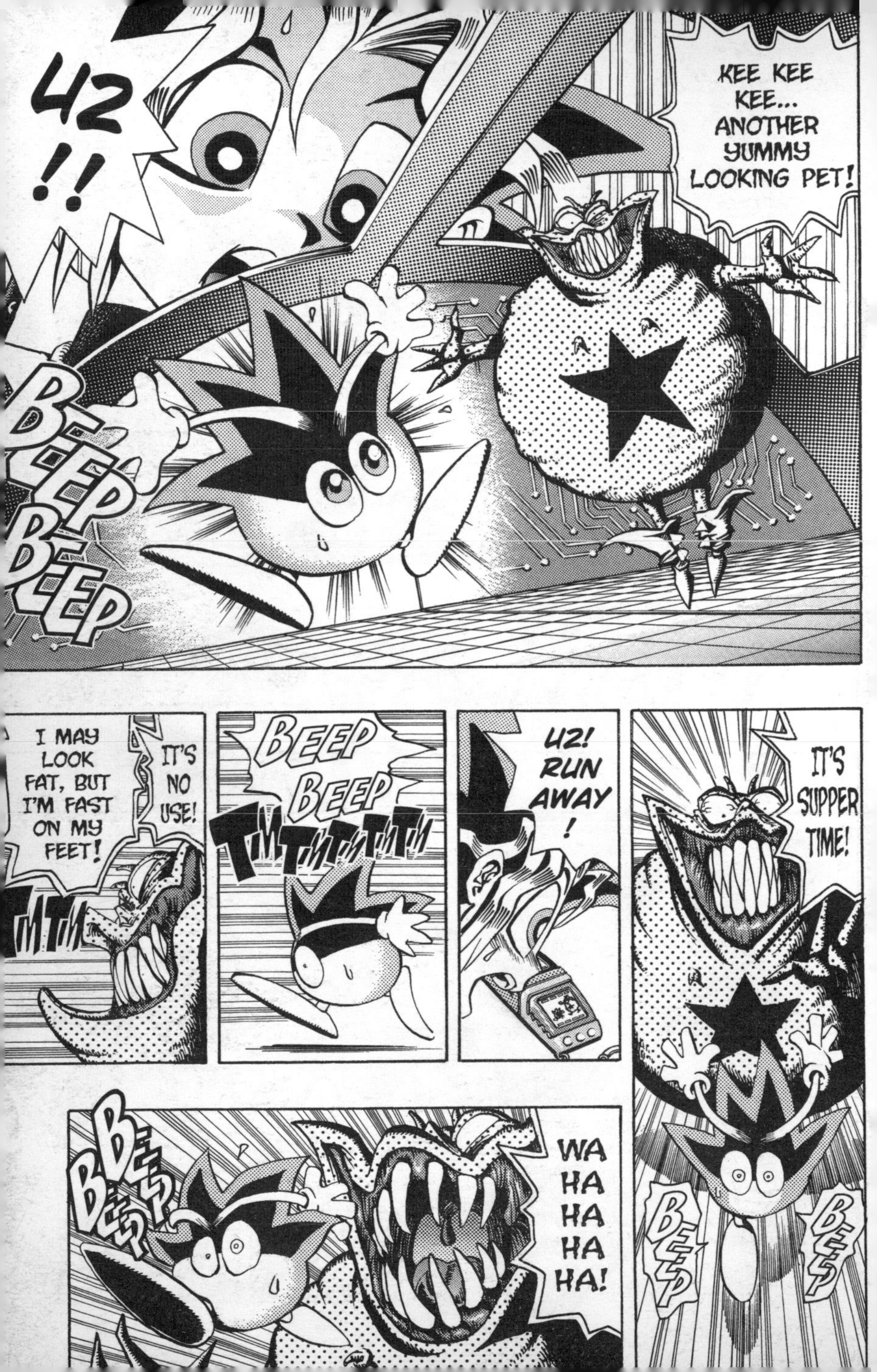
KEE KEE KEE... ANOTHER YUMMY LOOKING PET!
U2 !!
BEEP BEEP
IT'S SUPPER TIME!
U2! RUN AWAY!
BEEP BEEP
IT'S NO USE!
I MAY LOOK FAT, BUT I'M FAST ON MY FEET!
WA HA HA HA HA!

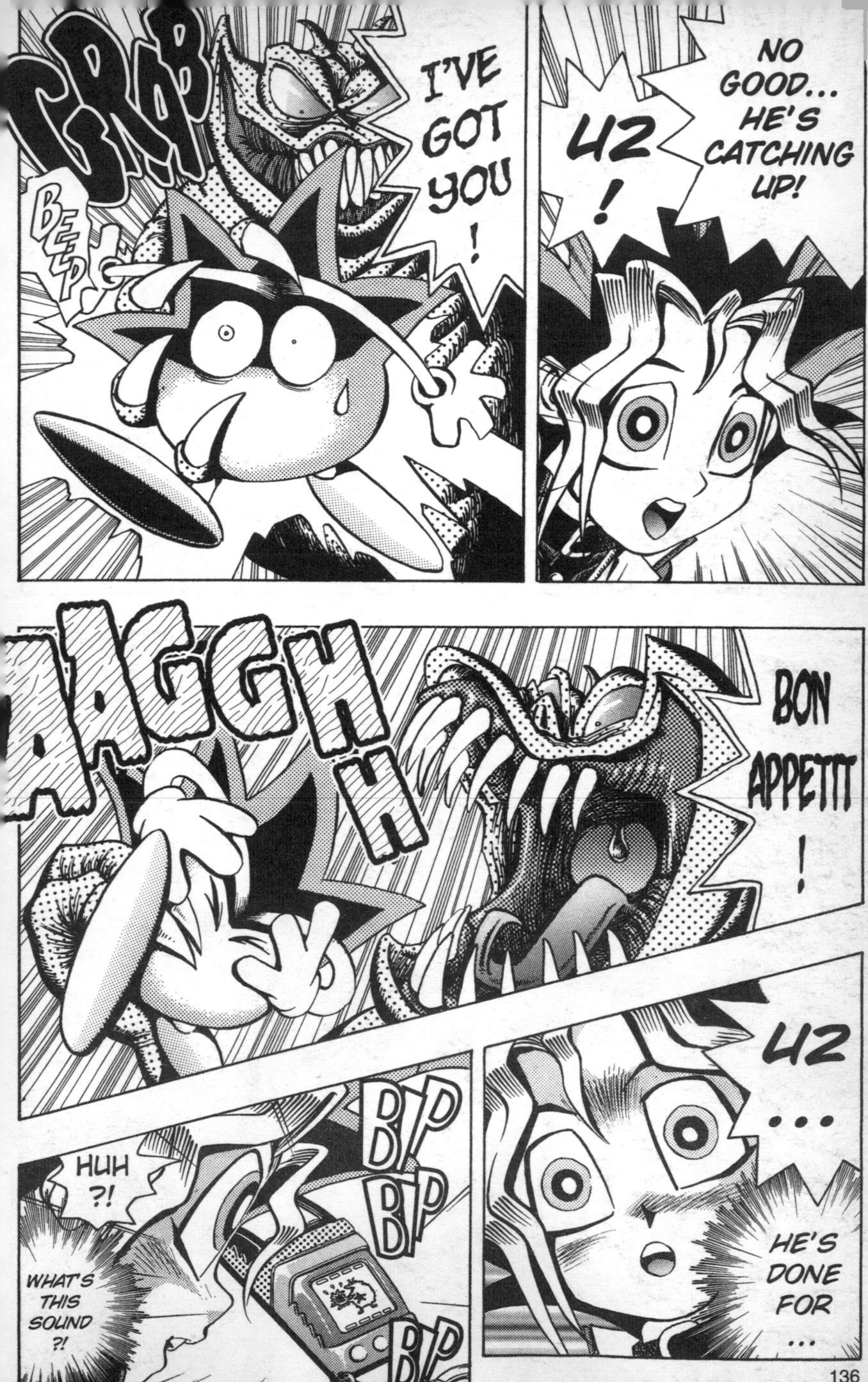
NO GOOD... HE'S CATCHING UP!
UZ!
I'VE GOT YOU!
GRAB
BEEP
BON APPETIT!
AAGGHH
UZ...
HE'S DONE FOR...
BIP BIP BIP
HUH?!
WHAT'S THIS SOUND?!

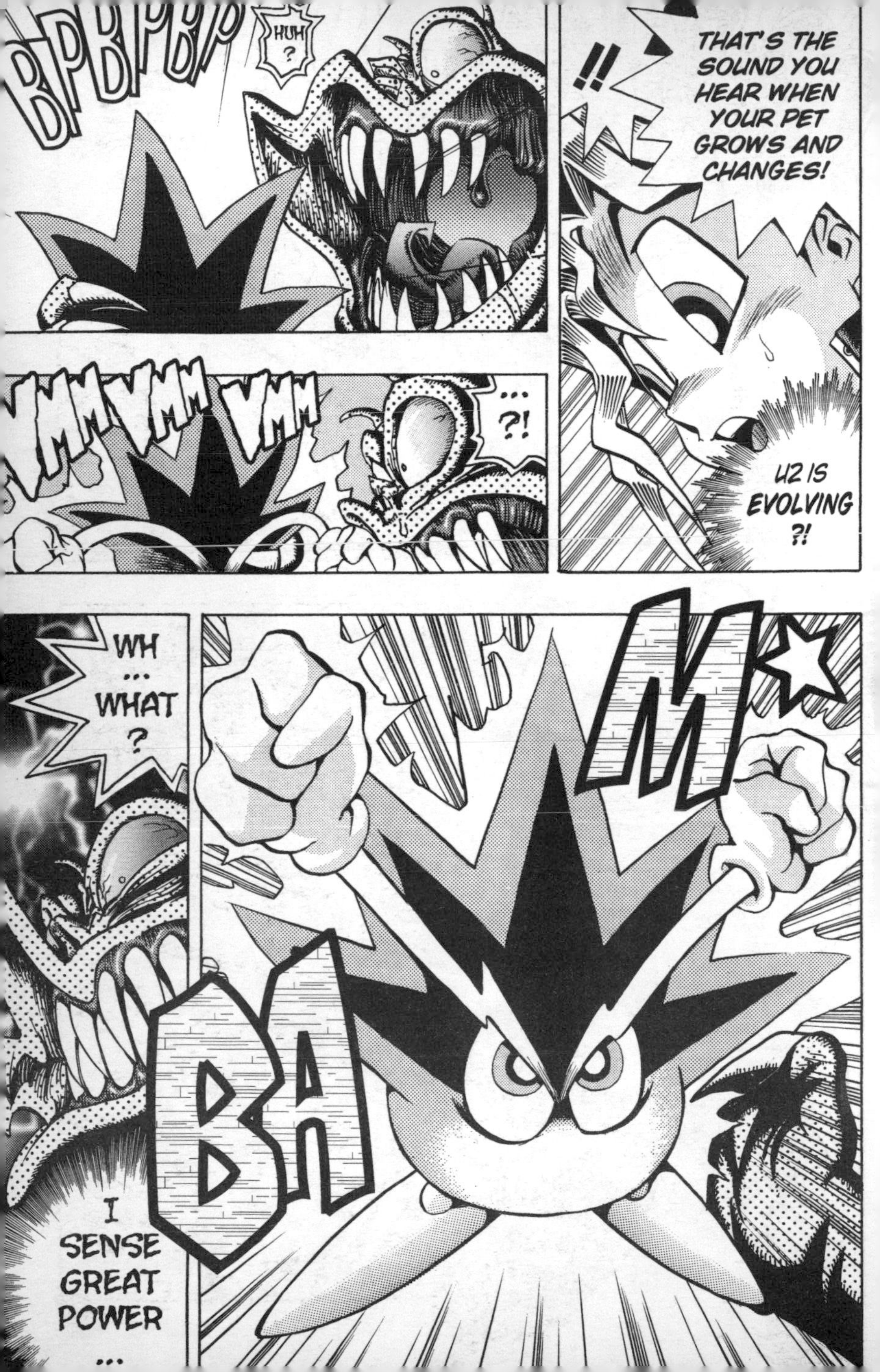
!!
THAT'S THE SOUND YOU HEAR WHEN YOUR PET GROWS AND CHANGES!
U2 IS EVOLVING ?!
HUH ?
BIPBIPBIP
... ?!
VMMVMM VMM
BA
M
WH ... WHAT ?
I SENSE GREAT POWER ...

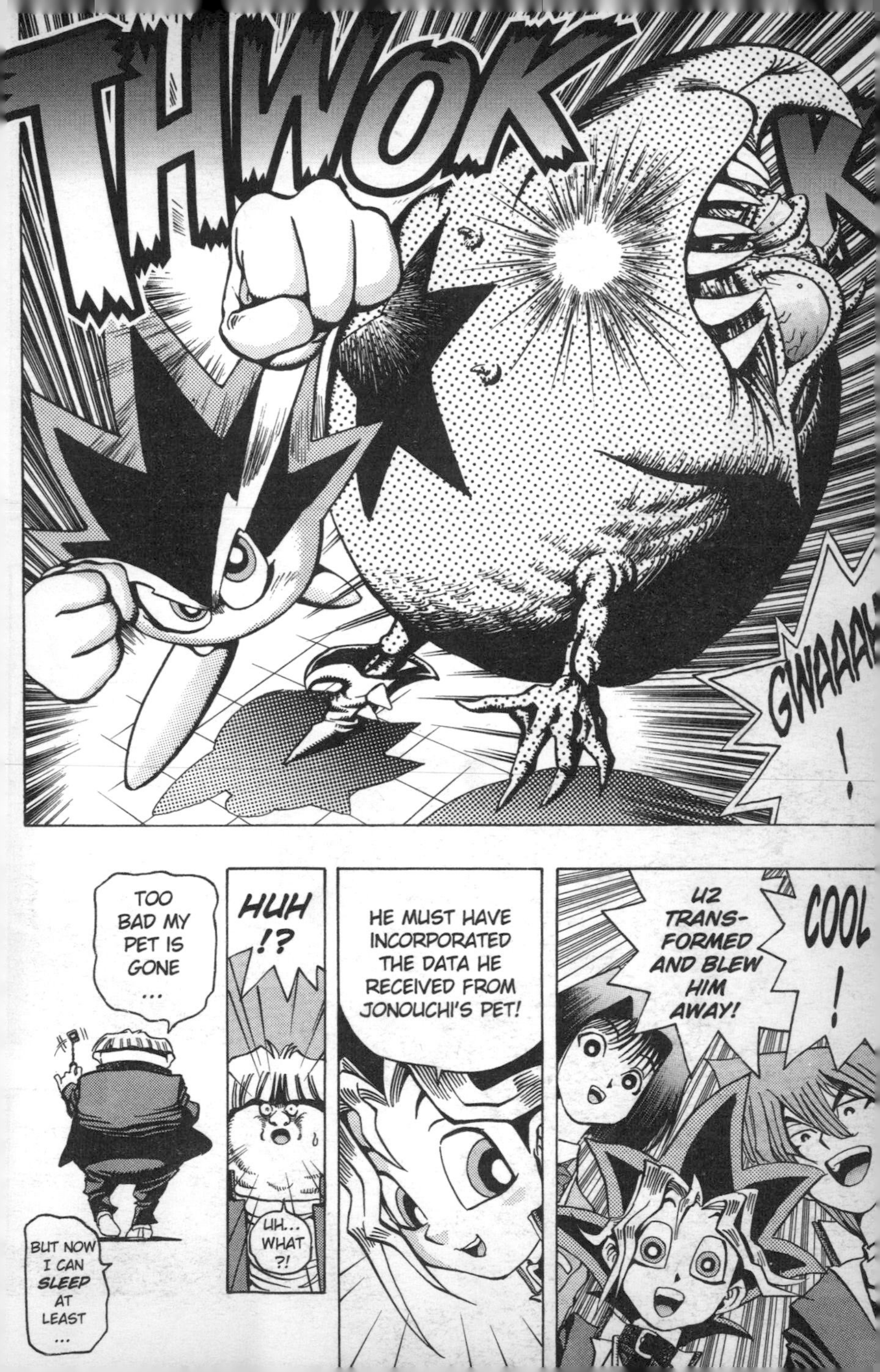
THWOK
GWAAA
!
COOL
!
U2 TRANS-FORMED AND BLEW HIM AWAY!
HE MUST HAVE INCORPORATED THE DATA HE RECEIVED FROM JONOUCHI'S PET!
HUH !?
UH... WHAT ?!
TOO BAD MY PET IS GONE ...
BUT NOW I CAN SLEEP AT LEAST ...

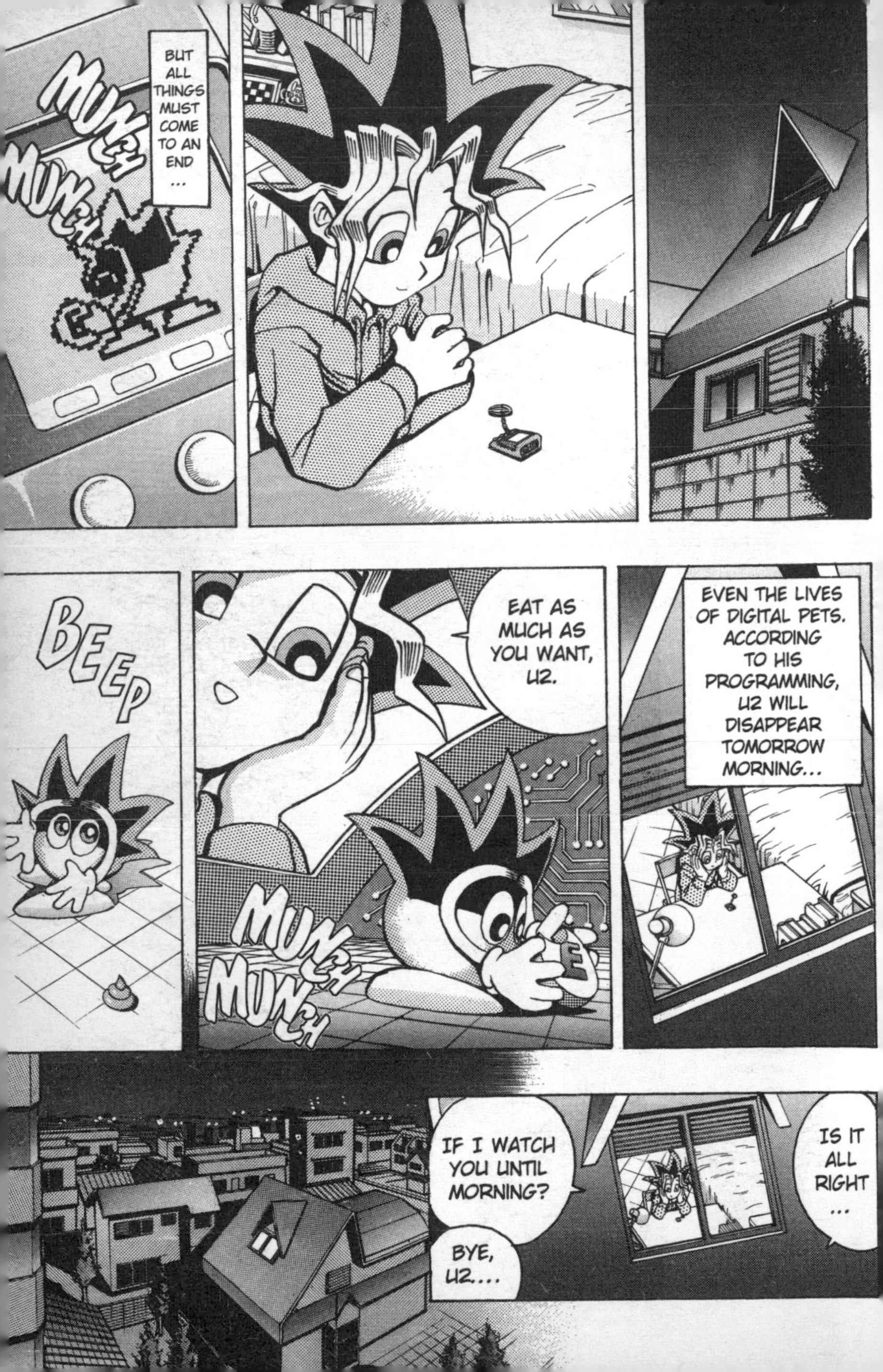
BUT ALL THINGS MUST COME TO AN END ...
MUNCH MUNCH
EVEN THE LIVES OF DIGITAL PETS. ACCORDING TO HIS PROGRAMMING, U2 WILL DISAPPEAR TOMORROW MORNING...
EAT AS MUCH AS YOU WANT, U2.
MUNCH MUNCH
BEEP
IS IT ALL RIGHT ...
IF I WATCH YOU UNTIL MORNING?
BYE, U2...

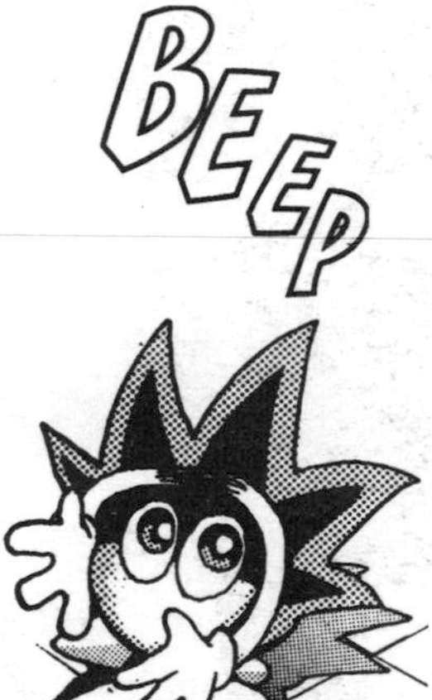
BEEP

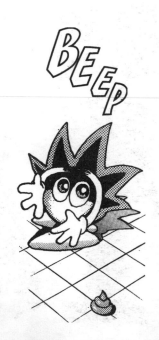

Duel 22:
American Hero
(Part 1)

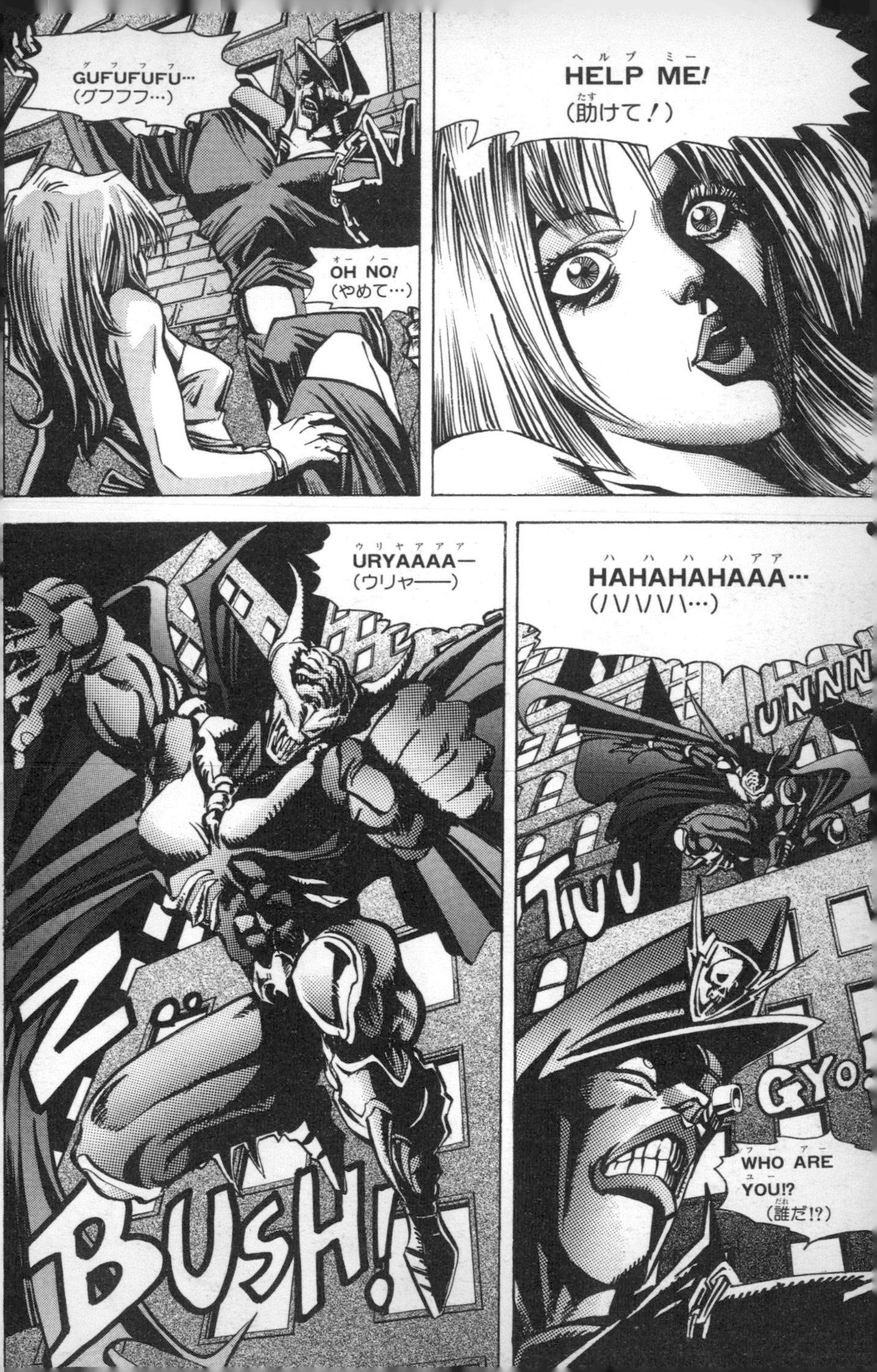
HELP ME!
(助けて!)
GUFUFUFU…
(グフフフ…)
OH NO!
(やめて…)
HAHAHAHAAA…
(ハハハハ…)
UNNN
TUU
GYO
WHO ARE YOU!?
(誰だ!?)
URYAAAA—
(ウリャ——)
BUSH!

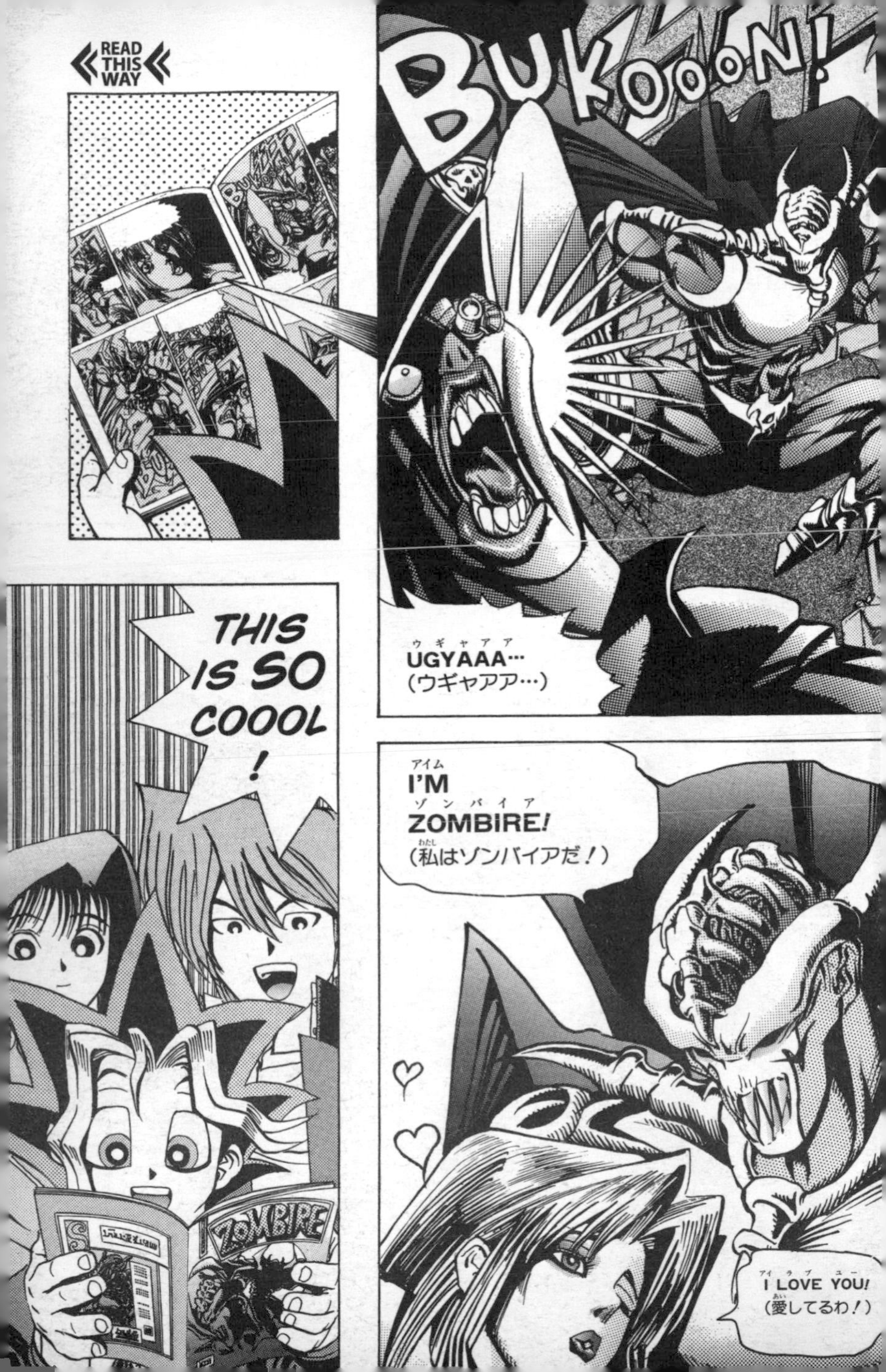
READ THIS WAY
BUKOOON!
UGYAAA…
(ウギャアア…)
I'M ZOMBIRE!
(私はゾンバイアだ！)
I LOVE YOU!
(愛してるわ！)
THIS IS SO COOOL!
ZOMBIRE

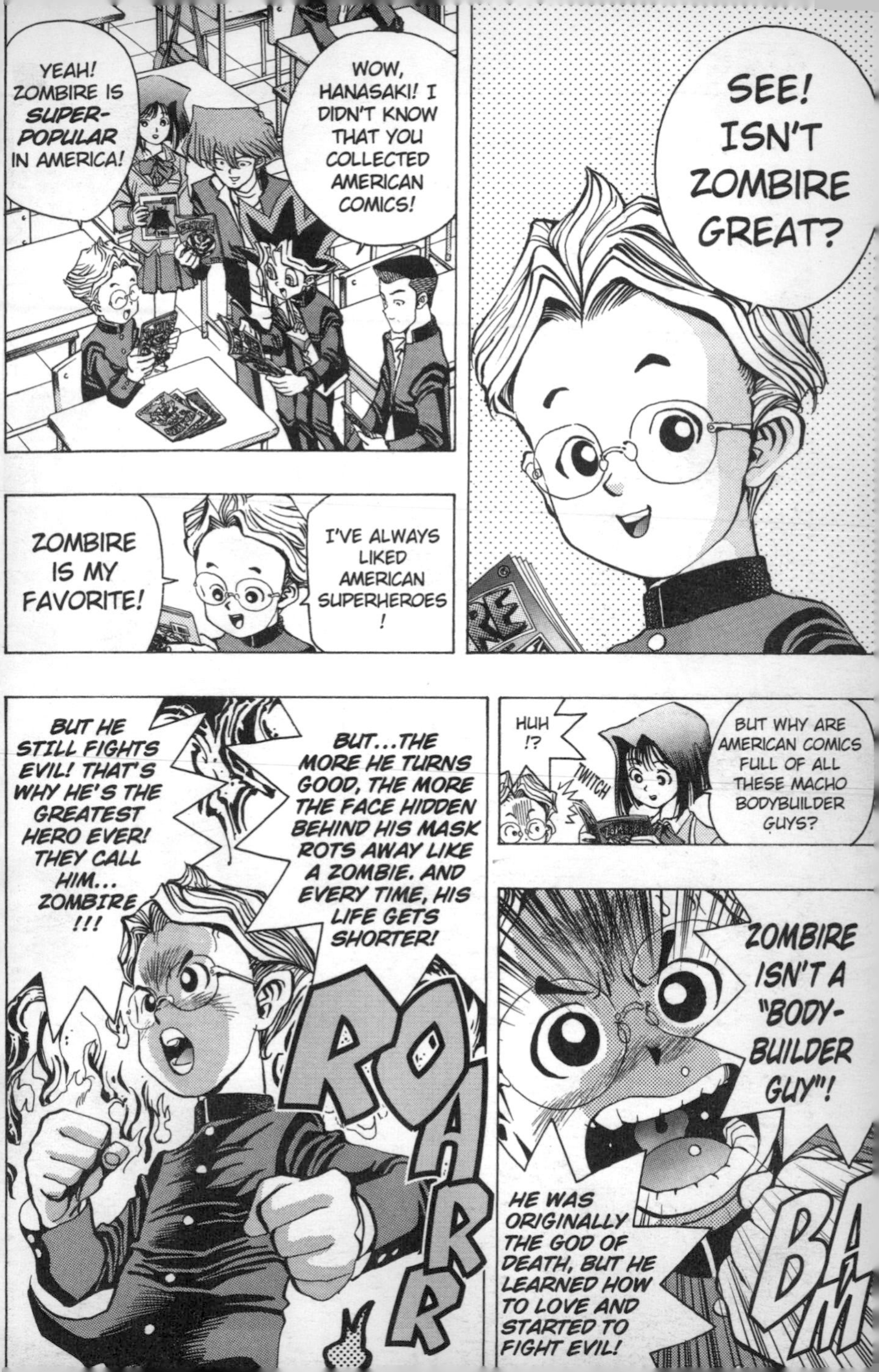
SEE! ISN'T ZOMBIRE GREAT?
WOW, HANASAKI! I DIDN'T KNOW THAT YOU COLLECTED AMERICAN COMICS!
YEAH! ZOMBIRE IS SUPER-POPULAR IN AMERICA!
I'VE ALWAYS LIKED AMERICAN SUPERHEROES!
ZOMBIRE IS MY FAVORITE!
BUT WHY ARE AMERICAN COMICS FULL OF ALL THESE MACHO BODYBUILDER GUYS?
HUH!?
TWITCH
ZOMBIRE ISN'T A "BODY-BUILDER GUY"!
HE WAS ORIGINALLY THE GOD OF DEATH, BUT HE LEARNED HOW TO LOVE AND STARTED TO FIGHT EVIL!
BAM
BUT...THE MORE HE TURNS GOOD, THE MORE THE FACE HIDDEN BEHIND HIS MASK ROTS AWAY LIKE A ZOMBIE. AND EVERY TIME, HIS LIFE GETS SHORTER!
BUT HE STILL FIGHTS EVIL! THAT'S WHY HE'S THE GREATEST HERO EVER! THEY CALL HIM... ZOMBIRE!!!
ROARRR

READ THIS WAY

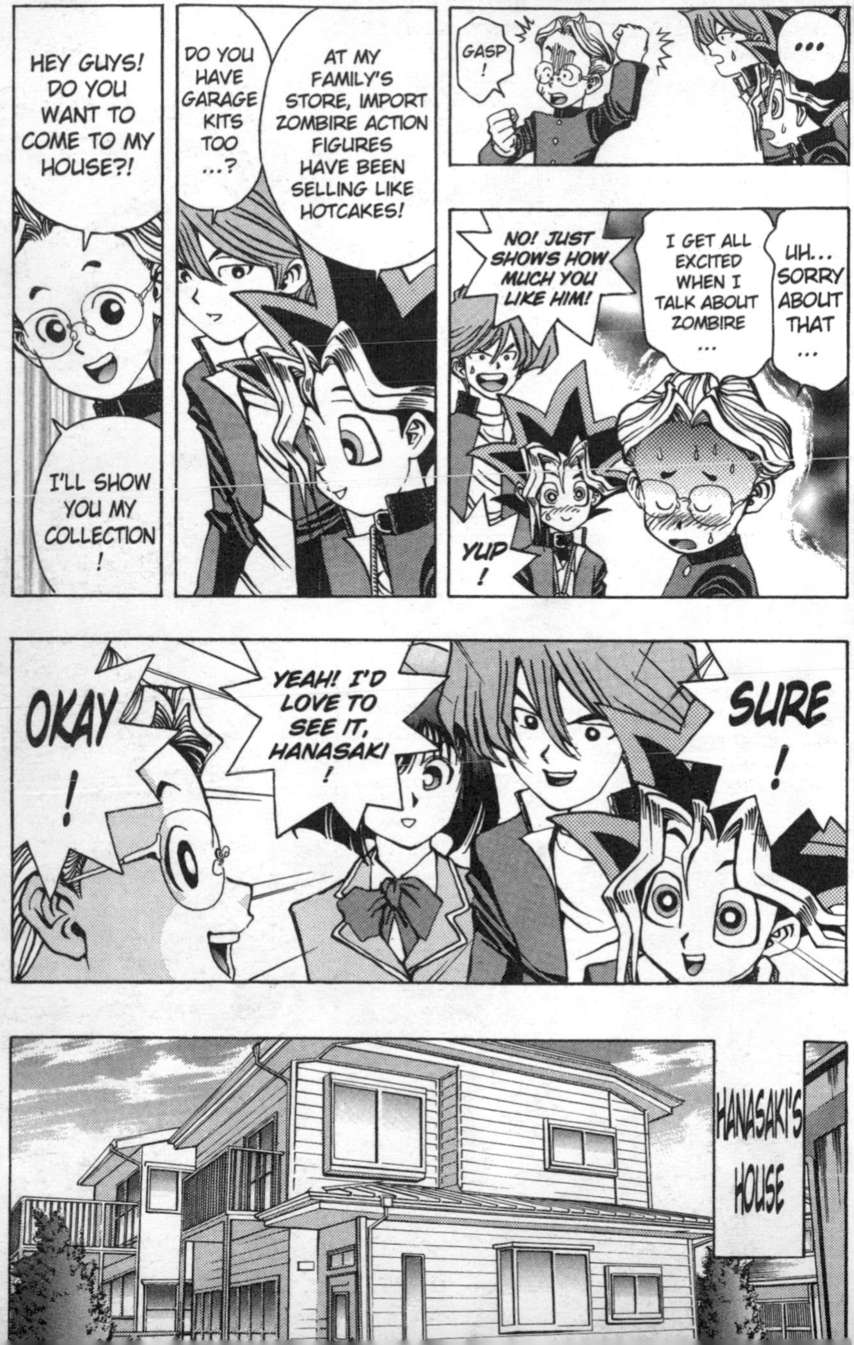
...
GASP!
UH... SORRY ABOUT THAT...
I GET ALL EXCITED WHEN I TALK ABOUT ZOMBIRE...
NO! JUST SHOWS HOW MUCH YOU LIKE HIM!
YUP!
AT MY FAMILY'S STORE, IMPORT ZOMBIRE ACTION FIGURES HAVE BEEN SELLING LIKE HOTCAKES!
DO YOU HAVE GARAGE KITS TOO...?
HEY GUYS! DO YOU WANT TO COME TO MY HOUSE?!
I'LL SHOW YOU MY COLLECTION!
SURE!
YEAH! I'D LOVE TO SEE IT, HANASAKI!
OKAY!
HANASAKI'S HOUSE

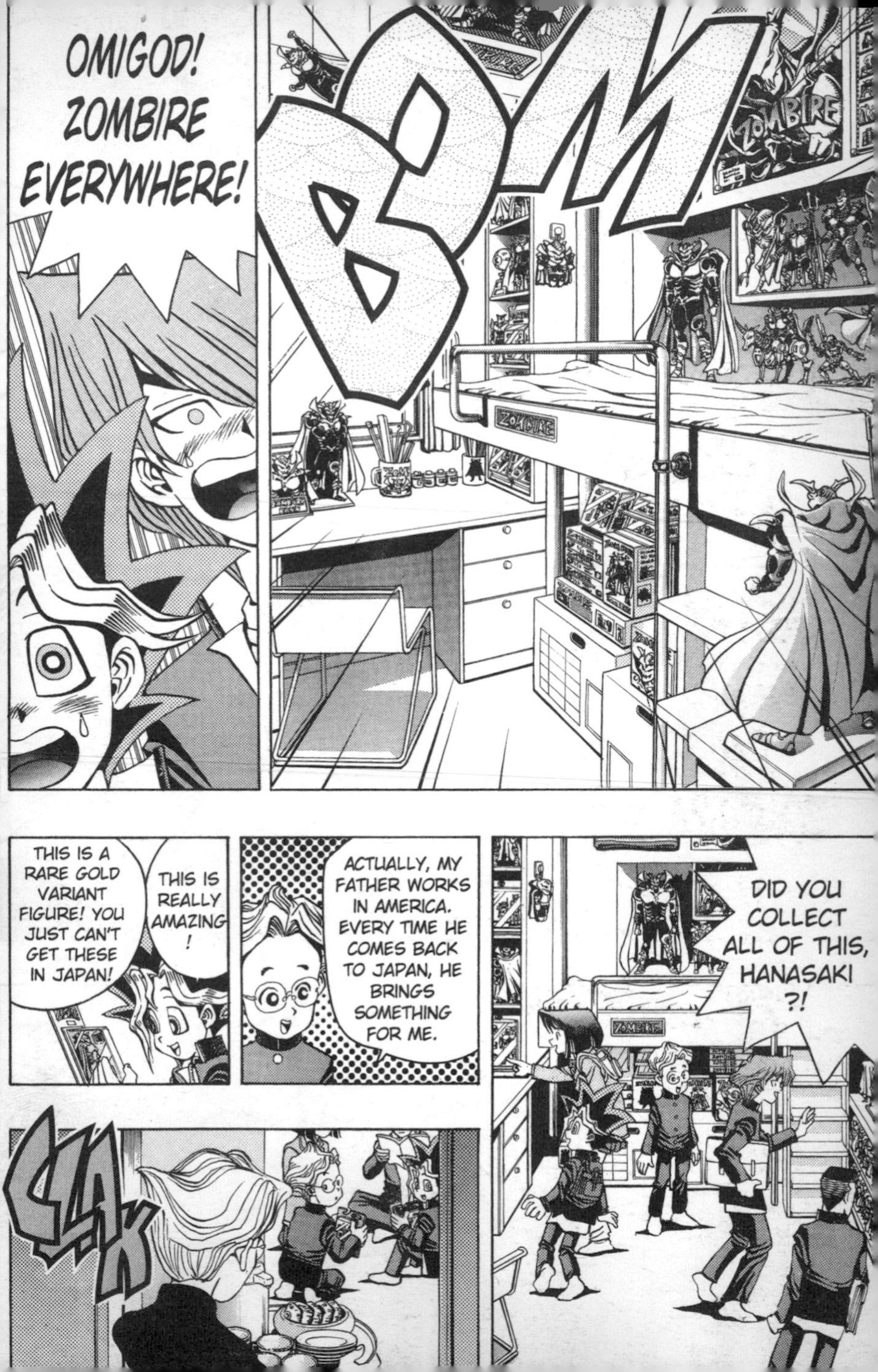
BOOM
OMIGOD! ZOMBIRE EVERYWHERE!
ZOMBIRE
DID YOU COLLECT ALL OF THIS, HANASAKI ?!
ACTUALLY, MY FATHER WORKS IN AMERICA. EVERY TIME HE COMES BACK TO JAPAN, HE BRINGS SOMETHING FOR ME.
THIS IS REALLY AMAZING!
THIS IS A RARE GOLD VARIANT FIGURE! YOU JUST CAN'T GET THESE IN JAPAN!
CLAK

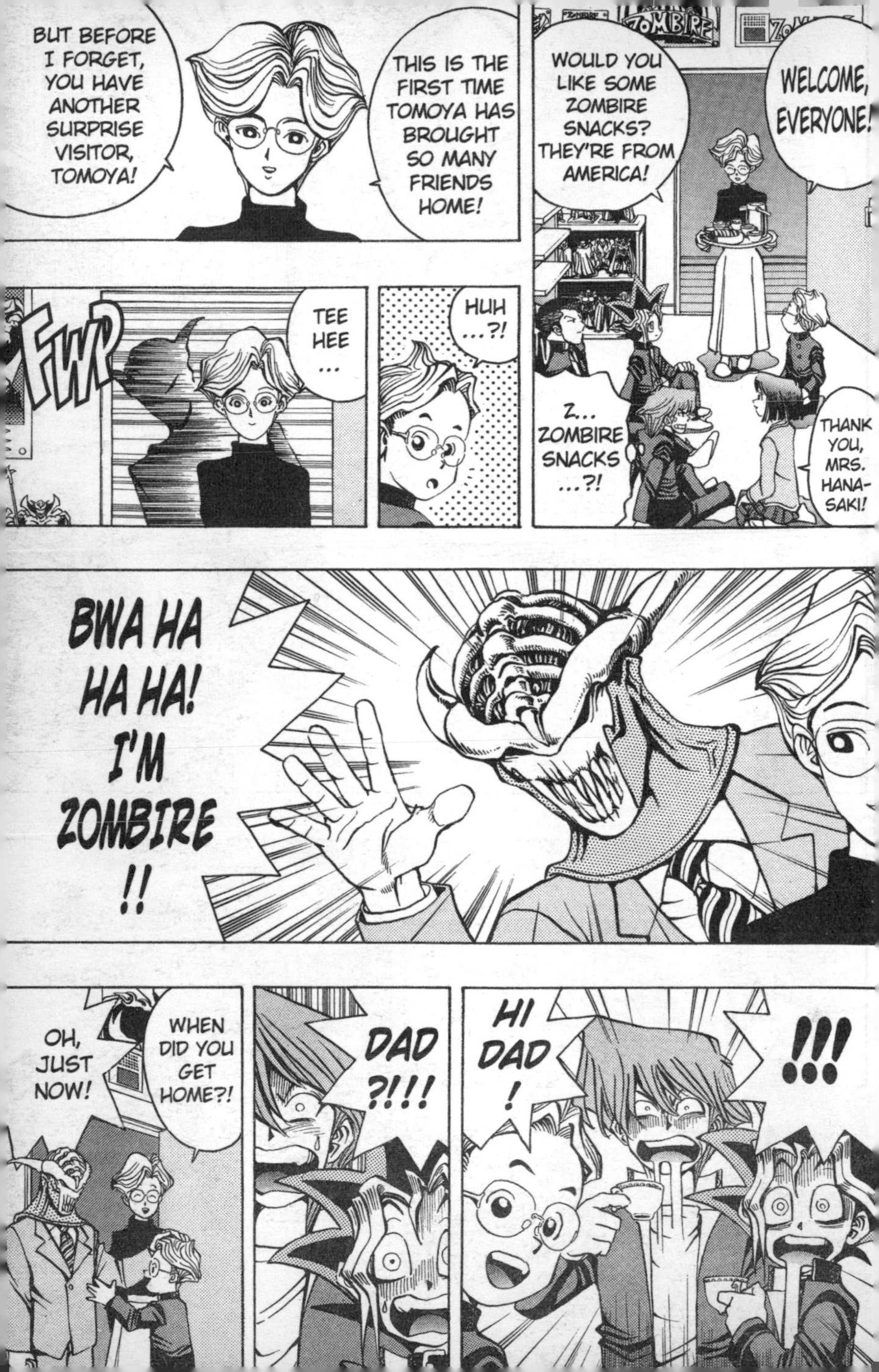
ZOMBIRE
WELCOME, EVERYONE!
WOULD YOU LIKE SOME ZOMBIRE SNACKS? THEY'RE FROM AMERICA!
THANK YOU, MRS. HANA-SAKI!
Z... ZOMBIRE SNACKS ...?!
THIS IS THE FIRST TIME TOMOYA HAS BROUGHT SO MANY FRIENDS HOME!
BUT BEFORE I FORGET, YOU HAVE ANOTHER SURPRISE VISITOR, TOMOYA!
HUH ...?!
TEE HEE ...
FWP
BWA HA HA HA! I'M ZOMBIRE !!
!!!
HI DAD !
DAD ?!!!
WHEN DID YOU GET HOME?!
OH, JUST NOW!

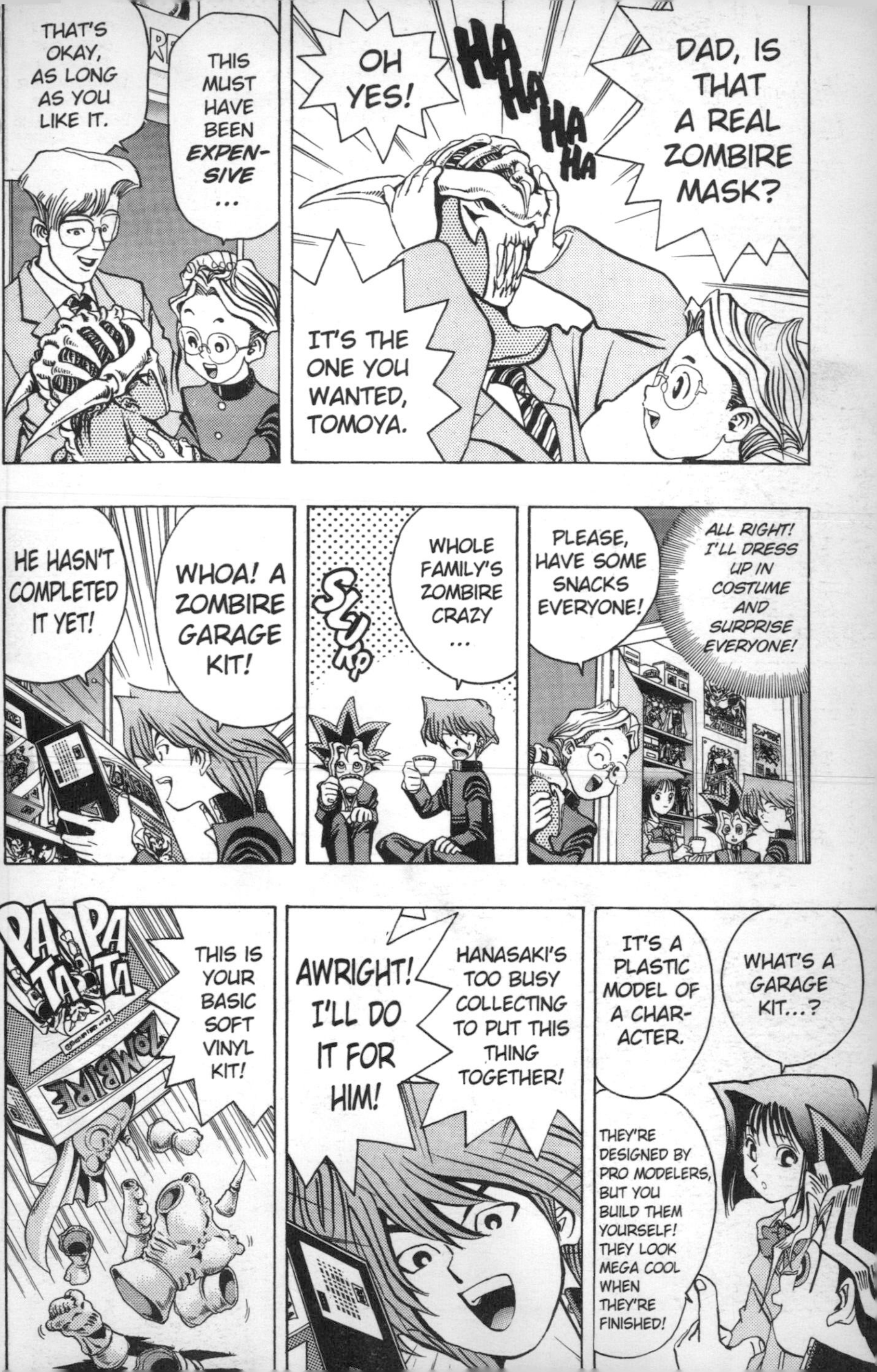
DAD, IS THAT A REAL ZOMBIRE MASK?
HA HA HA HA
OH YES!
IT'S THE ONE YOU WANTED, TOMOYA.
THIS MUST HAVE BEEN EXPENSIVE...
THAT'S OKAY, AS LONG AS YOU LIKE IT.
ALL RIGHT! I'LL DRESS UP IN COSTUME AND SURPRISE EVERYONE!
PLEASE, HAVE SOME SNACKS EVERYONE!
WHOLE FAMILY'S ZOMBIRE CRAZY...
SLURP
WHOA! A ZOMBIRE GARAGE KIT!
HE HASN'T COMPLETED IT YET!
WHAT'S A GARAGE KIT...?
IT'S A PLASTIC MODEL OF A CHARACTER.
THEY'RE DESIGNED BY PRO MODELERS, BUT YOU BUILD THEM YOURSELF! THEY LOOK MEGA COOL WHEN THEY'RE FINISHED!
HANASAKI'S TOO BUSY COLLECTING TO PUT THIS THING TOGETHER!
AWRIGHT! I'LL DO IT FOR HIM!
PA PA TA TA
THIS IS YOUR BASIC SOFT VINYL KIT!

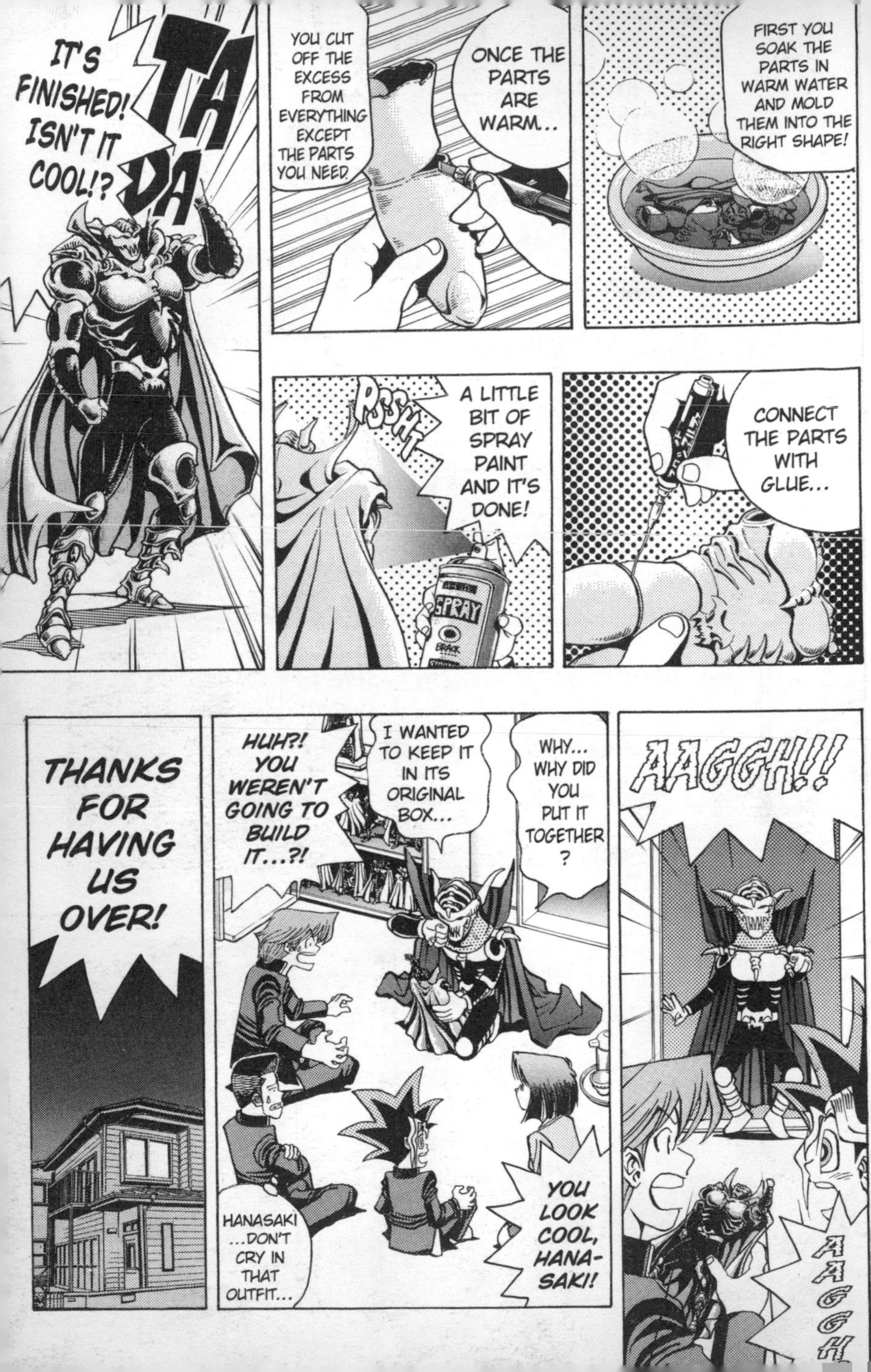
FIRST YOU SOAK THE PARTS IN WARM WATER AND MOLD THEM INTO THE RIGHT SHAPE!
ONCE THE PARTS ARE WARM...
YOU CUT OFF THE EXCESS FROM EVERYTHING EXCEPT THE PARTS YOU NEED.
CONNECT THE PARTS WITH GLUE...
PSSHT
A LITTLE BIT OF SPRAY PAINT AND IT'S DONE!
SPRAY
TA DA
IT'S FINISHED! ISN'T IT COOL!?
AAGGH!!
AAAGGGH
WHY... WHY DID YOU PUT IT TOGETHER?
I WANTED TO KEEP IT IN ITS ORIGINAL BOX...
HUH?! YOU WEREN'T GOING TO BUILD IT...?!
YOU LOOK COOL, HANA-SAKI!
HANASAKI ...DON'T CRY IN THAT OUTFIT...
THANKS FOR HAVING US OVER!

READ THIS WAY

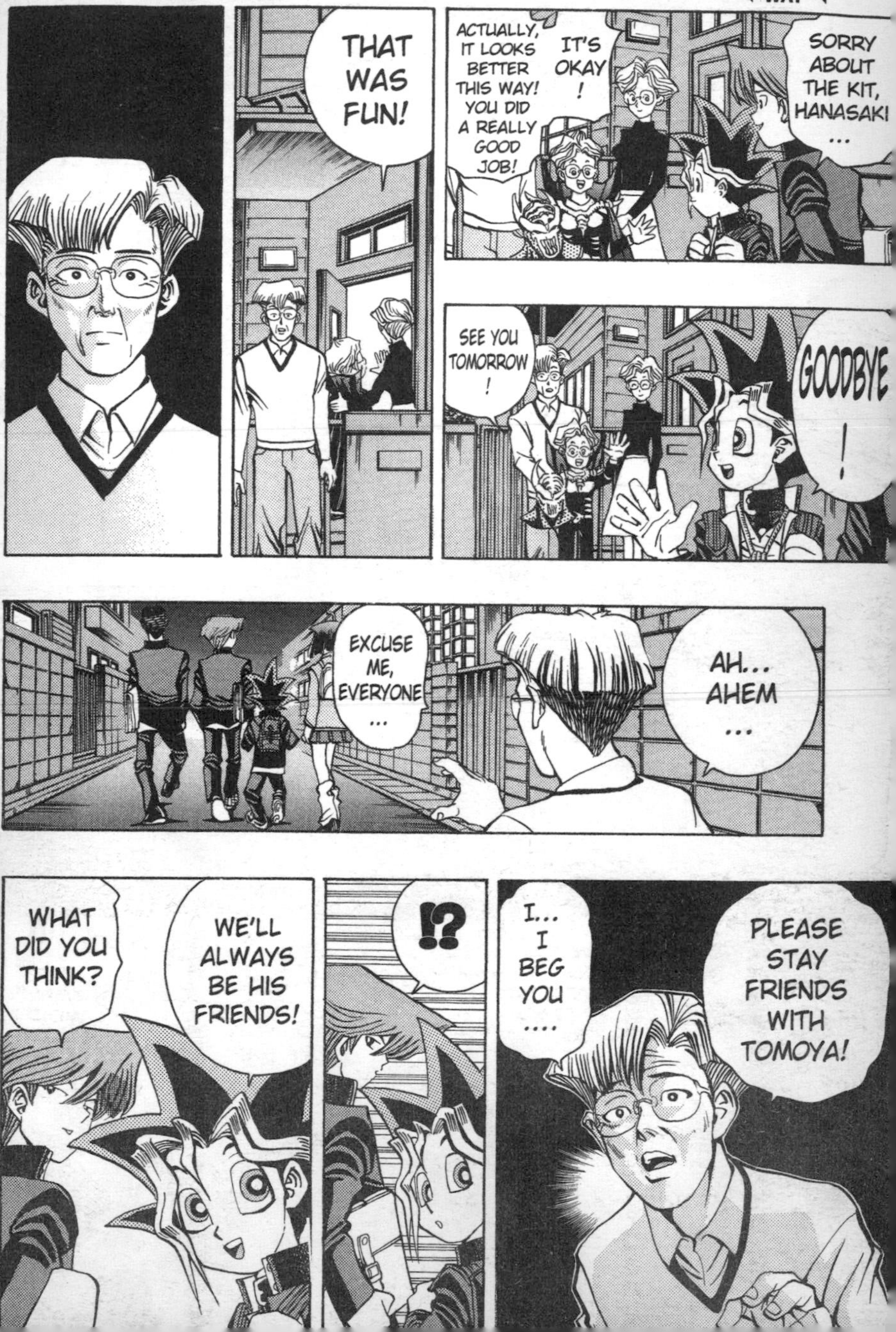

SORRY ABOUT THE KIT, HANASAKI...
IT'S OKAY!
ACTUALLY, IT LOOKS BETTER THIS WAY! YOU DID A REALLY GOOD JOB!
GOODBYE!
SEE YOU TOMORROW!
THAT WAS FUN!
AH... AHEM...
EXCUSE ME, EVERYONE...
PLEASE STAY FRIENDS WITH TOMOYA!
I... I BEG YOU....
!?
WE'LL ALWAYS BE HIS FRIENDS!
WHAT DID YOU THINK?

READ THIS WAY

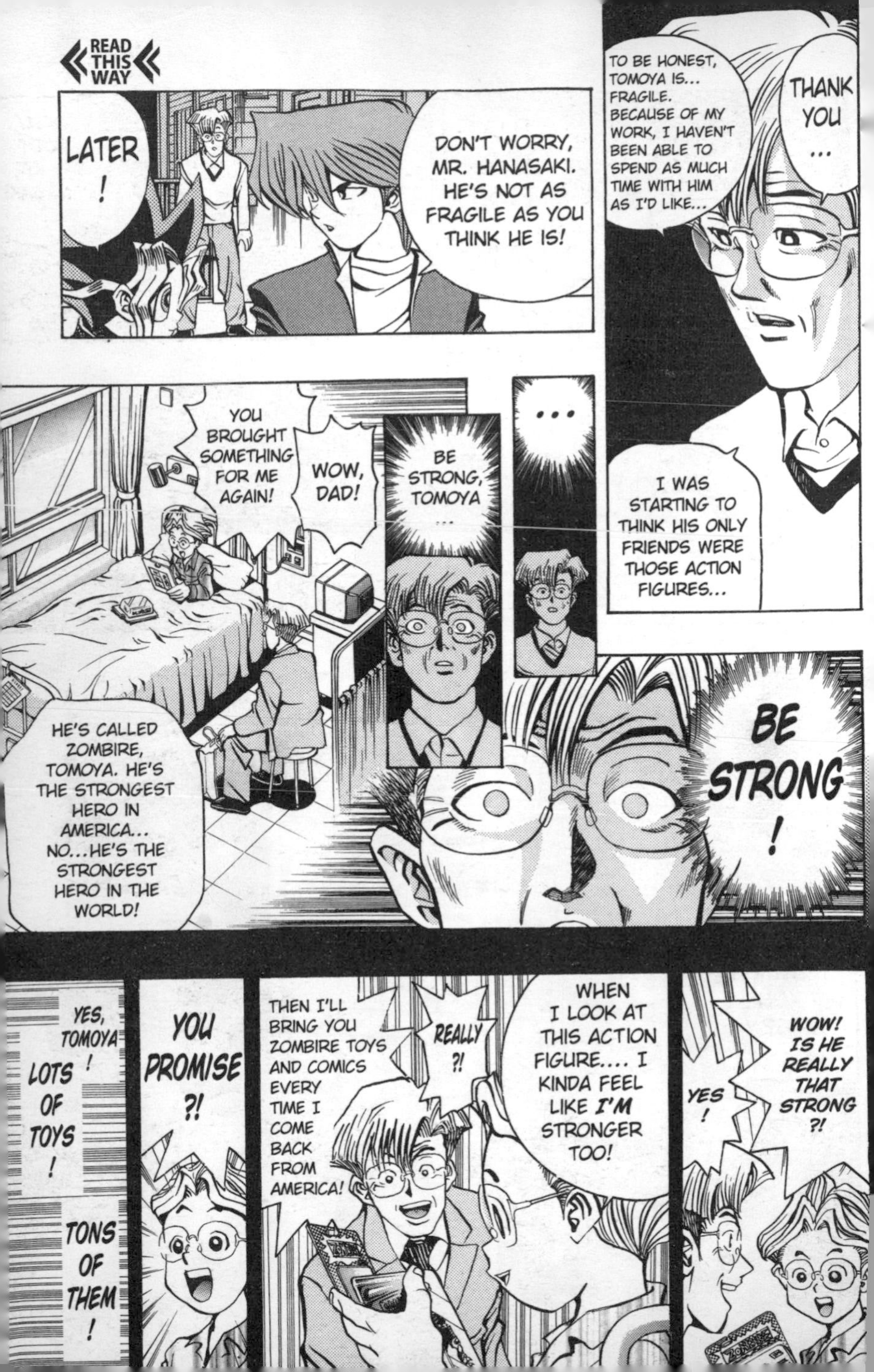
THANK YOU ...
TO BE HONEST, TOMOYA IS... FRAGILE. BECAUSE OF MY WORK, I HAVEN'T BEEN ABLE TO SPEND AS MUCH TIME WITH HIM AS I'D LIKE...
I WAS STARTING TO THINK HIS ONLY FRIENDS WERE THOSE ACTION FIGURES...
DON'T WORRY, MR. HANASAKI. HE'S NOT AS FRAGILE AS YOU THINK HE IS!
LATER!
...
BE STRONG, TOMOYA ...
BE STRONG!
WOW, DAD!
YOU BROUGHT SOMETHING FOR ME AGAIN!
HE'S CALLED ZOMBIRE, TOMOYA. HE'S THE STRONGEST HERO IN AMERICA... NO...HE'S THE STRONGEST HERO IN THE WORLD!
WOW! IS HE REALLY THAT STRONG?!
YES!
WHEN I LOOK AT THIS ACTION FIGURE.... I KINDA FEEL LIKE *I'M* STRONGER TOO!
REALLY?!
THEN I'LL BRING YOU ZOMBIRE TOYS AND COMICS EVERY TIME I COME BACK FROM AMERICA!
YOU PROMISE?!
YES, TOMOYA!
LOTS OF TOYS!
TONS OF THEM!

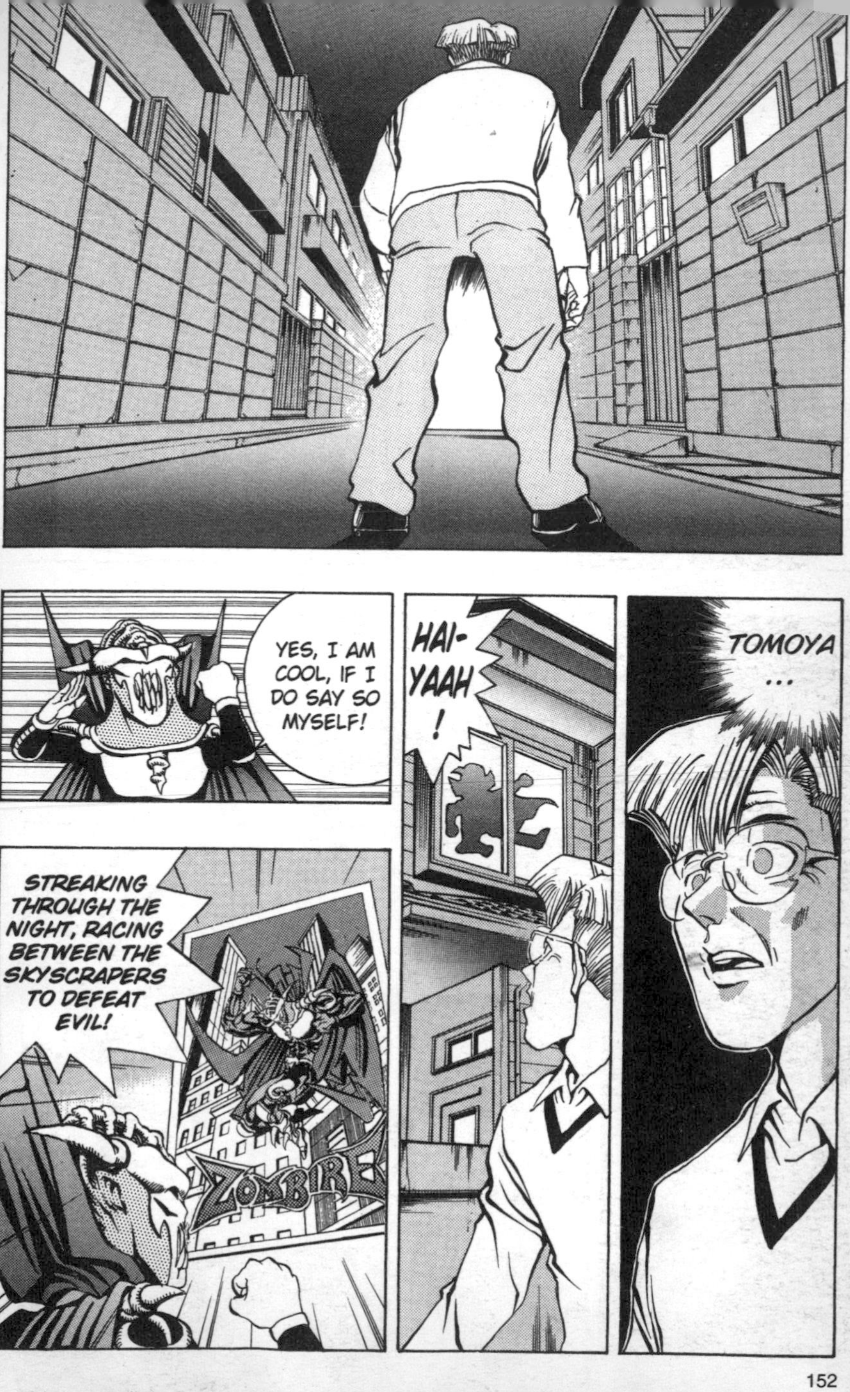
TOMOYA ...
HAI-YAAH!
YES, I AM COOL, IF I DO SAY SO MYSELF!
STREAKING THROUGH THE NIGHT, RACING BETWEEN THE SKYSCRAPERS TO DEFEAT EVIL!
ZOMBIRE

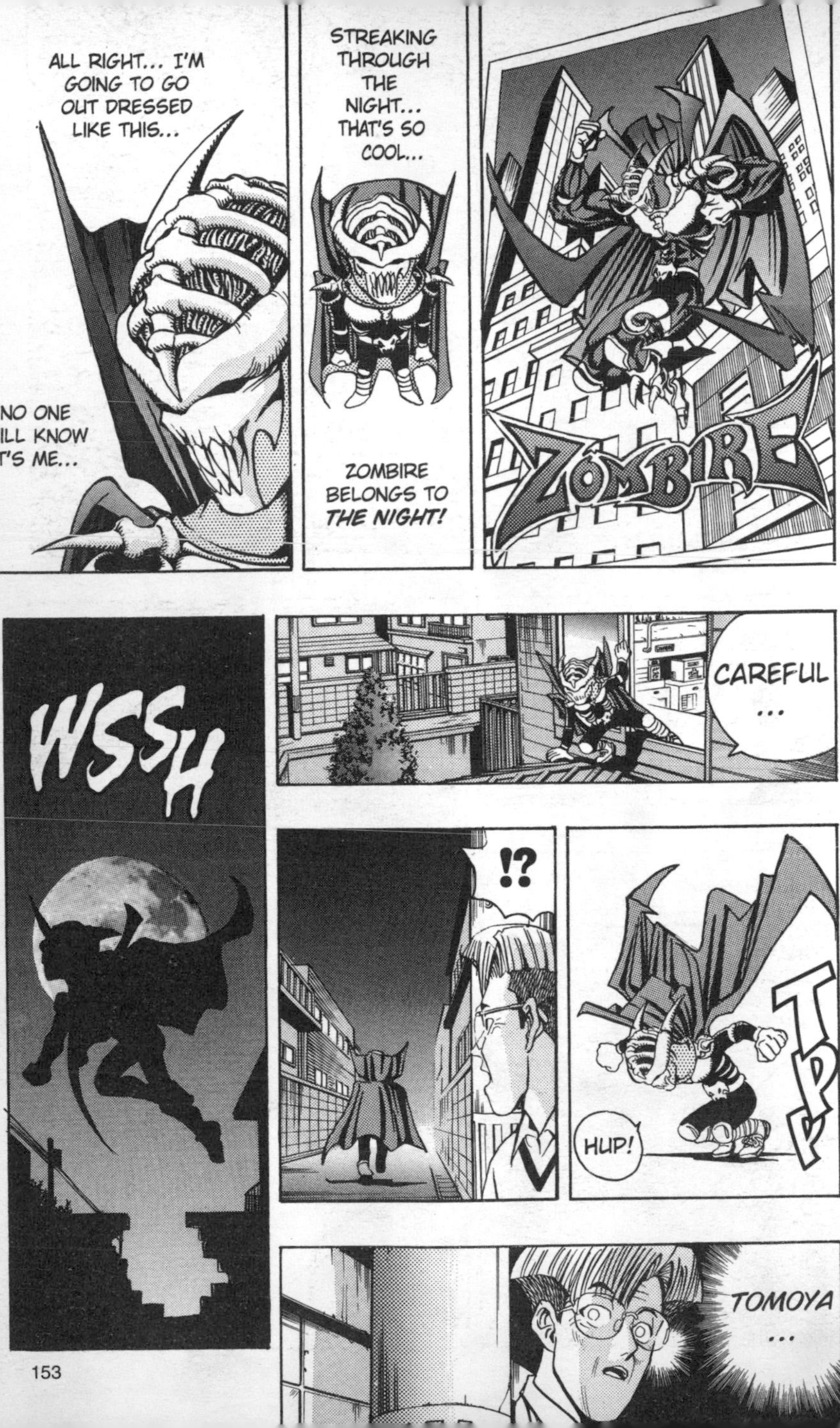
ZOMBIRE
STREAKING THROUGH THE NIGHT... THAT'S SO COOL...
ZOMBIRE BELONGS TO *THE NIGHT!*
ALL RIGHT... I'M GOING TO GO OUT DRESSED LIKE THIS...
NO ONE WILL KNOW IT'S ME...
CAREFUL ...
TPP
HUP!
!?
TOMOYA ...
WSSH

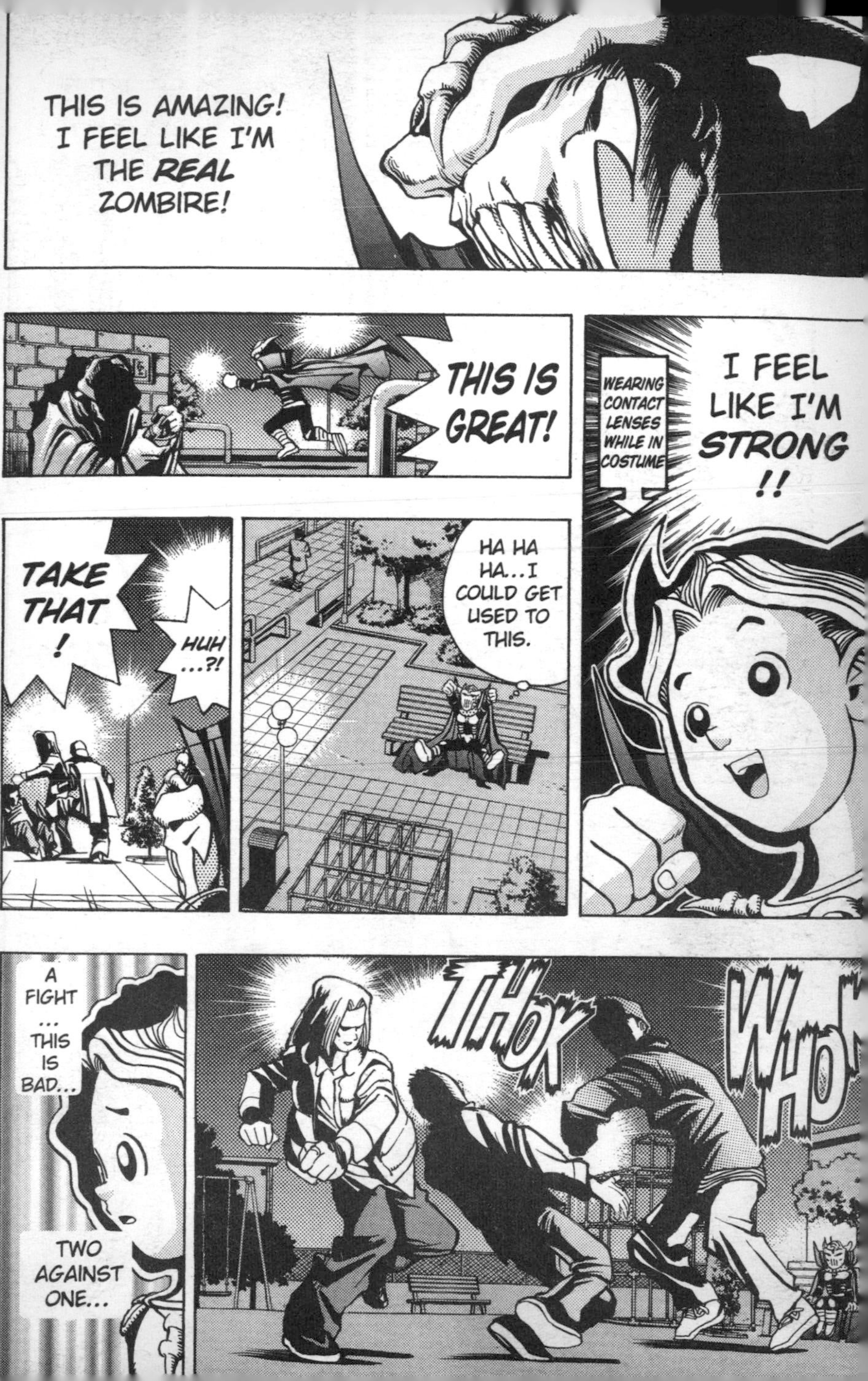
THIS IS AMAZING! I FEEL LIKE I'M THE *REAL* ZOMBIRE!
I FEEL LIKE I'M *STRONG* !!
WEARING CONTACT LENSES WHILE IN COSTUME
THIS IS GREAT!
HA HA HA...I COULD GET USED TO THIS.
TAKE THAT!
HUH...?!
A FIGHT... THIS IS BAD...
TWO AGAINST ONE...

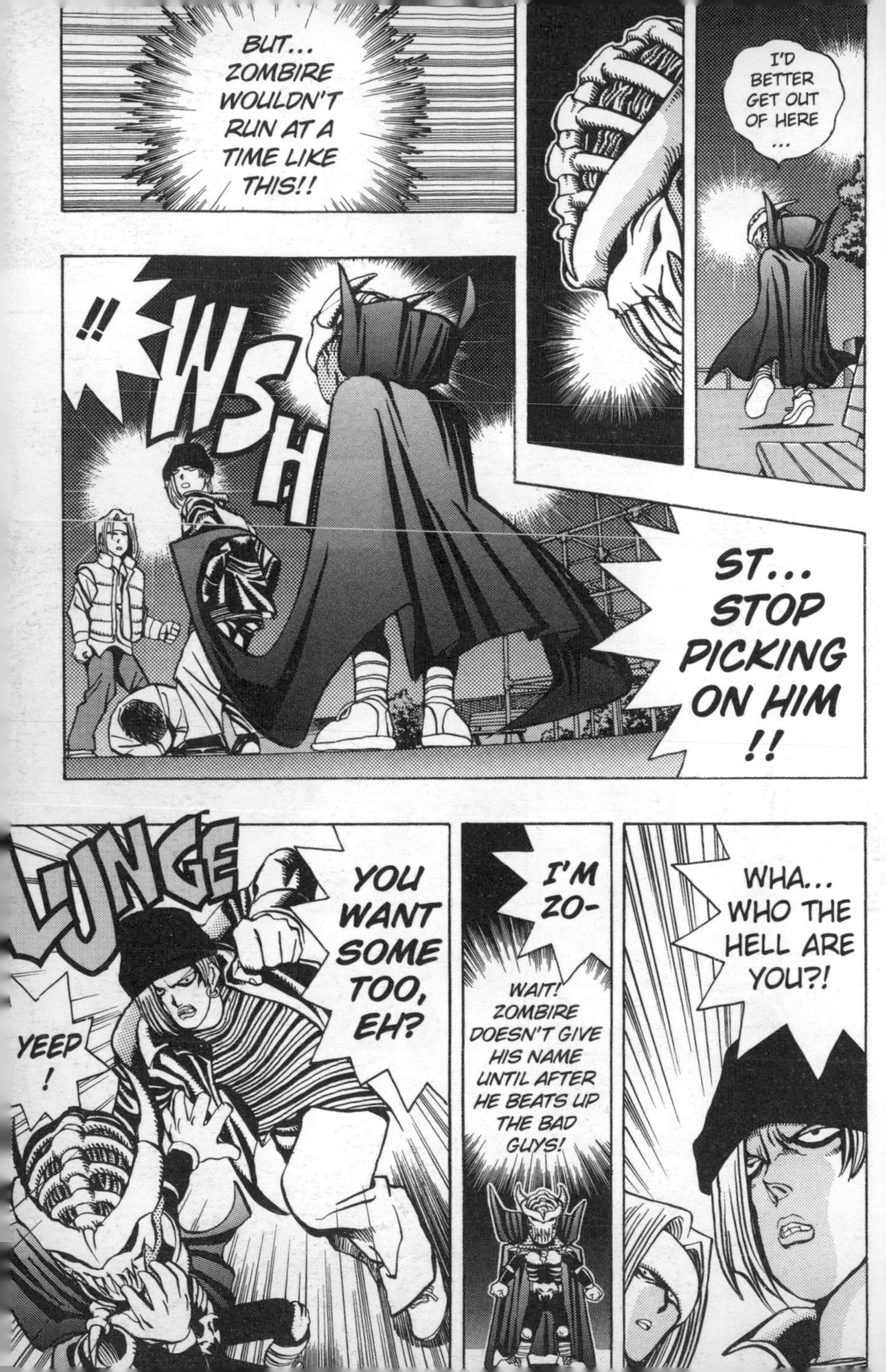
I'D BETTER GET OUT OF HERE ...
BUT... ZOMBIRE WOULDN'T RUN AT A TIME LIKE THIS!!
!!
WSH
ST... STOP PICKING ON HIM !!
WHA... WHO THE HELL ARE YOU?!
I'M ZO-
WAIT! ZOMBIRE DOESN'T GIVE HIS NAME UNTIL AFTER HE BEATS UP THE BAD GUYS!
LUNGE
YOU WANT SOME TOO, EH?
YEEP !

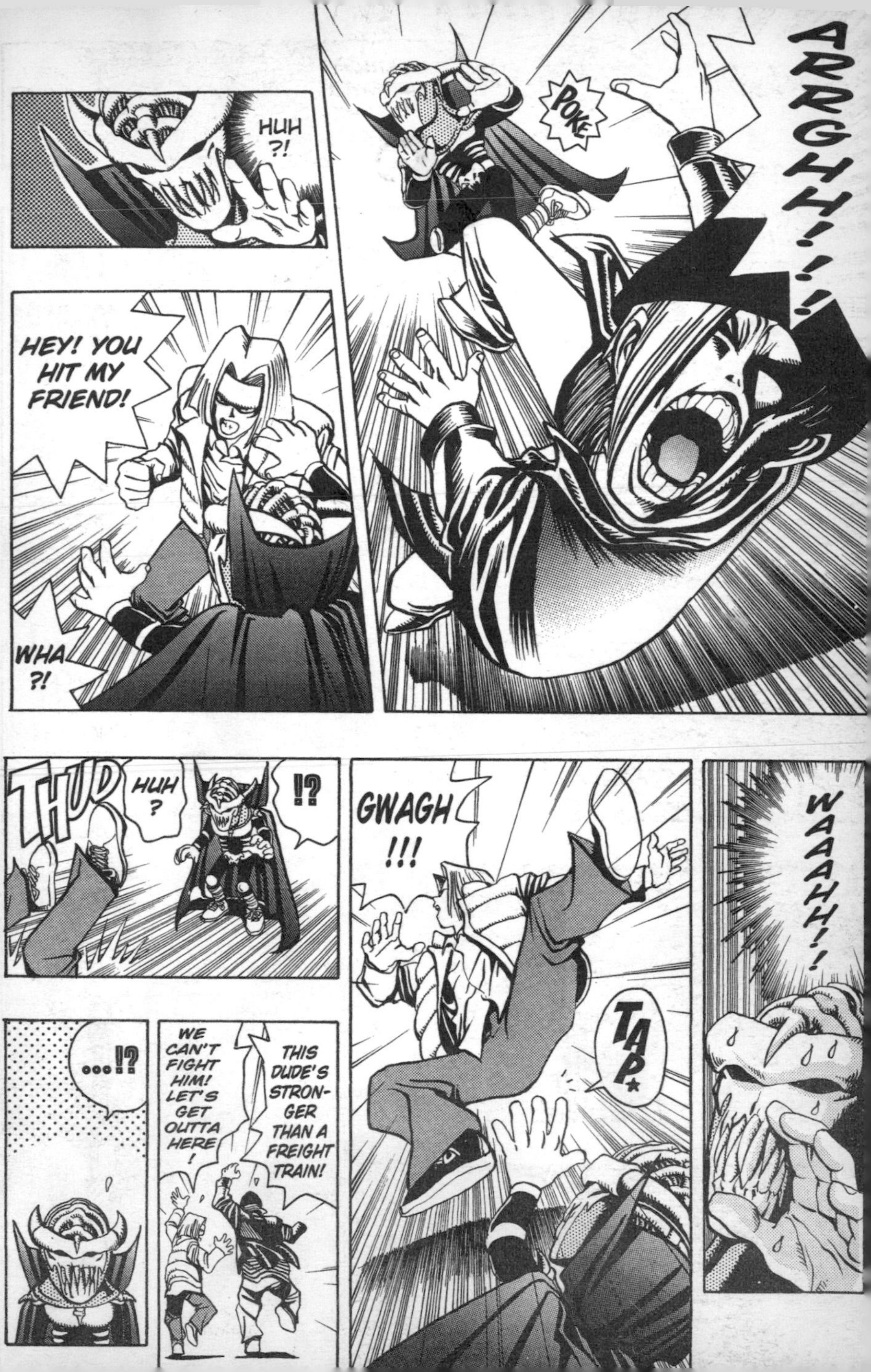
ARRGHH!!!!
POKE
HUH ?!
HEY! YOU HIT MY FRIEND!
WHA ?!
WAAAHH!!!
GWAGH !!!
TAP
!?
HUH ?
THUD
THIS DUDE'S STRONGER THAN A FREIGHT TRAIN!
WE CAN'T FIGHT HIM! LET'S GET OUTTA HERE!
...!?

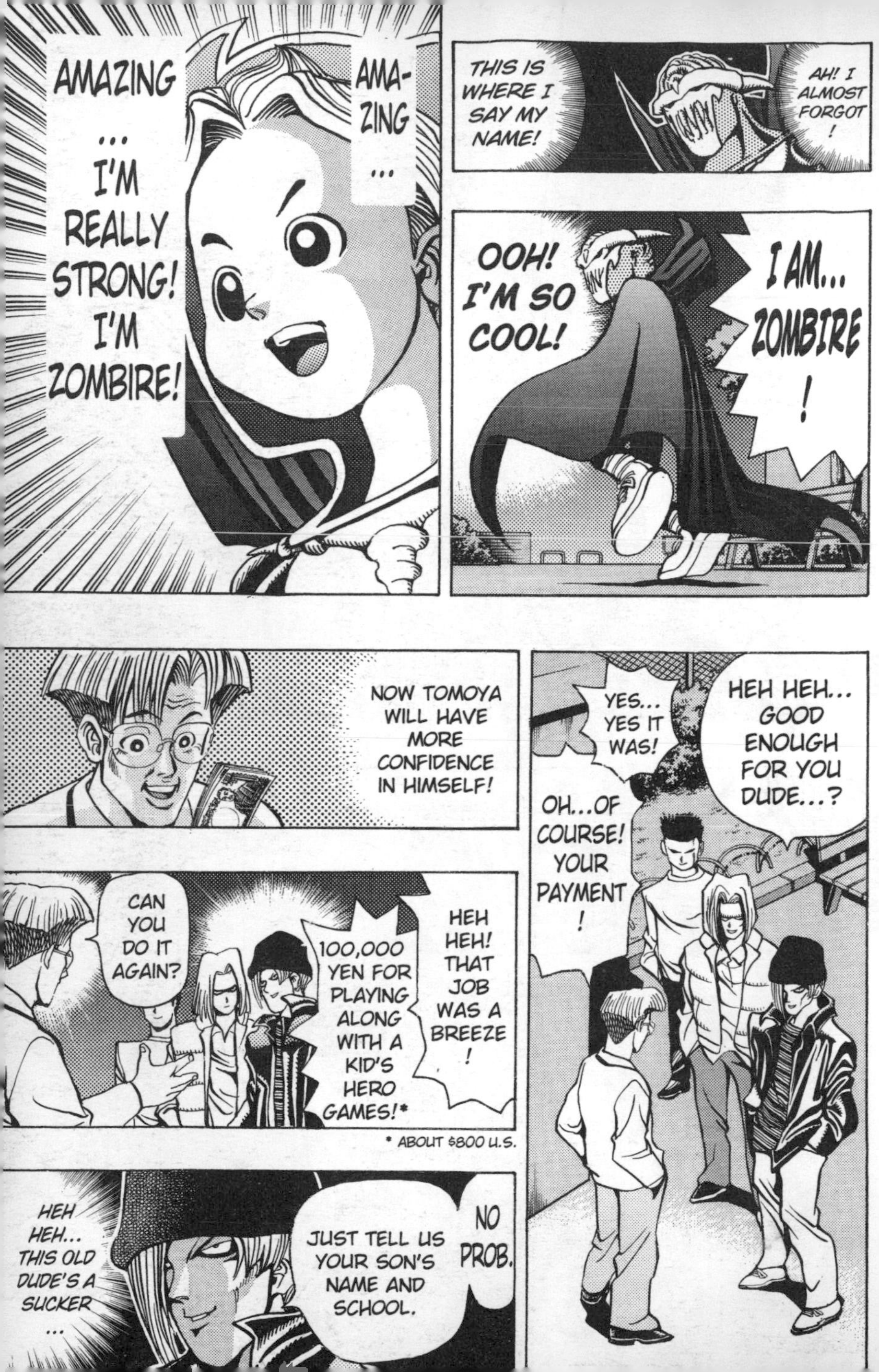
AH! I ALMOST FORGOT!
THIS IS WHERE I SAY MY NAME!
I AM... ZOMBIRE!
OOH! I'M SO COOL!
AMAZING...
AMAZING... I'M REALLY STRONG! I'M ZOMBIRE!
HEH HEH... GOOD ENOUGH FOR YOU DUDE...?
YES... YES IT WAS!
OH...OF COURSE! YOUR PAYMENT!
NOW TOMOYA WILL HAVE MORE CONFIDENCE IN HIMSELF!
HEH HEH! THAT JOB WAS A BREEZE!
100,000 YEN FOR PLAYING ALONG WITH A KID'S HERO GAMES!*
CAN YOU DO IT AGAIN?
* ABOUT $800 U.S.
NO PROB.
JUST TELL US YOUR SON'S NAME AND SCHOOL.
HEH HEH... THIS OLD DUDE'S A SUCKER...

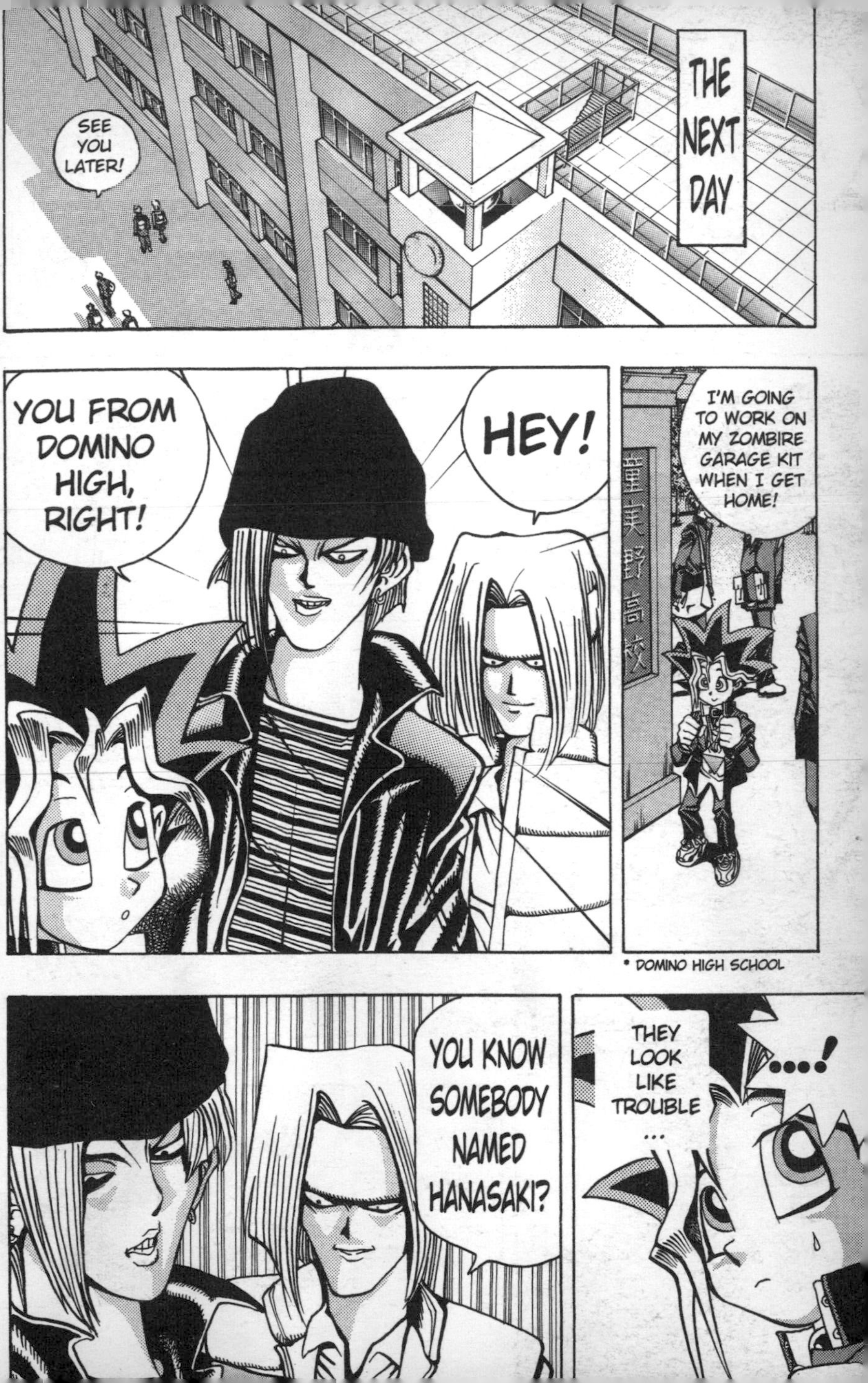
THE NEXT DAY
SEE YOU LATER!
I'M GOING TO WORK ON MY ZOMBIRE GARAGE KIT WHEN I GET HOME!
童実野高校
HEY!
YOU FROM DOMINO HIGH, RIGHT!
* DOMINO HIGH SCHOOL
...!
THEY LOOK LIKE TROUBLE ...
YOU KNOW SOMEBODY NAMED HANASAKI?

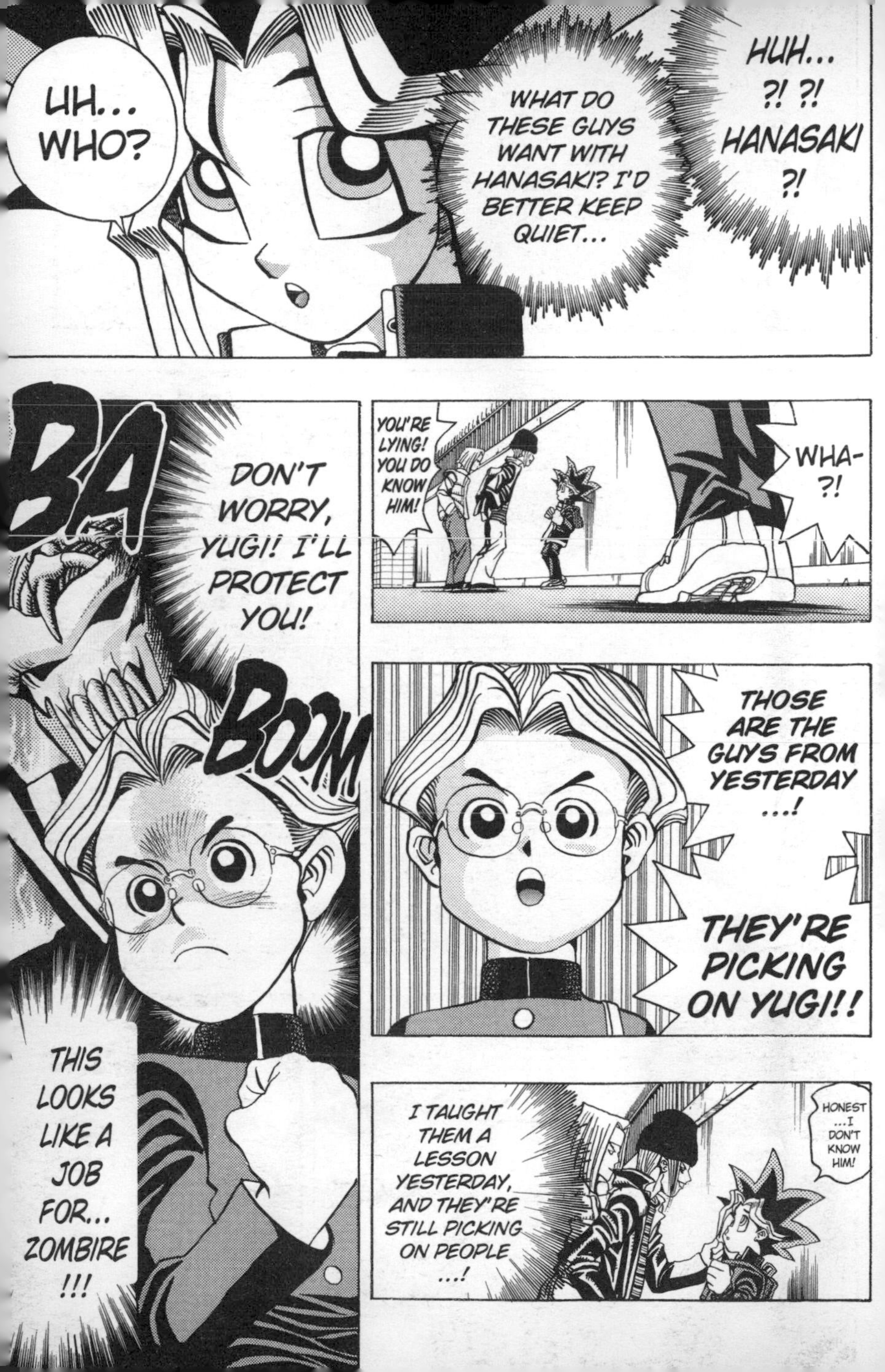
HUH... ?! ?! HANASAKI ?!
WHAT DO THESE GUYS WANT WITH HANASAKI? I'D BETTER KEEP QUIET...
UH... WHO?
YOU'RE LYING! YOU DO KNOW HIM!
WHA- ?!
THOSE ARE THE GUYS FROM YESTERDAY ...!
THEY'RE PICKING ON YUGI!!
HONEST ...I DON'T KNOW HIM!
I TAUGHT THEM A LESSON YESTERDAY, AND THEY'RE STILL PICKING ON PEOPLE ...!
BA
DON'T WORRY, YUGI! I'LL PROTECT YOU!
BOOM
THIS LOOKS LIKE A JOB FOR... ZOMBIRE !!!

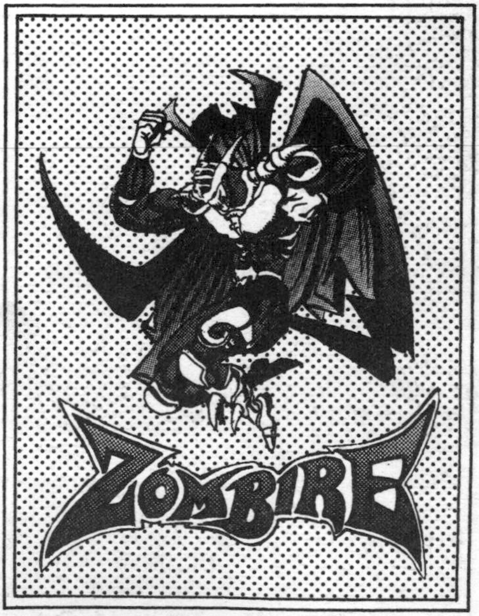
ZOMBIRE

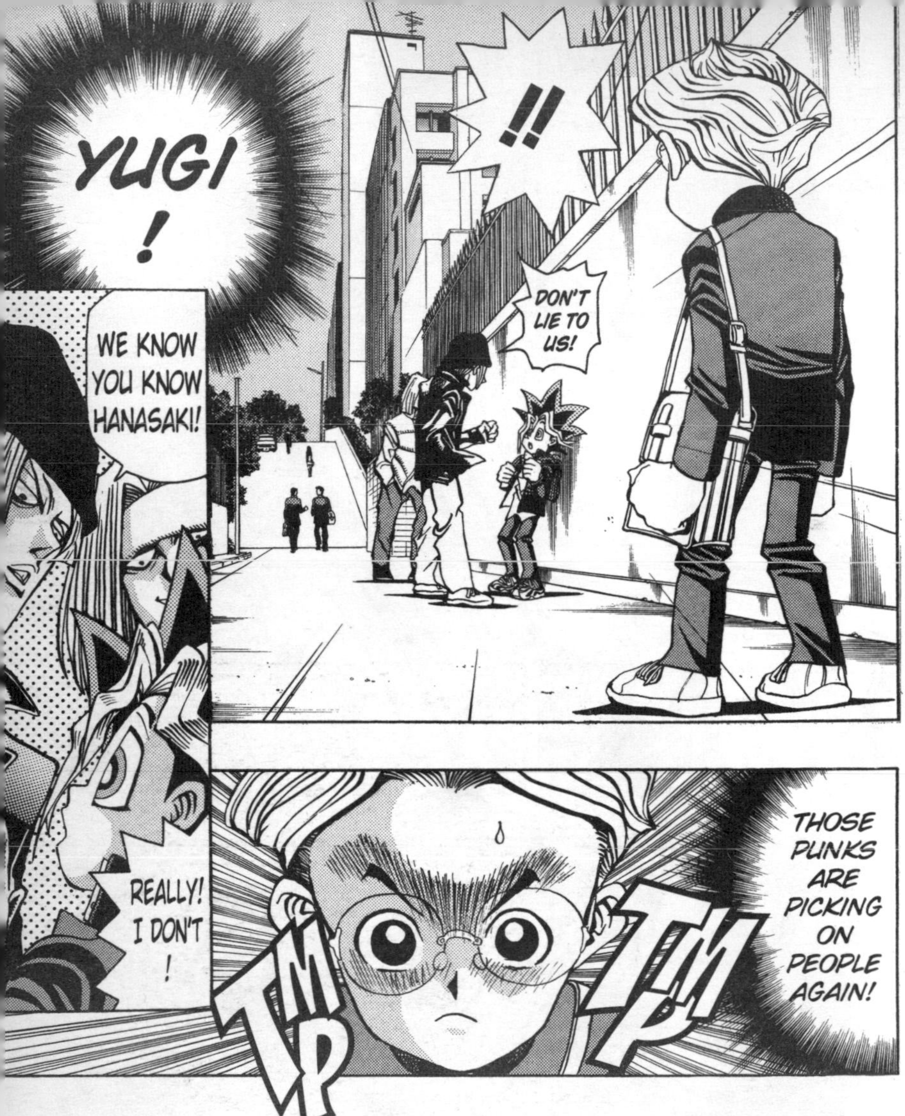
!!
DON'T LIE TO US!
TMP
TMP
THOSE PUNKS ARE PICKING ON PEOPLE AGAIN!
YUGI!
WE KNOW YOU KNOW HANASAKI!
REALLY! I DON'T!

Duel 23:
American Hero (Part 2)

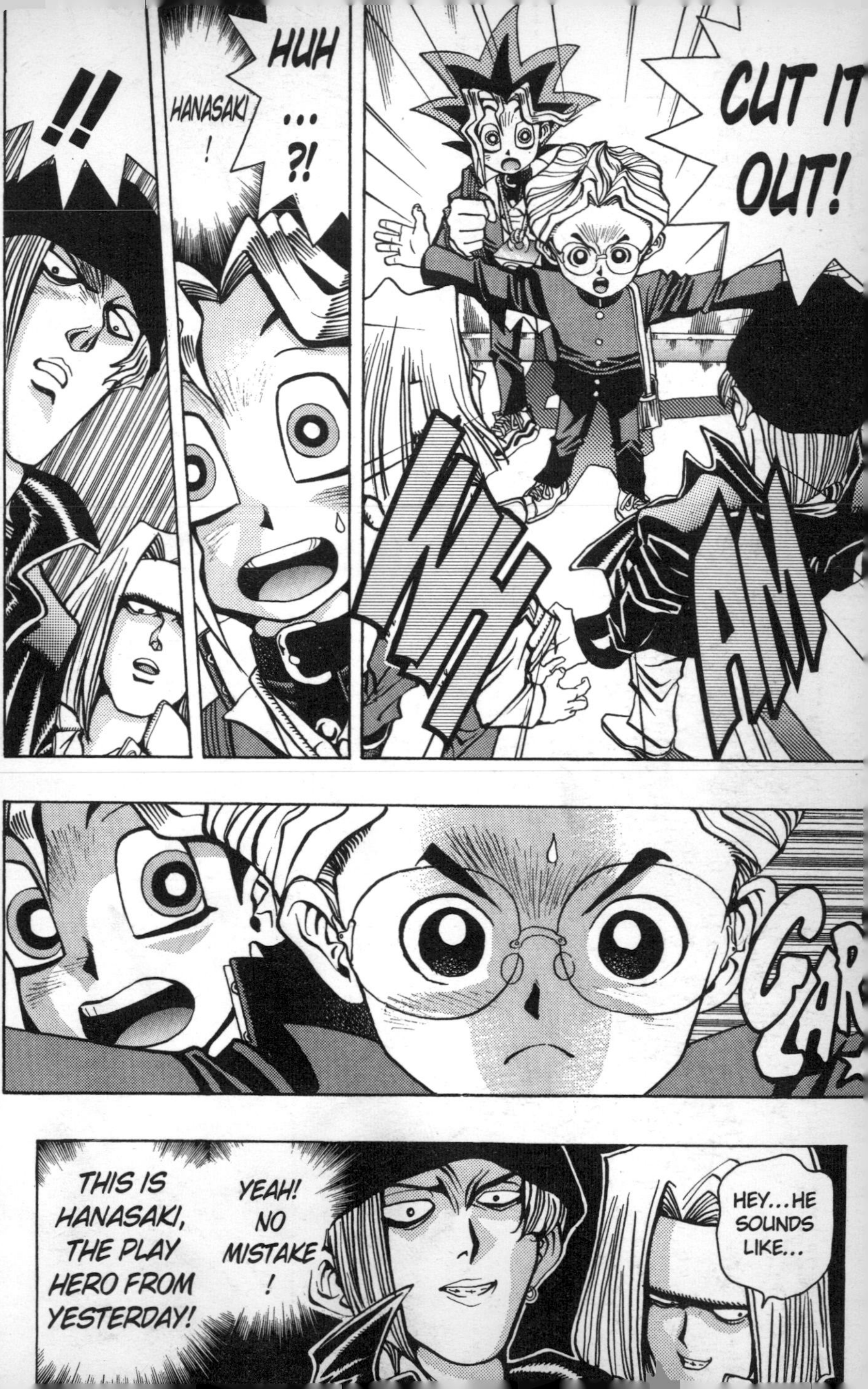
CUT IT OUT!
WH
AM
HUH
...?!
HANASAKI!
!!
HEY...HE SOUNDS LIKE...
YEAH! NO MISTAKE!
THIS IS HANASAKI, THE PLAY HERO FROM YESTERDAY!

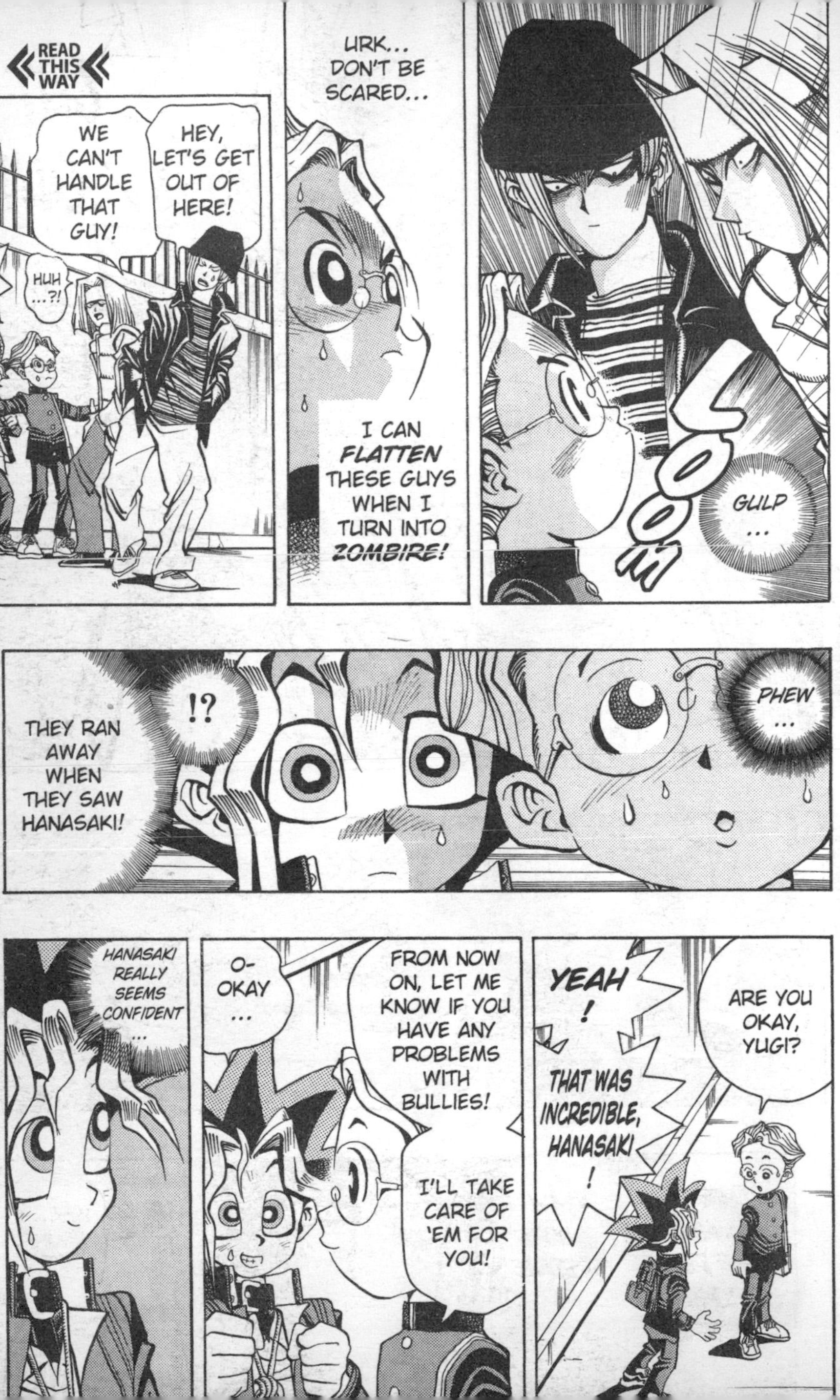
READ THIS WAY
GULP ...
LOOOM
URK... DON'T BE SCARED...
I CAN FLATTEN THESE GUYS WHEN I TURN INTO ZOMBIRE!
HEY, LET'S GET OUT OF HERE!
WE CAN'T HANDLE THAT GUY!
!
HUH ...?!
PHEW ...
!?
THEY RAN AWAY WHEN THEY SAW HANASAKI!
ARE YOU OKAY, YUGI?
YEAH!
THAT WAS INCREDIBLE, HANASAKI!
FROM NOW ON, LET ME KNOW IF YOU HAVE ANY PROBLEMS WITH BULLIES!
I'LL TAKE CARE OF 'EM FOR YOU!
O-OKAY ...
HANASAKI REALLY SEEMS CONFIDENT ...

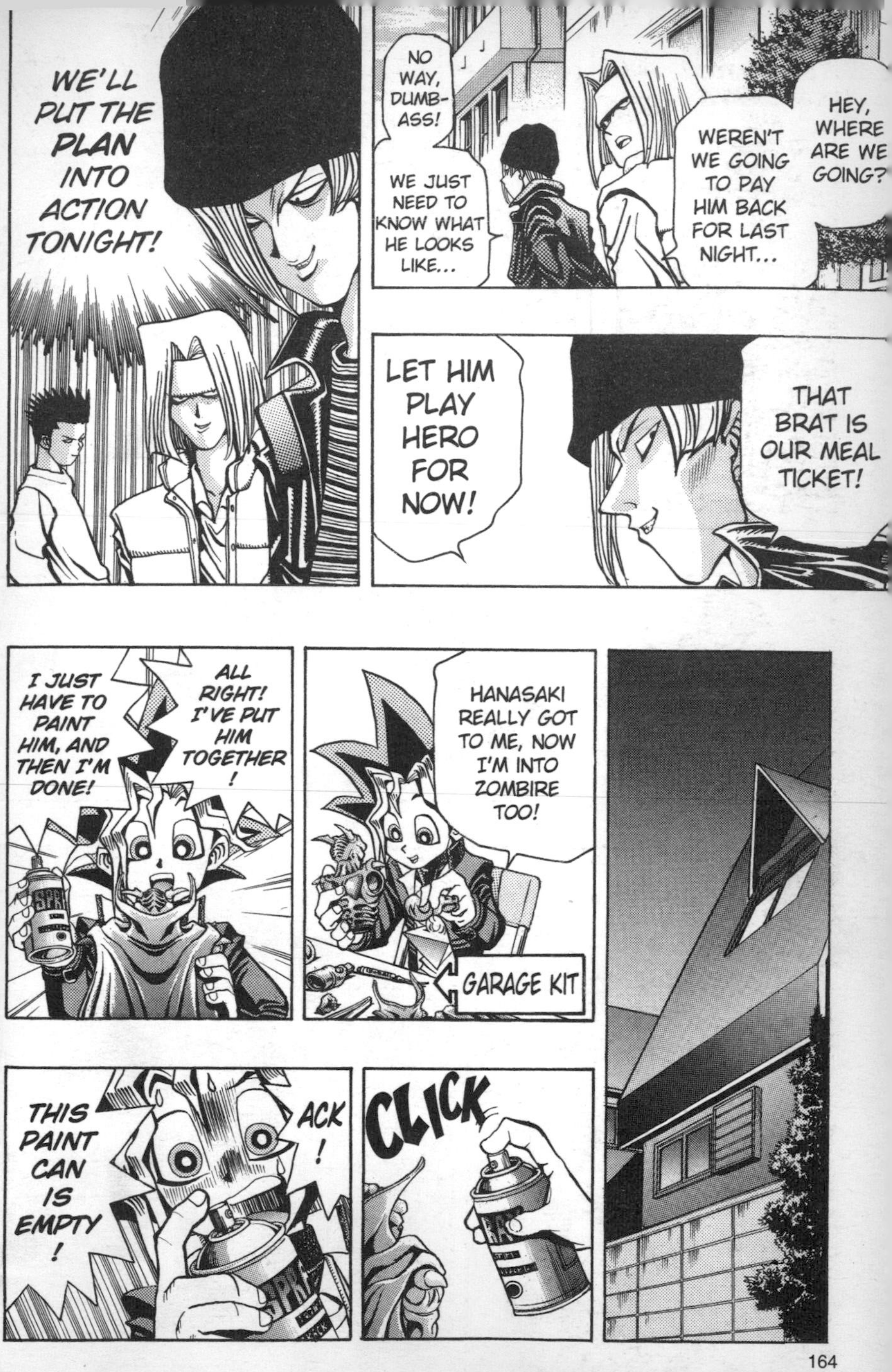
HEY, WHERE ARE WE GOING?
WEREN'T WE GOING TO PAY HIM BACK FOR LAST NIGHT...
NO WAY, DUMB-ASS!
WE JUST NEED TO KNOW WHAT HE LOOKS LIKE...
THAT BRAT IS OUR MEAL TICKET!
LET HIM PLAY HERO FOR NOW!
WE'LL PUT THE PLAN INTO ACTION TONIGHT!
HANASAKI REALLY GOT TO ME, NOW I'M INTO ZOMBIRE TOO!
GARAGE KIT
ALL RIGHT! I'VE PUT HIM TOGETHER!
I JUST HAVE TO PAINT HIM, AND THEN I'M DONE!
CLICK
ACK!
THIS PAINT CAN IS EMPTY!

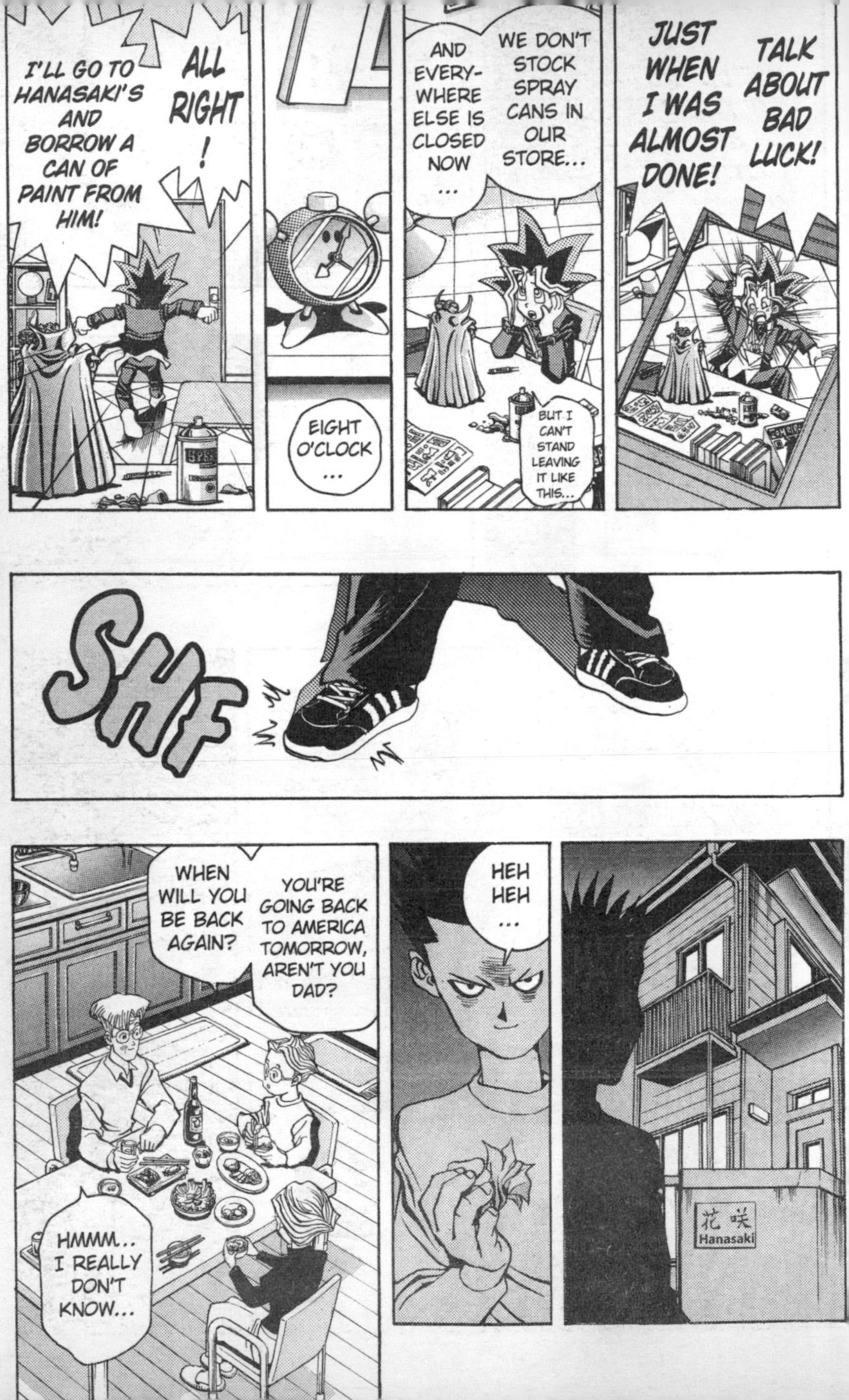
TALK ABOUT BAD LUCK!
JUST WHEN I WAS ALMOST DONE!
WE DON'T STOCK SPRAY CANS IN OUR STORE...
AND EVERY-WHERE ELSE IS CLOSED NOW ...
BUT I CAN'T STAND LEAVING IT LIKE THIS...
EIGHT O'CLOCK ...
ALL RIGHT !
I'LL GO TO HANASAKI'S AND BORROW A CAN OF PAINT FROM HIM!
SHF
花咲
Hanasaki
HEH HEH ...
YOU'RE GOING BACK TO AMERICA TOMORROW, AREN'T YOU DAD?
WHEN WILL YOU BE BACK AGAIN?
HMMM... I REALLY DON'T KNOW...

READ THIS WAY

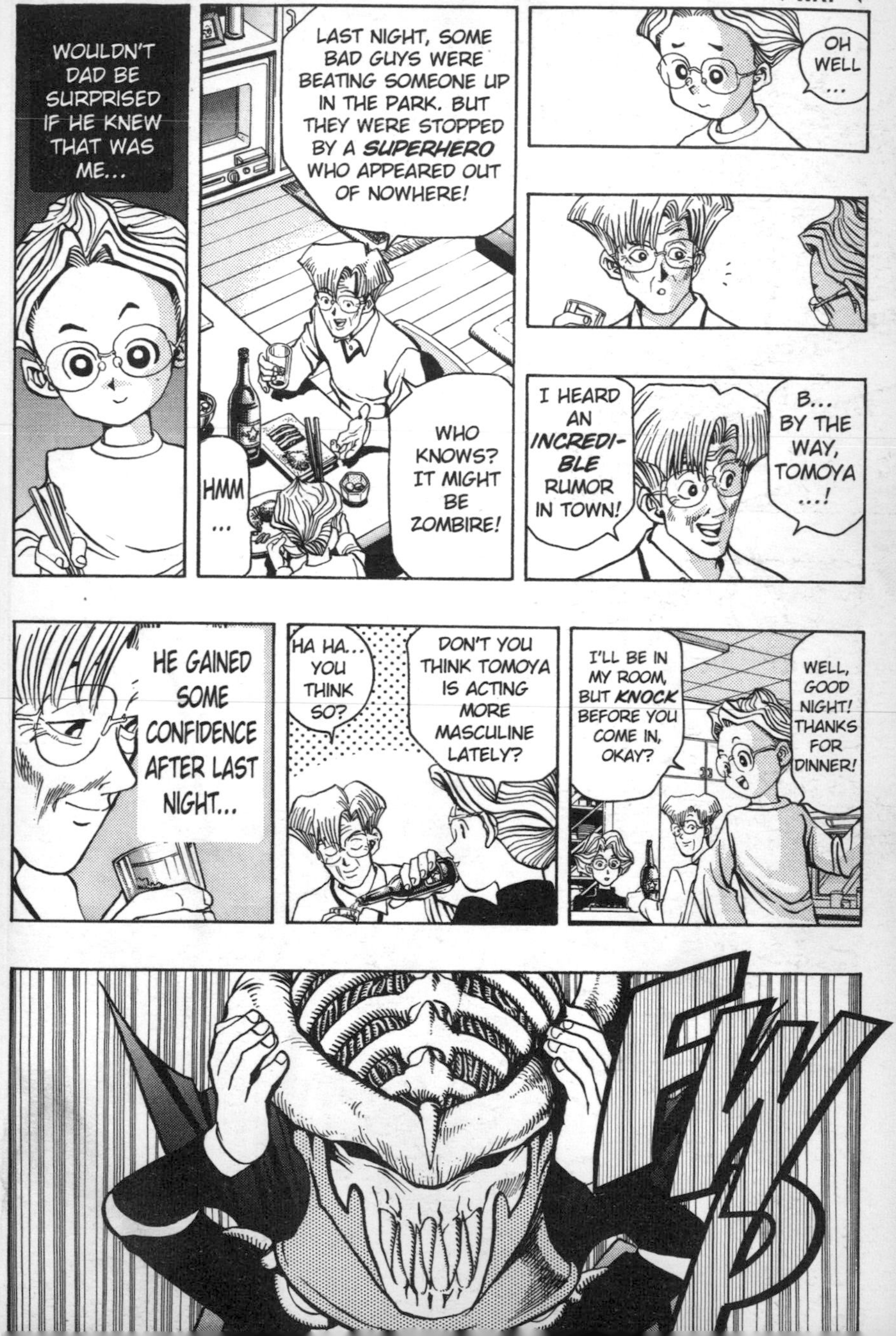
OH WELL...
B... BY THE WAY, TOMOYA...!
I HEARD AN INCREDIBLE RUMOR IN TOWN!
LAST NIGHT, SOME BAD GUYS WERE BEATING SOMEONE UP IN THE PARK. BUT THEY WERE STOPPED BY A SUPERHERO WHO APPEARED OUT OF NOWHERE!
WHO KNOWS? IT MIGHT BE ZOMBIRE!
HMM...
WOULDN'T DAD BE SURPRISED IF HE KNEW THAT WAS ME...
WELL, GOOD NIGHT! THANKS FOR DINNER!
I'LL BE IN MY ROOM, BUT KNOCK BEFORE YOU COME IN, OKAY?
DON'T YOU THINK TOMOYA IS ACTING MORE MASCULINE LATELY?
HA HA... YOU THINK SO?
HE GAINED SOME CONFIDENCE AFTER LAST NIGHT...

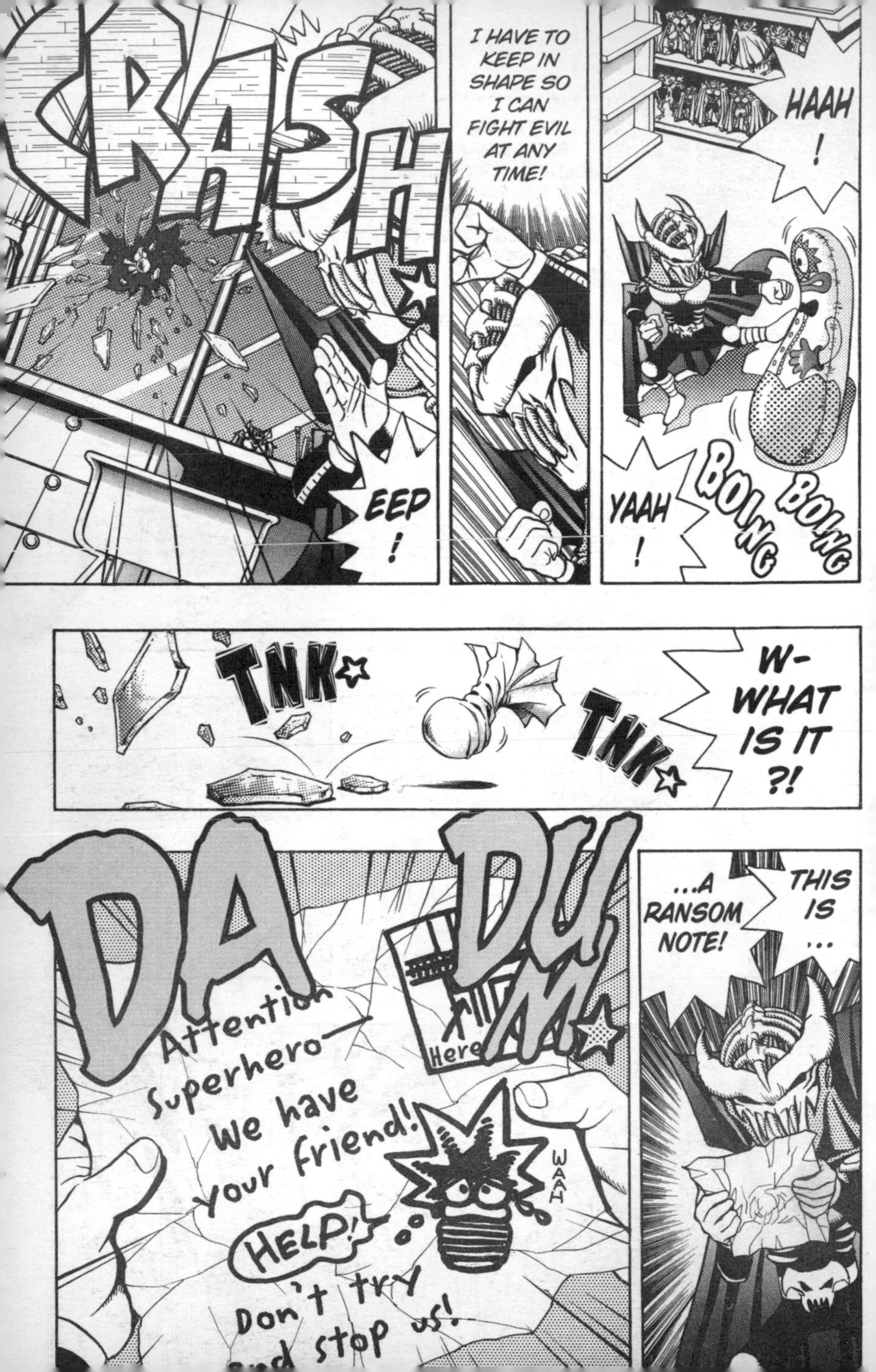
HAAH!
YAAH!
BOING
BOING
I HAVE TO KEEP IN SHAPE SO I CAN FIGHT EVIL AT ANY TIME!
CRASH
EEP!
W-WHAT IS IT?!
TNK
TNK
THIS IS...
...A RANSOM NOTE!
DA DUM
Attention Superhero—
We have your friend!
Here
WAAH
HELP!
Don't try and stop us!

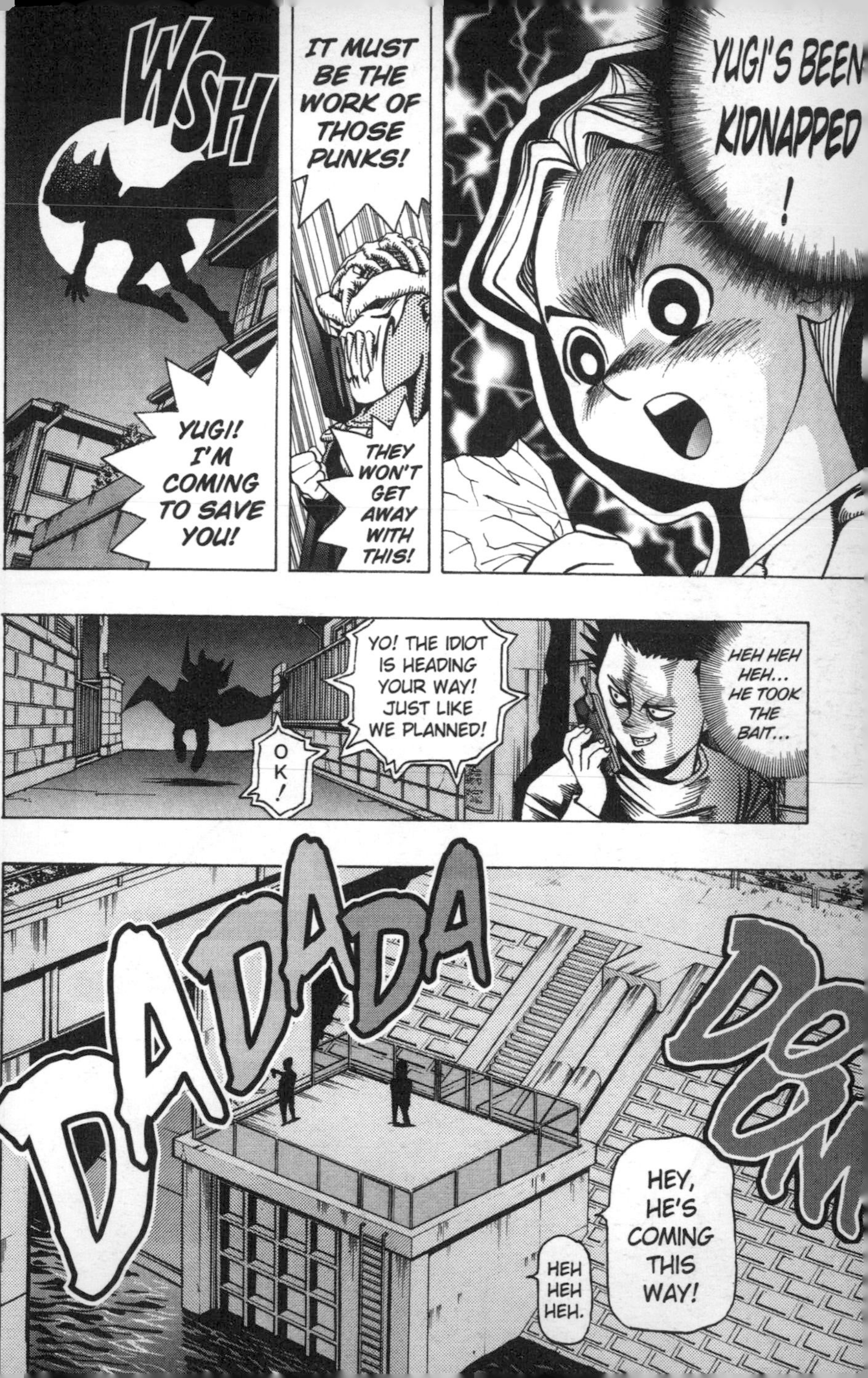
YUGI'S BEEN KIDNAPPED !
IT MUST BE THE WORK OF THOSE PUNKS!
THEY WON'T GET AWAY WITH THIS!
WSH
YUGI! I'M COMING TO SAVE YOU!
HEH HEH HEH... HE TOOK THE BAIT...
YO! THE IDIOT IS HEADING YOUR WAY! JUST LIKE WE PLANNED!
OK!
HEY, HE'S COMING THIS WAY!
HEH HEH HEH.
DADADA

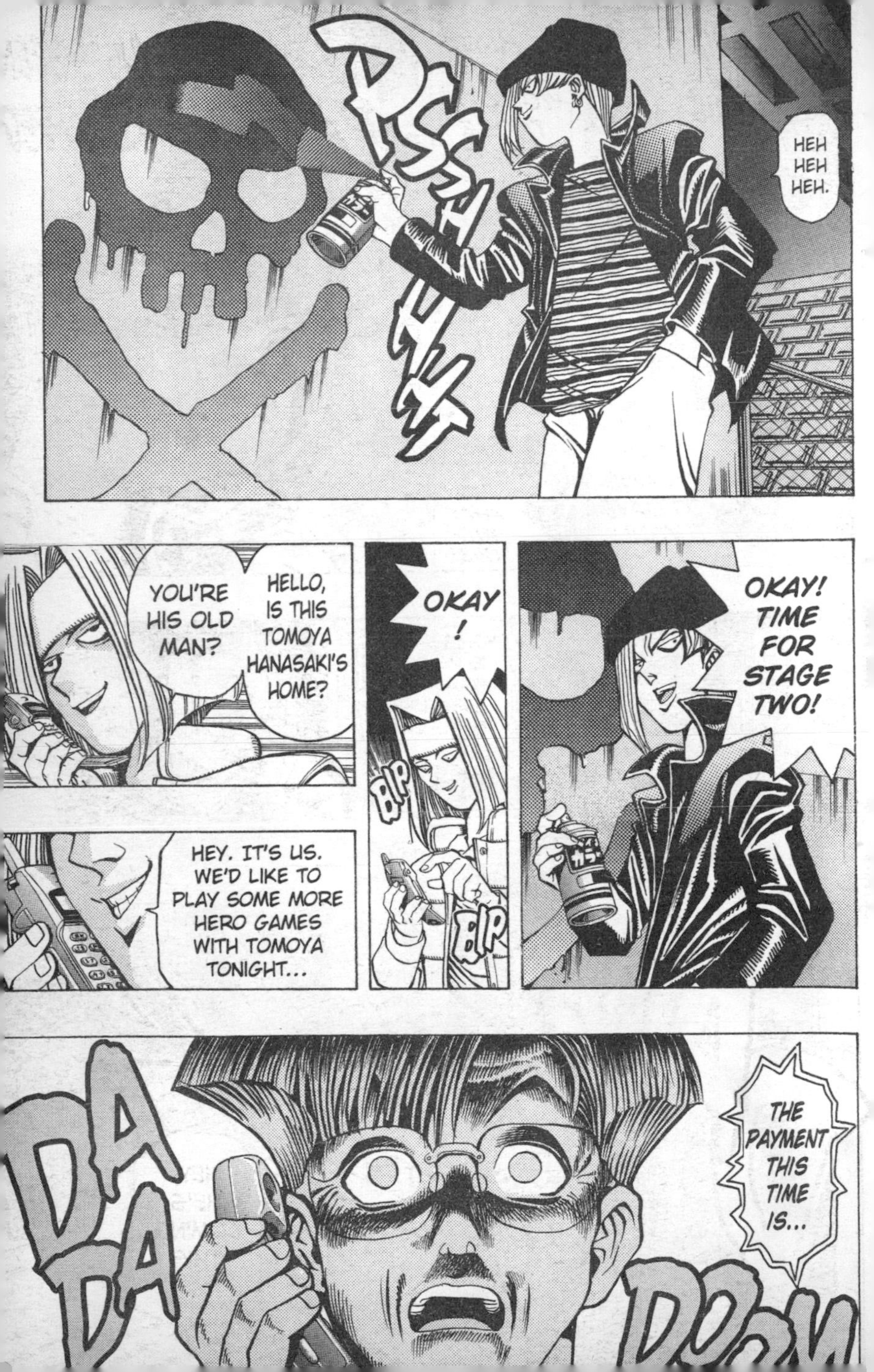
HEH HEH HEH.
OKAY! TIME FOR STAGE TWO!
OKAY!
BIP
BIP
HELLO, IS THIS TOMOYA HANASAKI'S HOME?
YOU'RE HIS OLD MAN?
HEY. IT'S US. WE'D LIKE TO PLAY SOME MORE HERO GAMES WITH TOMOYA TONIGHT...
THE PAYMENT THIS TIME IS...
DA DA
DOOM

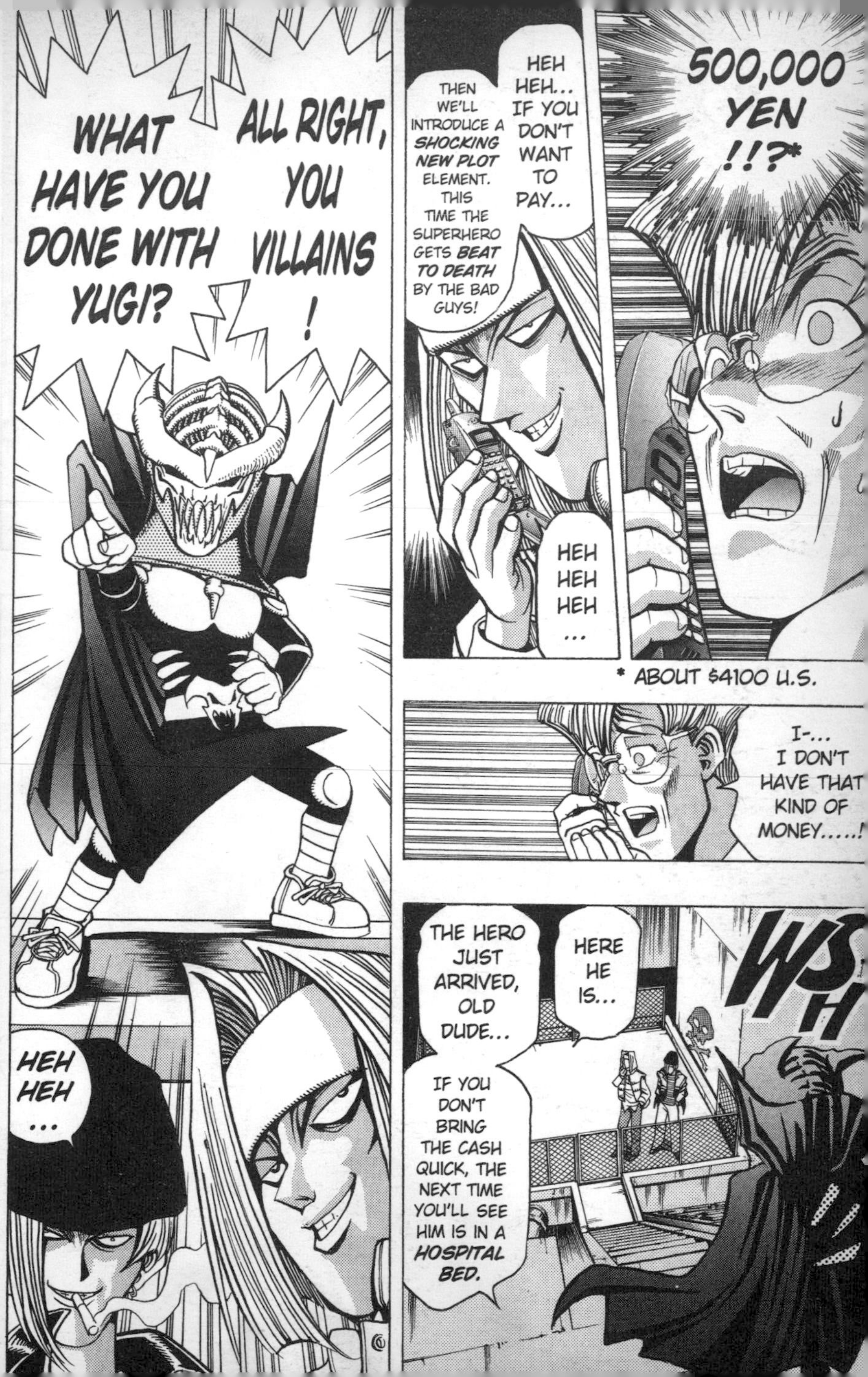
500,000 YEN !!?*
HEH HEH... IF YOU DON'T WANT TO PAY...
THEN WE'LL INTRODUCE A SHOCKING NEW PLOT ELEMENT. THIS TIME THE SUPERHERO GETS BEAT TO DEATH BY THE BAD GUYS!
HEH HEH HEH ...
I-... I DON'T HAVE THAT KIND OF MONEY.....!
WSH
HERE HE IS...
THE HERO JUST ARRIVED, OLD DUDE...
IF YOU DON'T BRING THE CASH QUICK, THE NEXT TIME YOU'LL SEE HIM IS IN A HOSPITAL BED.
ALL RIGHT, YOU VILLAINS !
WHAT HAVE YOU DONE WITH YUGI?
HEH HEH ...

* ABOUT $4100 U.S.

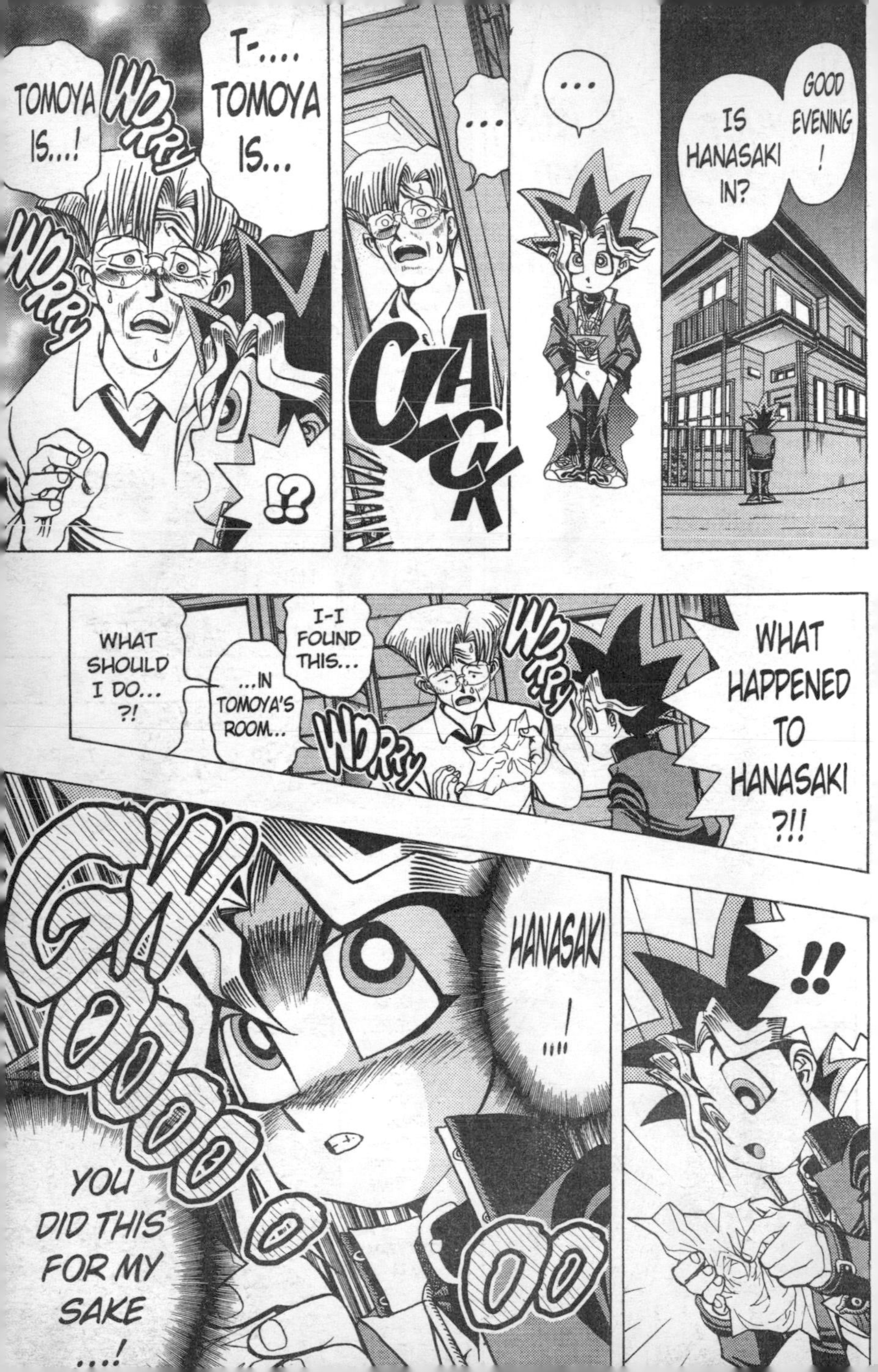
GOOD EVENING!
IS HANASAKI IN?
...
...
CLACK
T-.... TOMOYA IS...
WORRY
TOMOYA IS...!
WORRY
!?
WHAT HAPPENED TO HANASAKI ?!!
WORRY
I-I FOUND THIS...
...IN TOMOYA'S ROOM...
WORRY
WHAT SHOULD I DO... ?!
!!
HANASAKI ...!
GWOOOOOOOOO
YOU DID THIS FOR MY SAKE ...!

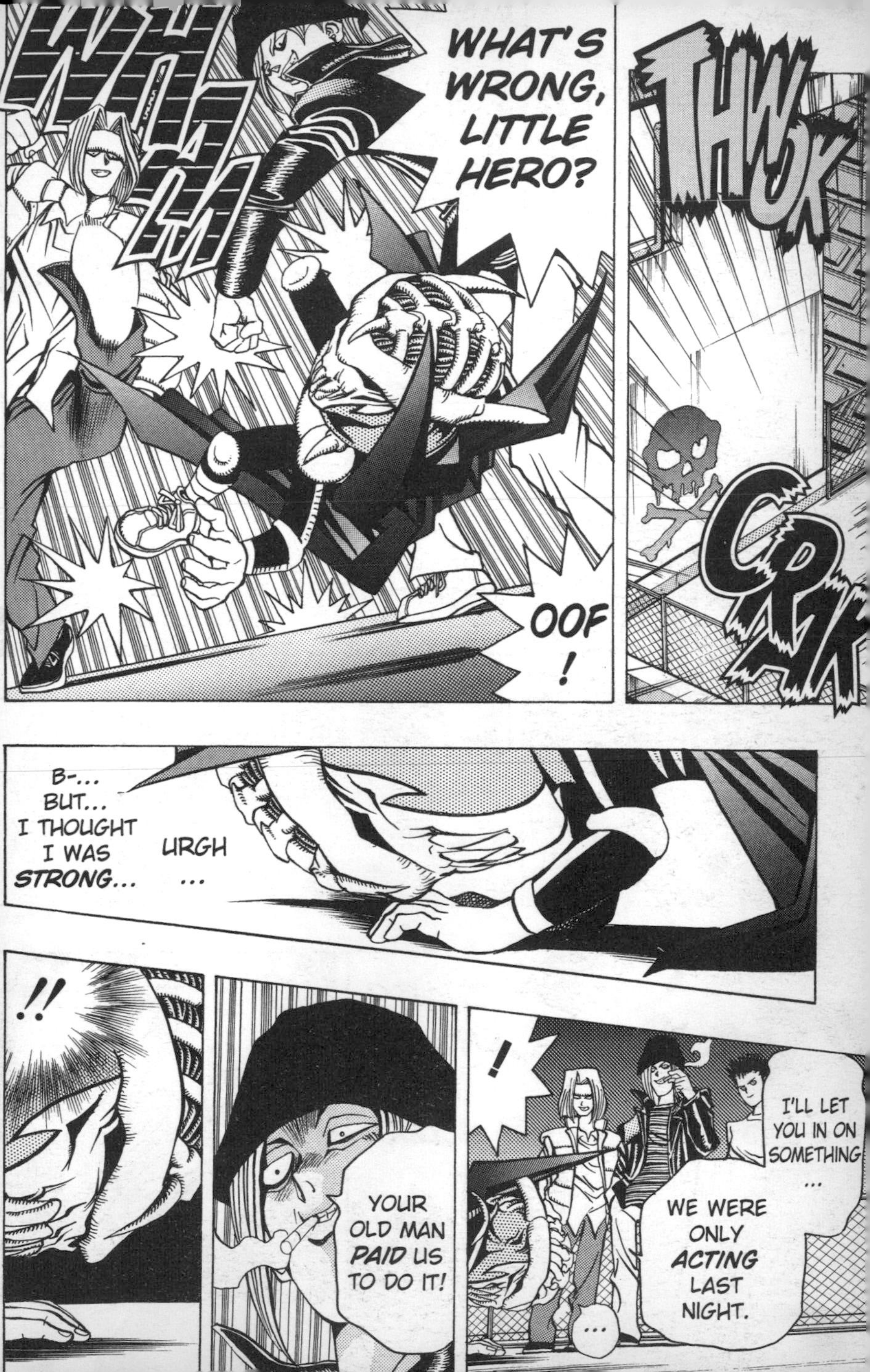
THWOK
CRAK
WHAT'S WRONG, LITTLE HERO?
OOF !
URGH ...
B-... BUT... I THOUGHT I WAS **STRONG**...
I'LL LET YOU IN ON SOMETHING ...
!
WE WERE ONLY **ACTING** LAST NIGHT.
...
YOUR OLD MAN **PAID** US TO DO IT!
!!

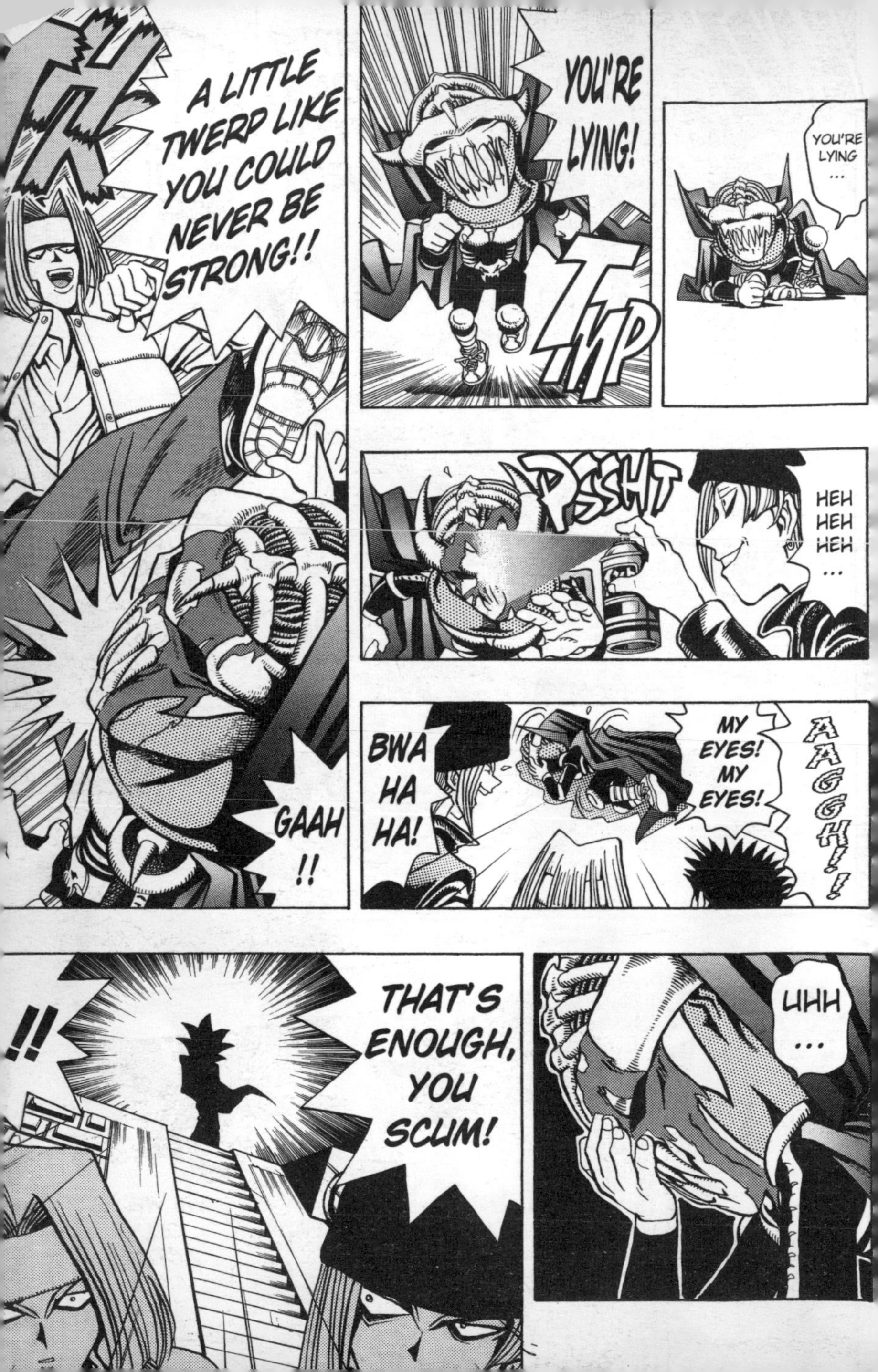
YOU'RE LYING ...
YOU'RE LYING!
TMP
HEH HEH HEH ...
PSSHT
AAGGH!!
MY EYES! MY EYES!
BWA HA HA!
A LITTLE TWERP LIKE YOU COULD NEVER BE STRONG!!
GAAH !!
UHH ...
THAT'S ENOUGH, YOU SCUM!
!!

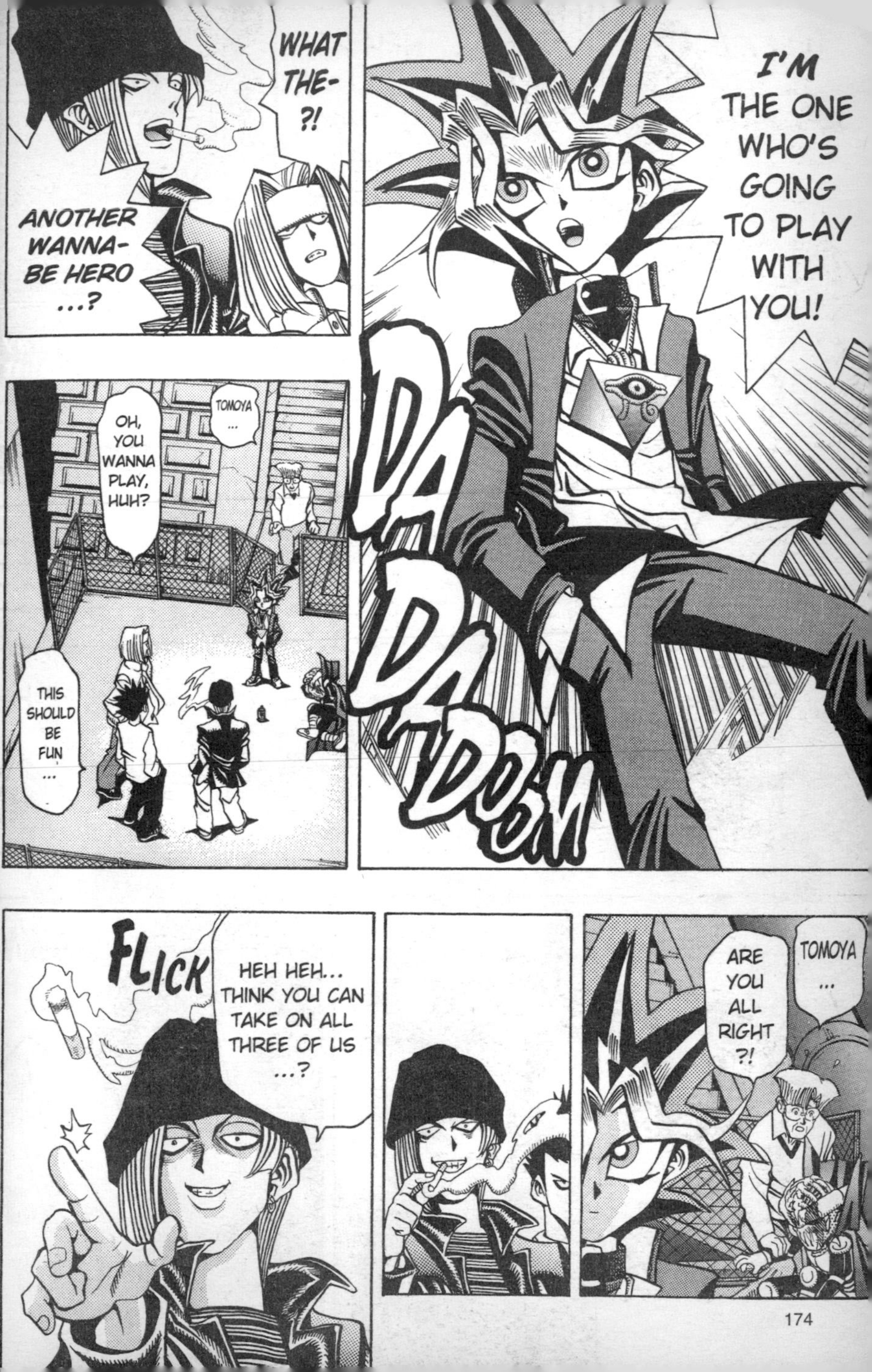
I'M THE ONE WHO'S GOING TO PLAY WITH YOU!
DA DA DOM
WHAT THE-?!
ANOTHER WANNA-BE HERO...?
TOMOYA...
OH, YOU WANNA PLAY, HUH?
THIS SHOULD BE FUN...
TOMOYA...
ARE YOU ALL RIGHT?!
FLICK
HEH HEH... THINK YOU CAN TAKE ON ALL THREE OF US...?

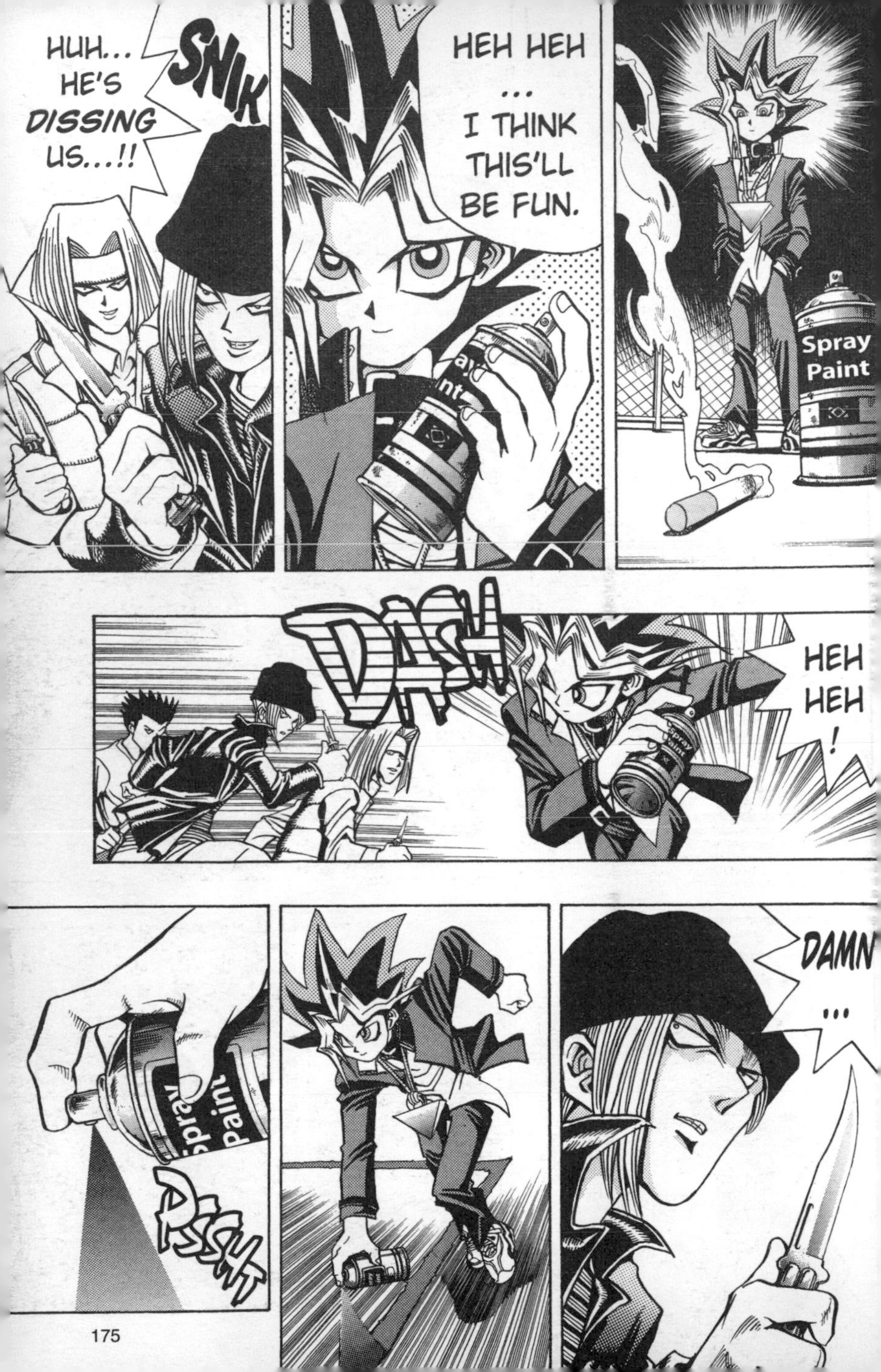
Spray Paint
HEH HEH ... I THINK THIS'LL BE FUN.
SNIK
HUH... HE'S DISSING US...!!
HEH HEH !
DASH
DAMN ...
Spray paint

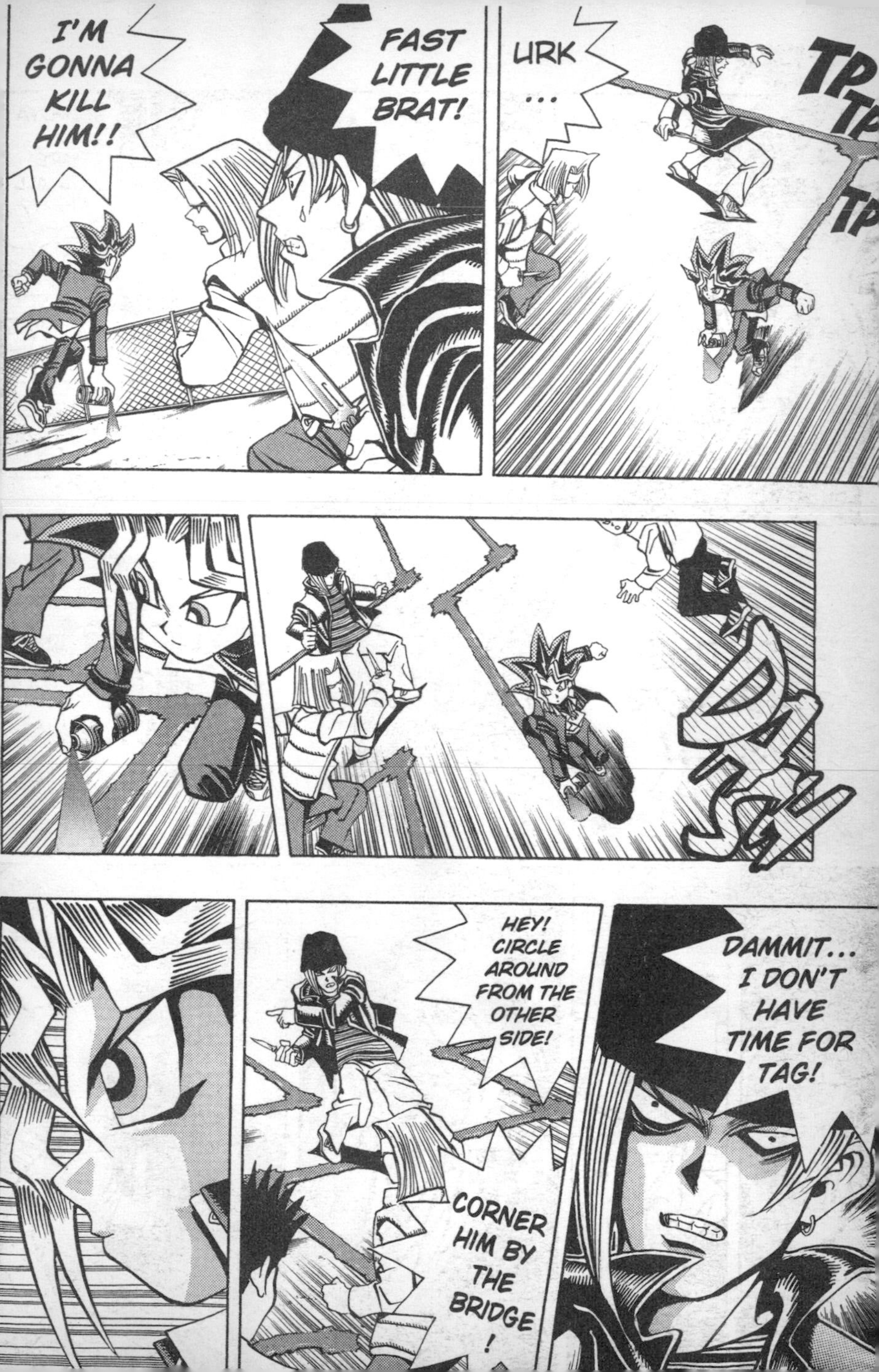
URK ...
TP TP TP
FAST LITTLE BRAT!
I'M GONNA KILL HIM!!
DAMMIT... I DON'T HAVE TIME FOR TAG!
HEY! CIRCLE AROUND FROM THE OTHER SIDE!
CORNER HIM BY THE BRIDGE!

READ THIS WAY

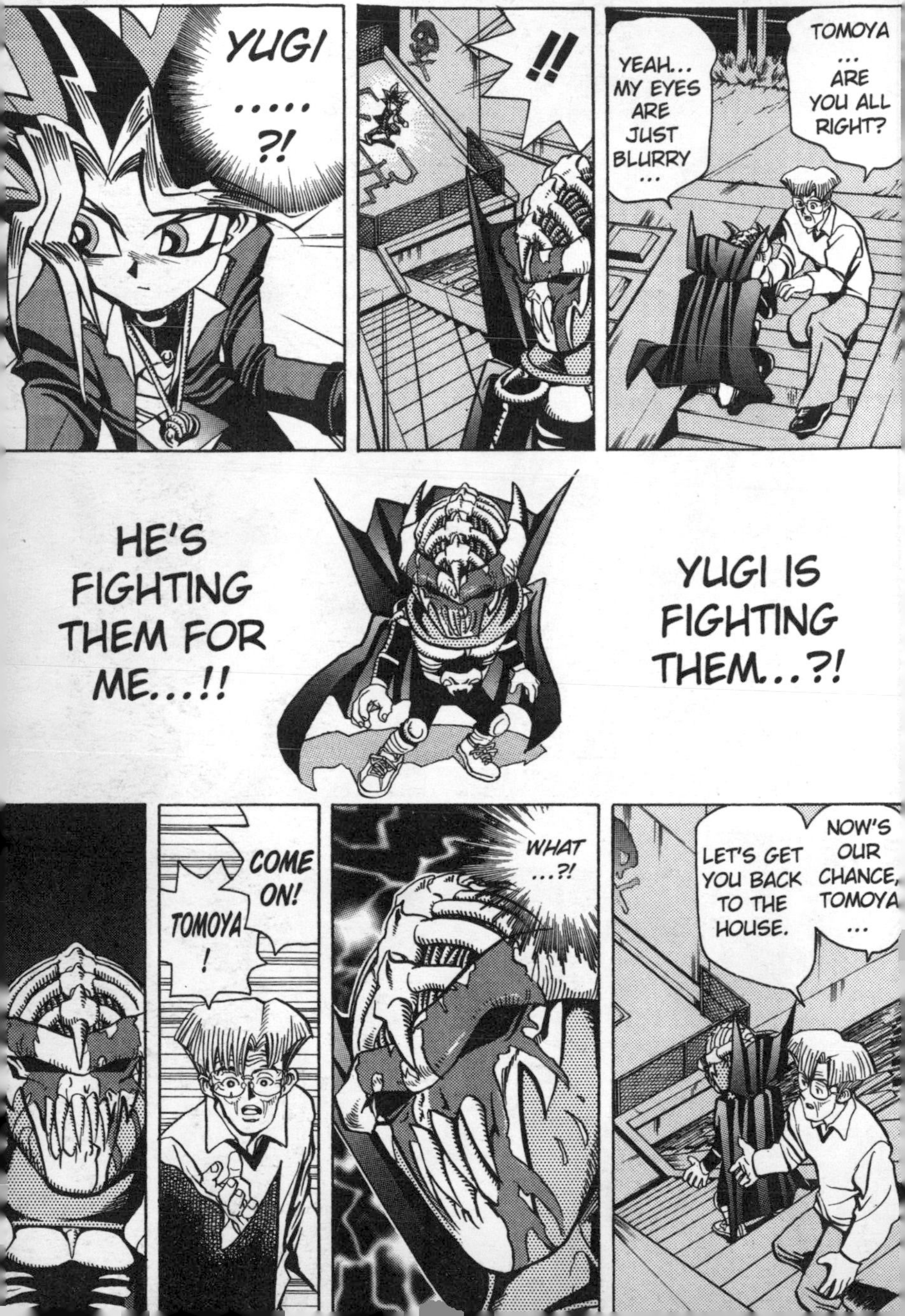
TOMOYA ... ARE YOU ALL RIGHT?
YEAH... MY EYES ARE JUST BLURRY ...
!!
YUGI ..... ?!
YUGI IS FIGHTING THEM...?!
HE'S FIGHTING THEM FOR ME...!!
NOW'S OUR CHANCE, TOMOYA ...
LET'S GET YOU BACK TO THE HOUSE.
WHAT ...?!
COME ON!
TOMOYA !

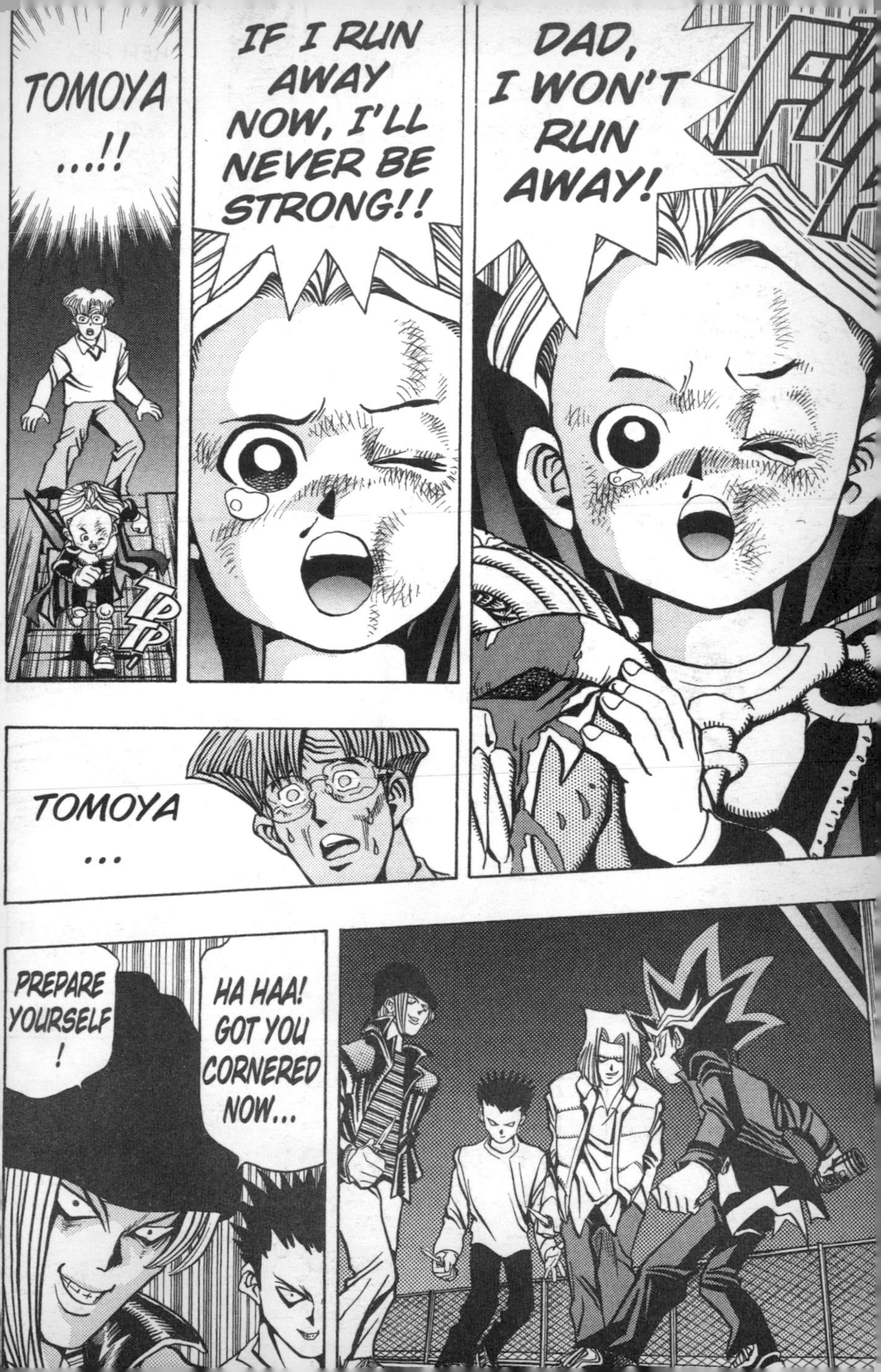
DAD, I WON'T RUN AWAY!
IF I RUN AWAY NOW, I'LL NEVER BE STRONG!!
TOMOYA ...!!
TP TP
TOMOYA ...
HA HAA! GOT YOU CORNERED NOW...
PREPARE YOURSELF!

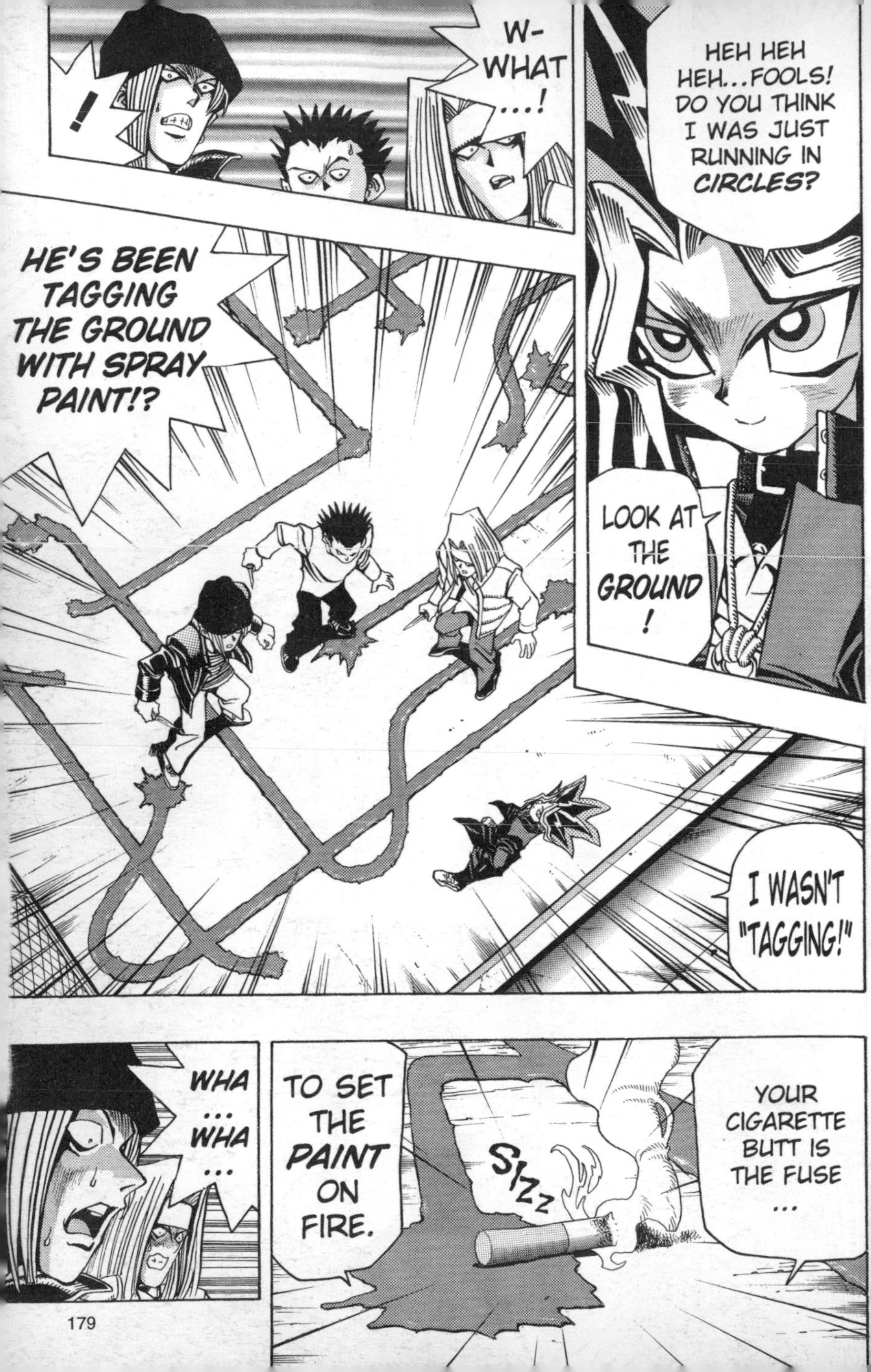
HEH HEH HEH...FOOLS! DO YOU THINK I WAS JUST RUNNING IN CIRCLES?
LOOK AT THE GROUND!
W-WHAT...!
!
HE'S BEEN TAGGING THE GROUND WITH SPRAY PAINT!?
I WASN'T "TAGGING!"
YOUR CIGARETTE BUTT IS THE FUSE...
TO SET THE PAINT ON FIRE.
SIZZ
WHA... WHA...

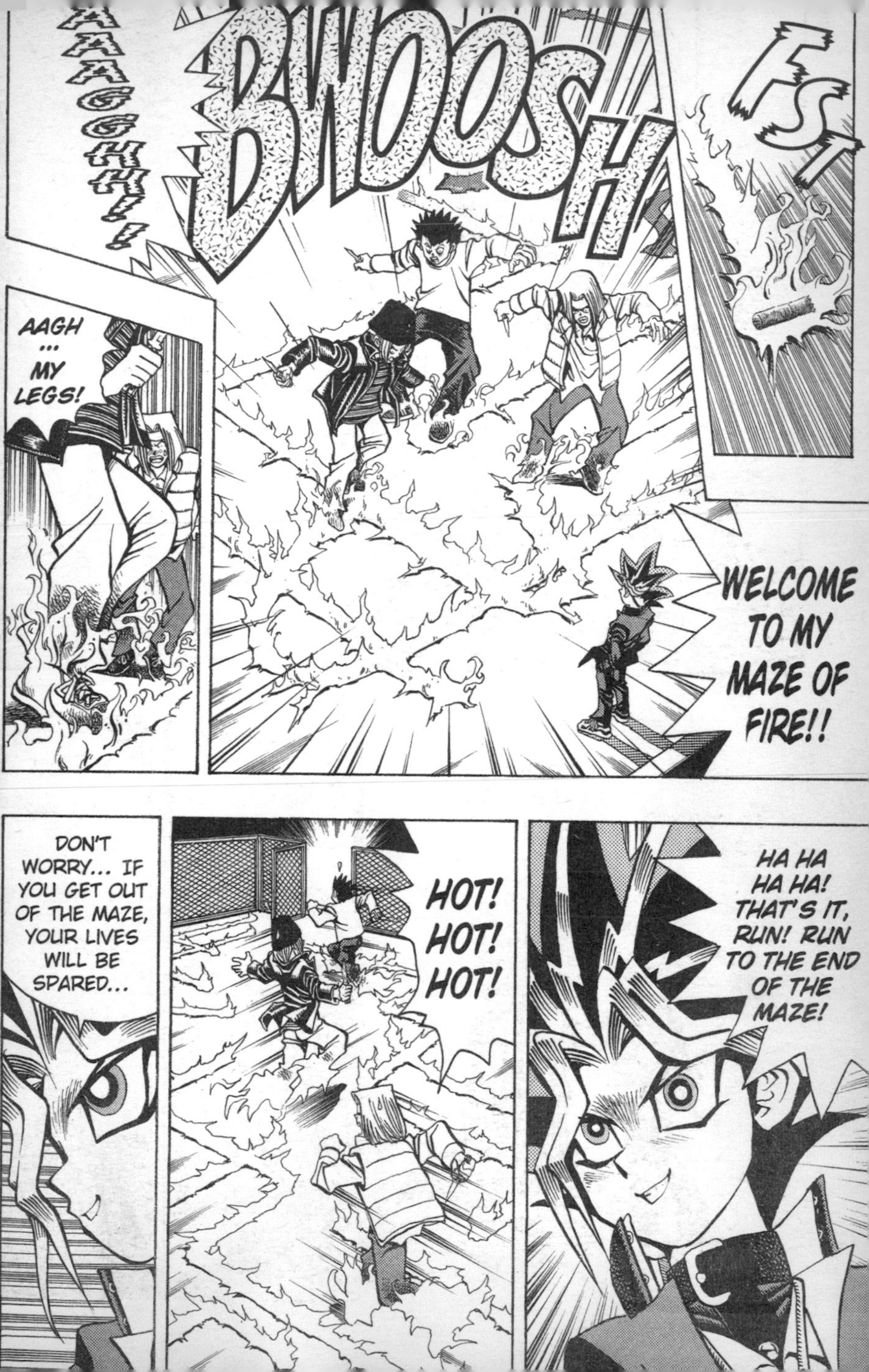
FST
BWOOSH
AAAGGHH!!
WELCOME TO MY MAZE OF FIRE!!
AAGH ... MY LEGS!
HA HA HA HA! THAT'S IT, RUN! RUN TO THE END OF THE MAZE!
HOT! HOT! HOT!
DON'T WORRY... IF YOU GET OUT OF THE MAZE, YOUR LIVES WILL BE SPARED...

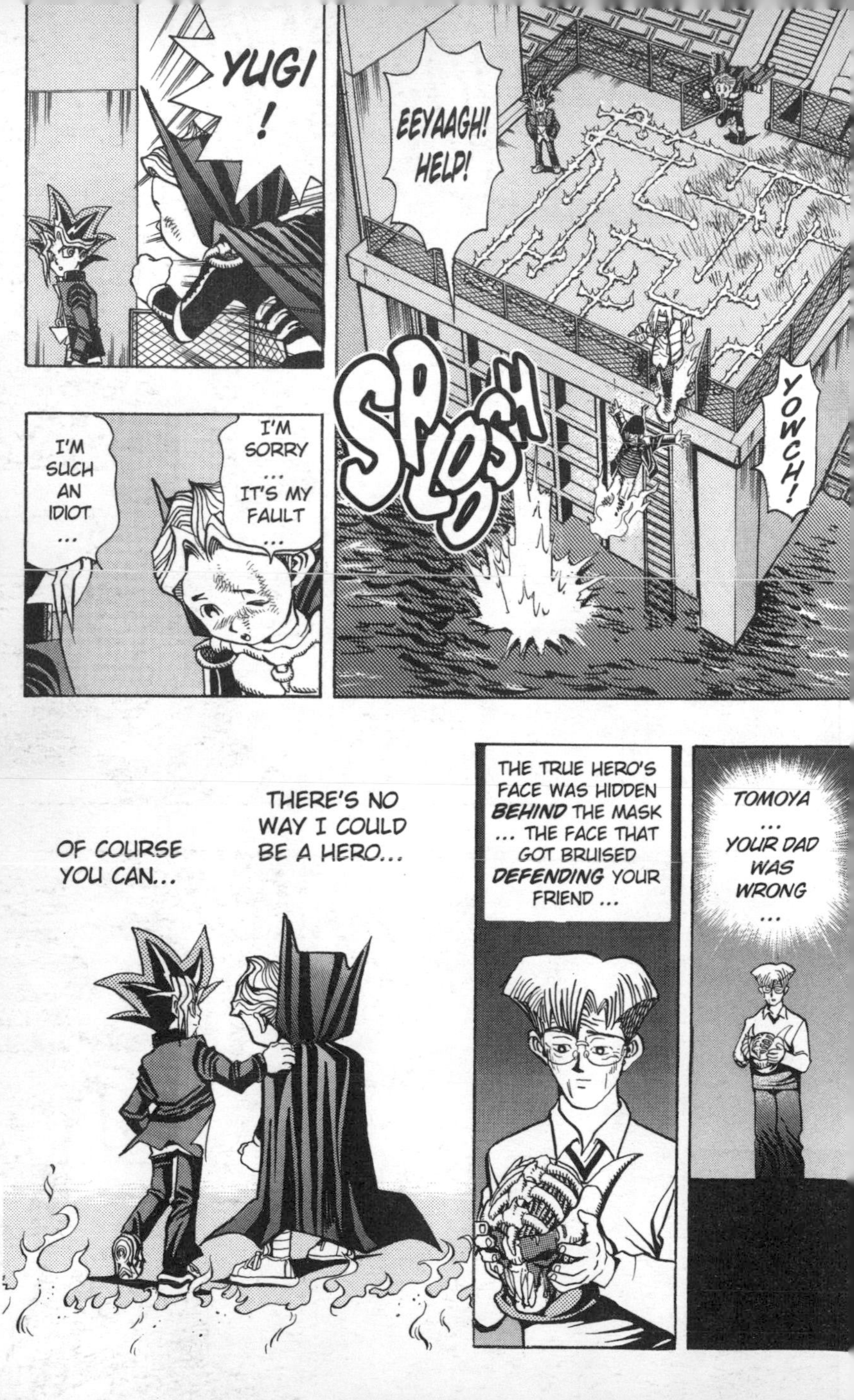
EEYAAGH! HELP!
YOWCH!
SPLOOSH
YUGI!
I'M SORRY ... IT'S MY FAULT ...
I'M SUCH AN IDIOT ...
TOMOYA ... YOUR DAD WAS WRONG ...
THE TRUE HERO'S FACE WAS HIDDEN **BEHIND** THE MASK ... THE FACE THAT GOT BRUISED **DEFENDING** YOUR FRIEND ...
THERE'S NO WAY I COULD BE A HERO...
OF COURSE YOU CAN...

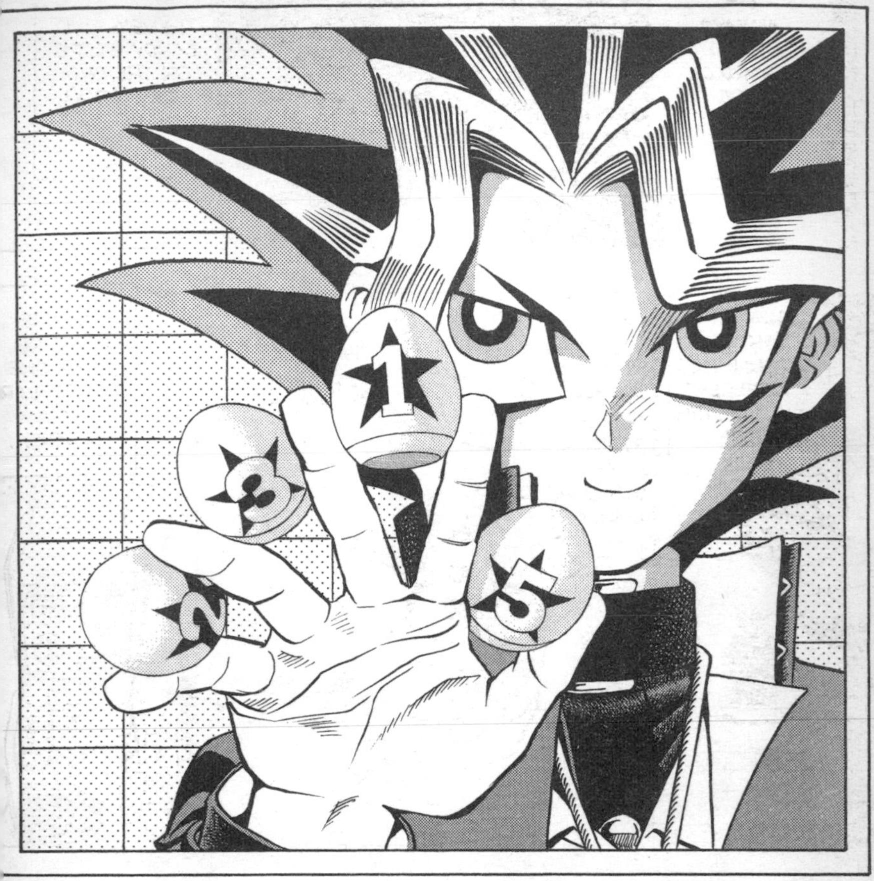
1
3
2
5

Duel 24:
Capsule Monster Chess

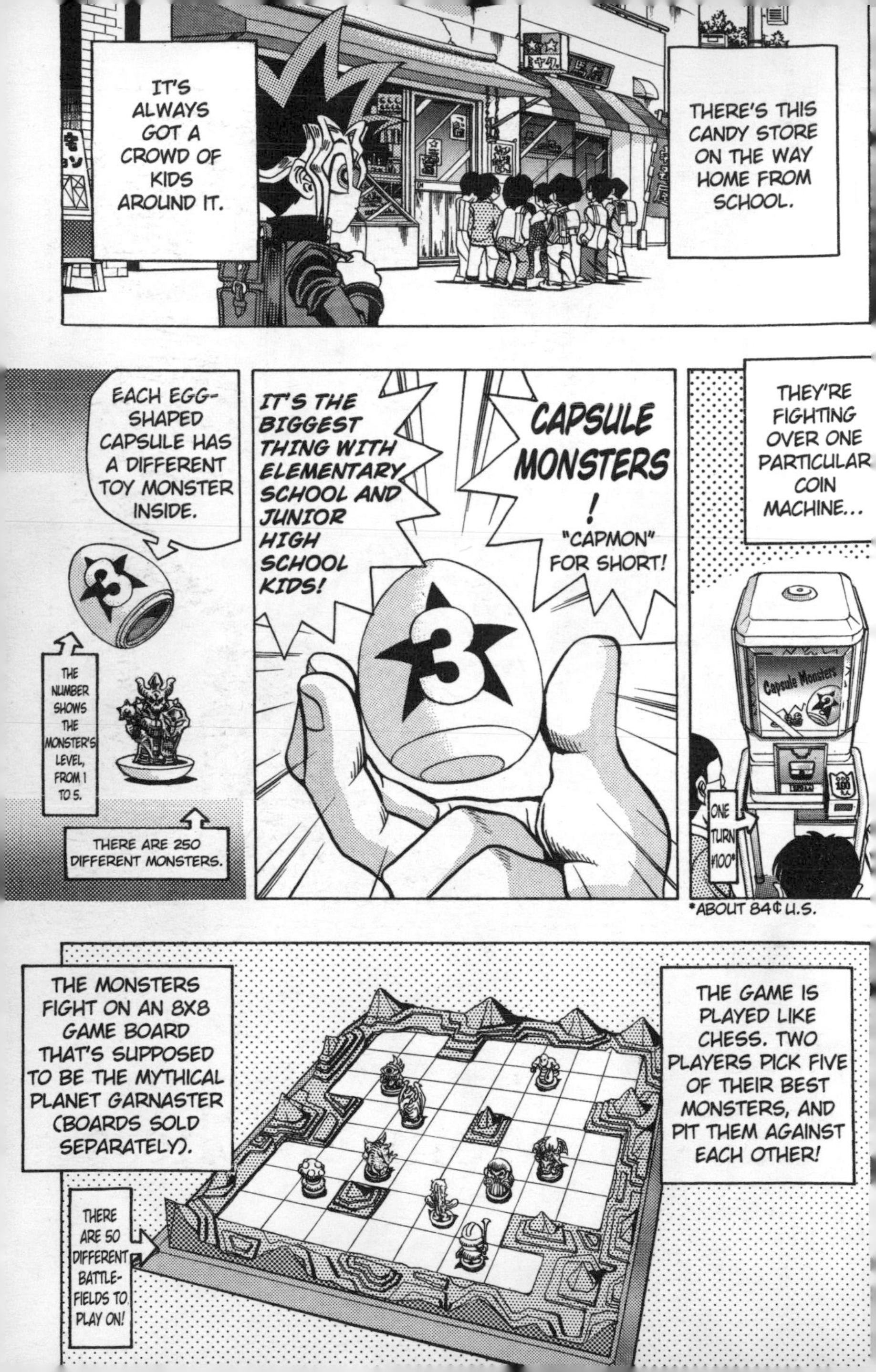
THERE'S THIS CANDY STORE ON THE WAY HOME FROM SCHOOL.
IT'S ALWAYS GOT A CROWD OF KIDS AROUND IT.
THEY'RE FIGHTING OVER ONE PARTICULAR COIN MACHINE...
Capsule Monsters
ONE TURN ¥100*
*ABOUT 84¢ U.S.
CAPSULE MONSTERS!
"CAPMON" FOR SHORT!
IT'S THE BIGGEST THING WITH ELEMENTARY SCHOOL AND JUNIOR HIGH SCHOOL KIDS!
EACH EGG-SHAPED CAPSULE HAS A DIFFERENT TOY MONSTER INSIDE.
THE NUMBER SHOWS THE MONSTER'S LEVEL, FROM 1 TO 5.
THERE ARE 250 DIFFERENT MONSTERS.
THE GAME IS PLAYED LIKE CHESS. TWO PLAYERS PICK FIVE OF THEIR BEST MONSTERS, AND PIT THEM AGAINST EACH OTHER!
THE MONSTERS FIGHT ON AN 8X8 GAME BOARD THAT'S SUPPOSED TO BE THE MYTHICAL PLANET GARNASTER (BOARDS SOLD SEPARATELY).
THERE ARE 50 DIFFERENT BATTLE-FIELDS TO PLAY ON!

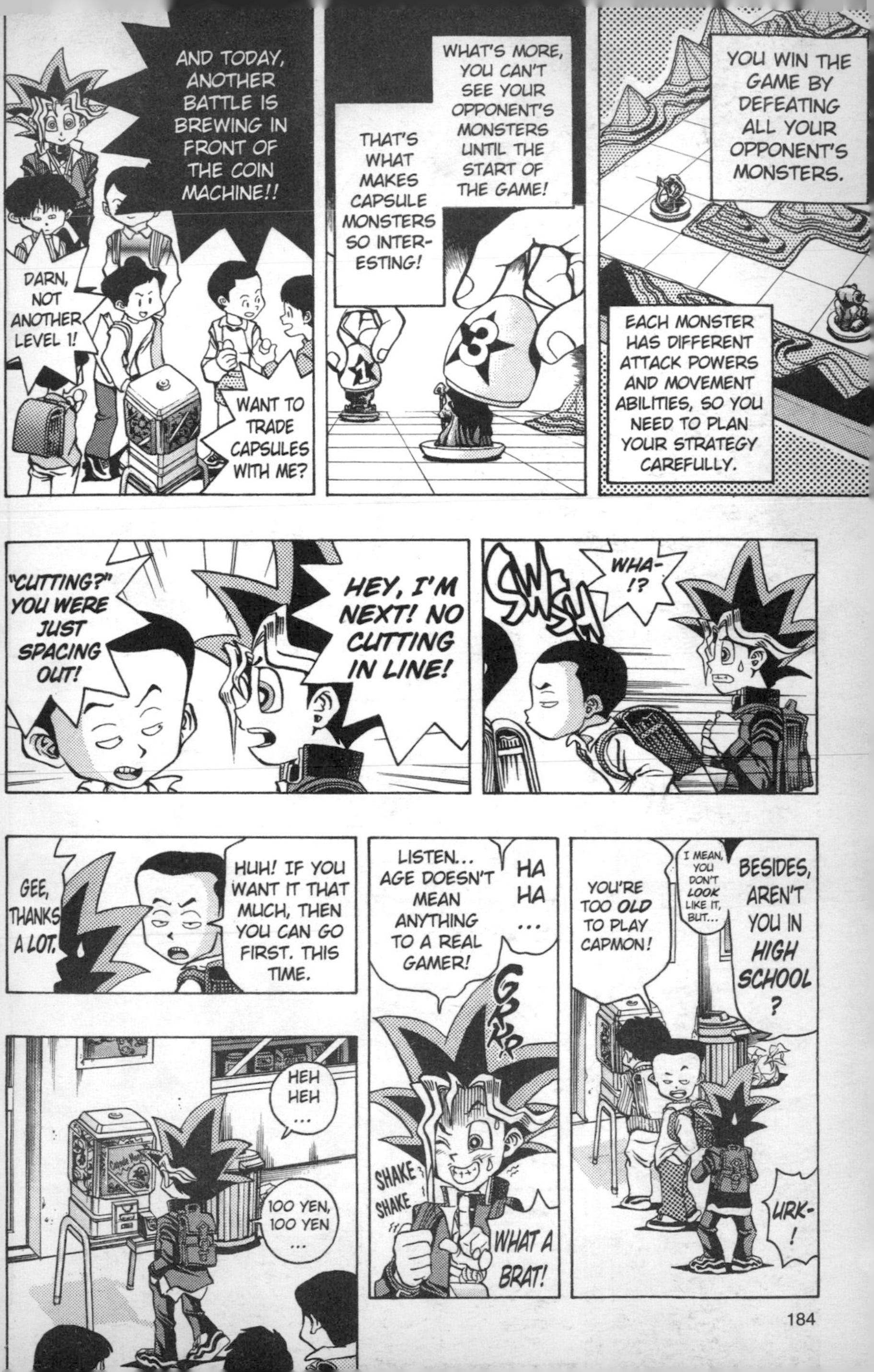

YOU WIN THE GAME BY DEFEATING ALL YOUR OPPONENT'S MONSTERS.
EACH MONSTER HAS DIFFERENT ATTACK POWERS AND MOVEMENT ABILITIES, SO YOU NEED TO PLAN YOUR STRATEGY CAREFULLY.
WHAT'S MORE, YOU CAN'T SEE YOUR OPPONENT'S MONSTERS UNTIL THE START OF THE GAME!
THAT'S WHAT MAKES CAPSULE MONSTERS SO INTER-ESTING!
AND TODAY, ANOTHER BATTLE IS BREWING IN FRONT OF THE COIN MACHINE!!
DARN, NOT ANOTHER LEVEL 1!
WANT TO TRADE CAPSULES WITH ME?
WHA-!?
HEY, I'M NEXT! NO CUTTING IN LINE!
"CUTTING?" YOU WERE JUST SPACING OUT!
BESIDES, AREN'T YOU IN HIGH SCHOOL?
I MEAN, YOU DON'T LOOK LIKE IT, BUT...
YOU'RE TOO OLD TO PLAY CAPMON!
URK-!
HA HA ...
LISTEN... AGE DOESN'T MEAN ANYTHING TO A REAL GAMER!
SHAKE
SHAKE
WHAT A BRAT!
HUH! IF YOU WANT IT THAT MUCH, THEN YOU CAN GO FIRST. THIS TIME.
GEE, THANKS A LOT.
HEH HEH ...
100 YEN, 100 YEN ...

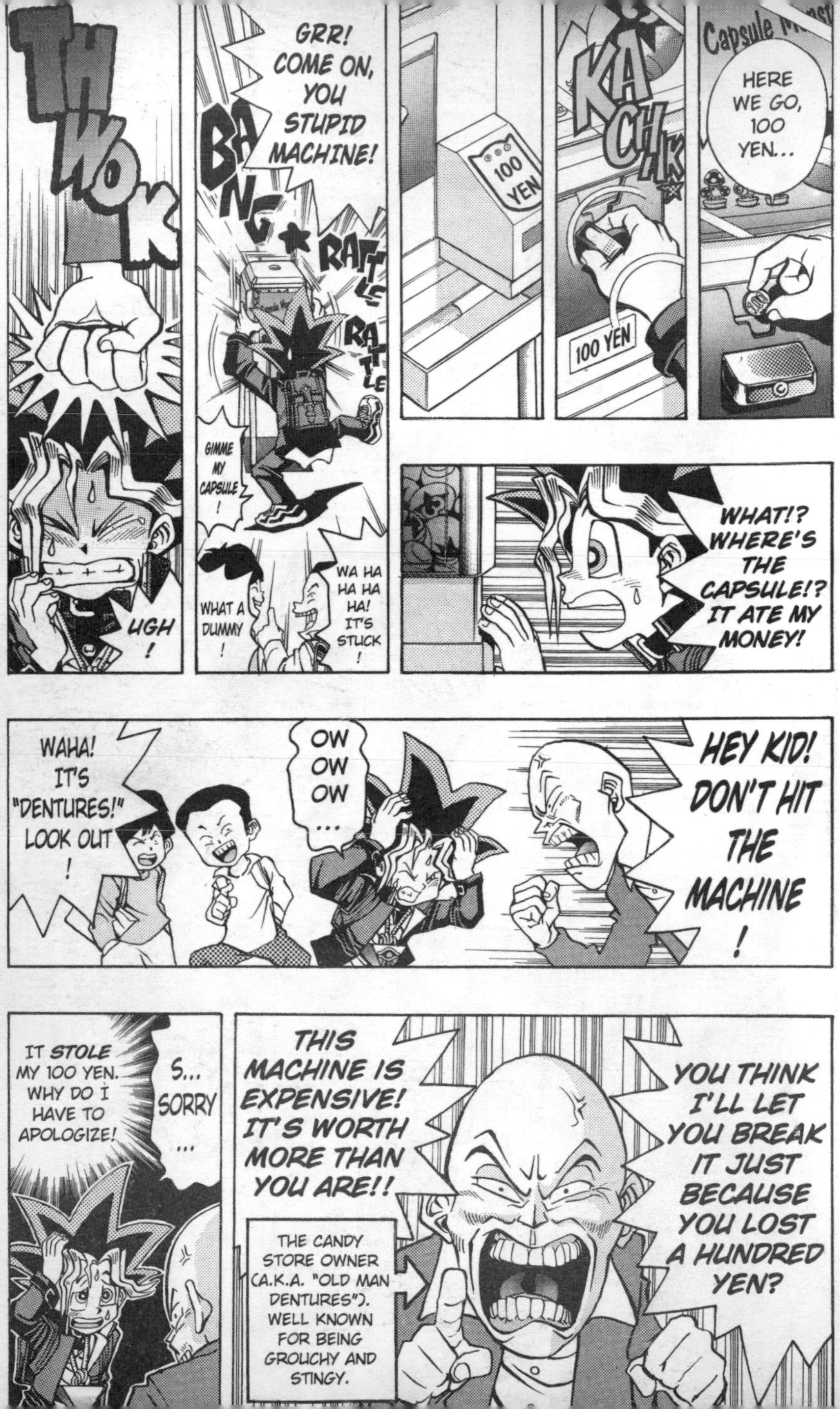

Capsule Mons
HERE WE GO, 100 YEN...
KA CHK
100 YEN
100 YEN
WHAT!? WHERE'S THE CAPSULE!? IT ATE MY MONEY!
GRR! COME ON, YOU STUPID MACHINE!
BANG
RATTLE
RATTLE
GIMME MY CAPSULE!
WA HA HA HA HA! IT'S STUCK!
WHAT A DUMMY!
THWOK
UGH!
HEY KID! DON'T HIT THE MACHINE!
OW OW OW...
WAHA! IT'S "DENTURES!" LOOK OUT!
YOU THINK I'LL LET YOU BREAK IT JUST BECAUSE YOU LOST A HUNDRED YEN?
THIS MACHINE IS EXPENSIVE! IT'S WORTH MORE THAN YOU ARE!!
THE CANDY STORE OWNER (A.K.A. "OLD MAN DENTURES"). WELL KNOWN FOR BEING GROUCHY AND STINGY.
S... SORRY...
IT STOLE MY 100 YEN. WHY DO I HAVE TO APOLOGIZE!

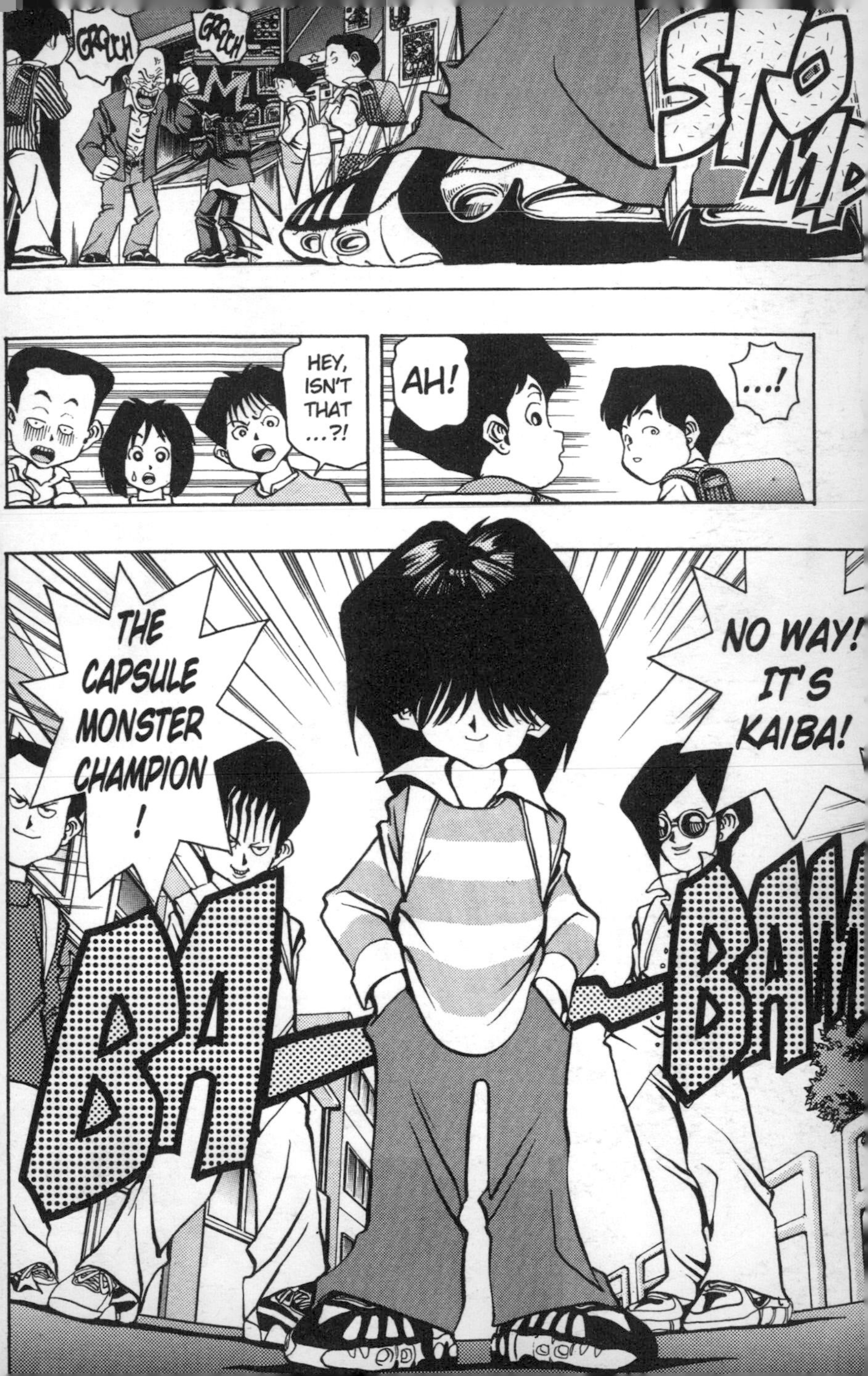
STOMP
GROUCH
GROUCH
...!
AH!
HEY, ISN'T THAT ...?!
NO WAY! IT'S KAIBA!
BAM
THE CAPSULE MONSTER CHAMPION!
BA

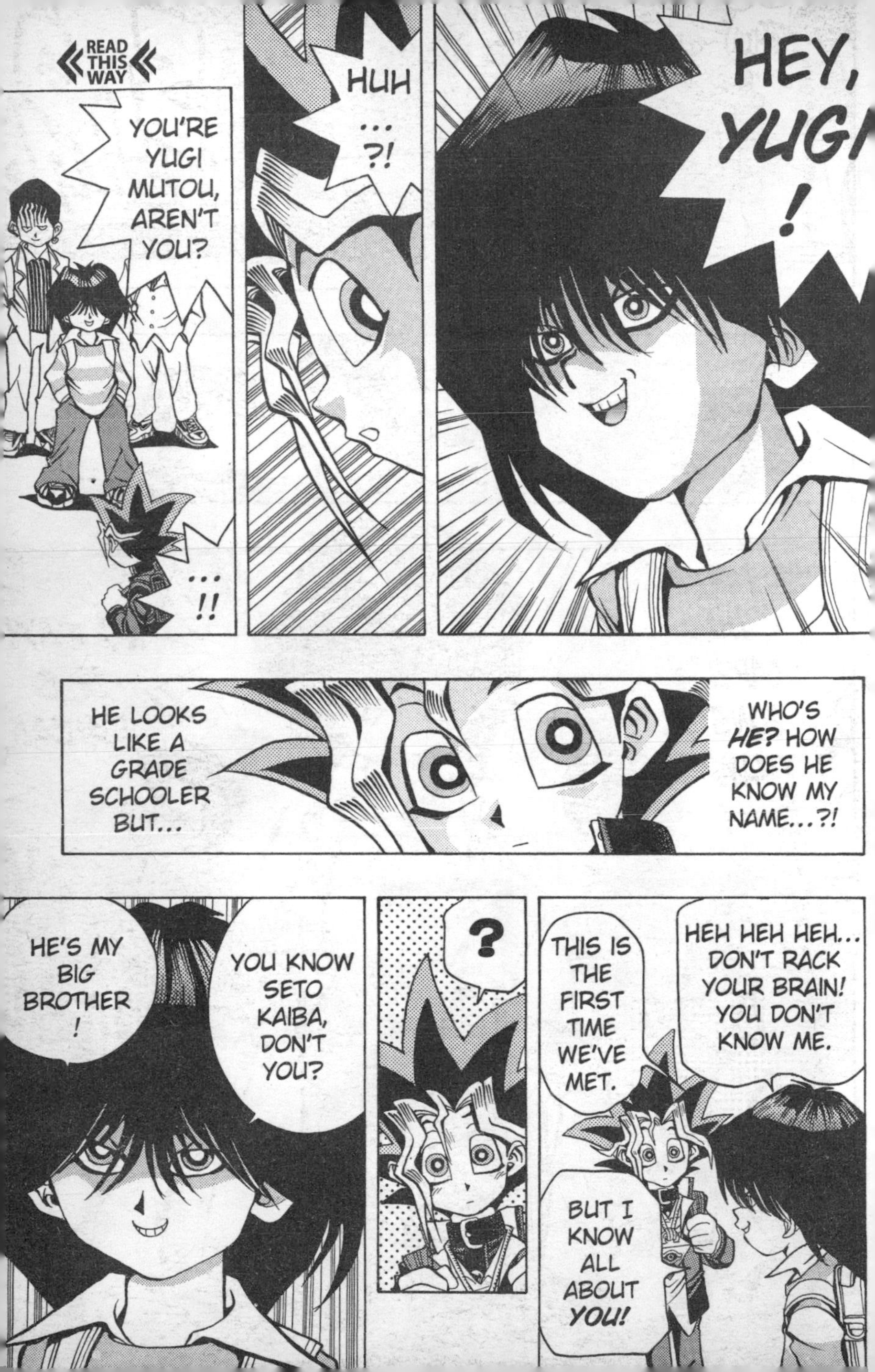
READ THIS WAY
HEY, YUGI!
HUH ...?!
YOU'RE YUGI MUTOU, AREN'T YOU?
...!!
WHO'S *HE?* HOW DOES HE KNOW MY NAME...?!
HE LOOKS LIKE A GRADE SCHOOLER BUT...
HEH HEH HEH... DON'T RACK YOUR BRAIN! YOU DON'T KNOW ME.
THIS IS THE FIRST TIME WE'VE MET.
BUT I KNOW ALL ABOUT *YOU!*
?
YOU KNOW SETO KAIBA, DON'T YOU?
HE'S MY BIG BROTHER!

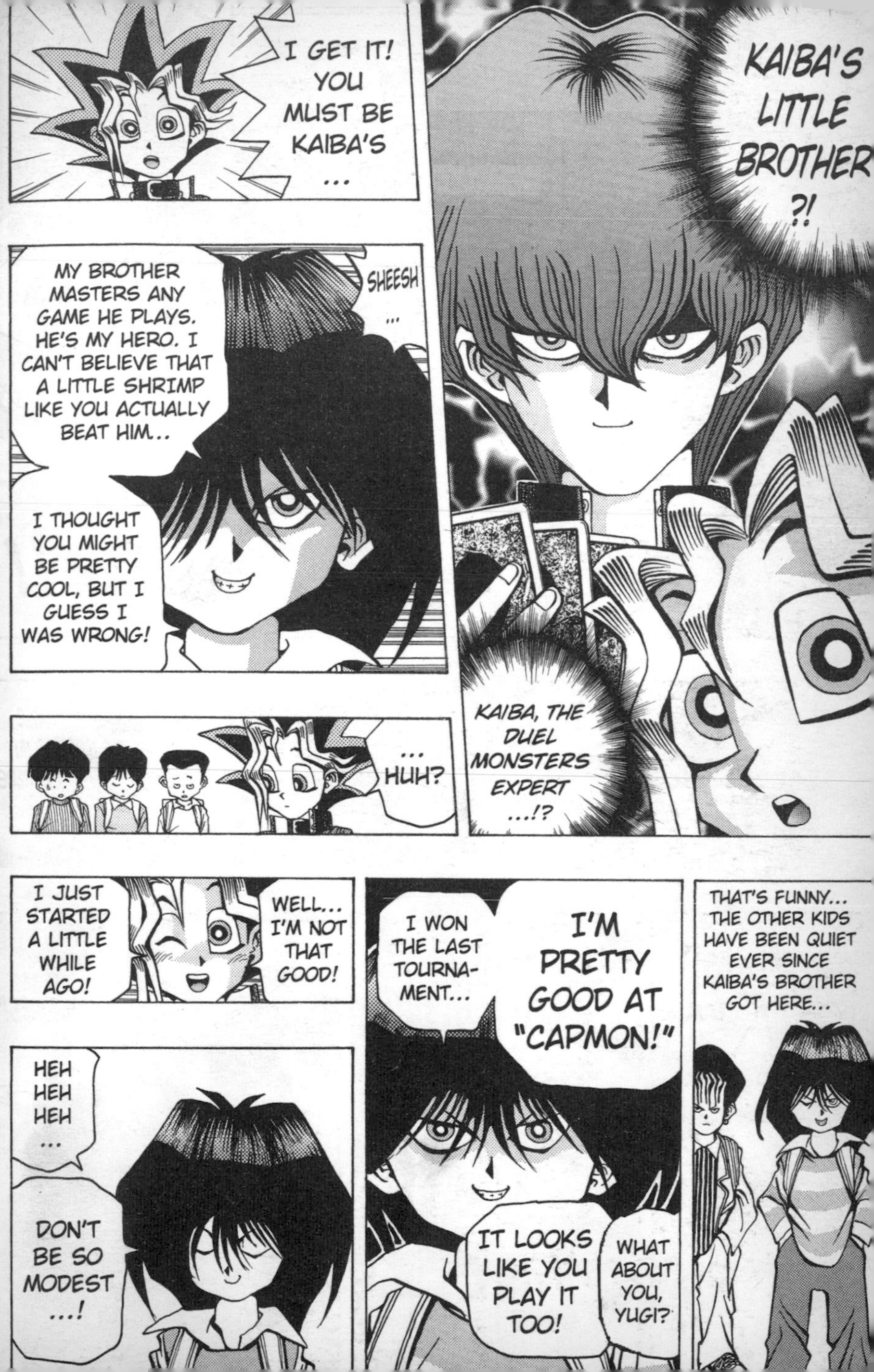
KAIBA'S LITTLE BROTHER ?!
KAIBA, THE DUEL MONSTERS EXPERT ...!?
I GET IT! YOU MUST BE KAIBA'S ...
SHEESH ...
MY BROTHER MASTERS ANY GAME HE PLAYS. HE'S MY HERO. I CAN'T BELIEVE THAT A LITTLE SHRIMP LIKE YOU ACTUALLY BEAT HIM...
I THOUGHT YOU MIGHT BE PRETTY COOL, BUT I GUESS I WAS WRONG!
... HUH?
THAT'S FUNNY... THE OTHER KIDS HAVE BEEN QUIET EVER SINCE KAIBA'S BROTHER GOT HERE...
I'M PRETTY GOOD AT "CAPMON!"
I WON THE LAST TOURNA-MENT...
WHAT ABOUT YOU, YUGI?
IT LOOKS LIKE YOU PLAY IT TOO!
WELL... I'M NOT THAT GOOD!
I JUST STARTED A LITTLE WHILE AGO!
HEH HEH HEH ...
DON'T BE SO MODEST ...!

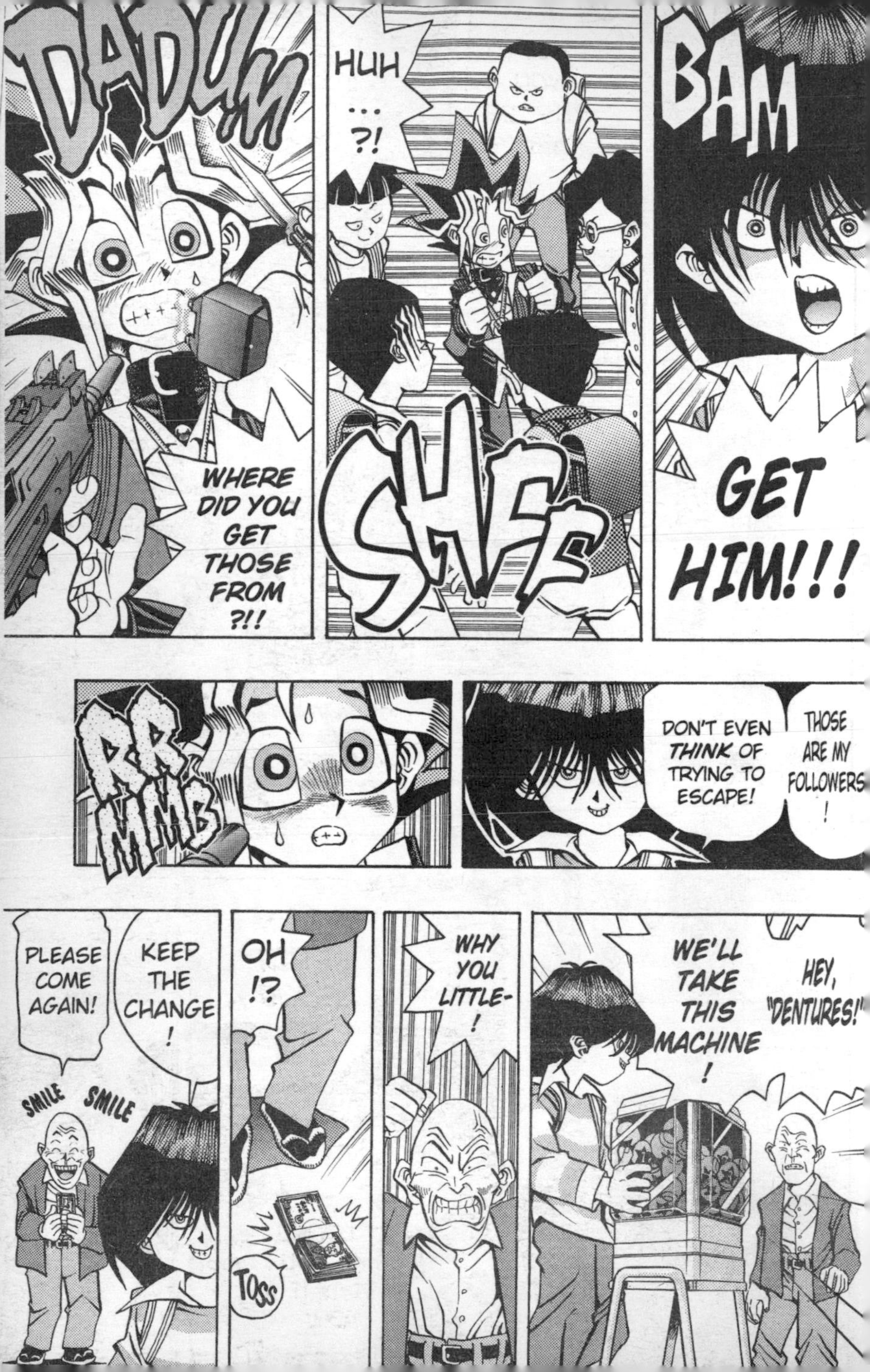
BAM
GET HIM!!!
HUH ... ?!
SHFF
DADUM
WHERE DID YOU GET THOSE FROM ?!!
THOSE ARE MY FOLLOWERS !
DON'T EVEN THINK OF TRYING TO ESCAPE!
RRMMB
HEY, "DENTURES!"
WE'LL TAKE THIS MACHINE !
WHY YOU LITTLE- !
OH !?
TOSS
KEEP THE CHANGE !
PLEASE COME AGAIN!
SMILE
SMILE

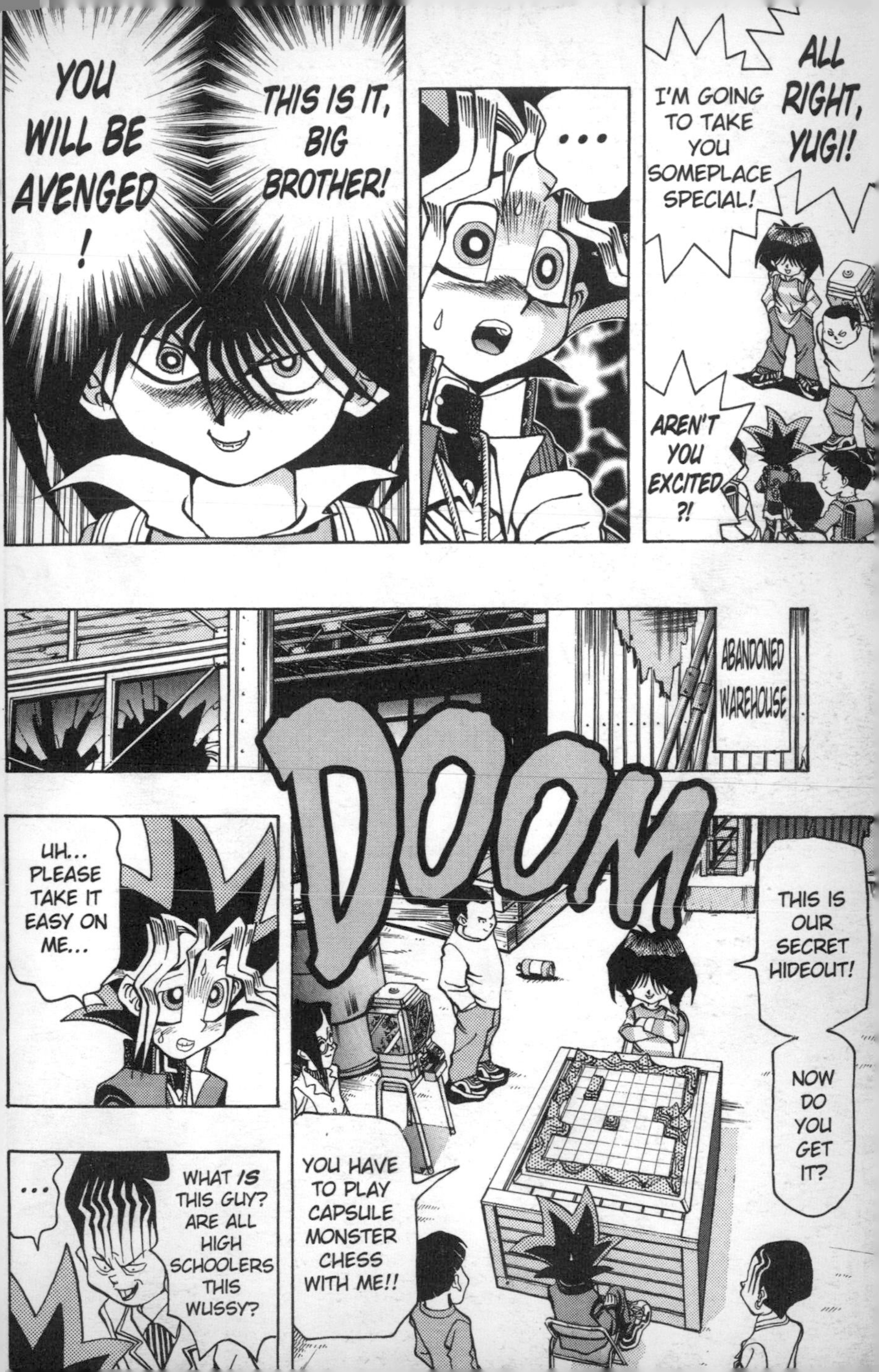
ALL RIGHT, YUGI!
I'M GOING TO TAKE YOU SOMEPLACE SPECIAL!
AREN'T YOU EXCITED?!
...
THIS IS IT, BIG BROTHER!
YOU WILL BE AVENGED!
ABANDONED WAREHOUSE
DOOM
THIS IS OUR SECRET HIDEOUT!
NOW DO YOU GET IT?
YOU HAVE TO PLAY CAPSULE MONSTER CHESS WITH ME!!
UH... PLEASE TAKE IT EASY ON ME...
WHAT IS THIS GUY? ARE ALL HIGH SCHOOLERS THIS WUSSY?
...

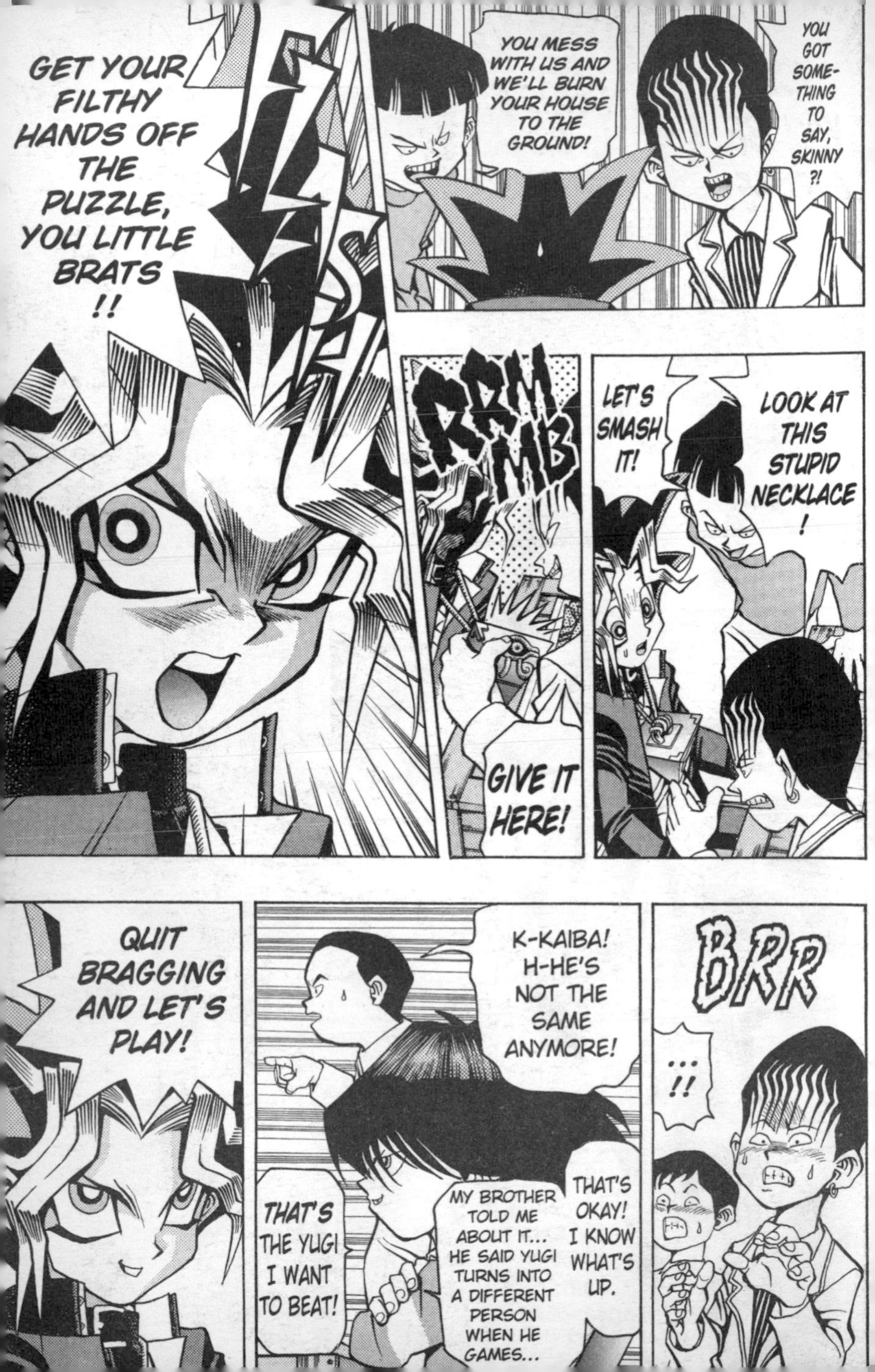
YOU GOT SOME-THING TO SAY, SKINNY?!
YOU MESS WITH US AND WE'LL BURN YOUR HOUSE TO THE GROUND!
LOOK AT THIS STUPID NECKLACE!
LET'S SMASH IT!
RRMMB
GIVE IT HERE!
GET YOUR FILTHY HANDS OFF THE PUZZLE, YOU LITTLE BRATS!!
BRR
...!!
K-KAIBA! H-HE'S NOT THE SAME ANYMORE!
THAT'S OKAY! I KNOW WHAT'S UP.
MY BROTHER TOLD ME ABOUT IT... HE SAID YUGI TURNS INTO A DIFFERENT PERSON WHEN HE GAMES...
THAT'S THE YUGI I WANT TO BEAT!
QUIT BRAGGING AND LET'S PLAY!

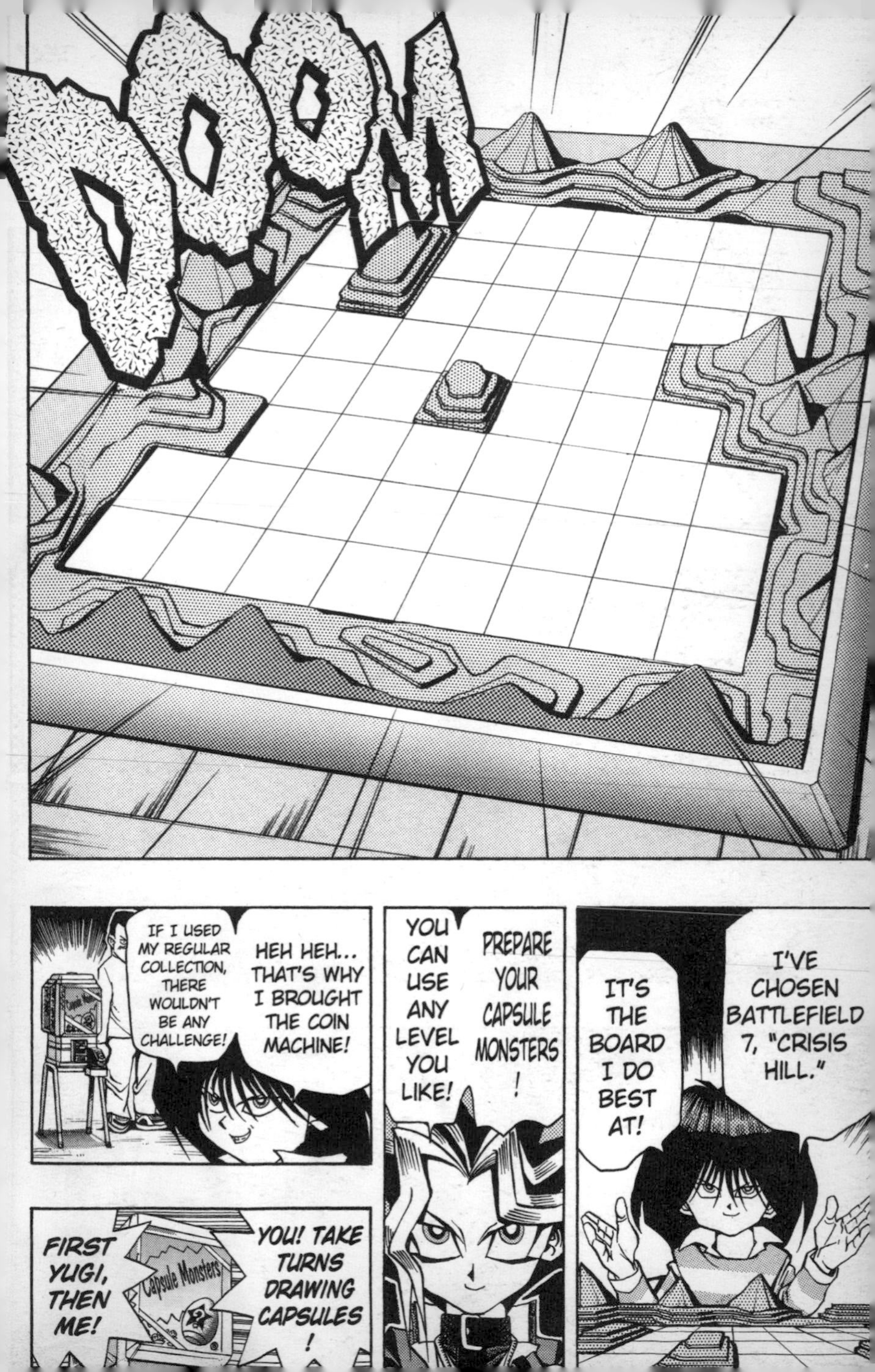
DOOM
I'VE CHOSEN BATTLEFIELD 7, "CRISIS HILL."
IT'S THE BOARD I DO BEST AT!
PREPARE YOUR CAPSULE MONSTERS!
YOU CAN USE ANY LEVEL YOU LIKE!
HEH HEH... THAT'S WHY I BROUGHT THE COIN MACHINE!
IF I USED MY REGULAR COLLECTION, THERE WOULDN'T BE ANY CHALLENGE!
YOU! TAKE TURNS DRAWING CAPSULES!
FIRST YUGI, THEN ME!
Capsule Monsters

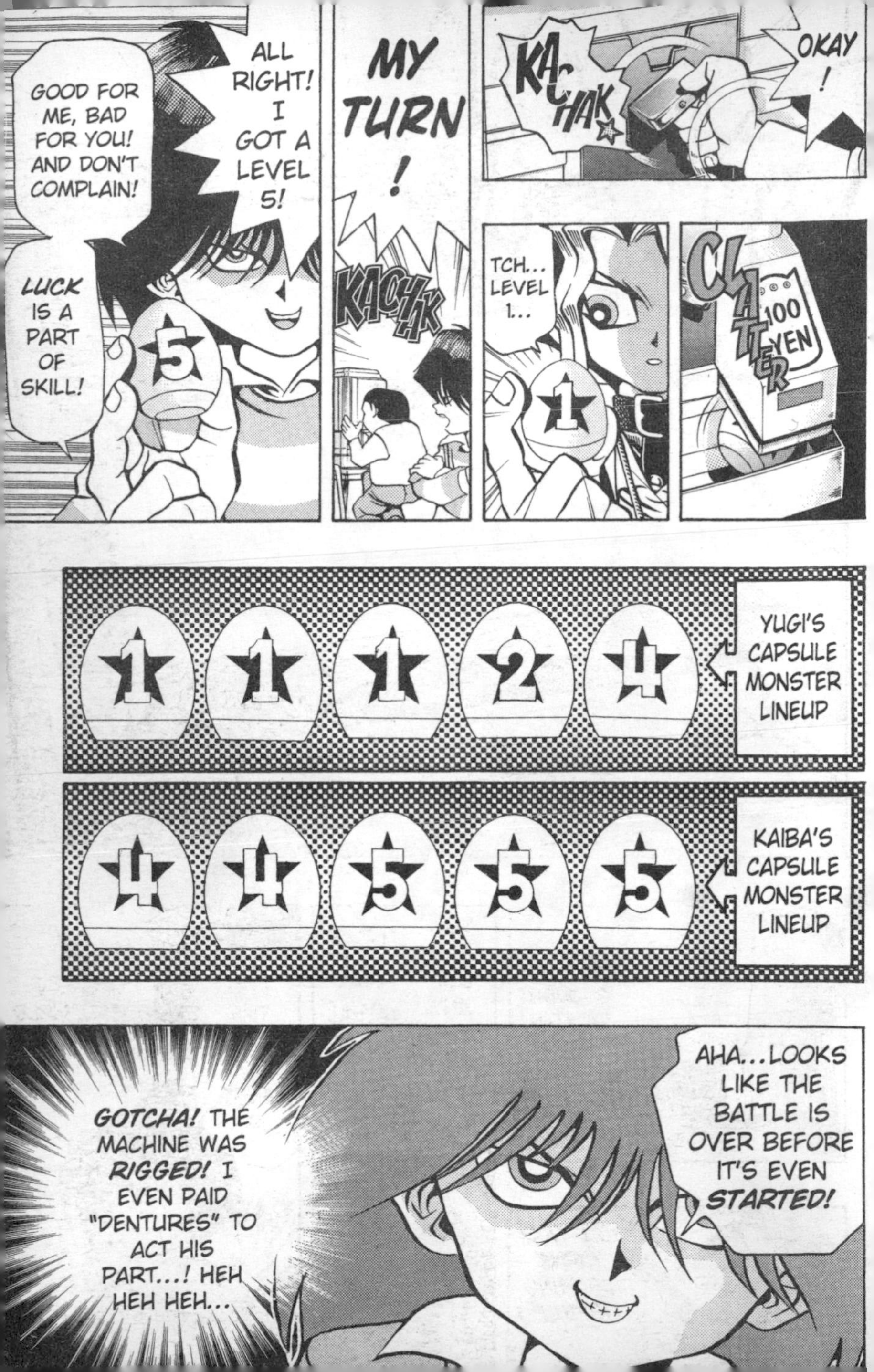
OKAY!
KACHAK
CLATTER
100 YEN
TCH... LEVEL 1...
1
MY TURN!
KACHAK
ALL RIGHT! I GOT A LEVEL 5!
GOOD FOR ME, BAD FOR YOU! AND DON'T COMPLAIN!
LUCK IS A PART OF SKILL!
5
YUGI'S CAPSULE MONSTER LINEUP
1 1 1 2 4
KAIBA'S CAPSULE MONSTER LINEUP
4 4 5 5 5
AHA...LOOKS LIKE THE BATTLE IS OVER BEFORE IT'S EVEN STARTED!
GOTCHA! THE MACHINE WAS RIGGED! I EVEN PAID "DENTURES" TO ACT HIS PART...! HEH HEH HEH...

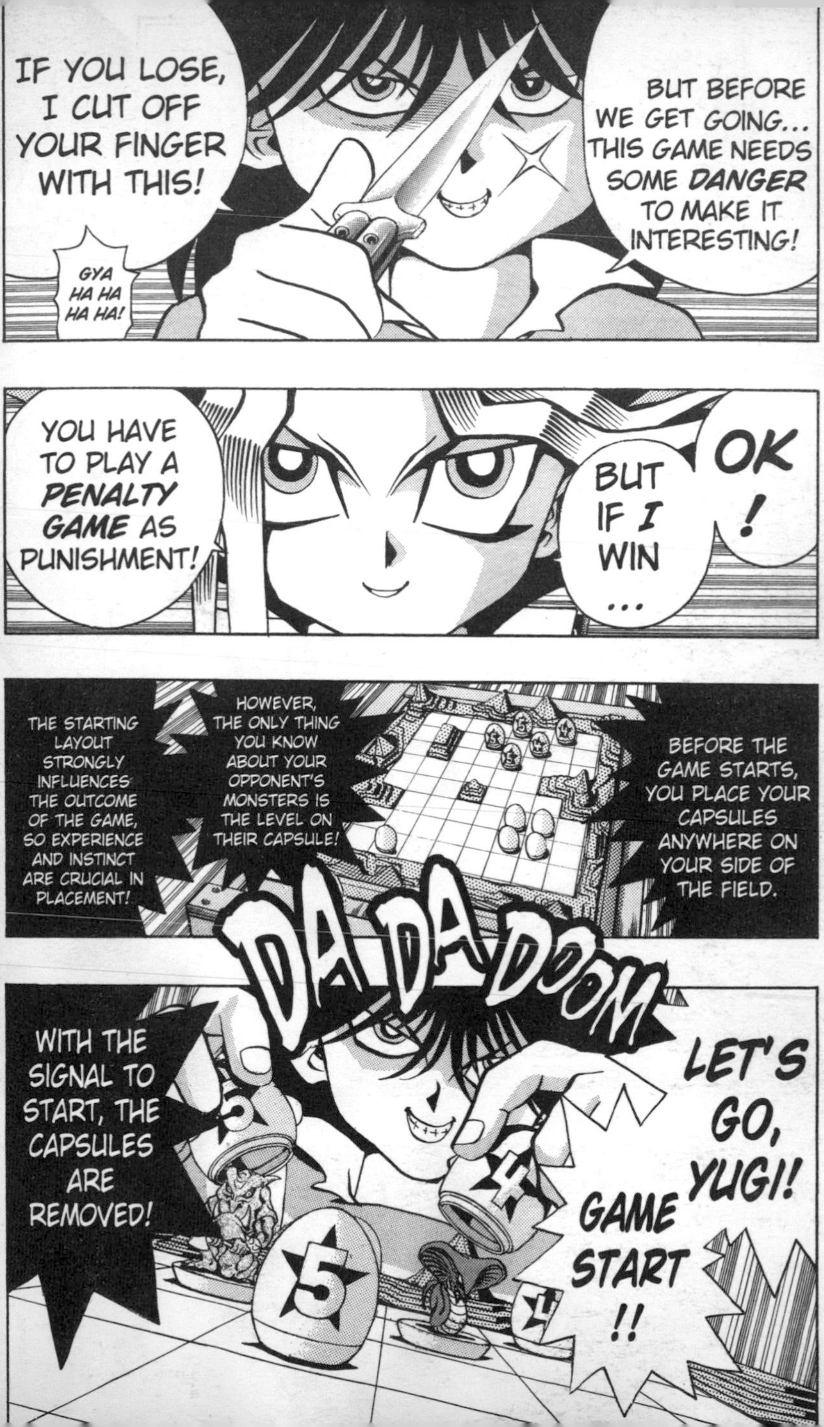
BUT BEFORE WE GET GOING... THIS GAME NEEDS SOME DANGER TO MAKE IT INTERESTING!
IF YOU LOSE, I CUT OFF YOUR FINGER WITH THIS!
GYA HA HA HA HA!
OK!
BUT IF I WIN...
YOU HAVE TO PLAY A PENALTY GAME AS PUNISHMENT!
BEFORE THE GAME STARTS, YOU PLACE YOUR CAPSULES ANYWHERE ON YOUR SIDE OF THE FIELD.
HOWEVER, THE ONLY THING YOU KNOW ABOUT YOUR OPPONENT'S MONSTERS IS THE LEVEL ON THEIR CAPSULE!
THE STARTING LAYOUT STRONGLY INFLUENCES THE OUTCOME OF THE GAME, SO EXPERIENCE AND INSTINCT ARE CRUCIAL IN PLACEMENT!
DA DA DOOM
LET'S GO, YUGI!
GAME START!!
WITH THE SIGNAL TO START, THE CAPSULES ARE REMOVED!

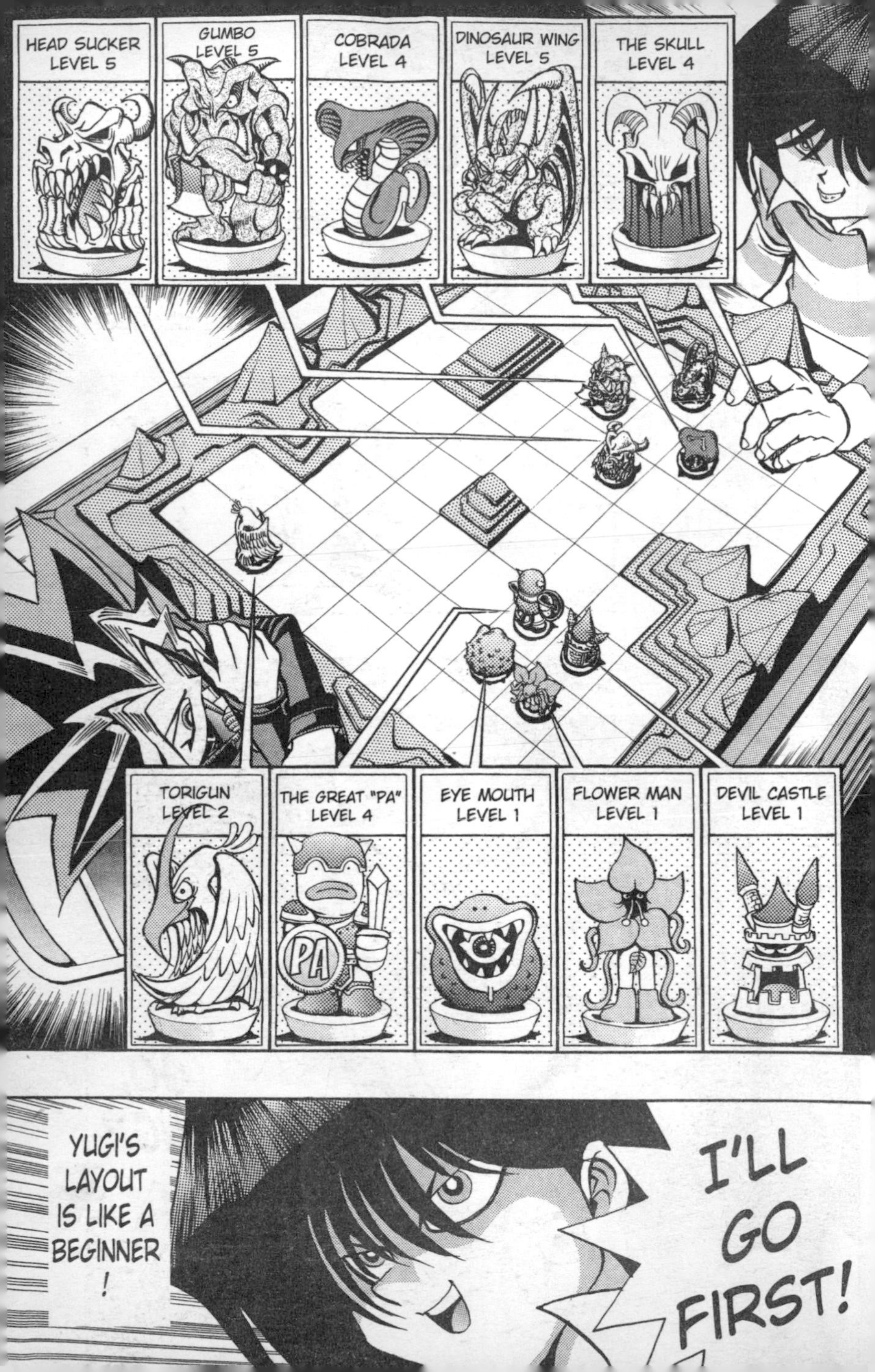
THE SKULL LEVEL 4
DINOSAUR WING LEVEL 5
COBRADA LEVEL 4
GUMBO LEVEL 5
HEAD SUCKER LEVEL 5
DEVIL CASTLE LEVEL 1
FLOWER MAN LEVEL 1
EYE MOUTH LEVEL 1
THE GREAT "PA" LEVEL 4
TORIGUN LEVEL 2
I'LL GO FIRST!
YUGI'S LAYOUT IS LIKE A BEGINNER!

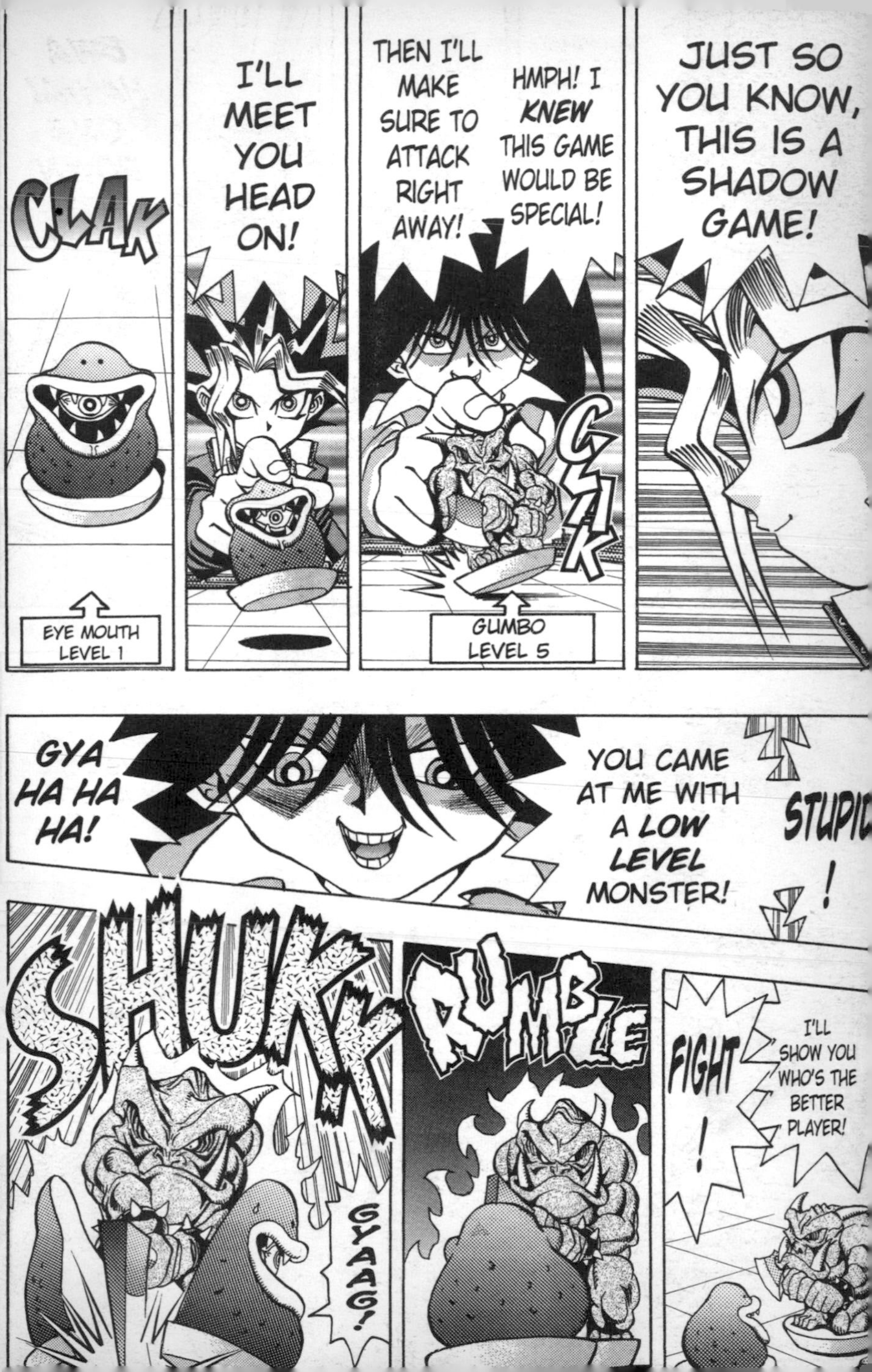
JUST SO YOU KNOW, THIS IS A SHADOW GAME!
HMPH! I KNEW THIS GAME WOULD BE SPECIAL!
THEN I'LL MAKE SURE TO ATTACK RIGHT AWAY!
CLAK
GUMBO LEVEL 5
I'LL MEET YOU HEAD ON!
CLAK
EYE MOUTH LEVEL 1
STUPI
!
YOU CAME AT ME WITH A LOW LEVEL MONSTER!
GYA HA HA HA!
I'LL SHOW YOU WHO'S THE BETTER PLAYER!
FIGHT !
RUMBLE
SHUK
GYAAAG!

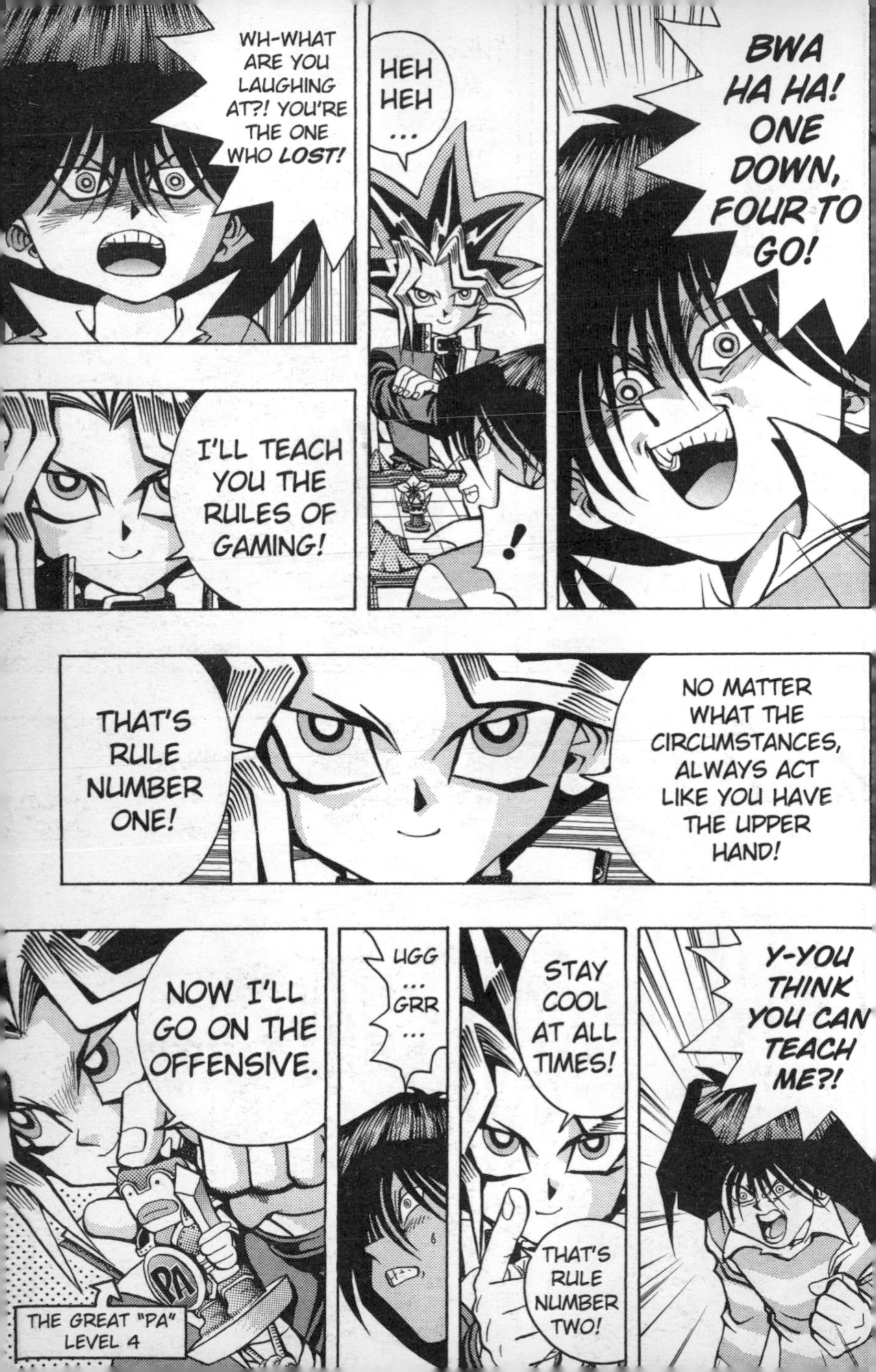
BWA HA HA! ONE DOWN, FOUR TO GO!
HEH HEH ...
!
WH-WHAT ARE YOU LAUGHING AT?! YOU'RE THE ONE WHO LOST!
I'LL TEACH YOU THE RULES OF GAMING!
NO MATTER WHAT THE CIRCUMSTANCES, ALWAYS ACT LIKE YOU HAVE THE UPPER HAND!
THAT'S RULE NUMBER ONE!
Y-YOU THINK YOU CAN TEACH ME?!
STAY COOL AT ALL TIMES!
THAT'S RULE NUMBER TWO!
UGG ... GRR ...
NOW I'LL GO ON THE OFFENSIVE.
PA
THE GREAT "PA" LEVEL 4

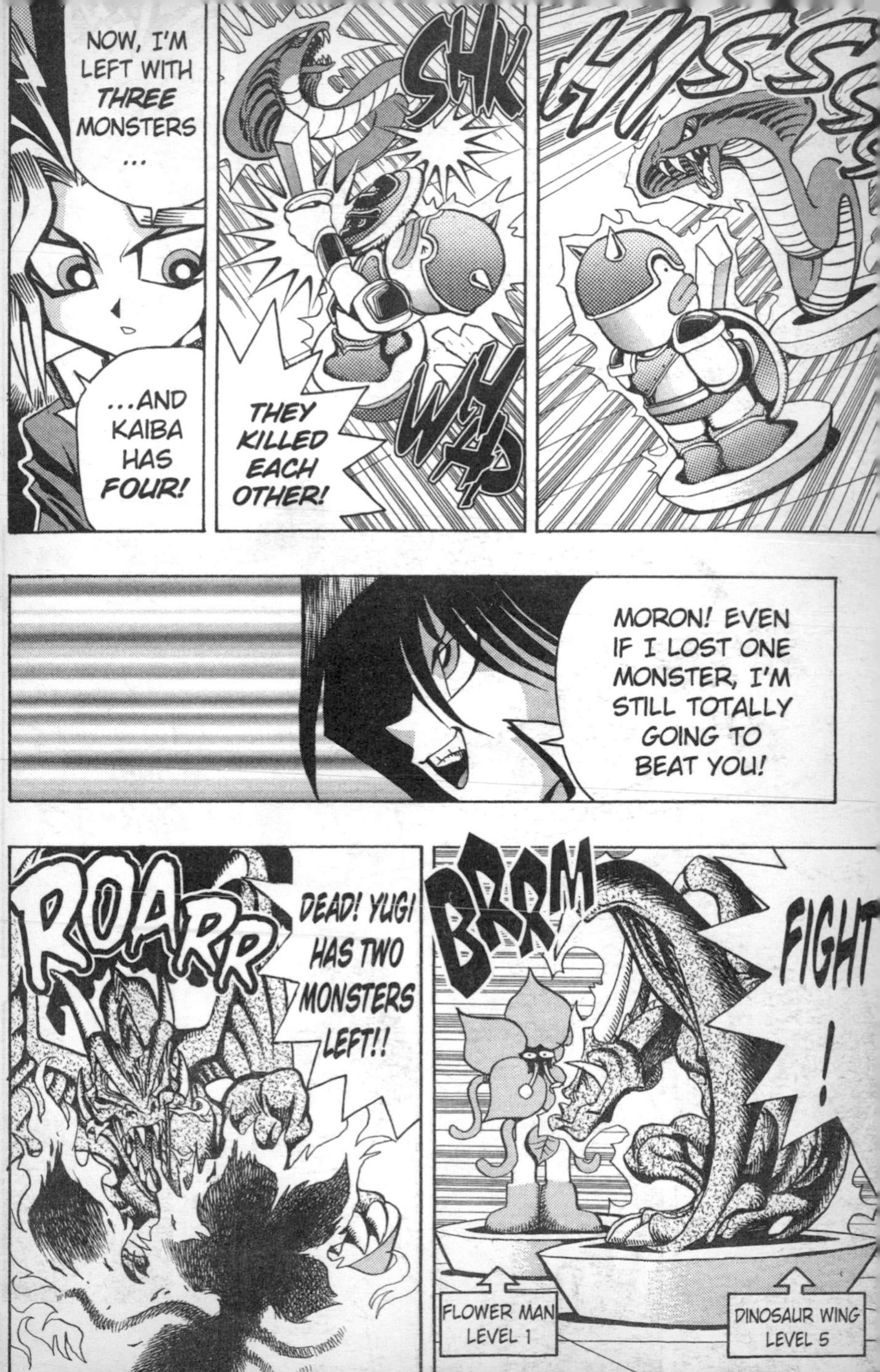
HISSS
SHK
THEY KILLED EACH OTHER!
NOW, I'M LEFT WITH THREE MONSTERS ...
...AND KAIBA HAS FOUR!
MORON! EVEN IF I LOST ONE MONSTER, I'M STILL TOTALLY GOING TO BEAT YOU!
BRRM
FIGHT!
FLOWER MAN LEVEL 1
DINOSAUR WING LEVEL 5
ROARR
DEAD! YUGI HAS TWO MONSTERS LEFT!!

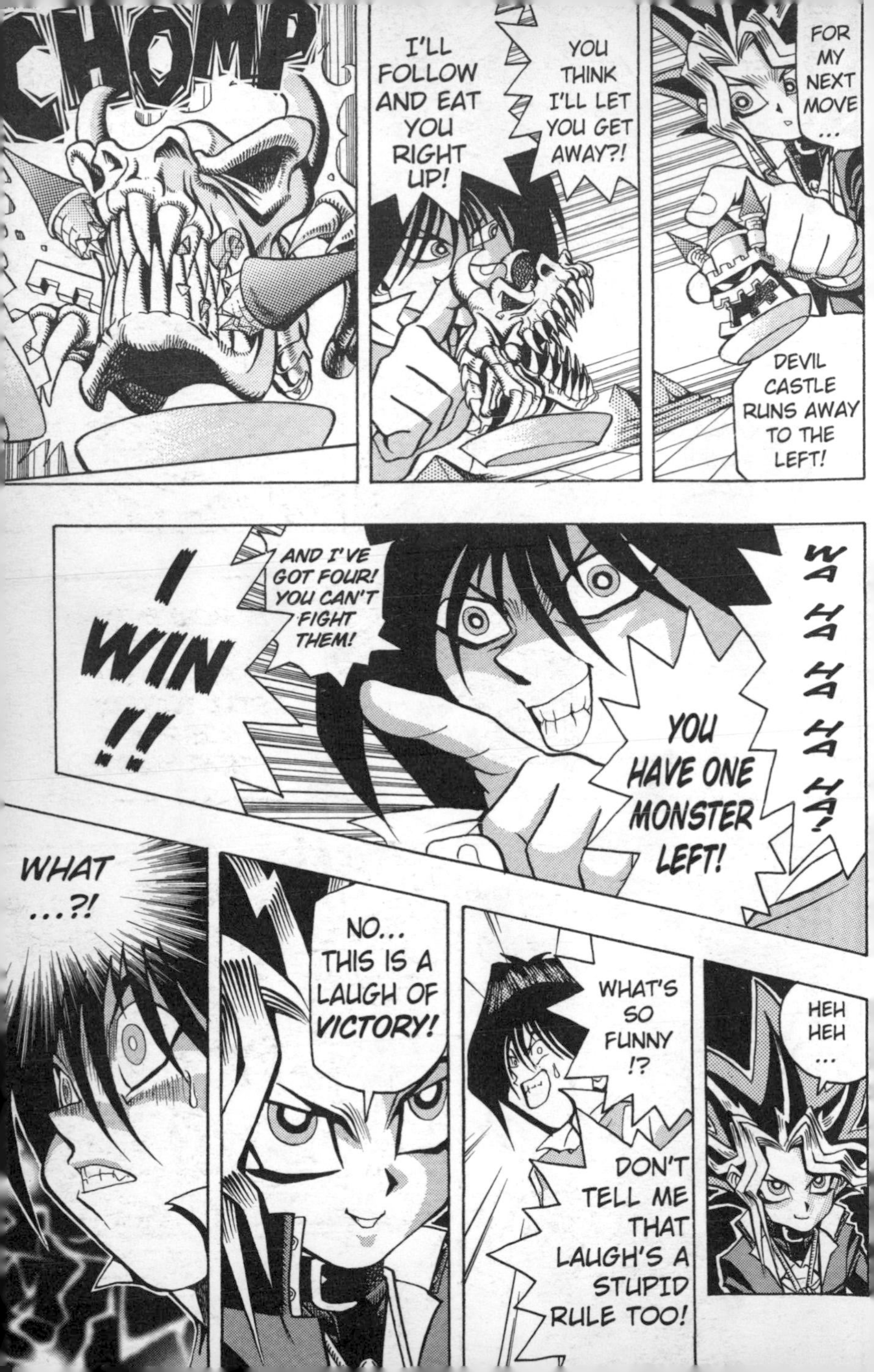
FOR MY NEXT MOVE ...
DEVIL CASTLE RUNS AWAY TO THE LEFT!
YOU THINK I'LL LET YOU GET AWAY?!
I'LL FOLLOW AND EAT YOU RIGHT UP!
CHOMP
WA HA HA HA HA HA!
YOU HAVE ONE MONSTER LEFT!
AND I'VE GOT FOUR! YOU CAN'T FIGHT THEM!
I WIN!!
HEH HEH ...
WHAT'S SO FUNNY !?
DON'T TELL ME THAT LAUGH'S A STUPID RULE TOO!
NO... THIS IS A LAUGH OF VICTORY!
WHAT ...?!

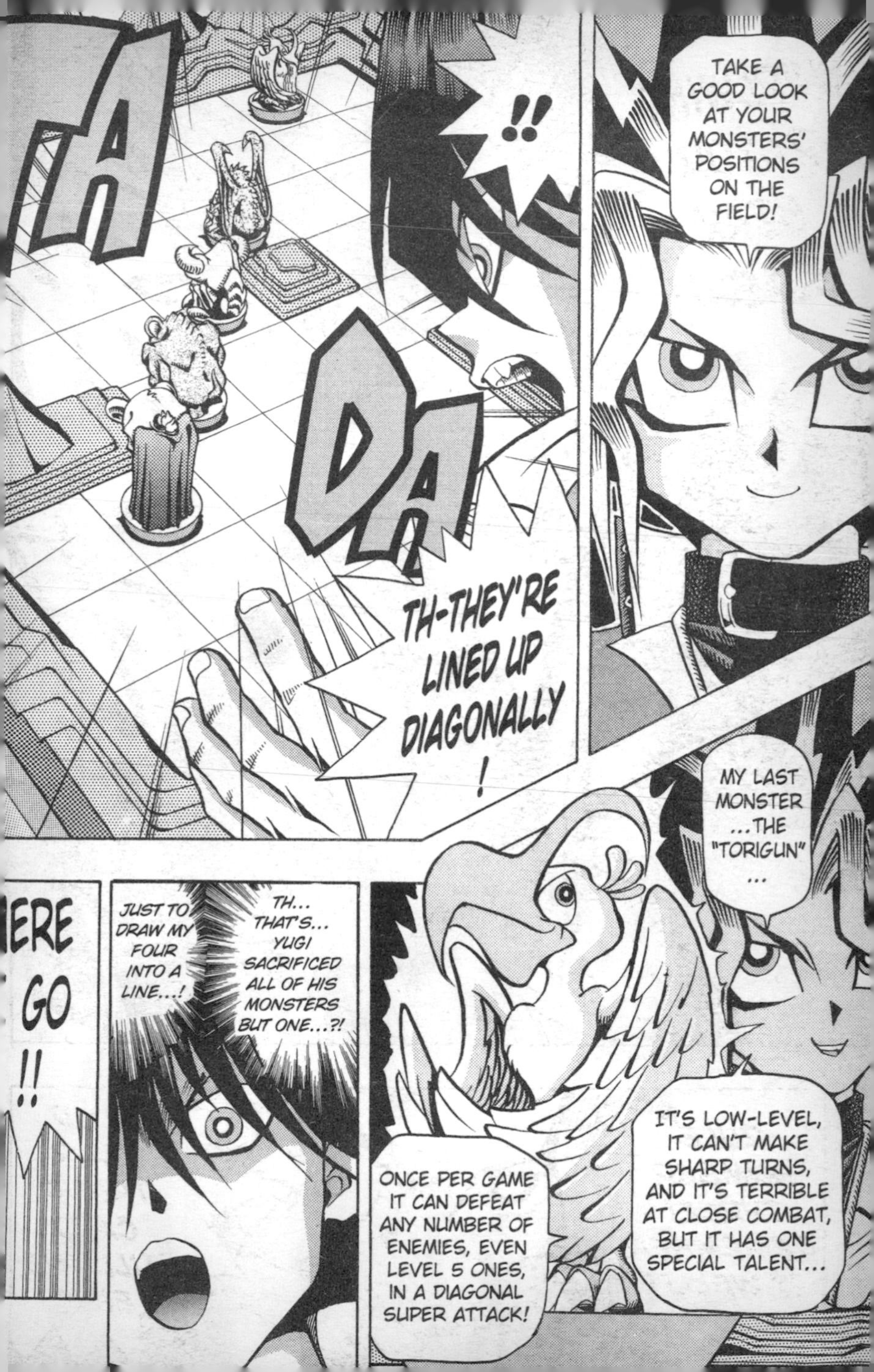
TAKE A GOOD LOOK AT YOUR MONSTERS' POSITIONS ON THE FIELD!
!!
A
DA
TH-THEY'RE LINED UP DIAGONALLY!
MY LAST MONSTER ...THE "TORIGUN" ...
IT'S LOW-LEVEL, IT CAN'T MAKE SHARP TURNS, AND IT'S TERRIBLE AT CLOSE COMBAT, BUT IT HAS ONE SPECIAL TALENT...
ONCE PER GAME IT CAN DEFEAT ANY NUMBER OF ENEMIES, EVEN LEVEL 5 ONES, IN A DIAGONAL SUPER ATTACK!
TH... THAT'S... YUGI SACRIFICED ALL OF HIS MONSTERS BUT ONE...?!
JUST TO DRAW MY FOUR INTO A LINE...!
ERE GO !!

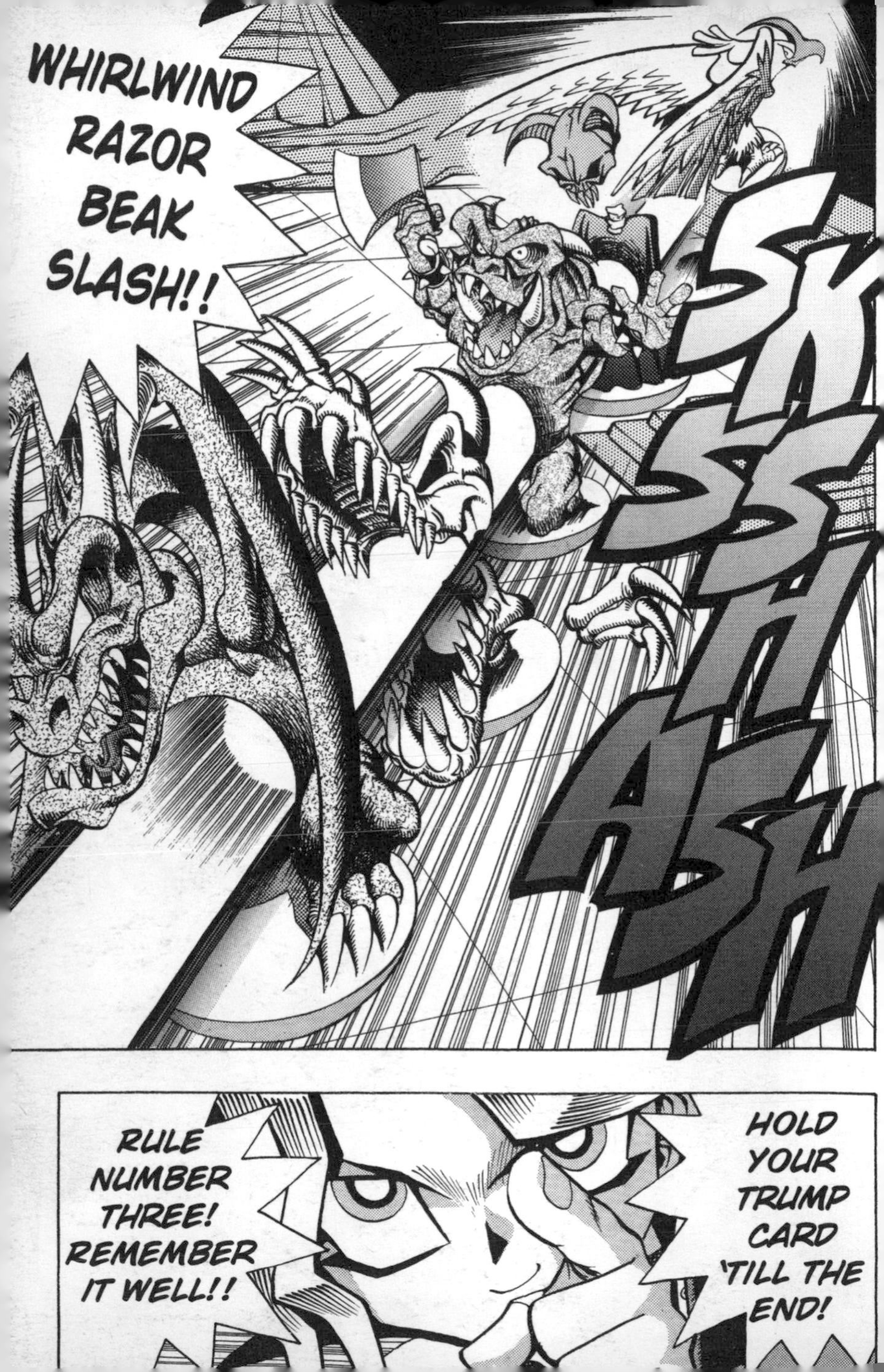
WHIRLWIND RAZOR BEAK SLASH!!
HOLD YOUR TRUMP CARD 'TILL THE END!
RULE NUMBER THREE! REMEMBER IT WELL!!

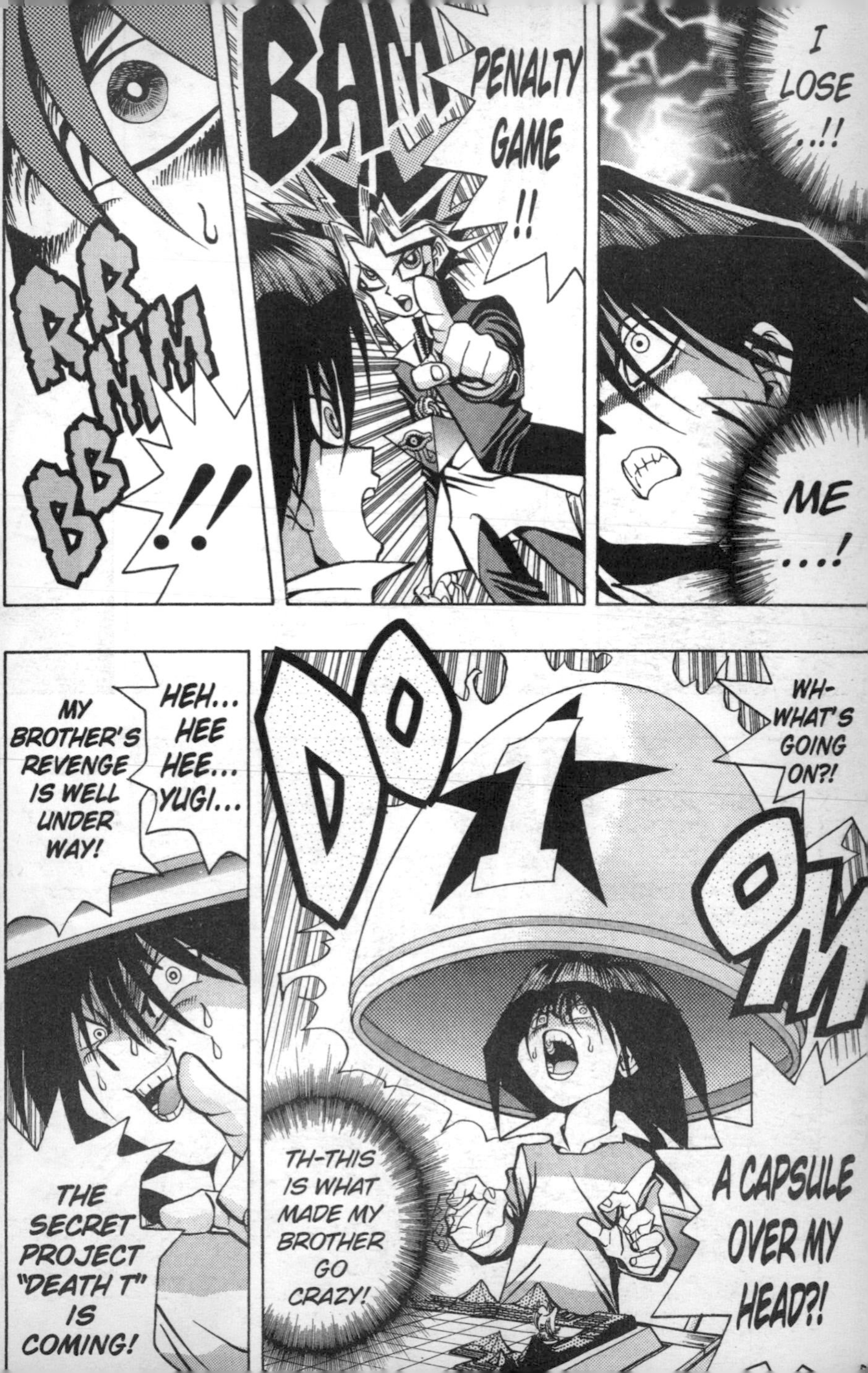
I LOSE ..!!
ME ...!
BAM
PENALTY GAME !!
RRMMBB !!
WH-WHAT'S GOING ON?!
DOOM
A CAPSULE OVER MY HEAD?!
TH-THIS IS WHAT MADE MY BROTHER GO CRAZY!
HEH... HEE HEE... YUGI...
MY BROTHER'S REVENGE IS WELL UNDER WAY!
THE SECRET PROJECT "DEATH T" IS COMING!

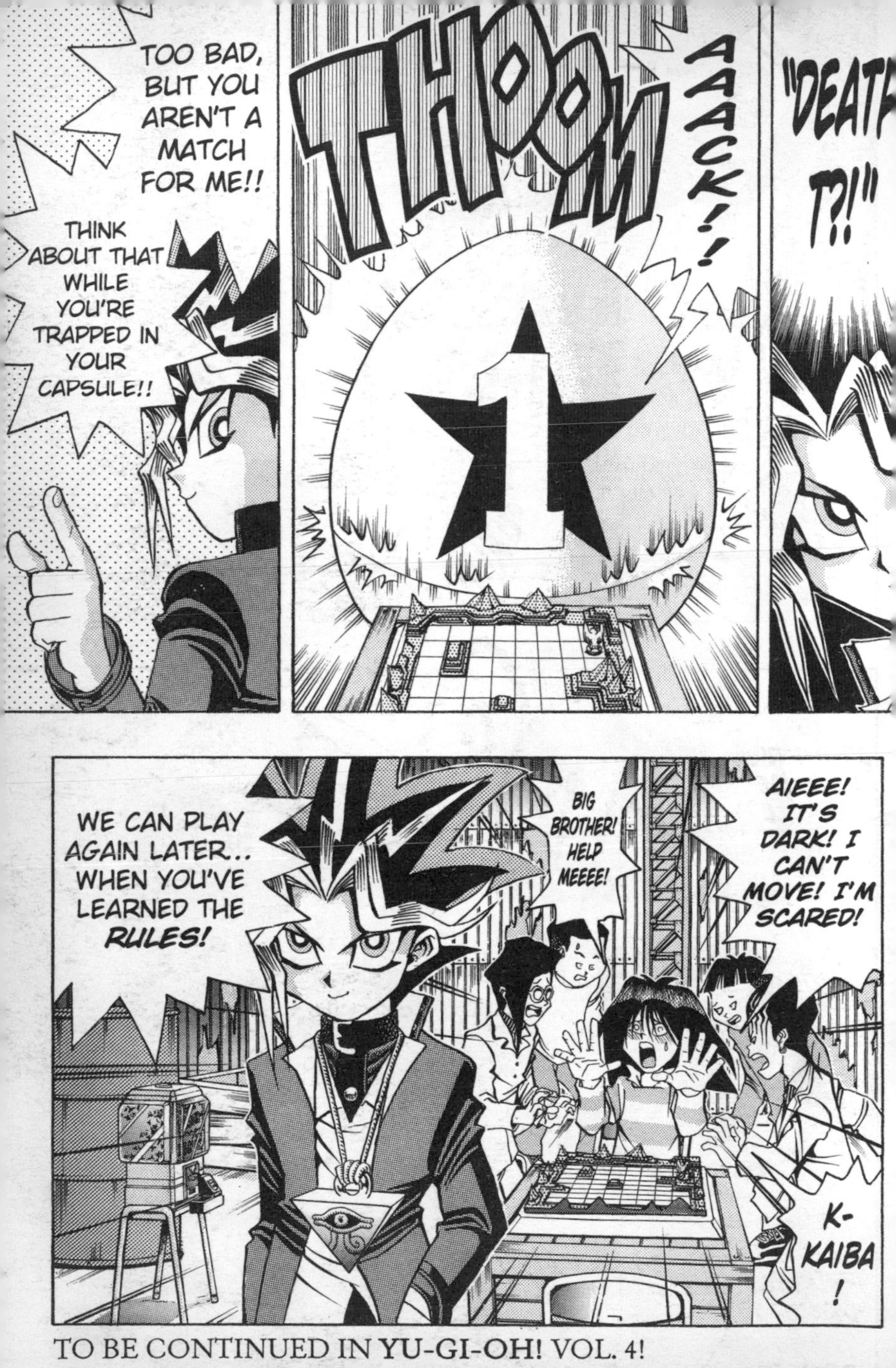
"DEATH T?!"
THOOM
AAAACK!!
TOO BAD, BUT YOU AREN'T A MATCH FOR ME!!
THINK ABOUT THAT WHILE YOU'RE TRAPPED IN YOUR CAPSULE!!
K-KAIBA!
AIEEE! IT'S DARK! I CAN'T MOVE! I'M SCARED!
BIG BROTHER! HELP MEEEE!
WE CAN PLAY AGAIN LATER... WHEN YOU'VE LEARNED THE RULES!

TO BE CONTINUED IN YU-GI-OH! VOL. 4!

COMPLETE OUR SURVEY AND
LET US KNOW WHAT YOU THINK!

❏ Please do NOT send me information about Gollancz Manga, or other Orion title, products, news and events, special offers or other information

Name: _____

Address: _____

Town: _____ County: _____ Postcode: _____

❏ Male ❏ Female   Date of Birth (dd/mm/yyyy): __ / __ / _____
                     (under 13? Parental consent required)

What race/ethnicity do you consider yourself? (please check one)

❏ Asian   ❏ Black   ❏ Hispanic

❏ White/Caucasian   ❏ Other: _____

Which Gollancz Manga title did you purchase?

Case Closed	Dragon Ball	Fushigi Yûgi	Yu-Gi-Oh!
❏ 1 ❏ 2	❏ 1 ❏ 2	❏ 1 ❏ 2	❏ 1 ❏ 2
❏ 3	❏ 3	❏ 3	❏ 3

What other Gollancz Manga do you own?

Case Closed	Dragon Ball	Fushigi Yûgi	Yu-Gi-Oh!
❏ 1 ❏ 2	❏ 1 ❏ 2	❏ 1 ❏ 2	❏ 1 ❏ 2
❏ 3	❏ 3	❏ 3	❏ 3

How many anime and/or manga titles have you purchased in the last year?
How many were Gollancz Manga titles?

Anime	Manga	GM
❏ None	❏ None	❏ None
❏ 1-4	❏ 1-4	❏ 1-4
❏ 5-10	❏ 5-10	❏ 5-10
❏ 11+	❏ 11+	❏ 11+

Reason for purchase: (check all that apply)

❏ Special Offer   ❏ Favourite title   ❏ Gift

❏ In store promotion If so please indicate which store: _____

❏ Recommendation   ❏ Other _____

Where did you make your purchase?

❏ Bookshop   ❏ Comic Shop   ❏ Music Store

❏ Newsagent   ❏ Video Game Store   ❏ Supermarket

❏ Other: _____   ❏ Online: _____

What kind of manga would you like to read?

❏ Adventure   ❏ Comic Strip   ❏ Fantasy

❏ Fighting   ❏ Horror   ❏ Mystery

❏ Romance   ❏ Science Fiction   ❏ Sports

❏ Other: _____

Which do you prefer?

❏ Sound effects in English

❏ Sound effects in Japanese with English captions

❏ Sound effects in Japanese only with a glossary at the back

Want to find out more about Manga?

Look us up at www.orionbooks.co.uk, or www.viz.com

THANK YOU! Please send the completed form to:

Manga Survey
Orion Books
Orion House
5 Upper St Martin's Lane
London, WC2H 9EA